To Mabili and Nadif, and to Ruby, who makes my futures possible, and for all our "rides on the elephant."

—Lou Turner

To Lillian and Krisman Neville and Sundiata Cha-Jua for modeling courage and fighting for the freedom of Black people everywhere.

—Helen A. Neville

Frantz Fanon's Psychotherapeutic Approaches to Clinical Work

Recognizing Frantz Fanon's remarkable legacy to applied mental health and therapeutic practices which decolonize, humanize, and empower marginalized populations, this text serves as a timely call for research, education, and clinical work to establish and further develop Fanonian approaches and practices.

As the first collection to focus on contemporary clinical applications of Fanon's research and practice, this volume adopts a transnational lens through which to capture the global reach of Fanon's work. Contributors from Africa, Australia, Europe, and North America offer nuanced insight into historical and theoretical methods, clinical case studies, and community-based innovations to place Fanon's research and practice in context. Organized into four key areas, including the Historical Significance of Fanon's Clinical Work; Theory and Fanonian Praxis; Psychotherapeutic and Community Applications; and Action Research, each section of the book reflects an impressive diversity of practices around the world, and considers the role of political and socioeconomic context, structures of gender oppression, racial identities, and their intersection within those practices.

A unique manifesto to the ground-breaking and immensely relevant work of Frantz Fanon, this book will be of great interest to graduate and post graduate students, researchers, academics and professionals in counseling psychology, mental health research, and psychotherapy.

Lou Turner is Clinical Assistant Professor in the Department of Urban and Regional Planning, and College of Fine and Applied Arts, University of Illinois at Urbana-Champaign, USA.

Helen A. Neville is Professor in the Department of Educational Psychology and Department of African American Studies at the University of Illinois at Urbana-Champaign, USA.

Explorations in Mental Health

Frantz Fanon's Psychotherapeutic Approaches to Clinical Work

Practicing Internationally with Marginalized Communities

Edited by Lou Turner and Helen A. Neville

Routledge
Taylor & Francis Group

NEW YORK AND LONDON

First published 2020
by Routledge
605 Third Avenue, New York, NY 10017

and by Routledge
2 Park Square, Milton Park, Abingdon, Oxon, OX14 4RN

First issued in paperback 2021

Routledge is an imprint of the Taylor & Francis Group, an informa business

Publisher's Note
The publisher has gone to great lengths to ensure the quality of this reprint
but points out that some imperfections in the original copies may be
apparent.

Library of Congress Cataloging-in-Publication Data
A catalog record for this book has been requested

ISBN 13: 978-1-03-223916-3 (pbk)
ISBN 13: 978-1-138-61157-3 (hbk)

Typeset in Baskerville
by Apex CoVantage, LLC

Contents

Preface and Acknowledgements

Lou Turner

One of the strategic aims of this collection has been to make the pedagogical case for the global incorporation of Fanon's socio-psychotherapy into the curricula of psychology programs of study for training psychologists and psychiatrists of color, or any student of psychology, interested in servicing underserved communities of color on the margins of mental health systems. It is a source of consternation that the response to the search question "Frantz Fanon" entered into the APA's *DSM 5* search engine comes back "No Matching Records found."

To rectify this academic-professional neglect, we have compiled a compelling collection of work that intersects Fanon's theoretical discourses and clinical applications. In demonstrating how they represent cases of Fanonian applications of psychotherapy, the contributions to *Frantz Fanon's Psychotherapeutic Approaches to Clinical Work: Practicing Internationally with Marginalized Communities* not only illuminate the contours of Frantz Fanon's therapeutic practices but the collateral effects of disclosing how seldom his therapeutic practices have been researched, analyzed, applied, or tested for their therapeutic efficacy or pedagogical potential. Until this collection of intense texts, Fanon's unique socio-psychotherapy existed on the margins of psychological disciplines, curricula, and pedagogy.

Along with clinical papers documenting contemporary Fanonian mental health practices, *Frantz Fanon's Psychotherapeutic Approaches to Clinical Work* is a "mixed-tape" of historical and theoretical engagements with the revolutionary psychotherapeutic practices of the radical anti-colonial therapist whom Dr. Richard Horton, editor of the global health journal *The Lancet*, calls the originator of the global health paradigm (2018). In that spirit, our aspiration for *Frantz Fanon's Psychotherapeutic Approaches to Clinical Work* is that it provokes sorely needed discussions of Fanon's clinical and psychotherapeutic practices in contemporary research and clinical and therapeutic spheres.

In the course of conceptualizing, collecting, and editing the contributions to this outstanding body of work, we have incurred the debt of a specific cohort of practitioners and scholars, beginning with the original set of prospective contributors we approached to contribute to this text. We were bolstered in our efforts by the immediate agreement of those we approached to contribute to this book. Even those few who for different reasons having to do with personal or professional reasons had to withdraw from the project were helpful in adding their views to the conceptual framework of the project. Whether it was Matthew B. Johnson, Associate Professor of Psychology at John Jay College of Criminal Justice, City University of New York, who widely published in the area of interrogation and false confessions, as well as in other areas involving psychology and law. Saths Cooper, who with the PAG (Psychology and Apartheid Group), formed in the mid-1980s by a group of Black psychologists, was instrumental in leading an academic boycott of organized psychology because its association with the Psychological Association of South Africa (PASA) failed to publicly show its abhorrence of apartheid, which produced deleterious consequences for the Black population's mental and psychological well-being. Ibrahim Makkawi of Birzeit University, on the West Bank of Palestine, who researches community psychology and contributed to the development of a master's program at Birzeit University in community psychology. Professor Makkawi traces community psychology on the West Bank back to the community organizing and grassroots activism of the first Intifada of 1987. Hussein A. Bulhan, Founder and President/Chancellor of Frantz Fanon University (FFU), Somaliland. FFU is an academic institution devoted to training a new cadre of professionals and paraprofessionals whose practice and social commitment follow the example of Frantz Fanon, while integrating state-of-the-art knowledge and technology with the culture, history, and beliefs of all individuals and communities served. Dr. Bulhan is a Fanon scholar whose book, *Frantz Fanon and the Psychology of Oppression* (1985) is still widely read since its publication almost 30 years ago.

While our greatest debt is to the extraordinary ensemble of scholars, researchers, and practitioners assembled in this first of its kind Fanonian text, we also want to acknowledge several key figures whose work and encouragement is reflected in *Frantz Fanon's Psychotherapeutic Approaches to Clinical Work*. Two seminal Fanon scholars have been of inestimable value to the trajectory of Lou Turner's work on Frantz Fanon over the years. Nigel Gibson (Emerson College) and Robert Bernasconi (Penn State University) provided engaging venues to present my theoretical research and to engage in invaluable discussions on the latest Fanon discourse and social movement activities inspired by Frantz Fanon. Conference, symposia and book opportunities were always forthcoming from Nigel and Robert, such that their selfless intellectual labors in the service of the work of others has been responsible for some of the profoundest discourse in Fanon Studies. More than 30 years of generosity of spirit and serious philosophic engagement in the thought of a revolutionary thinker as fertile as Fanon's, naturally, can never be repaid in full. However, for my part (Lou Turner), it is my hope that the turn that Helen A. Neville and I have taken Fanon Studies in editing this unique collection of Fanonian practices, research, and theoretical/historical engagements will be viewed as advancing our collective efforts to recover a "new Frantz Fanon" for a new generation which "must, out of relative obscurity, discover its mission, fulfill it, or betray it" (Fanon, 1966, p. 167).

References

Fanon, F. (1966). *The wretched of the earth* (C. Farrington, Trans.). New York: Grove Press.

Horton, R. (2018). Frantz Fanon and the origins of global health. *The Lancet*, *392* (10149). Retrieved from www.thelancet.com/journals/lancet/article/PIIS0140-6736(18)32041-5/fulltext.

Introduction

Lou Turner and Helen A. Neville

> Global health is not merely a constellation of diseases, a collection of national health systems, or even a set of values. It is a way of looking at our world. It seeks to observe, document, monitor, interpret, and eliminate the harms that accrue from national and transnational forces inimical to health—political, commercial, military, financial, diplomatic, legal, intersectional, and cultural. Global health is about power and poverty, violence and exploitation, oppression and silence, and collusion and exclusion. If one views global health using this broader lens, the historical turn that was the decisive and creative moment for the birth of global health was surely decolonization. It was decolonization, beginning in the 1950s with legacies that continue to this day, which illuminated the myriad pressures that shape the health of peoples worldwide. And the person who wrote the first manifestos for global health was Frantz Fanon.
>
> (Horton, 2018, np)

The prestigious global health journal, *The Lancet*, carried a provocative "Comment" by the journal's editor-in-chief, Richard Horton, entitled "Frantz Fanon and the origins of global health." Three days later, Johns Hopkins Bloomberg School of Public Health's e-newsletter *Global Health Now* picked up Horton's (2018) comment, retitling it "Frantz Fanon's Manifestos." The occasion of Horton's comments was to take exception to the "dangerous myth that has been cloaked around the young body of global health" (Horton, 2018) that the HIV/ AIDS epidemic was the initiating cause and modality of the global health movement. The HIV/AIDS origin story of global health is "a deception that erases important histories, marginalizes already neglected peoples, and prevents accurate understanding of why progress towards sustainable health improvements in some of the most resource-poor settings is so slow and erratic" (Horton, 2018, np). Horton challenged the global health community to assume "a more expansive view, starting with decolonization in the 1950s, and the crucial, unsung work of psychiatrist and activist Frantz Fanon" (Global Health Now, 2018, np).

In point of fact, the history of global health is not the only field in the medical sciences whose history is "cloaked in a dangerous [exclusionary] myth" (Horton, 2018) that has disappeared the work and contributions of Frantz

Fanon. Despite the fact that Fanon's contributions to postcolonial and critical theory are richly documented, his actual therapeutic practices have seldom been researched and analyzed. McCulloch (1983) and Bulhan (1985) are fugitive exceptions. That his unique socio-psychotherapy exists on the margins of psychology, psychiatry, psychoanalysis, and related mental health fields is in part because of the politicized character of his widely available published writings, but we also cannot ignore the negligence of Western scholars and practitioners to seek out the contributions of intellectuals from the African Diaspora. One overarching goal of this collection is thus to unveil Fanon's innovations and legacy in the applied mental health fields.

Our interest in uncovering the application of Fanon's work on mental health practice internationally predates the publication of Fanon's clinical papers (2015, 2018). In 1987, the critically acclaimed *Cry Freedom* premiered. In this biopic of sorts, Richard Attenborough explores the life and death of Steve Biko and the journalist who covered these events. It was the first time a major motion picture exposed in detail the horrors of apartheid South Africa. As a graduate student, I (Helen A. Neville) vividly remember seeing the movie with my mom at the Vista Theatre in Los Angeles. The venue is not as important as what happened after. I purchased from an activist who was staffing a stand outside of the theatre a copy of Lou Turner and John Alan's (1986) recently published monograph, *Frantz Fanon, Soweto, and Black American Thought*. The book with its coverage of Fanon and the connection among Black struggles internationally sparked a political awakening (Fanon, 1966) in me. As fate would have it, we (Lou Turner and Helen A. Neville) became colleagues in the Department of African American Studies at the University of Illinois at Urbana–Champaign nearly two decades later. Our mutual interests and expertise in Fanon Studies (Turner) and Black Psychology (Neville) led us to develop and offer a course on Black liberation psychology. Our work on the course served as the beginning of a dialogue and collaboration thinking through the contributions of Fanon's work in psychology. The real impetus for the current collection, however, emerged from Turner's persistent critique of the limited exploration of Fanon's clinical work and to a lesser degree Neville's frustration with the erasure of Fanon in much of the work in liberation psychology. The birth of this collection comes at the dawn of a Fanon renaissance; a point of time which propelled Horton (2018), the editor of most prestigious medical journal, to proclaim Fanon penned the "first manifesto for global health."

Fanon's now readily available clinical papers present us not only with a "new Frantz Fanon," but they provide evidence for his evolving therapeutic approaches that today are broadly construed as "cultural competency," "cultural humility," and social justice counseling. Fanon's clinical writings about *decolonizing the mind* serve as blueprints for contemporary efforts to decolonize psychiatry (Heaton, 2013), psychological science (Adams, Dobles, Gómez, Kurtiş, & Molina, 2015), nursing (McGibbon, Mulaudzi, Didham, Barton, & Sochan, 2014), and counseling related fields (Goodman & Gorski, 2014). The effort to decolonialize psychology is probably best captured by Bulhan's work in the Horn of Africa. Bulhan is the founding president of the Frantz Fanon University (FFU) which aims "to decolonize psychological science in teaching, social, and clinical practice" (FFU, 2014). As Fanon's clinical papers disclose, and the monographs collected in this text demonstrate, the challenge is:

> To decolonize psychological science, it is necessary to transform its focus from promotion of individual happiness to cultivation of collective well-being, from concern with instinct to promotion of human needs, from prescriptions for adjustment to affordances for empowerment, from treatment of passive victims to creation of self-determining actors, and from globalizing, top-down approaches to context-sensitive, bottom-up approaches. Only then will the field realize its potential to advance Frantz Fanon's call for humane and just social order.
>
> (Bulhan, 2015, p. 239)

The Fanonian Itinerary

Fanonian therapeutic approaches contain a sociospatial dimension in which the clinic/hospital, center, and/or community, feature prominently in the studies in this text, whether South Los Angeles' Fanon Research and Development Center (King, this volume), Centro Frantz Fanon in Turin, Northern Italy (Beneduce, this volume), the community-based Somali social service agency, Midaynta, in Toronto, Canada (Chioneso et al., this volume), Australian and Torres Strait mental health systems (Molloy this volume), or a community rape crisis center (Valgoi, this volume), or the Bellevue/NYU Program for Survivors of Torture (Smith & Gueu, this volume). The itinerary of Fanonian approaches is illustrative of transnational mental health researches and practices in marginalized communities.

At either end of the post-Fanon spectrum (i.e., the six decades since Fanon's death in 1961), multiple Fanon centers and one Frantz Fanon University testify to the institutionalization of the mental health revolution in psychotherapy that attaches to the name "Frantz Fanon." The 1974 establishment of the Fanon Research and Development Center in South Los Angeles' marginalized Black community and the 1996 initiation of Centro Frantz Fanon, in the northern Italian city of Turin, for displaced immigrants from Africa and the Middle East, converge across the spectrum of discourses in Fanonian psychopolitics to recapitulate and extend his itinerary. There are other examples, from the San Francisco Bay Area, to London's Black immigrant Brixton community, to the community-based sociotherapy initiatives in Rwanda. These centers translated Fanon's psychopolitcal thought into clinical practice. They incorporated Fanon's insights about the impact of racial violence on the human psyche for both the oppressor and the oppressed, the nature of the healing relationship (doctor–patient, psychologist–client), the role of disrupting and decolonizing health institutions to provide efficacious services to the most vulnerable in society (Giordan, 2011). As such, Frantz Fanon is the face of a new international revolution in mental healthcare

Rwanda is the site of perhaps the most significant instance of this new Fanonian revolution in healing practices from (neo)colonial violence. After the 1994 Rwanda genocide, the country embarked on an array of restorative justice initiatives, including "community-based sociotherapy." These healing strategies are designed to help restore Rwandan civil society from the mass trauma of the genocide and policy failures of international peacekeeping forces and aid agencies. Although the initiatives differ depending on the specific mission of a given organization, collectively they are designed to promote the restoration of human dignity, communal safety, and wellness in its broadest sense.

One of the central aims of this collection is to serve as a transnational call (manifesto) to establish and fund centers, collaboratives, and educational institutions to carry out and extend the kind of research and development of Fanonian approaches and practices articulated here. Another aim of the edited work is to provide Fanon-informed case studies to delineate ways in which scholars and practitioners can bring together political engagement and clinical intervention in racial states and neocolonial spaces.

A New Frantz Fanon: Implications for Clinical Research and Practice

With the long-awaited English translation of previously unpublished or unavailable writings of Frantz Fanon, *Frantz Fanon: Alienation and Freedom* (2018), we are at the dawn of discovering a "new Frantz Fanon." It is exciting to recognize that the work of so many contributors to *Frantz Fanon's Psychotherapeutic Approaches to Clinical Work: Practicing Internationally with Marginalized Communities* was already trending in the direction of the new Fanon we find in his recently published clinical papers and lectures. This is the first collection to focus on contemporary clinical applications of Fanon's research and practice *and* it adopts a transnational lens through which to capture the global reach of Fanon's work. The contributors represent scholars and practitioners from Africa, Australia, Europe, and North America. In addition, the book incorporates multiple methods, including historical and theoretical approaches, placing Fanon's research and practice in context; clinical case studies applying Fanon's principles to individual and group therapy, as well as community-based practice and research. And, we include interviews with Fanonian practitioners and researchers to highlight the voices of those working in the trenches. Although Fanon's work is far-reaching, the current collection concentrates on practice with racially-ethnically-culturally and economically marginalized communities globally. The contributions herein contribute to the discourse that the publication of his previously unpublished or unavailable work has instigated. Moreover, this book comes at a moment when a new generation of scholars, mental health practitioners, and activists are discovering a new Frantz Fanon. *Frantz Fanon's Psychotherapeutic Approaches* represents a collective intervention in Fanon Studies,

Black psychology, and other areas of psychology (e.g., liberation, critical counseling, community), psychiatry, social justice counseling, and community mental health engagements with underserved populations. The book is organized around four areas: (1) Fanon's Clinical Work in Historical Context; (2) History, Theory and Fanonian Praxis; (3) Fanon in Clinical Action: Psychotherapeutic and Community Applications; and (4) Fanonian Research in Action. Each section reflects the diversity of practices around the world and considers the roles of political and socioeconomic context, structures of gender oppression, racial identities and their intersection within those practices.

Fanon's Clinical Work in Historical Context

The chapters in the first section of *Frantz Fanon's Psychotherapeutic Approaches* set Fanon's psychotherapy within multiple sociohistorical settings. Camille Robcis locates Fanon as an emerging professional within the French revolution in psychiatry, which was centered in the radical setting of Saint-Alban Hospital, in Saint-Alban-sur-Limagnole, France. Lou Turner then situates Fanon's nine clinical papers in the broader historical medical and philosophical debates during colonialism and in the current trends in Fanon studies. In doing so, he traces Fanon's attempts to transfer Saint-Alban's institutional therapy, renamed sociotherapy, to the North African milieu undergoing radical mutations of decolonization. We end the section with an interview with Lewis M. King, founding director of the Fanon Research and Development Center in South Los Angeles. The interview serves as a bridge between Fanon's revolutionary thought at the fall of colonialism to later clinical application in racial states. The interview captures the African American context of the Black Power era of the early 1970s and the creation of the first Fanon Center.

In her chapter, "Frantz Fanon, Institutional Psychotherapy, and the Decolonization of Psychiatry," Robcis describes Fanon's psychopolitics as a function of the duality she locates in his concept of alienation, viz., psychological and political alienation. Each is intensified by the socioeconomic processes that Fanon's sociodiagnostics unpacks. Her interrogation commences with an examination of Fanon's 1956 "Letter of Resignation" as chief medical physician of Algeria's Blida-Joinville Psychiatric Hospital (BPH). Robcis attends to Fanon's treatment of the social and economic origins of alienation as it is racialized (epidermalized), that is, "inscribed in the body and in the skin" (p. 9). Robcis' discussion of the historical context of the revolution in French psychiatry and Fanon's theory of the subject as instrumental to his decolonizing psychiatry is critical in connecting Fanon's writing to contemporary practices of mental healthcare work with marginalized groups.

A contribution of Robcis' (this volume) chapter is her careful tracing of the history of the psychiatric revolution that led to institutional psychology at Saint-Alban during Fanon's internship as part of his course of study in psychiatry at the University of Lyon. In her history of the French psychiatric revolution, Robcis clarifies what Fanon's biographers (Gendzier, 1974; Macey,

2012) and commentators (McCulloch, 1983) find vexing, viz., Fanon's combining psychiatry and psychoanalysis. As Robcis insists, "The point was thus not to choose between psychiatry *or* psychoanalysis but to anchor psychiatry in a psychoanalytic understanding of the subject, a subject that resulted from conscious and unconscious representations that were constructed in relation to others" (p. 30). In part, Robcis owes her unique grasp of the institutional psychotherapy (IP) of Saint-Alban to having had the privilege of interviewing Jean Oury, an intern during the formative years of IP. Citing Francois Tosquelles' two articles on Fanon's stay at Saint-Alban, Robcis provides an unexpectedly revealing contextualization of Fanon's literary output, namely the two plays he wrote that are now available with the publication of *Alienation and Freedom* (2018). Robcis' chapter scopes out the innovations and therapeutic pedagogy in sociotherapy that Fanon instituted amongst Blida-Joinville Hospital staff. She also takes account of Fanon's failed experiment with sociotherapy on a Muslim men's ward and the journey it initiated in Fanon's discovery of the "total social fact" (p. 34) of Algeria.

Lou Turner picks up the thread of Fanon's "traveling theory" (Said, 1999) across the North African préterrain to his rendezvous with revolution. The geopsychiatry of Fanon's evolving approach to sociotherapy, or properly ethnopsychiatry (Gibson & Beneduce, 2017), with marginalized communities is embedded in conflicted ethnographic and normative biases of academic theories and research methods. Through Turner's discussion of Fanon's nine seminal clinical papers, he argues that the unearthed formerly unavailable works of Fanon confirm that the main texts of Fanon's published *oeuvre* were either contemporaneous with or had priority over some of the most compelling theorizing of the modern conjuncture of power, subjugation, and the possibilities for human liberation in the postwar world.

Turner's analysis, especially of the collaborative multi-authored clinical paper assessing the administrative challenges of psychiatric hospitalization in Algeria, exposes insights connecting Fanonian practice to contemporary concerns: (a) Fanonian criteria for assessment of mental health administration in terms of the medical infrastructure needed for his specific sociotherapeutic practice; (b) identification of problems that cultural competency was supposed to solve; (c) problems of "social re-adaptation" of psychiatric after-care for marginal or underserved communities; (d) the pedagogical particularities of institutional retraining and certification of staff for Fanonian applications; (e) the role of indigenous mental health workers and staff in Fanonian sociotherapy; and (f) the outline of what a Fanonian mental health infrastructure would look like.

Uncovering the influence of racial oppression on the psychological health of African Americans and also the pathways to healing and freedom from racial domination was the scientific imperative of the South Los Angeles Fanon Research and Development Center, founded and directed by psychologist Lewis M. King. In fact, King sees the Fanon Center (and, he adds, also the purpose of the present book) as "giving the 'subaltern' a voice. We the historically oppressed are now writing about ourselves. There is a certain organicity to it all that must be captured and represented. Deep reflection is necessary" (King, email correspondence, 2019). In lieu of the availability of Fanon's clinical papers, mental health research centers like the Fanon Center translated his published psycho-political treatises into Fanonian research paradigms. This transactional strategy made naming the Center after Frantz Fanon more than a question of "branding." As an outgrowth of the National Institute of Mental Health and its Center for the Study of Minority Group Mental Health Programs, established in 1970, the Fanon Center affiliated with the Department of Psychiatry of the Charles R. Drew Postgraduate Medical School, in turn affiliated with the Martin Luther King, Jr. General Hospital, in Compton, California beginning in September 1974 (Fanon Research and Development Center, 1976).

In our interview, King shared his own political development or "awakening"; seeds were planted as a youth in Trinidad and were fomented on the Howard University campus as a student-activist in 1965–66. He and fellow students like Stokely Carmichael and professors such as Nathan Hare were in daily discourse about "Black Power." These intellectual and activist pursuits lay the foundation for King's later professional identity as psychological researcher. King discussed the history of and impetus behind the Fanon Center. As a research and development center, we wanted to understand what a Fanonian approach to psychological research looked like in the Black Power era. How, in other words, did King and his collaborators see Fanon's theory and practice contributing to the psychopathological research needed to meet the mental health needs of African American communities, especially in Los Angeles?

In our conversation with King, we also wanted to gain a sense of the Fanon Center's frameworks, initiatives, and programs. King "restored" the significance of the late African American psychologist Dr. J. Alfred Cannon to the history of Los Angeles' Black mental healthcare and cultural communities. Cannon was motivated by the 1965 Watts rebellion to build cultural and mental health institutions in service to Los Angeles' Black cultural renaissance. (During the Black Power era of the late 1960s and 1970s, Cannon founded the Central City Community Mental Health Center, in 1973, was instrumental in establishing the Frederick Douglass Child Development Center, and with C. Bernard Jackson, co-founded the Inner-City Cultural Center.) Catalyzed by the Watts rebellion and, earlier, the passage of the federal Community Mental Health Act, Cannon organized Black psychiatrists to build mental health institutions in and for the Black community. One of these was the Drew Medical School as part of the Martin Luther King, Jr. Hospital in Compton, California, where the Fanon Research and Development Center would be housed.

King's recollection of the Fanon Center is a narrative of the transcontinental (Howard to UCLA) and diasporic student connections in which Frantz Fanon was first discovered and entered African American consciousness and struggle, from community to campus and back again. Fanon's thought and the emergent narrative of his revolutionary practice as a psychiatrist operated at the nexus of academia and the Black community. Lewis M. King and his fellow students, and later his professional colleagues, embodied the transdisciplinary and transactional itinerary represented by Frantz Fanon. As he maintains, "Fanon is NOT just a name." Because there is so little documented of the historic intersections between an HBCU (historically Black colleges and universities) like Howard University and a West Coast PWI (predominantly White institution) like UCLA, between Black students on university campuses and the Black communities they sought to impact and change with their education, between African American and Afro-Caribbean student-activists, and between Fanon and the emergent Black Power and Black Studies movements from the Civil Rights Movement, we have dedicated sufficient space for King's narrative of this little known history to move it from the margins to the center of the Black intellectual tradition in psychology.

History, Theory and Fanonian Praxis

The Wretched of the Earth posits the twin spheres of violence: (a) the violence of colonization and its elicitation of anti-colonial violence by the colonized and (b) Fanon's psychiatric practice with victims and perpetrators of violence and torture. The radical existentialism of Fanon's project sought to foster a "new humanism:"

> The struggle for freedom does not give back to the national culture its former value and shape; this struggle which aims at a fundamentally different set of relations between men [and women] cannot leave intact either the form or the content of the people's culture. After the conflict there is not only the disappearance of colonialism but also the disappearance of the colonized man.
>
> (Fanon, 1966, p. 197)

This new humanity cannot do otherwise than define a new humanism both for itself and for others. In a sense, *The Wretched of the Earth* is Fanon's *memoires* of decolonization, a counter-narrative to the *memoires* produced by the colons of the military-medical corps of the 19th and early 20th centuries. Such *memoires* of participant accounts of racial and ethnic typologies of conquered peoples have a long genealogy, from Roman antiquity to early modern European colonization of Asia, Africa, and the Americas. Such *memoires* were the terrain upon which scientific Enlightenment discourses on "race" operated to form a feedback loop of scientific-philosophic-militarist rationalizations of Western imperialist colonization of the global South.

In her monograph, "Therapy of/for the Oppressed: Frantz Fanon's Psychopolitical Pedagogy of Transformation," Erica Burman (this volume) engages the relationship between Fanon's theory of violence in the context of his sociotherapy. Fanon's psychopolitics and sociotherapy is cross-referenced with Paulo Freire, who is often cited in tandem with Fanon, based on the educational psychology of their "pedagogy of the oppressed." Burman unpacks discourses surrounding Fanon's therapeutic practice for their pedagogical functions. The clinical framing of his public discourse and the pedagogical framing of his political psychology means, according to Burman's argument, that our engagement with Fanon's concept of violence is inescapable. What is unique in Burman's reading of Fanon's controversial violence discourse is her making it a *teachable moment* to instruct the colonized to be actional instead of reactional. Burman concludes that "Fanon was an educator" (p. 120). She avers that we do not have an account of Fanon's practice as a therapist. Critical of Fanon's (and Tosquelles') use of electro-shock and insulin therapies, Burman observes:

> Even in his account of the day hospital he established at Tunis, Fanon emphasizes how this can still accommodate drug-induced comas and electro-shock sessions, the former known as either the Bini method, or annihilation therapy, explicitly so named on the basis that the maladaptive aspects of the patient's personality should be obliterated and so that more appropriate behaviors and characteristics could be imprinted. These, then, are aspects of Fanon's psychiatric practice that—true to his own practice of speaking truth to power, we should not shy away from condemning as complicit with an abusive psychiatric system.
>
> (p. 119)

Burman's monograph is preoccupied with the pedagogical dimensions of Fanon's psychotherapy of restorative reciprocity between human subjects. From his published works, *Black Skin, White Masks* and *The Wretched of the Earth*, she identifies a seldom recognized contribution of Fanon's to therapeutic practice, viz., the dialectic of conflictual-reciprocal encounters which enable the patient to authorize herself, a practice that Burman describes as "ethical-political practice in action" (p. 123). This is evidence of Fanon's "radical humanism," she contends, because it anticipates a state of independence, which links the individual back to the social. What is revolutionary in Fanon's concerns is the transformation of the alienated social relations of racialized or colonial society. Fanonian revolutionary theory and practice is privileged with enduring engagements with Italian postwar discourses in radical social science and humanities. Roberto Beneduce, founder of the Turin Frantz Fanon Centre, finds, in concert with Fanon, that *testimony* is essential in therapeutic practices especially for those experiencing trauma as a result of political events. Beneduce's (this volume) discussion of Fanonian critical ethnography in relation to the work of the Turin Frantz Fanon Centre with African immigrants demonstrates the premise of this book. The conceptual range of Beneduce's chapter, "The Psychic Life of History: Migration, Critical Ethno-Psychiatry, and the Archives of the Future," resonates with Fanon's deep theorization of psychiatry that we now have available with the publication of his University of Lyon dissertation, namely that "to approach the problem of history from a psychoanalytic and ontological angle, . . . history is nothing but the systematic valorization of collective complexes" (Fanon, 2018, p. 257).

Beneduce's nuanced discussion of the case studies and the embedded history, or historicity (being of history), of the trauma produced by colonialism over its *longue durée* into the postcolonial present of the immigrant, in North Africa and Europe, is an unmistakable contribution to extending Fanon, even as we are rediscovering his practices and his spectral interventions *via* his clinical papers and dissertation. The discursive drift of his monograph across complex ethnographies, psychoanalysis, psychotherapies, deconstructions of transnational literatures of oppression, displacement, foreclosure, memory, and mourning recollects Fanon's project in *Black Skin*. It is a Fanonian reflection that gives those who would engage Fanon's *Black Skin* confirmation of the interdisciplinarity of his genetic method of approach. In a word, Beneduce has globalized Fanon's approach.

Fanon in Clinical Action: Psychotherapeutic and Community Applications

The essays in this section traverse a fine line between the application of Fanon's clinical work and his phenomenological-existential discourse on the lived experience of human beings *in situs* (in situation). Fanon's writings have provided a conceptual approach to the provision of mental health services to underserved communities for more than 60 years in various transnational contexts. His approach to the mental health needs of oppressed communities has also served as a training framework for mental health professionals working in resource centers assisting refugees and immigrants from conflict zones. Victims of political repression or trauma induced by socioeconomic deprivation are treated with Fanonian therapeutic approaches that are also political and social forms of community health. Fanonian psychology thus offers an interactive therapeutic/political approach to race-based trauma, which is critical to social-emotional well-being and healing.

The chapters in this section present research—informed and Fanonian—inspired by clinical practices. Fanon developed his unique psychotherapeutic approach working with torture and trauma survivors (Turner, 2011). Thus, the focus of the section centers on a discussion of and case examples with survivors of torture, as well as victims of political repression and race-based trauma. For Fanon, "testimony" was an essential therapeutic tool in the treatment of adults and children suffering from various forms of trauma. In addition to the role of testimony in therapy, this section incorporates ways in which therapy can be interactive and political practice that aids in healing individuals and their communities.

Drawing on years of clinical experience in working with West and Central African refugees seeking mental health services at Bellevue Hospital, in New York City, Hawthorne E. Smith (Co-Director of Clinical Services for the Bellevue/NYU Program for Survivors of Torture) and his colleague, Mr. Gueu, describe the nature and expression of neocolonial trauma. They outline the limitations of Western conceptualizations of trauma assessment and treatment in working with torture survivors from Africa. Using insights from Fanon's work with torture survivors and refugees, Smith and Gueu identify culturally relevant expressions of trauma, which have implications for individual and community interventions. Their work with support groups for French-speaking African survivors of torture is powerful, merging trauma-informed therapy with insights from Fanon's clinical approach. Importantly, the work of the Bellevue/NYU Program for Survivors of Torture bridges the Fanon meme that went viral on social media at the time of the 2014 sidewalk choking murder of Eric Gardner by Staten Island, New York police: "When we revolt it's not for a particular culture. We revolt simply because, for many reasons, we can no longer breathe" (Fanon, 1967, p. 226).

Luke Molloy, Senior Lecturer in the School of Nursing, University of Wollongong, Australia begins his monograph in Fanonian fashion by providing a context for understanding the mental health needs of indigenous peoples of Australia and Torres Strait. Molloy conceptualizes psychiatric nursing practices of cultural safety with Australia's First Peoples through the lens of Fanon's ideas. His method of cultural contextualization fits within psychiatric nursing practices with indigenous populations. With 20 years of clinical experience in acute mental healthcare in Ireland and Australia, Molloy's teaching and researching mental health nursing at the University of Wollongong relies on ethnographic methods to explore both professional practices and health services. This was necessitated by the failure of mainstream mental healthcare services to provide culturally safe care for Aboriginal and Torres Strait peoples despite national reports and policies calling for reform of mental health systems serving indigenous peoples.

Not unlike Fanon's practice in Algeria's and Tunisia's mental health systems, Molloy considers how the ideas of Fanon can be used to promote cultural safety within Australian and Torres Strait mainstream mental health services. Beyond cultural safety in mental health nursing, Molloy uses Fanon's ideas as a strategy to prompt mental health nurses to critically reflect on the imbalances in power and social equality inherent in healthcare delivery to indigenous populations. Promotion of critical reflection on the relationship between colonialism and healthcare status in Australia has the potential to change the attitudes of nurses, in Molloy's view, from a posture that reinforces the colonial hegemony of mental health practices and systems to one that supports the structure of feeling of indigenous culture. Fanon's ideas and their potential for promoting cultural safety articulate a conceptual strategy for mental health nurses to critically navigate the asymmetric power relations and inequalities of healthcare delivery to marginal populations. Molloy's chapter guides mental health nurses' understanding of the colonial nexus between Australian and Torres Strait indigenous communities and the hegemony of the mental healthcare systems and practices that wittingly or unwittingly support their marginalization.

In "The Case of K: Looking to Frantz Fanon to Guide Cross-Racial Trauma-Informed Therapy," Maria Judith Valgoi (Assistant Professor at Governors State University in Illinois, USA) makes singular contributions to Fanonian psychotherapeutic practice on several levels. First and importantly, she situates herself as a White woman in the problematic of racial dominance and structural inequality at the interpersonal nexus of the lived experience of racialism. As Valgoi argues, it is "foundational to my development of a social consciousness as a practitioner and my ability to use interventions of liberation in the therapeutic context" (p. 199). In her work with an African American woman seeking services at a local rape crisis center, Valgoi centers her practice of Fanonian institutional therapy by making the ecosystem of the environment in which she practices representative of the social struggles of the people of color in the community in which she works, engaging in those struggles herself, and making it a point to familiarize herself with the leaders and community participants of those struggles by name. As a summation of this kind of "woke psychotherapy," Valgoi's intellectual and affective commitment to, in Gramscian terms, posit herself "as an element of the contradictions and elevate this contradiction to a principle of knowledge and therefore of action" (Gramsci, 1971), discloses an organic Gramscian–Fanonian connection. Moreover, the description of the psychopolitical environment of her therapeutic setting represents a compelling iteration of the institutional therapy of Fanon's mentor Francois Tosquelles. More to the point, Valgoi expresses Fanon's admonition that "psychiatry has to be political" (Cherki, 2006). The innovative design of the "case of K" is illustrative of Fanonian approaches to psychotherapy that are forward-facing to such contemporary methods as telepsychology/telehealth or the ways in which information communication technology can be creatively deployed in providing mental health services in marginalized communities.

The last contribution to this section is a discussion that the editors had with Imani Bazzell, producer and host of a community mental healthcare radio program called "ACCESS Live" in the central Illinois twin communities of Champaign–Urbana, where the research one campus of the University of Illinois is located. This section's trajectory brings us to the innovative production of community mental health, public service, and radio programming developed by Imani Bazzell for the African American community of Champaign–Urbana. "ACCESS Live" operated within a Fanonian frame for nearly a decade. It was a public service platform to which the editors (Turner and Neville) were often invited to contribute. Mindful of the different strands of development of Fanonian thought in the US—e.g., the Black Power Movement and the Black Panther Party, or Black Studies and Black Psychology in academia—we wanted to explore a strand that has seldom attracted much attention. Fanon's ideas would seem to resonate with the professional and community healthcare activists engaged in actual therapeutic practices in psychiatric centers or mental health facilities in community settings like Champaign–Urbana's Black community. However, just how a community activist and leader like Bazzell would deploy a Fanonian media platform to help the Black community come to grips with the politics of the psychological traumas to which it is daily prone is what Bazzell explores in dialogue with the editors.

Auspiciously, we interviewed Bazzell on the sixtieth anniversary of Fanon's *A Dying Colonialism*, one of whose many innovations was its chapter on the psychology of the radio. Initially a technology of colonial hegemony, the transistor radio underwent a dialectical inversion, becoming an instrument of the national liberation movement. Our discussion with Bazzell highlights the community setting as also a media environment in which Fanon's ideas and therapeutic practices operate in the marginalized communities, especially traumatized communities of color dating back to the beginning of the Black Power Movement, in the late 1960s. The role of information media (traditional and social) in messaging Fanon's ideas intertwined with mental health public service messaging in marginalized communities is inherently political, demonstrating that *the medium is the message* and affirming Fanon's claim that "Psychiatry [and by extension psychology] has to be political." Bazzell's engagements with Fanon's ideas over a life of social justice activism bears witness to the contention that Fanon was the precursor to what, today, is called liberation psychology. Bazzell's recounting the origin and development of the "ACCESS Live" community mental health initiative captures the kind of psychopolitical innovation in mental healthcare delivery that recovers Fanonian sociotherapy for marginalized communities as a liberation psychology.

Fanonian Research in Action

> Fanon's hope for mankind is a useful starting point for any study of man and particularly one that addresses social and cultural influences in human behavior with specific references to psychopathology. His hope that the tools never possess the man is our belief that research never mystify the man; his hope that the enslavement of man cease forever speaks to our principle that researchers must not participate in the process of oppression.
>
> (King, 1978, p. 405)

The two research initiatives in the last section return us to Fanon's engagement with the psychology of the subaltern and the marginalized, viz., to the scenes of subjection of colonial and neocolonial trauma and to racialized contestations over identity in the struggle for what Fanon called a "new humanism" (Fanon, 1966). Fanon's heightened awareness of the social and cultural context in which social science research is conducted instructs us to be sensitive to how the quality of the settings and social relationships between researchers and participants or patients influences the quality of the results from applied mental health research. From this frame, the validity of research in marginalized communities of color is reflected in the degree to which the research results are used to help those communities (a) come to terms with the histories of what we now call racial trauma and (b) become actional or awaken the liberatory impulses of marginalized communities. Both studies in this section explore several problematics of Fanonian research in action.

Nkechinyelum A. Chioneso and her collaborators, Mahad A. Yusuf and Shamso M. Elmi of the Toronto-based Somali social services agency, Midaynta (*Unity*, in Somali), report on an action research initiative using a Fanonian lens to study the etiology of youth violence. In their chapter—"Mending a Crack in the Sky: An Evolving Community Healing Case Study Among Somali Canadians"—they describe the push-pull factors driving Somali immigration to Canada and the oppressive policies and practices fueling violence in and around Toronto. Similar to a number of other postcolonial countries, Somalia experienced sovereign conflicts (namely with Western countries) which set the foundation for internal turmoil as expressed in civil wars and civic discontent. Somali refugees were lured to Canada with ideas of a multiracial democracy and a better life; yet, once they arrived to the global North they were met with policies that reinforced alienation through racial and gender oppression and economic stagnation. Chioneso and her colleagues, like other contributions in this collection, engage the human vulnerability rendered by these demographic, military, environmental, and economic forces.

The authors outline the development of the collaboration and the proposed three-phase action project: conducting a participatory action research, completing a community action plan, and producing a documentary film. In the same vein as Fanon's case study of sociotherapy on a Muslim men's ward, Chioneso and colleagues confront the tension between listening and responding to the needs of community members and adhering to Western ideals of science and practice. In their reflexive exploration of the local realities of conducting action research, the authors analyze barriers and present possible solutions. They discuss the importance of remaining flexible and fluid when navigating between traditional research methods and the development of intervention based on the emerging data or community voices resulting from these efforts. They illustrate the complexities of conducting culturally informed community-based research with at least one goal of political awakening (Fanon, 1966).

We come full circle with the ending of the collection. We (Turner and Neville) formalized our initial application of Fanon to contemporary Black psychology by using a phenomenological research design to explore the ways in which Black people experience recognition in racial states and neocolonial societies. The chapter is a reprint of our article titled "Race and Recognition: Pathways to an Affirmative Black Identity" published in the *Journal of Black Psychology*, and co-authored with Brigitte Viard, one of our students. In this work we operationalize Fanon's dialectic of recognition for research agendas dedicated to analyzing Black identity formation in the era of colorblind racism (the dominant ideology that serves to deny, minimize, and distort the existence of structural racism

In our model we strive to elevate attitudes of recognition/respect to a level of social behavior that involves action. Grounding our conceptualization is the assertion that complex networks of adaptive attitudes and behavior patterns are discernible in phenomena of racial recognition. Such networks are framed by larger societal processes, which is why Fanon's psychology is sociogenic. Black lived experience in a White world is inauthentic and alienated because, as Fanon argued, even the barest reciprocal recognition that the Black individual is *human* is withheld or suspended by White society. Respect is an inherent characteristic of Fanon's dialectic of recognition, making it more than a social class-labor struggle but, as well, a natural race-identity struggle for a new humanity, a new humanism

Our incorporation of respect/self-respect in the existential phenomena of recognition/reciprocity raises an interesting set of issues. Defined in its existential sense as establishing the ethical/moral relations between human beings *qua* human beings, recognition is existential, in the sense of affirming human existence, because it presupposes human reciprocity, (i.e., our existence as *social* individuals). Self-consciousness, more than our identity, regulates our existence for others. This is recognition proper or what we might call reciprocity or *existential recognition*. With the introduction of *respect* into the dynamics of the recognition process, we constitute a second-order form of recognition, or *respect recognition*, which is defined in the terms outlined in "Race and Recognition." This second form of respectful recognition is status governed and driven. Historically, what makes the struggle for recognition such a challenging phenomenon in the formation of Black identity is the confusion of these two forms of recognition. The great merit of Fanon's discovery of a second dialectic of recognition, distinguished from Hegel's notion of recognition, is that he unraveled the confusion surrounding the two forms of recognition. In other words, where Black folk believe that they are striving for respect recognition, they are in fact struggling literally for their lives, for existential recognition, (i.e., for the very right to exist).

Findings from the in-depth racial life narrative interviews with self-identified Black people in Australia, Bermuda, South Africa, and the United States provide insight about the ways in which people construct, experience, and seek recognition and respect. Narrators shared stories in which they felt disrespected because of their race—whether interacting with Whites or with members from their own racial-ethnic group within the context of White supremacy. Participants further delineated the ways in which they demanded respect and thus recognition for their full humanity. We situate the discussion of recognition/respect within the larger debates in the psychology literature around racial identity or the meaning making process around one's racial group membership. This conceptual and methodological approach recalls the psychogenetic method of Fanon's published works, which is now confirmed by his "new" writings. In the research we negotiated the challenge to avoid positivism by taking seriously the obstacles and pitfalls to achieving an internalized, positive racial identity.

Fanon in Action, Today

The contours of Fanon's *A Dying Colonialism* and *The Wretched of the Earth* are to be found in his clinical papers where his psychotherapeutic practices stand-in as analogies for decolonization. Similarly, Fanon's decolonization of the clinic is his analogue for the "new reality of the nation" being born out of the revolution. Psychology and psychiatry have never been placed on such a concrete sociohistorical level, that is, in and as an act of social revolution.

The question—what happens after the revolution?—for the practice of *post-colonial* psychotherapy is not fully answered in the current collection. However, the works here explicate contemporary connections between Fanon's scholar-activism during the decolonialization movements of the 1950s and 1960s to the application of his clinical insights in contemporary racial states and neocolonial spaces. The essays included are modeled on the sociogenic therapy and research frameworks of Fanon's dialectic; they contain the "bacilli" of revolution (Lenin, 1974). We hope this collection serves as a resource for locating the "revolutionary time" called for in Fanonian psychotherapeutic approaches to clinical work in marginal communities as well as responds to appeals for increased global mental health practices that promote liberation and wellness among those most affected by interlocking forms of oppression (race, nationality, class, gender, etc.). The mission statement of Frantz Fanon University, in Somaliland, captures the aims of this book:

> Those who read his books and study his practice find much that can guide them toward professional integrity and compassionate service to under-served populations. Frantz Fanon University seeks to not only preserve Fanon's revolutionary legacy but also advance his commitment to social justice by teaching, writing, and serving communities in action.
>
> (FFU, 2014)

Bibliography

Adams, G., Dobles, I., Gómez, L. H., Kurtiş, T., & Molina, L. E. (2015). Decolonizing psychological science: Introduction to the special thematic section. *Journal of Social and Political Psychology*, *3*(1), 213–238.

Agathangelou, A. (2014). *Frantz Fanon, clinic(al) time, and the event*. Paper given at Black Perspectives in Counselling, Psychology & Psychotherapy, 8th Critical Multicultural Counselling and Psychotherapy Conference, OISE, University of Toronto. Retrieved from www.oise.utoronto.ca/cdcp/UserFiles/File/Conference_Package_2014.pdf.

Basabose, J. (2014). Community based sociotherapy in Rwanda: Healing a post-violent conflict society. *Insight on Conflict*. Retrieved from www.peaceinsight.org/blog/2014/09/community-based-sociotherapy-rwanda/.

Batchlor, K. (2017). The translation of *Les Damnés de la terre* into English: Exploring Irish connections. In K. Batchlor & S. Harding (Eds.), *Translating Frantz Fanon across continents and languages*. London: Routledge.

Bernasconi, R. (2010). Fanon's *the wretched of the earth* as the fulfillment of Sartre's *critique of dialectical reason*. *Sartre Studies International*, *16*(2), 36–47.

Bloch, M. (1990). Foreword. In O. Mannoni (Ed.), *Prospero and Caliban: The psychology of colonization*. Ann Arbor, MI: University of Michigan Press.

Bulhan, H. (1985). *Frantz Fanon and the psychology of oppression*. New York: Plenum Press.

Bulhan, H. (2015). Stages of colonialism in Africa: From occupation of land to occupation of being. *Journal of Social & Political Psychology, 3*(1), 239–256.

Burman, E. (2019). *Fanon, education, action: Child as method*. London: Routledge.

Cherki, A. (2006). *Frantz Fanon: A portrait*. New York: Cornell University Press.

Cross, W. E., Jr. (1971). Discovering the Black referent: The psychology of black liberation. In V. J. Dixon & B. G. Foster (Eds.), *Beyond Black or White: An alternate America* (pp. 96–110). Boston: Little, Brown and Company.

Curry, T. (2017). *The man-not: Race, class, genre, and the dilemmas of black manhood*. Philadelphia: Temple University Press.

Department of Economic and Social Affairs Population Division (DESA). (2019). *World population prospects 2019 highlights*. New York: United Nations. Retrieved from https://population.un.org/wpp/Publications/Files/WPP2019_Highlights.pdf.

Desai, M. (2009). *The psychological, the sociopolitical, and interdisciplinary inquiry: Lessons from Frantz Fanon*. Paper presented at the 117th Convention of the American Psychological Association, Toronto, Canada.

Desai, M. (2014). Psychology, the psychological, and critical praxis: A phenomenologist reads Frantz Fanon. *Theory and Psychology, 24*(1), 1–18.

Etherington, B. (2016). An answer to the question: What is decolonization? Frantz Fanon's the wretched of the earth and Jean-Paul Sartre's critique of dialectical reason. *Modern Intellectual History, 13*(1), 151–178.

Fanon, F. (1966). *The wretched of the earth* (C. Farrington, Trans.). New York: Grove Press.

Fanon, F. (1967). *Black skin, white masks* (C. Markmann, Trans.). New York: Grove Press, (fifth printing).

Fanon, F. (1969). *Toward the African revolution* (H. Chevalier, Trans.). New York: Grove Press.

Fanon, F. (2015). *Frantz Fanon, Écrits sur l'aliénation et la liberté* (J. Khalfa & R. Young, Trans.). Paris: La Découverte.

Fanon, F. (2018). *Frantz Fanon: Alienation and freedom* (R. Young & J. Khalfa, Eds., S. Corcoran, Trans.). London: Bloomsbury.

Fanon Research & Development Center. (1976). *Fanon research & development center: An overview* [an informational brochure]. Los Angeles: Fanon Research & Development Center.

Faramelli, A. (2017). The decolonized clinic: Fanon with Foucault. *LJCT, 1*(2), 114–128.

FFU (Frantz Fanon University). (2014). Retrieved 2019, from http://fanonuniversity.org/index.html.

Gendzier, I. (1974). *Frantz Fanon: Critical study*. New York: Vintage Books.

Gibson, N., & Beneduce, R. (2017). *Frantz Fanon, psychiatry and politics*. Johannesburg, South Africa: Wits University Press.

Giordano, C. (2011). Translating Fanon in the Italian context: Rethinking the ethics of treatment in psychiatry. *Transcultural Psychiatry, 48*(3), 228–256.

Giordano, C. (2014). *Migrants in translation: Caring and the logics of difference in contemporary Italy*. Oakland, CA: University of California Press.

Global Health Now. (2018). *Frantz Fanon's manifestos*. Johns Hopkins Bloomberg School of Public Health. Retrieved from www.globalhealthnow.org/2018-09/frantz-fanons-manifestos.

Goodman, R. D., & Gorski, P. C. (Eds.). (2014). *Decolonizing "multicultural" counseling through social justice*. New York, NY: Springer.

Gramsci, A. (1971). Problems of Marxism. In *Selections from the prison notebooks of Antonio Gramsci*. New York: International Publishers.

Heaton, M. M. (2013). *Black skin, white coats: Nigerian psychiatrists, decolonization, and the globalization of psychiatry*. Athens, Ohio: Ohio University Press.

Hirschfeld, L. (1996). *Race in the making: Cognition, culture, and the child's construction of human kinds*. Cambridge, MA: MIT Press.

Horton, R. (2018). Frantz Fanon and the origins of global health. *The Lancet, 392*(10149). Retrieved from www.thelancet.com/journals/lancet/article/PIIS0140-6736(18)32041-5/fulltext.

Jackson, L. (2005). *Surfacing up: Psychiatry and social order in colonial Zimbabwe, 1908–1968*. Ithaca, NY: Cornell University Press.

Johnson, M. (2005). The central park jogger case-police coercion and secrecy in interrogation. The 14th Annual Frantz Fanon MD Memorial Lecture. *Journal of Ethnicity in Criminal Justice, 3*(1–2), 131–143.

Kellner, D. (1989). *Critical theory, Marxism, and modernity*. Baltimore, MD: Johns Hopkins University Press.

King, L. M. (1976). On the nature of a creative world: Toward a restoration of creativity in psychology. In *African philosophy: Assumptions and paradigms for research on Black persons*. Los Angeles: Fanon Center Publication.

King, L. M. (1977). *Notes toward a creative mental health model: Discourse on a 20th Century Paradigm*. Paper presented at the Third Annual J. Alfred Cannon Research Conference, Atlanta, GA.

King, L. M. (1978). Social and cultural influences on psychopathology. *Annual Review of Psychology, 29*, 405–433.

King, L. M., Dixon, V. J., & Nobles, W. W. (Eds.). (1976). *African philosophy: Assumptions & paradigms for research on Black persons*. J. Alfred Cannon Research Conference Series. Los Angeles: Fanon Center Publication, Charles R. Drew Postgraduate Medical School.

King, L. M., Dixon, V. J., & Wilson, E. B. (1976). *The Fanon center restoration model: An emancipatory strategy for the education of all children*. Report submitted to the National Institute of Education. Los Angeles: Fanon Center.

King, L. M., Price, E., & Myers, H. (1972). *The Black child*. Critical Psychological Issues. UCLA Manuscript.

Krader, L. (1975). *Asiatic mode of production: Sources, development and critique in the writings of Karl Marx*. Assen, Netherlands: Van Gorcum.

Lenin, V. I. (1974/1916). The discussion on self-determination summed up. In *Collected works* (Vol. 22). New York: International Publishers.

Macey, D. (2012). *Frantz Fanon: A biography*. London: Verso.

Makkawi, I. (2017). The rise and fall of academic community psychology in Palestine and the way forward. *South African Journal of Psychology, 4*, 482–492.

McCulloch, J. (1983). *Black soul, white artifact: Fanon's clinical psychology and social theory*. Cambridge: Cambridge University Press.

McGibbon, E., Mulaudzi, F. M., Didham, P., Barton, S., & Sochan, A. (2014). Toward decolonizing nursing: The colonization of nursing and strategies for increasing the counter-narrative. *Nursing Inquiry, 21*(3), 179–191.

Mirzeoff, N. (2011). *"We are all children of Algeria:" Visuality and counter-visuality, 1954–2011* (Vol. 3). Frantz Fanon. Retrieved from http://scalar.usc.edu/nehvectors/mirzoeff/jai-huit-ans-analysis.

Myers, H. F. (1976). Holistic definitions and measurements of states of non-health. In L. M. King, V. J. Dixon, & W. W. Nobles (Eds.), *African philosophy: Assumption & paradigms for research on Black persons*. Los Angeles: Fanon Center Publication.

Myers, H. F. (1979). Mental health and the Black child: The manufacture of incompetence. *Young Children, 34*(4), 25–31.

Razanajao, C. L., Postel, J., & Allen, D. F. (1996). The life and psychiatric work of Frantz Fanon. *History of Psychiatry, 7*, 499–524.

Robcis, C. (2016). François Tosquelles and the psychiatric revolution in postwar France. *Constellations, 23*, 212–222. https://doi.org/10.1111/1467-8675.12223.

Said, E. (1999). Traveling theory reconsidered. In N. Gibson (Ed.), *Rethinking Fanon: The continuing dialogue*. Amherst, NY: Humanities Books.

Smith, H., & Keller, A. (2007). The context in which treatment takes place: The multi-faceted stressors facing survivors of torture and refugee trauma. In *Like a refugee camp on First Avenue: Insights and experiences from the Bellevue/NYU program for survivors of torture*. New York: Bellevue and NYU Program for Survivors of Torture.

Smith, H., Keller, A., & Lhewa, D. (Eds.). (2007). *Like a refugee camp on First Avenue: Insights and experiences from the Bellevue/NYU program for survivors of torture*. New York: Bellevue and NYU Program for Survivors of Torture.

Tosquelles, F. (2017). Frantz Fanon in Saint-Alban: A 1975 interview with François Tosquelles. *Theory and Critique of Psychology, 9*, 223–229. Retrieved from www.teo cripsi.com/ojs.

Turner, L. & Alan, J. (1986). *Frantz Fanon, Soweto, and American Black thought*. Chicago: News & Letters.

Turner, L. (1996). On the difference between the Hegelian and Fanonian dialectic of Lordship and bondage. In L. Gordon, T. D. Sharpley-Whiting, & R. White (Eds.), *Fanon: A critical reader* (pp. 134–151). Oxford, England: Blackwell Publishers.

Turner, L. (2008). Self-consciousness as force and reason of revolution in the thought of Steve Biko. In A. Mgnxitama, A. Alexander, & N. C. Gibson (Eds.), *Biko lives! Contesting the legacies of Steve Biko* (pp. 69–82). New York: Palgrave Macmillan.

Turner, L. (2011). Fanon and the biopolitics of torture: Contextualizing psychological practices as tools of war. In N. Gibson (Ed.), *Living Fanon: Global perspectives* (pp. 117–130). New York: Palgrave Macmillan.

Section 1

Fanon's Clinical Work in Historical Context

1 Frantz Fanon, Institutional Psychotherapy, and the Decolonization of Psychiatry

Camille Robcis

In December 1956, Frantz Fanon resigned from his position as medical director of the psychiatric hospital of Blida-Joinville in Algeria. In a letter addressed
to the Resident Minister and Governor General Robert Lacoste, Fanon (1967)
explained that after three years of arduous work to improve the mental health
of the local population, the reality of colonialism, its "tissue of lies, cowardice,
[and] contempt for man" had finally convinced him to leave:

> Madness is one of the means man has of losing his freedom. And I can say,
> on the basis of what I have been able to observe from this point of vantage,
> that the degree of alienation of the inhabitants of this country appears to
> me frightening. If psychiatry is the medical technique that aims to enable
> man no longer to be a stranger to his environment, I owe it to myself to
> affirm that the Arab, permanently alien [*aliéné permanent*] in his own coun-
> try, lives in a state of absolute depersonalization.
>
> (p. 53)

By choosing the adjective *aliéné* to describe the colonized Algerians, Fanon
was playing with the double meaning of the term in French: estranged and
foreign—even in their own land—but also mentally unstable, crazy, insane.
More broadly, Fanon was articulating a point that he reiterated throughout his
life: colonialism had a direct psychic effect. It could literally render someone
mad by hijacking their person, their being, and their sense of self. The confisca-
tion of freedom and the alienation brought about by colonialism and by racism
were always political and psychic at once.

By the time Fanon wrote this letter in 1956, the war in Algeria had turned
increasingly violent. Guy Mollet, the new prime minister elected earlier that
year, was greeted by tomatoes and furious crowds in Algiers in February 1956.
The following month, the French legislature voted to grant the government
"special powers," giving the army free reign to reestablish order in Algeria.
Fanon had followed the intensification of the war closely and by 1956, he was
already involved with the Front de Libération Nationale (FLN) which had
reached out to him in his capacity as a doctor to provide drugs and medical advice—including psychiatric help—for the combatants. As Fanon (1967)

explained in his letter to Lacoste, he had finally come to realize that his "absurd gamble" to promote progressive psychiatric reforms while serving the French State was hopeless. As he put it, it had become increasingly obvious that "the social structure existing in Algeria was hostile to any attempt to put the individual back to where he belonged. . . . The events in Algeria are the logical consequence of an abortive attempt to decerebralize a people" (p. 53). Violence, in other words,—political, social, and psychic—was constitutive of colonialism: it was the structure of the land, a structure that had come to condition individuals in their very psyche.

Fanon's letter gives us a particularly good entry-point into his conception of the psychiatric which is the subject of this essay. More precisely, I wish to highlight two of the hypotheses that Fanon formulates in his letter: first, that the political and the psychic are intimately tied; and second, that the social space and the physical environment of the colony, the enclosure and the segregation on which they are premised, fundamentally shape the psyche of the colonized. Fanon had intuited these theses from his most early work, especially in *Black Skin, White Masks* and "The North African Syndrome," both published in 1952. However, as I wish to argue here, it was his residency at the hospital of Saint-Alban from 1952 to 1953, his encounter with François Tosquelles, and his discovery of institutional psychotherapy that ultimately confirmed for him, on an empirical level, that alienation was always social and psychic at once.

Institutional psychotherapy played a key role in Fanon's thought and medical practice not only by giving him the tools to diagnose what Tosquelles called the concentrationist logic of asylums (but also, as Fanon would suggest, of the colonial world). It also offered Fanon an example of what disalienation, freedom, and emancipation could look like within the hospital and also within society at large. After leaving Saint-Alban, Fanon tried to enact these experiments inspired by institutional psychotherapy, both in his clinical work in Algeria and Tunisia and in his political writings. As I want to show, Fanon neither applied nor adapted a model of Western psychiatry to the colonial settings of Algeria and Tunisia. Rather, he revised the very foundations of this framework in order to promote what he considered a truly disalienated and disalienating psychiatry, a psychiatry close to the notion of "national culture" that Fanon theorized in his last and best-known book, *The Wretched of the Earth*.

To be sure, the fact that Fanon practiced psychiatry throughout his life is not new (Bulhan, 1985; Cherki, 2000; Keller, 2007a; Khalfa, 2015; Macey, 2012; Mbembe, 2016; Ranzanajao & Postel, 2007; Vergès, 1997). My aim in this chapter is thus not to underscore once again the importance of psychiatry in Fanon's work. Rather, I want to argue that the evolution of Fanon's thought across institutional and political/decolonial contexts explains as much about the history, promise, and achievements of institutional psychotherapy as it does about his political thinking. My point is to highlight the significance of Fanon in the genealogy of what is generally called "Western radical psychiatry."[1]

Fanon's Theory of the Subject

Fanon left his native island of Martinique to study medicine in Lyon in 1946. He chose to specialize in psychiatry in 1949 under the supervision of Jean Dechaume, an expert in psychosurgery, neuropsychiatry, and neurology. At the time, French university training in the domain of psychiatry was dominated by an organicist and neuropsychiatric approach to mental illness, and this was especially true of Lyon. Fanon admired Dechaume's scientific rigor and he retained a certain inclination for this type of empiricism throughout his life. However, he quickly felt constrained by the theoretical narrowness of psychiatry and turned to other fields, including literature, anthropology, philosophy, and psychoanalysis. While at Lyon, he attended the lectures of the anthropologist André Leroi-Gourhan and of the philosopher Maurice Merleau-Ponty. He read extensively and engaged the main intellectuals of his period: Claude Lévi-Strauss, Marcel Mauss, Karl Marx, Vladimir Lenin, G.W.F. Hegel (mediated by Alexandre Kojève and Jean Hyppolite), Martin Heidegger, and Jean-Paul Sartre. During these years, Fanon also immersed himself in psychoanalysis through Freud and Lacan, and in Gestalt theory through Kurt Goldstein. Finally, he wrestled with the theses of Henri Ey and other French psychiatrists gathered around the journal *Évolution Psychiatrique* who had been trying to reconcile psychiatry and psychoanalysis since 1925. From existentialism and anthropology, Fanon learned the importance of relationality in the construction of the self. Through Marxism, he came to appreciate the decisive effect of politics on the human condition. Psychoanalysis and phenomenology offered him a theory of embodiment that complemented social construction. Bringing together these different currents and disciplines, Fanon spent much of his time in medical school thinking about psychic causation, trying to untangle the biological from the psychological, and separating the role of phylogeny, ontogeny, and sociogeny in the constitution of the self.

Fanon's medical thesis centered on Friedreich's ataxia, a hereditary disease that causes progressive damage to the nervous system. As he explained in his introduction (2018), this illness was of particular interest to him because despite the fact that the state of general paralysis was "eminently neurological," it was usually accompanied by "a certain psychiatric symptom cluster" (p. 206). The close study of Friedreich's ataxia was thus for Fanon a way to ponder a fundamental medical—but also philosophical—quandary: "At what point can a neurological disease be suspected of triggering psychic alterations? At what point can it be said that the thought processes are disturbed?" (p. 224). This was another way to delimit neurology and psychiatry, to reflect on the problem of specialization and disciplinary borders (p. 247). In order to think through these questions, Fanon turned to the works of Henri Ey, Jacques Lacan, and Kurt Goldstein—three of his contemporaries who were also crucial for the doctors at Saint-Alban. In his thesis, Fanon mapped out the substantial differences between their respective approaches before suggesting that the three figures were linked by their desire to undercut the dichotomy between the neurological and the physiological. Ey, Fanon wrote, remained committed to a neurological framework despite the fact that he underscored the psychic nature of pathogenesis (p. 255). For Goldstein, "every organic manifestation . . . is the fruit of global mechanisms. For him, the organism acts as a whole" (p. 255). In both cases, Fanon observed, neurological and psychiatric troubles went hand-in-hand.

Significantly, Fanon ended his thesis with an extended discussion of Lacan whose work appeared closest to his own position. Referring to Lacan as an "eminently controversial figure," Fanon highlighted two concepts in Lacan's early work that he found especially helpful (p. 262). The first was his concept of desire, which provided a link between on the one hand the biographical development of the subject and, on the other, his lived experience (his *Erlebnis*—a term that Fanon would take up in *Black Skin, White Masks*), his ego ideal and his relationships (and tensions) with others (p. 264). The second was Lacan's notion of personality, especially important in his 1932 thesis on paranoia, which Lacan defined phenomenologically as both grounded in genetics and able to integrate human relations of the social order (p. 265).[2] According to Fanon, through his concepts of desire and of personality, Lacan stressed the fact that madness always had something to do with the social.

Fanon's wish to complicate the classic (but by then much-contested) medical dictate that every symptom requires a lesion was not, however, simply motivated by his wide range of readings. It was also inspired by his first experiences in the medical field even before he chose to specialize in psychiatry. Indeed, throughout medical school, Fanon was regularly asked to accompany doctors who had to attend emergencies in a predominantly Muslim neighborhood of Lyon. Fanon describes finding patients in dirty beds, in sordid rooms, with friends and family weeping and screaming because they were convinced that the patient was on the brink of death. Fanon and the supervising doctors would proceed to an examination that would generally reveal no significant illness. Eventually, and in response to further complaints by the patient, the doctor would recommend further testing. Three days later, the same person would show up completely cured and the French doctors would conclude that "the North African's pain, for which we can find no lesional basis, is judged to have no consistency, no reality" (Fanon, 1967, p. 6). This verdict confirmed what colonial psychiatry, especially the Algiers School, had argued for years and what much of French racism corroborated: "when you come down to it, the North African is a simulator, a liar, a malingerer, a sluggard, a thief" (p. 7). For Fanon, however, the pain described by these patients was not imaginary but all too real. As he contended, this illness did have symptoms but they were not necessarily physiological. He called it "the North African syndrome."

Fanon's essay on "The North African Syndrome" provides yet another confirmation of the interdependence of psyche and soma, of medicine and politics. As Fanon (1967) put it: "it so happens that there is a connection" between "the North African on the threshold of the French Nation" and "the North African in a hospital setting":

Threatened in his affectivity, threatened in his social activity, threatened in his membership in the community [*appartenance à la cité*]—the North African combines all the conditions that make a sick man. Without a family, without love, without human relations, without communion with the group, the first encounter with himself will occur in a neurotic mode, in a pathological mode; he will feel himself emptied, without life, in a bodily struggle with death, a death on this side of death, a death in life.

(p. 13)

As this passage makes clear, the existence of these real-yet-imaginary illnesses displayed by North African immigrants confirmed with striking clarity the structural effects of racism and discrimination on the psyche.

"The North African Syndrome" first appeared in 1952 in the left-leaning Social-Catholic journal *Esprit* where Fanon had published a few months earlier another essay, "The Lived Experience of the Black Man"—which eventually became the fifth chapter of *Black Skin, White Masks*. These two *Esprit* articles gave Fanon wide exposure as they brought his ideas out of the world of psychiatry into the mainstream French intellectual scene and into a broader conversation around racism, colonialism, and psychiatry. Indeed, *Esprit* had been critical not only of French colonial policy but also of mainstream psychiatry, as evidenced by its December 1952 issue titled "The Misery of Psychiatry" to which Lucien Bonnafé, François Tosquelles, Georges Daumézon, Louis Le Guillant and other "radical psychiatrists" associated with Saint-Alban had contributed. It was through *Esprit* that Fanon eventually found a publisher for *Black Skin, White Masks* (originally titled "Essay for the Disalienation of the Black Man") which Jean-Marie Domenach, the journal's editor-in-chief, passed on to Francis Jeanson at the Éditions du Seuil and which appeared in French bookstores in the spring of 1952.

Fanon wrote *Black Skin, White Masks* while he was finishing medical school. As he indicates in one of his early chapters, his original idea was to submit the manuscript as his medical thesis but Dechaume was quick to reject it on the predictable grounds that it defied all existing academic and scientific norms (Macey, 2012, pp. 136–137). It is in this context that Fanon turned to the more conventional topic of Friedreich's disease, somewhat reluctantly and hastily, so that he could graduate. As his initial title suggests, the question of "disalienation"—with its double meaning in French as a political and psychic process—was at the heart of *Black Skin, White Masks*. As Fanon wrote in his introduction (2008), even though his analysis was primarily psychological, "it remains, nevertheless, evident that . . . the true disalienation of the black man implies a brutal awareness of the social and economic realities" (p. xiv). If racism did indeed produce an inferiority complex, Fanon continued, it began as an economic process that was later internalized, "epidermalized"—inscribed in the body and in the skin.

In *Black Skin, White Masks* like in his medical thesis and in his article on "The North African Syndrome," Fanon turned to a wide array of texts and disciplines to study the phenomenon of racial alienation. He referred to his book as a "clinical study" and in that sense, we can read it in line with these two other works, as a complementary text, as three attempts to explore the question of causality in mental illness and to elaborate a theory of subjectivity that drew on psychiatry, psychoanalysis, phenomenology, and politics. Fanon's subject was defined by a structure of conscious and unconscious relations rather than by biological essentialism or brain chemistry. This structural analysis allowed Fanon to highlight the importance of the social (especially of structural racism) but also of alterity, of others, in the construction of the self.

Fanon's Encounter With Institutional Psychotherapy: Saint-Alban

Fanon first heard about Saint-Alban in medical school, through one of his fellow students, a family friend of Paul Balvet who had directed the hospital since 1937 (Macey, 2012, p. 139). At the end of his medical studies, Fanon had accepted a short internship in the psychiatric hospital of Saint-Ylie of Dole in the Jura where, as the only intern for a hundred and fifty patients, he was exposed to the dire conditions of French psychiatric hospitals (Ranzanajao & Postel, 2007, p. 149). After a brief—and equally demoralizing—return to Martinique as a temporary locum at the Colson hospital (Tristram, 2007), Fanon arrived at Saint-Alban in April 1952, in the midst of the psychiatric revolution that came to be known as institutional psychotherapy—but which Fanon more frequently referred to as *socialthérapie*.

Institutional psychotherapy was very much a product of the Second World War and the particular set of circumstances that brought together a group of physicians frustrated with the biological essentialism of mainstream psychiatry, communist and anarchist refugees fleeing fascism, artists and intellectuals—especially Surrealists—who had long been fascinated with madness, and local inhabitants. Despite these various backgrounds, the community at Saint-Alban shared a vision of psychiatry as a deeply political practice. Indeed, institutional psychotherapy was first and foremost a reaction against the massive mortality rate in psychiatric hospitals during the war, in Germany but also, as it was less known, in France. As is by now well documented (von Platen, 2001; Proctor, 1988), eugenics and the forced euthanasia of the "incurably sick" were integral to the Third Reich's program of racial purification. "Action T4," as this policy was later called, resulted in 70,000 official deaths, but according to some historians, the number was closer to 200,000. Although the Vichy regime never had an explicit policy of extermination, between 1940 and 1945 roughly 40,000 patients died in French psychiatric hospitals. Many of these deaths were because of food shortage, the rationing system, and the harsh living conditions that all of France experienced during these years, but several historians (Bueltzingsloewen, 2007; Lafont, 1987) maintain that the Vichy regime silently endorsed the Nazi State's policies by encouraging a "soft extermination" of the mentally ill. At Saint-Alban, hospital administrators began to hoard extra food with the help of the local population in order to feed the patients. More generally, the war and fascism made them realize the extent to which the political and the psychic were linked. From the experience of Occupation, they had learned that psychiatry needed to fight on both fronts—psychic and political—if it wanted to avoid becoming complicit with genocidal practices.

Among the most important doctors at Saint-Alban during the war was François Tosquelles who, I would suggest, was also Fanon's most important mentor. Tosquelles was a Catalan-born psychiatrist and one of the founders of the POUM, the anarchist-inspired and anti-Stalinist leftist movement that flourished in the Republican Spain of the 1930s. After fighting Franco's army during the Spanish Civil War, Tosquelles fled to France where he was placed in a refugee camp before arriving at the hospital of Saint-Alban. Both at the front and in the camp, Tosquelles set up therapeutic communities where, with the help of other soldiers and prisoners, he would treat the combatants and the refugees who had been severely affected psychologically by the violence of the war. These improvised psychiatric experiments convinced Tosquelles that psychiatry could be practiced anywhere (Faugeras, 2007; Pain, Polack, & Sivadon, 1989; Robcis, 2016).

Tosquelles liked to repeat that in the course of his life he had been exposed to multiple physical and ideological "occupations": as a Catalan citizen fighting Spanish imperialism; as an activist in the POUM struggling against Stalinist domination; as an opponent to fascism first in Spain and later in the Resistance in Vichy France; as a refugee incarcerated in the deplorable conditions of French concentration camps. These various forms of segregation, colonization, or incarceration had rendered him particularly sensitive to the dangers of "concentrationism"—which he also called *le-tout-pouvoir* [the-all-power]. "Concentrationism" was the potential of any institution or any group to become authoritarian, oppressive, discriminatory, and exclusionary. As the war had made clear, "concentrationism" threatened not only our modes of social and political organization: it was also a behavior, a psychic disposition. As such, alienation was always social and psychic at one. In this sense, Tosquelles referred to Marx and Freud as the "two legs" of institutional psychotherapy: when one leg walked, the other needed to follow. Both were complementary and indissociable to understand and to fight against the "voluntary servitude" in which humans lived.

It is at this crossroad of Marxism and psychoanalysis that institutional psychotherapy was born as a tool to diagnose but also to fight against this "double alienation." Because institutional psychotherapy never sought to become a totalizing philosophy, it is difficult to pinpoint a general model or method. However, its practitioners did rely on a couple of key texts and basic principles. Among these was the belief that theory and practice were inextricably linked. As Tosquelles and his colleagues had realized from their medical training, much of the problem with psychiatry that they were encountering stemmed from its misconception and misunderstanding of psychosis. On the one hand, mainstream psychiatry still considered psychosis as an exclusively neurological phenomenon located and locatable on the brain and the field as a whole remained hostile to any insights from the social and human sciences. On the other hand, most of Freudian psychoanalysis had concluded that psychosis was really outside its realm. As Freud had observed in his famous Schreber case, psychotics had a different relationship to language and to transference (and to what Lacan would later call the Symbolic), and hence they could not be treated by the same principles of the "talking cure."

As the practitioners of institutional psychotherapy observed, however, psychotics could indeed have various transferential relations but they were not one-on-one and intersubjective, as in the case of neurosis: they were collective. Social relations thus offered a privileged lens to observe the operations of the psychotic unconscious, to analyze the projection of desires and fantasies, to study identifications, and to eventually try to work therapeutically with them. The point was thus not to choose between psychiatry *or* psychoanalysis but to anchor psychiatry in a psychoanalytic understanding of the subject, a subject that resulted from conscious and unconscious representations that were constructed in relation to others. For this purpose, one of the most helpful thinkers was Jacques Lacan, who in his early work—especially his 1932 thesis *On Paranoid Psychosis and its Relations to the Personality*—urged psychiatry to stop looking for neurological automatisms and to turn to psychoanalysis instead to understand the construction of a "personality." However, unlike Lacan who eventually abandoned psychiatry in favor of psychoanalysis, institutional psychotherapy insisted on the specificity of the medical practice, on the materiality of the "medical technique" to use Fanon's term in the opening quote.

These were some of the theoretical premises that guided Tosquelles and his colleagues at Saint-Alban as they set up a series of concrete practices that would favor this transferential constellation and that would complement their medical treatments: group therapies, general meetings, self-managed unions of patients (also known as "the Club"), ergotherapy workshops (printing, binding, woodwork, pottery . . .), libraries, publications, and a wide range of cultural activities (movies, concerts, theater . . .). The idea was to constantly imagine and reimagine institutions that would produce new vectors of transference, different forms of identifications, and alternative social relations. Every therapeutic intervention was grounded in the practice, all in the hope of dis-alienating not only the patients but also the collectivity as a whole. As Tosquelles's colleague Jean Oury (2016) put it, the main goal of institutional psychotherapy was to set up "mechanisms to fight, every day, against that which can turn the whole collective towards a concentrationist or segregationist structure" (p. 9). In this sense, institutional psychotherapy was a form of medical treatment but also a philosophy and a practice of everyday life that would prevent the reappearance of these political and psychic "concentrationisms." The goal was to devise structures that could be constantly rethought, reworked, and remapped as antidotes to this recurring concentrationist threat. In the words of Tosquelles, institutional psychotherapy was an attempt to cure not only the patients, not only the doctors, but an "attempt to cure life."

Fanon never wrote directly about his experience at Saint-Alban, but we know from Tosquelles who devoted two essays to Fanon's psychiatric legacy that he was an enthusiastic participant in the various social activities of the hospital. During his fifteen months there, Fanon helped set up plays, musical productions, and ergotherapy stations, and he wrote several pieces for the hospital's newsletter *Trait d'union* (Tosquelles, 2007a, 2007b, pp. 75–76). During this time, Fanon also co-wrote two medical papers with Tosquelles which they presented at national congresses on psychiatry and neurology. As Tosquelles put it, Fanon was fully immersed in the Saint-Alban adventure because he welcomed it as an alternative to the dry version of organicist psychiatry that he had encountered in Lyon. Saint-Alban was the site of a "hypothesis" to use Tosquelles' term, a hypothesis that stipulated that if you could get together a group of people in an open space, some crazy and some not, and give them the means to articulate and rearticulate who they were and how they were shaped by history, they could, eventually, feel better (Tosquelles, 2007a, pp. 11–12).

Institutional Psychotherapy in North Africa

Deeply marked by the Saint-Alban experiment and the desire to revolutionize psychiatric care, Fanon passed his medical exams in 1953 and applied to various positions in psychiatric hospitals throughout France. He eventually accepted a post at the hospital of Blida-Joinville, the largest psychiatric institution in North Africa, where he arrived in November 1953. The idea of creating a state-of-the-art facility to treat the mentally ill in Algeria was spearheaded by Antoine Porot, the chair of psychiatry at the medical school of Algiers, the principal architect of French Algeria's network for psychiatric care, and one of the figures whom Fanon attacked throughout his life as emblematic of the racism of colonial medicine. As Richard Keller has shown (2007b), the Blida hospital, which had opened in 1938, encapsulated many of the paradoxes inherent in the French project of colonial medicine: modernizing while racializing, reforming while conservative (p. 48). Similarly, Porot was a complex figure, someone who considered himself a true reformist, the "Pinel of Algeria" who fought tirelessly to create a health system independent of the metropole while positing at the same time some of the most racist theories about "native psychology" (Bégué, 1996; Berthelier, 1994; Cherki, 2000; Keller, 2007b; Macey, 2012; Vergès, 1996).

By the time Fanon was recruited at Blida, the hospital was overcrowded with two thousand patients for eight hundred beds, underfunded, and in desperate need of reform. Like Saint-Alban before the war, the hospital looked and felt essentially like a prison. As many testimonies—including Fanon's—confirm, living conditions at Blida were truly dehumanizing. Patients wandered in rags when they were not tied to their beds or to trees in the garden (Cherki, 2000; Murard, 2008; Zahzah & Ridouh, 2008). But Blida suffered not only from the set of infrastructural problems common to most French psychiatric institutions in the postwar period: it also functioned as a microcosm of Algerian colonial society with all of its racism and segregation. Medicine as a field of study was still mostly restricted to Algeria's white population and when Fanon arrived, none of the psychiatrists working at Blida were of Arab descent. The patients were divided into gender-specific pavilions, some reserved for Europeans and the others for Muslims. Upon his arrival at Blida, Fanon joined four other doctors, *chefs-de-service,* who were not in any way interested in psychiatric innovation or in anti-colonial activism.

Yet, Fanon was vocal about his objections to colonialism and to the way psychiatry was practiced—which made working with his white colleagues arduous. As he recounted in a letter to his friend Maurice Despinoy, a psychiatrist whom he had met at Saint-Alban and who had moved to Martinique, it was difficult to practice institutional psychotherapy at Blida when people had a completely different "understanding of psychiatry and the mental life of the patients." As an example, Fanon mentioned that his desire to institute bimonthly meetings was received with generalized apathy on the part of the patients and the staff: "No overall project, no collaboration, no cooperation; and the worst is that at the start of meetings everyone is already tired as if all dialogue was simply in vain" (2018, p. 350). As a result, Fanon surrounded himself with a group of interns that included Alice Cherki, Jacques Azoulay, Charles Géronimi, and François Sanchez, all young, politically engaged, and enthusiastic about the possibility of using psychiatry to advance a decolonial revolution (Cherki, 2000; Macey, 2012). With the help of these interns, Fanon applied some of the techniques that he had learned at Saint-Alban in a "fifth division" which he supervised. This division was composed of four pavilions: one of European women and three of Muslim men.

As he had learned from Tosquelles, institutional psychotherapy needed to "cure the hospital" before it could cure its patients. The staff thus played an essential role in this mission and Fanon insisted on the importance of training his nurses and interns. To that effect, he organized classes and seminars for his employees and he encouraged them to record their daily observations in diaries. He incited them to eat with the patients—something which had been previously forbidden (Zahzah & Ridouh, 2008). He insisted on removing all uniforms to fight against depersonalization. He set up a café, Le Café Bon Accueil, to function as the kind of Club that he had witnessed in Saint-Alban. As Fanon put it (2018), the café was a "space to re-learn the gestures of the outside" and to "institute the social" (p. 331). He organized daily meetings, built a library, set up ergotherapy stations—weaving, pottery, knitting, gardening— and promoted sports, especially soccer, which he argued, could play an important role in the re-socialization of patients. He planned field trips to the beach, arranged parties and holiday celebrations, encouraged drama, singing, and other artistic productions, screened a series of movies, and invited professional singers to perform at the hospital.

These various activities which were meant to reconstitute "the social architecture of the hospital," were advertised in the hospital's newspaper, *Notre journal,* which was printed by the patients in one of the ergotherapy stations (Archives IMEC FNN1.20; FNN1.21; FNN1.22). Like at Saint-Alban, these newsletters had a double purpose: they advertised the events of the day but they also had a more therapeutic goal. As one editorial put it: "To write means to want to be read. In the same stroke it means to want to be understood. In the act of writing there is an effort being made; muddled and vague [thoughts] are combatted, surpassed" (Fanon, 2018, p. 325). Finally, the newsletters allowed Fanon and his staff to communicate with the patients and to explain the theoretical principles underlying institutional psychotherapy: "If care is not taken, the hospital establishment which is above all a curative establishment, a therapeutic establishment, is gradually transformed into a barracks [*caserne*] in which children-boarders [*enfants-pensionnaires*] tremble before parent-ordelies [*infirmiers-parents*]" (Fanon, 2018, p. 346). This was in accordance with Fanon's reflections in more scholarly publications during this time, including an article on agitation for the journal *Maroc médical*. As he explained, isolating agitated patients in solitary confinement could only aggravate their symptoms: "shutting the patient in a cell, isolating him, fixing him to the bed—this amounts to printing the conditions for hallucinatory activity" (Fanon, 2018, p. 442). Instead, the hospital needed to function as a healing collective, as the knot of social relations, the site of production of "dis-alienating" forces (Fanon, 2018, p. 440).

Fanon meticulously documented these practices in a fascinating article that he co-wrote with one of his interns, Jacques Azoulay, in 1954 for *L'Information psychiatrique*. As Fanon and Azoulay observed, institutional psychotherapy was instantly successful within the ward of European women. From the first months, "the very atmosphere of the ward had changed. . . . Not only had asylum life become less distressing for many, but the rhythm of discharges had already markedly increased" (Fanon, 2018, p. 357). In the Muslim section, however, things were much more complicated. Fanon and Azoulay described their first months as a "total failure" (p. 357). The meetings designed to plan the parties, the movies, the newsletter—meetings designed to "transform that abstract and impersonal multitude into a coherent group driven by collective concerns"—did not interest the patients in the least (p. 358). The sessions were eventually shortened but the patients remained indifferent and the staff resented the meetings as an additional burden. Fanon and Azoulay were also disheartened to realize that the newsletter, the "social cement" of the collective, did not appeal to these male patients who neither cared to read nor to contribute to it. In the first months, only one text had been written by an Arab patient. In the ergotherapy sessions, the patients remained still, "unoccupied, completely indifferent to the accomplishment of shared work [*travail commun*]" (p. 360). Neither the theater nor the movies managed to capture the patients' attention. As Fanon and Azoulay concluded, after three months and despite their sustained efforts, they were unable to get the Muslim patients involved in the collective life that was flourishing in the European pavilion. Instead, the atmosphere in the Arab quarters was "oppressive, stifling [*irrespirable*]" (p. 361).

In the second half of their article, Fanon and Azoulay tried to come to terms with the reasons behind this failure:

We had naively taken our division as a whole and believed we had adapted to this Muslim society the frames of a particular Western society. . . .

We had wanted to create institutions and we had forgotten that all such
approaches must be preceded with a tenacious, real and concrete interrogation into the organic bases of the indigenous society. How can we have
been so misguided as to think that a Western-inspired social therapy could
be simply applied to a ward of Muslim patients? How was a structural
analysis possible if the geographic, historical, cultural and social frames
were bracketed?

(p. 362)

As Fanon and Azoulay made clear, their attempt to impose a Western grid
in Algeria was a form of violence that was ultimately complicit with imperialism. Instead of "adopting a policy of assimilation," psychiatry needed to
embrace a "revolutionary attitude," it needed to shift from a "position in which
the supremacy of Western culture was evident, to one of cultural relativism"
(pp. 362–363). As Fanon and Azoulay specified, the "cultural relativism" they
were advocating was not the cultural relativism of ethnopsychiatry as practiced
by Porot and the Algiers School. Rather, what they had in mind was to consider Algeria as a "total social fact" in Marcel Mauss's sense, to pass "from the
biological level to the institutional one, from the natural existence to cultural
existence" (p. 363). The point was not to return to a traditional Algerian society
untouched in the past but rather to observe and take into account its irreversible transformation under colonialism.

In their attempt to discern this "national culture," this "total social fact,"
Fanon and Azoulay began to travel throughout Algeria. Little by little, they
came to understand why this initial form of institutional psychotherapy had
failed in Blida. The first obstacle that they mentioned was the language barrier and the fact that none of the doctors—including Fanon—spoke Arabic.
Moreover, most of the Muslim patients were illiterate and so reading and
writing in the newsletter was simply not an option. For most of the Muslim patients, Fanon and Azoulay observed, parties were primarily religious or
familial celebrations so it was difficult to get them excited about the abstract
idea of a party. A majority of these patients had never been exposed to the
theater, which only existed in large urban centers. Instead, Fanon and Azoulay noticed that the more pervasive form of entertainment in Algeria were
professional storytellers who traveled from village to village and recited epic
poems grounded in the local folklore. Similarly, Fanon and Azoulay recognized that the kinds of activities proposed in the ergotherapy stations, weaving
for example, were considered intrinsically feminine. Finally, they realized that
if the patients seemed uninterested in the movies that they were showing, it
was because their plots were too "western." If they avoided playing the games
that were being proposed (like hide-and-seek), it was because these were not
recognizable.

With this new knowledge, Fanon and his interns began to adapt institutional
psychotherapy to the Algerian context. They changed their movie selection and
privileged action-filled films; they picked games that were familiar to Algerians;

they celebrated the traditional Muslim holidays; they invited Muslim singers to perform in the hospital; and they hired a professional storyteller to come speak to the patients. What Muslim men most seemed to enjoy doing after work was gathering amongst themselves in a café where they could play cards or dominos. Thus, Fanon and his team inaugurated a *café maure* which, they claim, rapidly became a popular socializing space. Each day, the number of patients involved in these activities grew and soon enough, institutional psychotherapy had changed the social fabric of the hospital: it had literally *instituted* the social. As Fanon concluded, this was "only a beginning, but already we believe we have eliminated the methodological errors" (p. 371). Unlike the "assimilated psychiatry" that Fanon had arrived with, this was a truly dis-alienated and dis-alienating psychiatry.

Decolonizing Intellectual History

Fanon was expelled from Algeria in January 1957 soon after sending his letter of resignation to Lacoste. He moved to Tunisia—which had achieved independence in 1956—where he continued to work as a psychiatrist and to experiment with institutional psychotherapy until he died of leukemia in December 1961. During these last years of his life, Fanon also deepened his links with the FLN. Every week, he was part of a convoy of doctors sent to treat Algerian combatants and refugees who were hidden in a farm near the border. Some of these patients eventually became the case studies in the last chapter of Fanon's *The Wretched of the Earth* (Cherki, 2000, p. 164). As Fanon observed (2004), once again stressing the structural link between the psychic and the political, the war had become a "breeding ground for mental disorders" (p. 182–183). It was also during these last years that Fanon wrote most of his political texts, which were published by François Maspero, an editor sympathetic to anti-colonialism and Third-Worldism but also to psychiatric reform. These included a series of articles for the FLN newspaper *El Moudjahid*, conference papers, and political speeches which were gathered in *Toward the African Revolution*, published posthumously in 1964; *The Year Five of the Algerian Revolution* in 1959; and finally, Fanon's most famous book, *The Wretched of the Earth*, in 1961.

After a serious accident at the Moroccan border that left his upper body in a cast, Fanon decided to dictate *The Year Five* and *The Wretched of the Earth* to Marie-Jeanne Manuellan, a social worker who was one of his assistants at the Charles-Nicolle day center in Tunis, Fanon's last post. Fanon and Manuellan would meet from seven to nine in the morning before Fanon began his consultations of the day. Fanon would speak and Manuellan would type. As Manuellan recalls, Fanon liked to repeat that madness was a "pathology of freedom" and that the goal of psychiatry was to produce free men (Manuellan, 2017). More generally, we could say that Fanon's political works were literally intertwined with his psychiatric practice, both on a practical and on a theoretical level. More specifically, I want to suggest that the kind of institutional psychotherapy that Fanon advocated in Blida and in Tunisia, especially after he revised it for his Muslim patients, was close to the kind of national culture that he celebrated in *The Wretched of the Earth*.

Unlike *The Year Five of the Algerian Revolution*, which in many ways was still written for a French public, a public that Fanon wanted to make aware of the horrors of colonialism, *The Wretched of the Earth* was primarily directed towards the nascent Third World, the African, Latin American, and Asian populations who were fighting for independence during the Cold War. "Come, comrades," Fanon wrote in the last pages of *The Wretched of the Earth* (2004), "the European game is finally over, we must look for something else. We can do anything today provided we do not ape Europe, provided we are not obsessed with catching up with Europe" (p. 236). "It is all too true," Fanon specified, "that we need a model, schemas, and examples." "For many of us," Fanon continued, "the European model [was] the most elating" (p. 236) but European history, as his book had shown, was one of systematic "hatred, slavery, exploitation, above all . . . bloodless genocide" (p. 38).

In *The Wretched of the Earth*, Fanon was never clear on what this other "model, schema, or example" for reconstruction would look like in concrete terms. However, it would seem that his notions of "national liberation" and of "national culture"—which are linked—come close. In Fanon's argument, "national culture" is never a stable or tangible prototype but rather a regulatory ideal that decolonized peoples should strive for, a little like the concept of "human emancipation" in Marx's work. Although it is difficult to find precise definitions of "national culture" or of "human emancipation" in Fanon's work, it is easier to discern what these notions are opposed to. Indeed, for Fanon, neither the search for an untainted past (which, according to him, crucially hindered *négritude* and tribalism) nor the superposition of a foreign model (whether it be classical nationalism, American capitalism, or Soviet-style communism) could bring about "national culture" as he understood the term. Instead, the national culture that he wanted to defend—a national culture synonymous with national liberation—was to be grounded in the past and in local tradition while being radically oriented towards the future; it was culturally specific and yet universal; it could serve as an instituting vector for both the subject and for popular will.

Institutional psychotherapy, as Fanon revised it in Blida, was also anchored in the language, customs, and everyday life of Algeria while remaining open to the future. It could provide the necessary tools to diagnose and combat the political, social, and psychic violence of racism and colonialism. By emphasizing the role that institutions played in the process of alienation and dis-alienation of the political, the social, and the subjective, institutional psychotherapy was perhaps one of the "model, schema, or example" that Fanon alluded to in *The Wretched of the Earth*. It was not a rigid template or framework that ought to be applied independently of context but rather an ethics, a practice of everyday life that could prevent the appearance of "concentrationisms" and ultimately lead to a freedom that would be collective and personal at once.

In the history of institutional psychotherapy, Fanon's name is rarely mentioned, especially in comparison to Tosquelles, Jean Oury, or Félix Guattari.

Similarly, most of the scholarship on Fanon that mentions his psychiatric training has not examined him in this particular constellation of thinkers influenced or interested by institutional psychotherapy, which aside from these three figures includes Gilles Deleuze, Georges Canguilhem, and Michel Foucault. Yet, the point of institutional psychotherapy was precisely to scrutinize all social and psychic formations, to unearth all traces of authoritarianism, to prevent reification and stagnation—to "defamiliarize, de-oedipalize, decode, and deterritorialize" to use the vocabulary that Deleuze and Guattari would claim a few years later (1983, p. 381).[3] If this is the case, then Fanon's work in North Africa was perhaps the most perfected example of institutional psychotherapy. Instead of simply applying a model that he had learned in the metropole and that was clearly not working in the colonial context, Fanon "deterritorialized" and transformed the practices and the theories themselves. In this sense, his psychiatric work was radical not necessarily for its content but for forcing us to "decolonize" intellectual history and to rethink the supposedly European parameters of the history of medicine, psychiatry, and what is generally referred to as "French theory."

Notes

1. There is, of course, no single definition of radical psychiatry but in general terms, I would characterize it as a psychiatric current that developed in the postwar period and that sought to treat the asylum as a microcosm for society at large in the hope of promoting non-hierarchical and non-authoritarian political and social structures. Some of the names most often associated with this radical psychiatric tradition include (but are not limited to) Franco Basaglia in Italy, David Cooper and R.D. Laing in the UK, Thomas Szasz in the US, and François Tosquelles, Jean Oury, and Félix Guattari in France. I prefer the term "radical psychiatry" to anti-psychiatry since anti-psychiatry in its Italian and British versions was explicitly committed to the destruction of the asylum whereas Tosquelles and Oury were deeply invested in retaining—and using—the medical potential of psychiatry. Furthermore, both adamantly refused the idea that mental illness was a mere "social construction."
2. On Lacan's relationship to psychiatry in the context of his thesis, see (Sédat, 2004) and (Roudinesco, 1993).
3. Deleuze and Guattari do cite Fanon a few times but in relation to colonialism and not to institutional psychotherapy.

References

Bégué, J.-M. (1996). French psychiatry in Algeria (1830–1962): From colonial to transcultural. *History of Psychiatry*, 7, 533–548.

Berthelier, R. (1994). *L'homme maghrébin dans la littérature psychiatrique*, préf. de Rachid Bennegadi. Paris: L'Harmattan.

Bueltzingsloewen, I. V. (2007). *L'hécatombe des fous: la famine dans les hôpitaux psychiatriques français sous l'Occupation*. Paris: Aubier.

Bulhan, H. A. (1985). *Frantz Fanon and the psychology of oppression*. New York: Plenum Press.

Cherki, A. (2000). *Frantz Fanon: Portrait*. Paris: Seuil.

Deleuze, G., & Guattari, F. (1983). *Anti-Oedipus: Capitalism and schizophrenia*. Minneapolis: University of Minnesota Press.

Fanon, F. (1967). *Toward the African revolution: Political essays* (H. Chevalier, Trans.). New York: Grove Press.

Fanon, F. (2004). *The wretched of the earth* (R. Philcox, Trans., 1st ed.). New York: Grove Press.

Fanon, F. (2008). *Black skin, white masks* (R. Philcox, Trans., 1st ed.). New York: Grove Press.

Fanon, F. (2018). *Alienation and freedom* (J. Khalfa and R. Young, Eds., S. Corcoran, Trans.). London: Bloomsbury.

Faugeras, P. (Ed.). (2007). *L'ombre portée de François Tosquelles*. Ramonville Saint-Agne: Eres.

Keller, R. C. (2007a). Clinician and revolutionary: Frantz Fanon, biography, and the history of colonial medicine. *Bulletin of the History of Medecine, 81*, 823–841.

Keller, R. C. (2007b). *Colonial madness: Psychiatry in French North Africa*. Chicago: University of Chicago Press.

Khalfa, J. (2015). Fanon and psychiatry. *Nottingham French Studies, 54*(1), 52–71.

Lafont, M. (1987). *L'extermination douce: la mort de 40000 malades mentaux dans les hôpitaux psychiatriques en France, sous le Régime de Vichy*. Ligné: Editions de l'Arefppi.

Macey, D. (2012). *Frantz Fanon: A biography* (2nd ed.). London and New York: Verso Books.

Manuellan, M.-J. (2017). *Sous la dictée de Fanon*. Paris: L'Amourier.

Mbembe, A. (2016). *Politiques de l'inimitié*. Paris: La Découverte.

Murard, N. (2008). Psychothérapie institutionnelle à Blida. *Tumultes, 31*(2), 31–45.

Oury, J. (2016). *La psychothérapie institutionnelle de Saint-Alban à la Borde*. Paris: éditions d'une.

Pain, F., Polack, J.-C., & Sivadon, D. (Writers). (1989). *Francesc Tosquelles: Une politique de la folie*. www.film-documentaire.fr/4DACTION/w_fiche_film/4904.

Proctor, R. (1988). *Racial hygiene: Medicine under the nazis*. Cambridge, MA: Harvard University Press.

Ranzanajao, C., & Postel, J. (2007). La vie et l'œuvre psychiatrique de Frantz Fanon. *Sud/Nord, 22*(1), 147–174.

Robcis, C. (2016). François Tosquelles and the psychiatric revolution in postwar France. *Constellations, 23*(2), 212–222.

Roudinesco, E. (1993). *Jacques Lacan: Esquisse d'une vie, histoire d'un système de pensée*. Paris: Fayard.

Sédat, J. (2004). Lacan et la psychiatrie. *Topique, 88*(3), 37–46.

Tosquelles, F. (2007a). Frantz Fanon à Saint-Alban. *Sud/Nord, 22*(1), 9–14.

Tosquelles, F. (2007b). Frantz Fanon et la psychothérapie institutionnelle. *Sud/Nord, 22*(1), 71–78.

Tristram, D. (2007). Frantz Fanon, le "chaînon manquant" de la psychiatrie martiniquaise. *Sud/Nord, 22*(1), 39–43.

Vergès, F. (1996). Chains of madness, chains of colonialism. In A. Read (Ed.), *The fact of blackness: Fanon and visual representation*. London: Institute of Contemporary Arts.

Vergès, F. (1997). Creole skin, black mask: Fanon and disavowal. *Critical Inquiry, 23*(3), 578–595.

von Platen, A. R. (2001). *L'Extermination des malades mentaux dans l'Allemagne nazie*. Toulouse: Erès.

Zahzah, A., & Ridouh, B. (Writers). (2008). *Frantz Fanon, mémoire d'asile* [Images animées]. In Paris: Centre national de la cinématographie. http://fondation-frantzfanon.com/frantz-fanon-memoire-dasile-2/.

2 "Psychiatry Has to Be Political"

The Préterrain to a New Fanon

Lou Turner

In a 2014 research article, "Race and Recognition: Pathways to an Affirmative Black Identity" (Neville, Viard, & Turner, 2014) published in the *Journal of Black Psychology*, counseling psychologist Helen A. Neville, in association with research assistant Brigitte Viard and myself (Lou Turner), summarized several years of research and interviews conducted across three continents and the Caribbean on the role of recognition in the psychology of self-identity of African-descended people. In our article (a reprint of which is included in this collection), we explicitly connected Frantz Fanon's concept of recognition to contemporary expressions of Black racial identity. Across contexts, we uncovered the core theme Global Recognition or the push people feel to gain recognition of their humanity as individuals and racialized beings.

In this research, we received approval from and adhered to Institutional Review Board (IRB) protocols. Contemporary IRB protocols demand that researchers and clinicians follow ethical and accepted practices to ensure informed consent, minimize harm, and protect the well- being of participants. Although it is unclear whether Fanon and his colleagues operated under the formal auspices of an evaluative review board, he, in effect, adhered to the criteria of such review board protocols at the Blida-Joinville Psychiatric Hospital in Algeria, the Manouba Razi Hospital, Fanon's first residency in Tunisia on the outskirts of Tunis, and the Charles-Nicolle General Hospital in the center of Tunis.

It will likely be objected that this flies in the face of Fanon's use of electroconvulsive therapy (ECT) and insulin shock therapy. However, as these were sanctioned psychiatric procedures at the time in both global North and South clinical settings, Fanon's, and previously his and his mentor François Tosquelles' ethical concerns about their use of these procedures at Saint-Alban Hospital, in France, are reflected in conference reports on their research and practices (Fanon, 2018, pp. 285–290, 291–298). The late 1960s and '70s movement against ECT should be contextualized. ECT, an effective psychiatric therapy when employed with rigorous safeguards, was misused to subdue "troublesome" patients and was contrary to Fanon's and Tosquelles' norms of institutional therapy (Gibson & Beneduce, 2017, p. 278). An indiscriminate, ahistorical critique of Fanon's use of ECT, while extolling his sociotherapy, is at odds with the dynamics of ECT and the strong criticisms of its misuse (see Sabbatini, 2019 for a useful synopsis of the history of shock therapy.)

Given the colonial setting of Fanon's research and practice, his transformation of mental health institutionalization anticipates the protocols of the Belmont Report (1978) issued by the National Commission for the Protection of Human Subjects of Biomedical and Behavioral Research and, in part, exceeds today's IRB requirements on protection of human participants in research and therapeutic practices. Particularly, he fought to humanize patients and participants in ways that were not commonly practiced in psychiatry. In fact, his work countered the over-pathologizing of black and marginalized populations as a result of misdiagnosis of their mental health concerns. Retrospectively, part of the impetus for our article stemmed from our earlier collaboration in co-teaching a class on black liberation psychology, featuring the work of Frantz Fanon, as a special topics course of the Department of African American Studies at the University of Illinois Urbana-Champaign. It seemed only natural to "apply" Fanon's concepts and theories of alienation, recognition, and reciprocity to the racial life narratives from Africa and the African diaspora. Fanon's concepts of racialized psychological development and dynamics have seldom been tested, let alone employed in actual research, research design, or applied in data analysis. Instead, a half century of engagements with Fanon's work have, through various "waves" of Fanon Studies discourse (Gordon, Sharpley-Whiting, & White, 1996), been heavily discursive, rhetorical, epistemological, and speculative. The analytical validity of Fanon's work—i.e., his interpretation of the psychological phenomena of racialized experience, critical engagements with multidisciplinary fields and schools of thought—as well as his own theory construction has rarely been tested, demonstrated, or applied in real-world contexts. One exception is William Cross' repurposing and extension of Fanon's theory of black self-consciousness into the Nigrescence model of black identity development (Cross, 1971).

As a Fanon scholar I welcomed the opportunity to collaborate on Neville's transcontinental research study. We worked on the assumption that nothing could be more natural than to apply Fanonian categories to the empirical data on black identity development. Engagement with testing Fanonian categories within the parameters of established research protocols produced two shocks of recognition for me. First, it struck me that there have been few research projects designed to test Fanon's categories of black psychogenic development, or documentation of Fanonian therapeutic practices. The second realization involved my own "empirical turn" toward a different encounter with Fanon's work than I had formerly pursued. By "empirical turn," I do not mean anything as chimerical as positivistic "evidence-based medicine" that elevates objective data as the standard of truth-claims about lived experience. Fanon was a proto-poststructuralist critic of scientism and methodological hegemony. Although this is evident throughout *Black Skin*, from his trenchant statement about methods ("There is a point at which methods devour themselves" (Fanon, 1967a, p. 14)) to his incisive criticisms of various schools of psychological thought, his critique of the Algiers School of ethnopsychiatry reveals his perception of the pitfalls of colonial scientism.

To be sure, I had engaged in bringing to light the real-world significance of Fanon's thought in the sociopolitical context of South Africa's anti-apartheid Black Consciousness Movement as that revolutionary moment unfolded in real-time, privileging the Fanonian engagements of BCM leader and theoretician Steve Biko (Turner & Alan, 1986). The point is, Fanon Studies has had little in the way of an agenda of empirical social research, analysis, and testing of Fanon's categories. These lacunae became more problematic with the recent publication of Fanon's clinical papers (2015, 2018).

With word of the imminent publication of Fanon's "clinical papers" in 2014 by Palgrave Press under the editorship of Nigel Gibson, new ground for an "empirical turn" was at hand. A translation of "Frantz Fanon's Clinical Studies (1954–1960)" had been produced by Mazi Allen as part of his 2011 dissertation for the State University of New York at Binghamton. With the unfortunate and unconscionable sidelining of Gibson's publication of Fanon's clinical papers for wide public circulation and research, engagement with a "new Frantz Fanon" was postponed. In 2015, *Écrits sur l'aliénation et la liberté* was published, edited by Jean Khalfa and Robert Young. After several postponements, the English translation was published as *Frantz Fanon: Alienation and Freedom*, September 2018. The "new Fanon" that we finally encountered with the publication of his clinical papers is one who is more empirical and research-oriented than the portrait that has come down to us of the revolutionary psychiatrist and political theorist over the last six decades. Posting the bibliographic inventory of Frantz and Josie Fanon's library, held at the Centre National de Recherches Préhistoriques, Anthropologiques et Historiques, on the web in 2013 opened the aperture wider on the optics of a new Fanon. The bibliographic inventory is found at www.cnrpah.org/data/fonds_frantz_fanon.pdf.

The recent resurfacing of an earlier and for the most part unknown Frantz Fanon who grappled with problems of ethnopsychiatry, the psychotherapeutics and research of traumatized populations, institutionalization, and medical ethics in marginalized communities under colonial domination compels a retracing, a reconnoitering, of the terrain he covered on the way to revolution. What this new dimension of Fanon's thought discloses is the geopsychiatric préterrain that he reconnoitered as he traveled to the field of action of both a new liberation psychology and the vicissitudes of revolution and counter-revolution in the decolonization process in which he was an eyewitness and on which he wrote more perspicaciously than anyone of the period. One of Fanon's last writings (1969), which captures him in action like none of his other writings, viz., his field notebook from the reconnaissance mission he undertook through Mali to open a munitions supply route on Algeria's southern frontier to supply the interior forces of the National Liberation Front in the summer of 1960 (see Turner, 1999), illumines the préterrain analogy used in the following section. Fanon's coverage of the préterrain to the theatre of revolutionary war with French colonialism is where we find some of his most incisive theorization of

Africa's revolutionary present and uncertain future. It is the préterrain or the forefield traversed on the way to revolution, as much as the actual terrain of the revolution of decolonization that determined "this Africa to come" (Fanon, 1969, p. 177). Until the publication of his clinical papers, we had no idea how deep Fanon's theorization of the psychopathology of colonization/decolonization ran in his dialectics of revolution. Reconnoitering the préterrain of Fanon's psychotherapeutic and research practices as his very original pathway to revolution is the burden of this monograph.

The Préterrain: Productions of Colonized and Decolonized Psychological Knowledge

This chapter stages several engagements at multiple sites from which to trace the trajectory of Frantz Fanon's development, practice, and impact as a subaltern psychiatrist of subaltern alienation, domination, and liberation. First, the milieu of his research and therapeutic practice was defined by the transformation of Western territorial colonialism into momentary national independence of subject nations, pursuant to the postcolonial restoration of neocolonialism that Fanon anticipated in his last work, *The Wretched of the Earth* (1961). Secondly, it is apparent to me that recognition of an ethnographic moment in Fanon's clinical papers is indispensable to comprehending his work as the decolonization of colonial psychiatry, a moment which speaks profoundly to the politics of global health policy in the neoliberal formation of the postcolony, today (Horton, 2018). Fanon's ethnopsychiatry is not only distinguished from the scientific racism of Algiers School ethnopsychiatry but from left-liberal French social science (Bourdieu, 1958). In formulating a decolonized ethnopsychiatry, Fanon contributed to political decolonization and to the creation of the "new reality of the nation" (Fanon, 1967, p. 159). Beyond the sociological frame of *Studies in a Dying Colonialism*, Fanon arrives at the *socialized* sphere of *The Wretched of the Earth* where national consciousness of the nationalist stage of the struggle must be quickly transformed into social consciousness via a method of searching for the truth of national independence in "local attitudes" as a "collective affair" (Fanon, 1966, p. 159). Because the discovery of the truth of the nation is found in the "local attitudes" of the people and methodologically involves a collective mode of inquiry and thought of the people, Fanon argues that the criteria for such a mode of truth in the political education of the people "is [1] to make the totality of the nation a reality to *each citizen*. It is [2] to make the history of the nation part of the *personal experience* of each of its citizens" (Fanon, 1966, p. 159—emphasis in original).

In their introduction to *Colonial Subjects: Essays on the Practical History of Anthropology* (2000), Peter Pels and Oscar Salemink discuss the problem of production of colonial knowledge and disciplinary discourses, and thereby the construction of colonial subjects, both the colonized and the social scientist. From a disciplinary vantage point, the production of practical ethnographic knowledge by coeval collaborators, viz., the local informant or patient and the ethnographic fieldworker/therapist, is reified in the institutional settings and procedures of academic publications, conferences, professional symposia, clinical rounds, grand rounds, etc. In the ritualized disciplinary context of the academy or hospital, the practical ensemble of relationships between fieldworker/therapist and his/her local coproducers, which formed the field/space/zone/landscape/terrain that transformed the inequality between therapist/ethnographer and "the other" into coeval collaborators in the coproduction of colonial knowledge, is summarily vitiated. Human relations undergo the universalizing normative discourse of social science methods, categorization, and abject purification of existential authenticity. Disciplinary knowledge is obedient to a dialectic of desire, which, on the one hand, falls in love with the subalternity of the other and, on the other, falls out of love in its desire to be wedded to another practicality and power, viz., the colonial/academic enterprise.

Fanon's divorce from the latter meant that he understood the colonial logic of social science epistemology. Although there is no doubt that the precipitating event was the Algerian revolution, the more salient point is that the revolution generated its own praxeology and its own dialectic of desire for knowledge, both disciplinary and revolutionary. *Sans* comprehension of this, Fanon remains a mystery to Fanon Studies, an enigma of appositional speculation of discursive noise. Fanon stood on the opposite side of the intellectual barricades from Bourdieu who sought disciplinary legitimacy whether within or outside the academy. The animus Bourdieu reserved for Sartre as a "public intellectual" was projected onto Fanon, who was no "public intellectual."

> What Fanon says corresponds to nothing. It is even dangerous to make the Algerians believe the things he says. This would bring them to a utopia. And I think these men [Sartre and Fanon] contributed to what Algeria became because they told stories to Algerians who often did not know their own country [sic!] any more than the French who spoke about it, and, therefore, the Algerians retained a completely unrealistic utopian illusion of Algeria. . . . [T]he texts of Fanon and Sartre are frightening for their irresponsibility. You would have to be a megalomaniac to think you could say just any such nonsense.
> (Bourdieu interview with Le Sueur, quoted in Burawoy, 2012)

The question is: How did Fanon intend to confront the colonial logic of social science epistemology, when it was no longer only theoretical, or when the field was no longer the metropole but the colony? In other words, what was Fanon's strategy? What tactical measures did he take?

For Pels and Salemink (2000) "It is necessary to locate discursive strategies in the contexts of their use, in the tactics of specific relationships of power and exchange that actualize and determine the value of these discursive strategies" (pp. 3–4). Strategy implies a "proper" location or "subject position outside the targeted group" as distinguished from tactics as "a bricolage of political calculations in which subject and target are coeval" (Pels & Salemink, p. 4).

The discursive strategies of the social sciences delimit the coeval relationship between ethnographer and the target population by erasing the social scientist from the zone of contact, vitiating the coproduction of ethnographic knowledge by the fieldworker/therapist and the local/indigenous resident, who had been raised out of the subaltern inequality of his/her colonial existence. The practical coproduction of knowledge is negated by the disciplinary strategies that return the colonial subjects (i.e., the subaltern colonized and the colonial social scientist) to their positions of socio-spatial and socio-epistemic inequality.

The relationship between scientific *observer* and the colonized *observed* was rendered through social encounters and the apparatus of institutional intake systems and administrative or therapeutic practices, which were uniquely renegotiated through practice in the case of Fanon and his colleagues. At one level, Fanon ran the risk of de-historicizing these relationships in the psychiatric profession and in his administrative practices, despite the radical ethos of Tosquelles' institutional therapy at Saint-Alban. Fanon mitigated the risk of recapture of the radical humanistic relationship of his therapeutic encounter by (1) iteratively resetting clinical settings and practices, and (2) by re-contextualizing ethnopsychiatry within the dialectics of decolonization, "where we have watched men [and women] being created by revolutionary beginnings" (Fanon, 1966, p. 153). He resorted to dramaturgical discourse in *A Dying Colonialism* in his observations of Algerian women whose revolutionary emergence on the historic stage was "an authentic birth in a pure state, without preliminary" (Fanon, 1967, p. 50).

The vector (direction and relationality) of Western social sciences as they operated in colonial fields of study and research was redirected in Fanon's fieldwork/therapy. His task was not only to decolonize psychotherapy but to historicize the discursive strategies he deployed in his clinical papers to bring about a new humanism, or what the term "Third World" signified, viz., the Third Age of humanity. In this, Fanon's clinical papers are distinguished from other psychiatric practices of the period. This is what Tosquelles (2017) meant by Fanon's life being consumed by risking the extension of psychiatry:

> What is the space of madness? . . . What [are] the limits of the field of professional action of psychiatrists? Where do we exercise said action of mental hygiene, even therapy? The "sick" attend, participate, and are outside the hospital. Families of the sick, as well. What we said was, here is a sector, an extension of psychiatry. You will see the risks. Fanon has consumed his life in it.
>
> (p. 224)

Ethnopsychiatry was an indispensable colonial technology for turning human encounters on the ground. That is, in the practice of ethnopsychiatry many professionals essentialized the identities and roles of "the Indian," "the Oriental," "the African," "the Arab," through travel to the geographical location of the subaltern "native." The social sciences, including psychiatry, traveled the routes of trade, conquest, conversion, settlement, and tourism of the occupier. The subaltern African became an object of investigative desire for knowledge of the dark other. The practical relationships formed through fieldwork and therapy gave way to the contemplative practice of theory in which formerly coproductive relationships were denied "in order to emphasize the Europeans' self-image of distanced, 'universal' observation" (Pels & Salemink, 2000, 4). It is tempting to mythically suppose that when Fanon entered the revolution, he overturned or decolonized this colonial methodology. Instead, we find evidence that it was his decolonizing of colonial ethnopsychiatry that was the vector of his entry into the revolution. His 1956 letter of resignation is evidence of this.

In a January 1956 letter to Maurice Despinoy, earlier his mentor at Saint-Alban, Fanon assures Despinoy that he is "currently unable to make the least promise" (Fanon, 2018, p. 417) to rejoin him professionally at the Colson mental institution on Fanon's home island of Martinique. However, there are several other points of interest in this letter, written the same year as his letter of resignation to Robert Lacoste, the Resident Minister and governor-general of Algeria, following the legislative election of a new socialist coalition in postwar France, headed by Guy Mollet (1956–57). First, the letter reveals Fanon's guarded optimism that the recall of Jacques Soustelle meant a change in French colonial policy. Soustelle was a trained anthropologist and brutal governor-general of Algeria whose rightwing politics later led him into the terrorist OAS (Organisation Armée Secrète). A colonial paramilitary precursor of the OAS, the Red Hand, is thought to be behind the attempt on Fanon's life in Rome in the summer of 1959. Guy Mollet had supported Mendes-France's granting of independence to Morocco and Tunisia, as well as France's retreat from Vietnam. The collateral supposition was that Algeria would follow suit with a second term of the Socialists in power. In this vein, Fanon apprises Despinoy that "Big things are brewing here [Algeria] and I am happy to witness them" (Fanon, 2018, p. 417). By the end of the year, Fanon resigned as chief of medicine at Blida-Joinville Hospital, marking another moment of his disenchantment with French Socialists. The second point of interest in the letter to Despinoy is his claim that "Colonialist psychiatry as a whole has to be disalienated" (Fanon, 2018, p. 417). This assessment frames his letter of resignation to Lacoste, December 1956.

Thirdly, there is an interesting passage in which the editors of *Alienation and Freedom* intimate that François Tosquelles ("Tosq?") is the subject of critique by Fanon and Despinoy:

> you and no one but you had finally situated the problem. What you say about [Tosq?] is spot on. [Tosq] must be fought. Being more impertinent than you, less timid (I call timidity the absolute respect of the other's subjectivity), struggle arises more quickly for me. We get to what is essential more quickly. Or we do not. It remains, however, that this often proves trying.
>
> (Fanon, 2018, p. 418)

Fanon's failed attempt to institute Tosquelles' institutional therapy on a Muslim men's ward had occurred less than two year earlier. So, "the problem" that Fanon claims Despinoy had "finally situated" in his practice in the French colony of Martinique was likely the problem Fanon encountered in the French colony of Algeria. Importantly, Despinoy's testimony that "had Fanon remained at Saint-Alban, he 'would have done his dissertation in biochemistry'" is evidence, according to Khalfa, that "we have no reason to underestimate Fanon's continued interest in the biological aspects of clinical psychiatry" (Fanon, 2018, p. 172).

Fanon's paper at Blida-Joinville summarizing his experiment with institutional psychotherapy on a European women's and a Muslim men's ward (Fanon & Azoulay, 1954), which resulted in *creative failure*, is the vector from which we should map the préterrain of Fanon's reconnaissance of the occupied territory of the colonial psyche. Tosquelles advises us to "read the thesis of [Jacques] Azoulay [on the subject-matter of his and Fanon's 1954 study] if we want to understand the itinerary of Fanon at Blida and its aftermath: nothing more or nothing less than its commitment to sector psychiatry" (Tosquelles, 2017, p. 226). Fanon supervised Azoulay's dissertation. That the Fanon–Azoulay experiment in institutional psychotherapy on two wards at Blida-Joinville Psychiatric Hospital would lead to Fanon's rethinking of the Eurocentricity of Tosquelles' Saint-Alban institutional therapy and that Tosquelles would advise us to read Azoulay's thesis to "understand the itinerary of Fanon at Blida and its aftermath" is at once telling and delimiting. Although Tosquelles sees Fanon consumed with risking "the extension of psychiatry," Fanon's "itinerary at Blida and its aftermath" is limited to "sector psychiatry," which was short of Fanon's political psychiatry of revolution and revolution as political psychiatry. The ambivalence surrounding Tosquelles' reference to the "aftermath" of Fanon's itinerary at Blida could be understood in terms of the latter, or merely as a reference to sector psychiatry. In what follows, we will see that these are not mutually exclusive. The ambiguity surrounding Tosquelles' statement may also be a matter of the very different trajectory of the historical moment in which he was interviewed (1975) versus the trajectory of Fanon's revolutionary moment, two decades earlier.

If Fanonian ethnopsychiatry is as he asserts, then we must lift his clinical papers out of their anoriginal heterogeneity in institutional therapy to comprehend their simple totality as an event in psychiatry and in the philosophy of history of revolution. This is, in part, intimated in Fanon's statement in his thesis on Friedreich's ataxia (1951) that he intended to demonstrate, in a book he was working on [*Black Skin?*], an approach to "the problem of history from a psychoanalytic and ontological angle, [which will] show that History is nothing but the systematic valorization of collective complexes" (Fanon, 2018, p. 257—translation altered). The anoriginality of this onto-epistemological process means that the abstract universal used to name the event of encounter between fieldworker/therapist and local subject gives rise to the need to (re)think social relationality. What is anorginal is the ontological fact that relationality is *a priori* (Benjamin, 2016), i.e., it always already functions in the abstract universalism of the science of the scientist and the ethnoscience of the ethnic other/informant/patient whose existence comes under the normative gaze of the scientist outside of or at a distance from the "field" of encounter where their field knowledge was coproduced.

Fanonian ethnopsychiatry not only undermines the monopoly of academic ethnography, but the institutional basis of psychiatry (even Tosquelles' institutional therapy). Strangely, Pels and Salemink (2000) privilege the practical men of the colonial enterprise as breaking up the academic monopoly on "ethnographic representation" (p. 8), viz., the administrative assemble of the colony on whose path ethnographic fieldworkers-cum-academic-anthropologists traveled to the colonial ethnographic field. On this view, Fanon's ethnopsychiatry is elided when it undermines or destructures the monopoly of academic ethnography and psychiatry. As he observed in *Wretched*, "The natives' challenge to the colonial world is not a rational confrontation of points of view. It is not a treatise on the universal, but the untidy affirmation of an original idea propounded as an absolute" (Fanon, 1966, p. 33). The knowledge Fanon collaborated in coproducing with his colleagues and patients or "guests," as Fanon referred to the women, men, and children under his care, according to Alice Cherki (Gibson & Beneduce, 2017, p. xv), bore the socio-spatial stamp of geopsychiatry undergoing decolonization.

Fanon confronted French colonial social science in his encounter with the colonized in Africa. At the time of his encounter, social scientists in various disciplines had not broken with the idealism of social science methods that distilled the lived experiences of subaltern subjects into essentialized categories of universal theorization. Even where a radical few discarded such idealism, and even more claim to have, today, "it still lingers in their historical self-conceptions" (Pels & Salemink, 2000, p. 9). Today, the so-called "activist-intellectual," "public intellectual," and "academic-activist" is supposed to call this disciplinary self-conception into question, if not destructure its academic/professional identity. The *risk* that Tosquelles tells us consumed Fanon's life is a singularity, an event horizon, in the destructuration of the academic/professional roles and methods of the intellectual's will to knowledge and power (prestige and privilege). The historic moment in which Fanon desired to know the subaltern subject of colonialism was at the same time the culmination of the subject's will to revolution, to disoccupy his/her socio-spatial geography and sociopsychology. Its *aftermath*, to reference Tosquelles, can as much be understood in terms of the problem of history that Fanon felt could be demonstrated as "the systematic valorization of collective complexes" (Fanon, 2018, p. 257) as the psychology of colonization that he theorized as undergoing destructuration commensurate with political decolonization.

Hybridity and Geopsychiatry

The present chapter traces the *préterrain* of the socio-spatial field of Fanon's ethnopsychiatry assembled in the recent publication of Fanon's "Clinical

Papers" that we can now traverse to a "new Frantz Fanon" nearly sixty years after his death. Encounters with Fanon, whether with his published political works or the recently published clinical papers, are overdetermined by the "specific location . . . of an academic relationship with the outside world in which scientific distinction is attained through the construction of 'pure' knowledge" (Pels & Salemink, 2000, p. 9). It would be "profitable to consider how such transformations of practical relationships," found in Fanon's clinical papers, overdetermine the current discursive exhaustiveness of Fanon Studies. More apropos, we must consider how Fanon subverted academic transformations of his practical relationships with subaltern subjects into the abstract constructs prefigured in the discursive strategies and methods of academic and professional disciplines.

Fanon's practice of institutional therapy, reiterated as sociotherapy, produced new locations (geography) and sociological localities in the transition from colonial Algeria to neocolonial Tunisia. In Pels' and Salemink's (2000) usage, hybridities are prefigured in the préterrain traversed on the way to the ethnographic field of study (practice of theory). The encounter of cultures and societies contributes not only to the cultural hybridity of Western and non-Western but to hybrid political economic systems, i.e., colonialism (see Turner, 2003). The préterrain commensurate with the hybridity of colonialism is the historical material precondition of ethnographic work, viz., modes of production, modes of reproduction of the administrative apparatus of colonial domination and inequality, etc., as well as cultural, discursive, and disciplinary modes of representation. According to Pels and Salemink, the préterrain also defines "the possibility and necessity of going 'out there'" (p. 13). The narrative of Fanon's oft recounted biography, up to his 1953 entrance onto the "field" of North Africa's political psychological landscape, maps the préterrain that defined the possibility and necessity of his "going 'out there.'" Camille Robcis' treatment of the revolution in French psychiatry expands the map of Fanon's préterrain. (See chapter one in this section.)

James Clifford's concept of *préterrain* conceptually maps the originary discourses and networks toured to arrive at the field of work (fieldwork) which organizes the ethnographic encounter between theorist and subject. The theoretical task embedded in Fanon's journey across the préterrain of postwar discourses and networks to the African revolution is etymologically recovered by Clifford:

> The Greek term theorein: a practice of travel and observation, a man sent by the polis to another city to witness a religious ceremony. "Theory" is a product of displacement, comparison, a certain distance. To theorize, one leaves home. But like any act of travel, theory begins and ends somewhere. In the case of the Greek theorist the beginning and ending were one, the home polis. This is not so simply true of traveling theorists in the late twentieth century.

(1989)

Discovering a "new Fanon" in his previously unavailable writings of 1954–60 from the North African settings of Algeria and Tunisia undergoing decolonization, specifically, the urban-rural environs of Algiers and Tunis, is an event in Fanon Studies. Camille Robcis (this volume) provides another part of the "backstory" to the "new Fanon," one which casts him in the revolution in French psychiatry staged at Saint-Alban Hospital with François Tosquelles, as well as other figures like Maurice Despinoy and such peers as Georges Canguilhem, who influenced philosophers of the French poststructuralist turn, such as Foucault, Derrida and Althusser. Of the many tributes to the influence of Canguilhem, none, except Deleuze and Guattari, mention the influence of Fanon in the Saint-Alban cohort (Deleuze & Guattari, 2009, p. 96).

Importantly, Saint-Alban and Blida-Joinville operated in the political context and geographic vicinity of resistance movements in which both institutions engaged—Saint-Alban during the waning years of the World War II underground Resistance and Blida-Joinville at the time of the French-Algerian revolutionary war. Thus, the geopsychiatry of the sociotherapy pursued by both institutions was neither merely a matter of breaching the barriers between the clinic and the community, nor only a matter of enhancing the cultural competency of the therapeutic setting and practices of the colonial milieu. Psychotherapy was made operable in the context of dynamic, often violent, changes and transformations in both instances. Psychotherapists at Saint-Alban and Blida-Joinville articulated the intersection of psychotherapy and social transformation; not the practice of psychotherapy within the inertial field of social stasis of the status quo, but the practice of psychotherapy on the combined ground of psychoanalytic and Marxian comprehension of the historicity of sociopsychological and political economic transformation.

The socio-spatial dialectic entailed in these consecutive historical transformations—World War II anti-fascist resistance and post-World War II anticolonial resistance—followed a dialectical logic of negation of negation, or *absolute negativity*. The negation of European fascism by the European Resistance, in which colonial subjects like Fanon participated as a young recruit in the Free French Army, became the Social Democratic object of a second negation in the conflagration of postwar anticolonial resistance, for which Fanon was arguably the epoch's most significant theorist and practitioner. (For an examination of the Frankfurt School precursor, namely, its critical discourse on the psychology of fascism, especially Adorno et al.'s *Authoritarian Personality*, see Turner (2002).) In a word, *Frantz Fanon was the embodiment of the dialectic of absolute negativity of the epoch*. Marxist Humanist philosopher Raya Dunayevskaya's (1989) treatment of "absolute negativity as new beginning" (p. 3), as the dialectical-historical determination of the postwar epoch of revolution, locates Fanon at this historic intersection. This subserves a collateral explanation of what attracted South Africa's Steve Biko to Fanon's theory of self-consciousness as a revolutionary category in articulating the politics of Black Consciousness for a resurgent anti-apartheid social movement coterminous with the Black Power Movement in the US and the neocolonial cul-de-sac of the national independence movements in Africa (Turner & Alan, 1978/1986). Fanon scholar-activist Nigel Gibson has made numerous theoretical contributions to mapping the sustained engagements between Fanon and the continuous emergence of generations of South African resistance to neo-apartheid and neoliberal nationalism (Gibson, 2011). Robcis' (2016) recovery of Fanon in the history of the postwar French revolution in psychiatry and psychoanalysis has yet to find an adequate echo in the delinquent recovery of Fanon in the French Hegel renaissance (Baugh, 2003; Mudimbe & Bohm, 1994) and in the antecedents of French poststructuralism. More is currently underway to recover Fanon in "Third World Marxism" with more nuanced and complex studies than previously articulated.

A seemingly anomalous site to stage an encounter with the "new Fanon" may be found in the editors' interview with Lewis M. King (this volume), the Executive Director of the Fanon Research and Development Center in Los Angeles, California. Fanon's work and example served as a model for Fanon Center psychologists, researchers, and practitioners in no small part because a decade of Black Power radicalism and theoretical exploration at the end of the Civil Rights Movement made African Americans the largest mass audience of Fanon's ideas in the 1960s and 1970s (Turner, 2011b). One measure of the popularity of Fanon in the Black Power era is reflected in the mass distribution publication of the 1965 American edition of *The Wretched of the Earth*, which went through seven printings in its first year alone. Moreover, it was Fanon's relationship to the Algerian revolution that persuaded African American radicals that Algiers was a safe haven beyond US imperialist reach, especially members of the Black Panther Party, in the late 1960s and 1970s (Mokhtefi, 2018).

This "new Fanon" is not only diasporic, but as King noted, the African American locus and global reach of Fanon's impact provided the model for the "research and development center" established in his name. As such, the Fanon Center reflected his thought and significance back to the Black World. Fanonian engagements of the Black Power era contributed to the transnational influence of Frantz Fanon that resurfaced with Steve Biko and the Black Consciousness Movement in the mid-1970s (Turner & Alan, 1986). Post-Black Power, the 1990s saw diverse postcolonial discoveries of Fanon by a new Global South generation.

The multilinear pathways to the "new Fanon" reflect an interdisciplinarity that was already present in Fanon's first work, *Black Skin, White Masks* (1952) and that is now deepened with the wide availability of his clinical papers and other writings. A contemporary encounter with this new Fanon was staged at a two-day symposium at Penn State University's Rock Ethics Institute, January 12–14, 2018, organized by Robert Bernasconi. I gave an invited address on "Fanon in Question: Destructuring the Possibility of Race" (Turner, 2018). The paper focused on the seldom examined subject of Fanon's concept of race and its relationship to the psychophysiological basis of Fanon's genetic method which, with the publication of the clinical papers, is now discernible throughout his *oeuvres* (Turner, 2018). For example, in his 1956 Letter of Resignation as chief medical director of the Blida-Joinville Hospital, in the context of the lead up to the Battle of Algiers (see Turner, 1999), Fanon complained that recent events of French colonialism in Algeria "are the logical consequence of an abortive attempt to decerebalize a people" (Fanon, 1969, p. 53). Colonialism made it impossible to practice a psychiatry that put the colonized back where they belonged, inasmuch as the social structures of colonialism were entirely inimical to the objectives of such professional ethics. Fanon's clinical papers reflect his genetic method, which privileged a physiological psychology that gave substance to his view that "Psychiatry has to be political." Between the socio-spatiality of the land and psychic structures of the colonized and colonizer is the biopolitics of the ethnopsychiatry that Fanon and his colleagues practiced, to which we now turn.

Fanon's Itinerary: The Clinical Papers

The contours of Fanon's therapeutic practices have seldom been researched, analyzed, applied, or tested. That his unique socio-psychotherapy exists on the margins of psychology and psychiatry no doubt is because of the politicized character of his published writings and the decentering of his clinical papers from their function in structuring his social theory. In addition to such biographical accounts as Irene Gendzier (1974) and David Macey (2000), earlier treatments of Fanon's clinical papers can be found in Jock McCulloch (1983), Hussein Bulhan (1985), and more recently in histories of psychiatry in North Africa by Richard Keller (2007a, 2007b), Marnia Lazreg (2007), and a forthcoming treatment of Fanon and his contemporaries at Saint-Alban Hospital in Camille Robcis' account of the history of France's post-World War II "psychiatric revolution." A personal insider's account of Fanon's psychotherapeutic practice is provided by one of his former interns, Alice Cherki (2006). Jean Khalfa (2015) and his section introduction to Part II of *Alienation and Freedom* (2018), which collects Fanon's "Psychiatric Writing," is an extensive engagement with Fanon's clinical papers. Finally, Nigel Gibson and Roberto Beneduce (2017) represent, in my view, the most incisive analysis of the clinical papers. In 2011, as appendix to his dissertation, *Frantz Fanon's Clinical Studies (1954–1960)*, Mazi Allen provided translations of nine of Fanon's clinical papers and lecture notes, coauthored with various colleagues and interns.

Fanon's clinical papers evidence the pragmatism of his thought and are arguably the source of his development of therapeutic approaches that are today broadly construed as "cultural competency" in psychotherapy. In lieu of the ready availability of Fanon's clinical papers, practitioners, clinics, diverse psychological professionals, and community psych centers inspired by his work translated his readily available published works into "Fanonian" therapies and applications. An example of this transactional strategy was evident in the establishment of the Fanon Research and Development Center in Los Angeles, California, in 1974.

The global diversity of the applications of Fanon's socio-psychotherapy anticipates what we are currently discovering in his clinical papers. First, Fanon's clinical papers present the portrait of a practicing clinician, psychotherapist, and hospital administrator critically applying and retooling his unique approach to what his mentor, François Tosquelles called "disoccupying the psyche." In discussing her work-in-progress, "Disoccupation: The Psychiatric Revolution in France, 1945–1975," Camille Robcis gives this biographical synopsis of Tosquelles' influence on French psychiatry:

> During the war, Saint-Alban [Hospital] had emerged as a particularly vibrant center of psychiatric reform under the impulse of François Tosquelles. . . . Tosquelles had studied psychiatry in Barcelona with Emil [Mira] y Lopez who had introduced him to phenomenology, psychoanalysis, and especially to the work of Jacques Lacan who remained a crucial reference for Tosquelles throughout his life. Tosquelles had also been in the POUM [Partit Obrer d'Unificacio Marxista], the anti-Stalinist and Trotsky-inspired workers' movement particularly important in Catalonia. After fleeing the Franco regime in 1939, Tosquelles was placed in a concentration camp for Spanish refugees in the southwest of France before he was eventually recruited by the director of the Saint-Alban hospital. This early experience of multiple "occupations" (Spanish in Catalonia, Stalinist within communist parties, fascist in Spain and in Vichy France, and German in the French territory) had convinced Tosquelles that occupation was not only a social and political reality but also a psychic structure. Thus, the search for a true freedom needed to go through a form of psychic "disoccupation." To think through these issues, the psychiatric hospital appeared to offer a perfect platform. . . . At Saint-Alban, Tosquelles collaborated with other communist psychiatrists . . . but also with intellectuals who were in the Resistance such as Georges Canguilhem [and] Frantz Fanon who interned at Saint-Alban.
>
> (Meyers, 2014)

Fanon translated the socio-therapeutic approach he learned from Tosquelles during his internship at Saint-Alban into a kind of situationism for "decolonizing" the colonized psyche in works like *Black Skin, White Masks* (1952), *A Dying Colonialism* (1959), and *The Wretched of the Earth* (1961). In providing a window into his critical applications, Fanon's clinical papers give us a direct means of engaging and evaluating Fanonian applications that have relied on these published works in lieu of the availability of his clinical papers. Second, Fanon's clinical practice intimates a research agenda for a diverse array of disciplines and sub-disciplines, from liberation psychology to cultural competences in counseling psychology and psychiatric nursing, from research in identity psychology to community psychology, from mental health administration, medical ethics and medico-legal issues (forensic psychiatry) to psychometric testing, and from the latest research on stress and trauma pathogenesis to critical deconstructions of trauma pathologization of global mental health responses in conflict zones by Western medical aid and non-governmental organizations.

Because the essays collected in this volume traverse a fine line between the application of Fanon's insights into clinical practice and his phenomenological-existential discourse on the lived experience of human beings *in situs* (in situation), a sampling of his clinical papers helps contextualize the scope of the essays in this collection. In the sections below, we unpack the most salient insights and incisive conclusions to be drawn for the momentum of the current historic moment. Now, as at the time of Fanon's dying colonialism, we live, as Gramsci observed, in an interregnum in which the old is dying and the new is not yet born wherein a great variety of morbid symptoms present themselves.

The Algiers Papers (1954–56): Practicing Sociopsychiatry of a Dying Colonialism

The results of the first of Fanon's clinical papers, the 1954 report coauthored with his intern Jacques Azoulay on the difficulties encountered in instituting sociotherapy on a Muslim men's ward at Blida Psychiatric Hospital (Fanon & Azoulay, 1954), were summed up a year later by Fanon in a discussion with another intern, Charles Geronomi. He responded to Geronimi's inquiry about the lessons he drew from the attempt to implement sociotherapy on a Muslim men's ward that "Psychiatry has to be political" (Cherki, 2006, p. 72). Elaborating on his self-critical assessment, Fanon confessed that he had not foreseen the problems and ultimate failure of attempting to institute sociotherapy on a Muslim men's ward at Blida-Joinville.

> You can only understand things with your gut, you know. It was not simply a matter of imposing imported methods that had been more or less adapted to the *native mentality*. I also had to demonstrate a number of things in the process: namely, that the values of Algerian culture are different from those of colonial culture; that these structuring values had to be embraced without any complexes by those to whom they pertained—the Algerian medical staff as well as the Algerian patients. I needed to have the support of the Algerian staff in order to incite them to rebel against the prevailing method, to make them realize that their competence was equal to that of the Europeans. The burden of suggesting appropriate forms of socialization and integrating them into the sociotherapy process had to be placed on the Algerian staff. That's what happened. Psychiatry has to be political.
> (Cherki, 2006, pp. 71–72)

The "creative failure" of the attempt to operationalize Western institutional psychotherapy for a Muslim male cohort is a strategy Fanon utilized on occasion to demonstrate Western psychotherapy's lack of cultural competency when applied to mental illness in non-Western societies (Desai, 2014). Cherki (2006) ponders whether "Fanon's attempt to impose European 'methodologies' on Muslim patients [was] a genuine 'mistake,' or had he consciously implemented a plan that he knew was doomed to failure from the outset?" (p. 71)

The study's political subtext demonstrated that "Algeria is [*not*] French" *contra* the colonialist claim voiced by then-Socialist Interior Minister, François Mitterand, in reasserting French hegemony over its prized North African colony after the defeat of France at Dien Bien Phu, Vietnam, in 1954. Given Fanon's engagements with Hegelian dialectic, it is worth noting Hegel's principle, "Error . . ., when it is uplifted and absorbed, is itself a necessary dynamic element of truth" (Hegel, 1874, para. 212); and his contention that "What calls itself the fear of error reveals itself as a fear of the truth" (Hegel, 1977, p. 74). These passages from Hegel's treatment of the teleological design of scientific inquiry and research resonate with Fanon's deep theorization of revolutionary dialectic in the sociopsychological transformation of individuals and institutions in colonial society. The logic, function, protocols, and method of Fanon's application of Saint-Alban's institutional therapy outside of its European context inaugurated Fanonian sociotherapy.

Sociotherapeutic Schema (Blida Case Study)

I. Sociotherapy

    i. Organization
    ii. Activities

II. Problems on Muslim Men's Ward

    i. Attempts
    ii. Cultural Competency

III. Assessment

    i. Clinical Environment
    ii. Cycle of Agitation, Restraint, Agitation

IV. Re-Assessment

    i. Self-Criticism

V. Political Psychology

    i. Colonial Socialization
    ii. Adaptation & Assimilation
    iii. Algiers School of Ethnopsychiatry & Critique

VI. Realignment

    i. Muslim Women
    ii. Functional Analysis (Sociological)
    iii. Functional Analysis (Marxian)

VII. Failure Assessment

    i. Language & Interpretation

       (a) Dialectics of Language

    ii. Cultural Alienation

    iii. Group & Game Therapy

    iv. Cinema

    v. Journal

    vi. Ergotherapy (Work Therapy)

VIII. Conclusion: Dialectic of Creative Failure

Sociotherapy

"Psychiatry has to be political." This is how Fanon summed up the failure of his and Azoulay's experiment to introduce sociotherapeutic methods on a Muslim men's ward at the Blida Psychiatric Hospital (Cherki, 2006, p. 72). Fanon cites the "lack of objectivity (on our part) which made many of our errors possible" (Fanon, 2018, p. 353), which refers to their imposition of Eurocentric socialization on Muslim men suffering from psychoses that originated from or were complicated by French colonialism's quest to assimilate Algerians and alienate them from their own culture.

Fanon and Azoulay were humbled by the failure of their experience, which made them engage Algerian culture with "the consciousness of our patients' double alienation—due to the tyranny of subjectivity and to what Piaget has termed sociocentrism" (Fanon, 2018, p. 354). They reoriented their research in "an entirely different direction" (Fanon, 2018, p. 354). Fanon's experience with institutional therapy at Saint-Alban was the model for his experiment at Blida. For his inaugural application of sociotherapy, Fanon cowrote a document based on Azoulay's thesis work while in the doctoral program at the University of Algiers (Gibson & Beneduce, 2017, p. 25). In the Blida experiment 165 European women and 220 Muslim men participated in a sociotherapy intervention. The application of sociotherapy was carried out in an inpatient unit in which four or five psychiatrists were responsible for 600 and later 400 patients.

The intervention of sociotherapy was comprehensive and involved an integrated care approach. Below is an outline of the organizational schedule and activities related to the sociotherapy intervention:

Organization

- Biweekly collective meetings
- Separate staff meetings
- Bimonthly events involving patients

- Patients, physicians, and nursing staff attended events
- A "social architecture" was formed producing possibilities of more social encounters
- European women's ward progressed with sociotherapy
- Capstone event was the Christmas festival organized by patients and two nurses

Activities

- Other socialized events:
- Cinema
- Discotheque
- Publication, *Notre Journal*, which includes contributions by staff and patients
- Chorus at Christmas festival

Ergotherapy

- Domestic work
- Knitting workshop (managed by nurse)
- Embroidery and needlework, including of patients' apparel

Problems on a Muslim Men's Ward

Language served as the main barrier in the first attempt of sociotherapy in the experiment. The difficulties Fanon and Azoulay encountered on a Muslim men's ward at Blida-Joinville were characterized as application of the same order of sociotherapeutic efforts in different settings produced successive failures. Group therapy was pursued only after a series of meetings with nursing staff. Engagement with Muslim patients was difficult because of physicians' (Fanon, et al.) inability to speak Arabic or Kabyle. However, the ethnic background of the nursing staff became a means to establish difficult patient contact. Using interpreters also presented problems of linguistic distancing and alienation in patient encounters. Fanon and Azoulay found that Muslim male patients ignored attempts to engage them or to inform them of events and activities associated with sociotherapy. After several weeks of attempted engagement, the experiment was abandoned.

In the second iteration of sociotherapy on the Muslim men's ward, Fanon and Azoulay became aware of the significance of the radio. Specifically, in this attempt, they charged psychiatric nurses to work with groups of ten patients by conducting nightly discussions, games and songs. Nurses wrote nightly reports on these activities. The reports described growing indifference on the part of the patients toward the games and activities. Instead, patients ended up listening to "Oriental music (on the radio)" (Fanon, 2018, p. 359). This is one of Fanon's earliest observations about the significance of the radio in Muslim culture.

The relevance of cultural competency emerged from the third attempt of applying sociotherapy on the men's ward. As part of the intervention, monthly festivals were organized along with the nightly activities. However, the organization of the festivals failed because of lack of interest on the part of the nurses. The festivals were similar to the activities conducted in the European women's ward (e.g., choral and theatrical performances). The nurses perhaps knew that such activities were culturally alien to the patients. Festivals, cinema showings, and initiation of a ward journal were activities organized with various degrees of success but essentially with little affect among Muslim men. Nurses did not buy into the program either, which undermined Fanon's strategy.

Ergotherapy (work therapy) was no more successful. The experience with ergotherapy and the workshop created to manufacture raffia mats, straw hats, and baskets is instructive: When nurses were not paying attention, patients would desert the workshop and go help a fellow patient clear a plot of land with a pick and shovel. In other words, patients organized their own culturally affirming collective milieu in response to and rejection of the "neo-society" Fanon tried to organize.

Assessment

Fanon's first assessment of the sociotherapy intervention was bleak. "After three months, not only could we not continue—despite our efforts to interest Muslim patients in commencing the type of collective life we had organized on the European women's ward—the atmosphere remained tense" (Fanon, 2018, p. 361). Because of remission of their symptomology, the patients required more attention and cleaning-up after, which consumed most of the staff's time, leaving little time for new therapeutic activities. In this and later papers, Fanon connected the organization of the clinical environment with the symptomology of patient behavior and how it militated against changing that environment. Patient pathology originated, in part, in the environment of the asylum, which reproduced forms of racial alienation of colonized society. This was manifested in conflicts between patients (the colonized) "into which nurses only would intervene at their own risk" (Fanon, 2018, p. 361). The clinic assumed the aspect of a menacing environment.

A cycle of agitation, restraint, agitation ensued, "reinforcing the totalitarian spirit of the ward" (Fanon, 2018, p. 361). Fanon's efforts at reform of the status quo on the ward were met with "inertia" (Fanon, 2018, p. 361). On the Muslim men's ward, the cycle of restraint and agitation prevailed, despite Fanon's and his colleagues' efforts to reform the environment through sociotherapy. "We had taken a wrong turn and had to figure out why: we had to clear this impasse" (Fanon, 2018, p. 362).

Reassessment

To clear the impasse, Fanon resorted to his background in sociology. He studied both the social setting of the Muslim men's ward in depth and "their milieu of origin (outside of the hospital)" (Fanon, 2018, p. 362). Fanon and his colleagues thought it merely a matter of adapting "Western contexts to a Muslim society" and that as a "matter of technical evolution" (Fanon, 2018, p. 362). Fanon confessed that "we had forgotten that every step on this path must be preceded by a tenacious interrogation of the concrete, real, and organic bases of the preexisting society" (Fanon, 2018, p. 362). In a later paper, Fanon would argue, with evidence, that day-hospitalization procedures, which were suited for modern Western clinical settings, had been successfully transplanted for the first time to a non-Western society in Tunis. Fanon's reference to the "the bracketing of the geographic, historical, cultural, and social contexts" (Fanon, 2018, p. 362) originated in his philosophical debt to phenomenology and was continuous with his use of phenomenological reduction as a discursive instrument for positing the lived experience of subaltern populations in the "fieldwork" of Western social science. Fanon and Azoulay reassessed their judgement, and thereby its underlying premise in institutional psychotherapy, that in the interest of focusing on the institutional experience of Muslim patients they had "bracketed," i.e., suspended, analysis and judgment of the "geographic, historical, cultural and social contexts" of those patients.

This discussion is complicated by the fact that the structural racism of the ethnopsychiatry of the Algiers School of Antoine Porot was allegedly oriented to Muslim culture. So, Fanon's self-criticism of his initial efforts to import Western sociotherapy to a Muslim men's ward led to (1) a reassessment that involved a deeper sociopsychological understanding of the Muslim cultural milieu in and outside of the hospital setting, and (2) a more successful reorganization of his sociotherapeutic procedures to coincide with Muslim cultural norms in Algeria. This was (3) later followed by his successful instantiation of Western-style day-hospitalization in Tunis with close attention to the sociology of Muslim cultural patterns.

Political-Psychiatry: Adaptation and Assimilation

It is essential to understand the political implications of Fanon's clinical work: If the ideological/political basis on which France sought to retain Algeria as a colony was that "Algeria is French," the evidence from Fanon's sociotherapeutic experiment on two psychiatric wards—a European women's ward and a Muslim men's ward—profoundly undermined that political position. Fanon's report of its failure was more than a scientific assessment of psychological models and clinical procedures. His observations revealed the underlying colonial assumption of the assertion "Algeria is French." In order for this assertion to hold true, North Africans must fully assimilate, in which case their "culture must disappear for the benefit of the other" (Fanon, 2018, p. 362). In doing so, the assimilation is unidimensional. Fanon makes a similar claim concerning the lack of reciprocity in the dialectic of recognition *Black Skin* (Fanon, 1967; Turner, 1996).

The problem of using an interpreter in therapy surfaces several times in Fanon's work. He notes that the attitudes of the therapists were not adapted to the patients on the Muslim men's ward. Instead, "a revolutionary attitude was necessary—for we needed to pass from a position where the supremacy of one culture [French] was self-evident to one of cultural relativism" (Fanon, 2018, pp. 362–363). Fanon then references Piaget on questions of adaptation and assimilation in order to understand the nature of the failure of sociotherapy on the Muslim men's ward.

Critique and Resolution (Case of Muslim Women)

Importantly, for the development of his psychotherapy, Fanon found it necessary to deconstruct the prevailing Algiers School of ethnopsychiatry. It was a critique and resolution of the problems encountered when attempting to implement sociotherapy on a Muslim men's ward in which Muslim women became instrumental. Until his clinical papers were available, it was thought that his criticism of the Algiers School was ideological—i.e., that his aim was to expose its bio-racism. The clinical papers reveal a more complex picture, one which shows Fanon taking the School's ethnographic claims seriously, as he had in the case of his critique of Octave Mannoni's ethnopsychological study of Madagascar, in *Black Skin*, even as he subjected both to sharp criticism. Because his point of departure was the cultural specificity of North Africans, Fanon credited the Algiers School of ethnopsychiatry with having revealed "several particularities of the North African" (Fanon, 2018, p. 363). Nevertheless, it did not deliver on its stated aim to proceed to "the functional analysis which they profess to be indispensable" (Fanon, 2018, p. 363). Then, with stunning theoretical sweep, Fanon sums up the problematic and proposes its resolution:

> [W]e must grasp the facts of North African society from within that very "totality". . . . This would entail a leap to efficacy, a transmutation from values to their realization. Thus, we must pass from the biological to the institutional, from the natural to the cultural—and in fact, the biological, psychological, and sociological are intrinsically tied (only held as separate through a mental aberration). It was thus because we had not integrated the notion of Gestalt and contemporary anthropology into our everyday practice that we encountered the difficulties mentioned above [i.e., the failure of the sociotherapy on the Muslim men's ward].
>
> (Fanon, 2018, p. 363)

The example Fanon gives of the "transmutation from values to their realization . . . into our everyday practice" is of Muslim women who passively participated in the activities on the European women's ward but who became very actively engaged "once a Muslim orchestra arrived at the hospital for a performance" and responded with "short, high-pitched, repetitive vocal modulations" (Fanon, 2018, p. 363). "It was evident to us," Fanon concluded, "that we need to find the gestalt which similarly facilitated reactions already inscribed on such definitively elaborate personalities" (Fanon, 2018, p. 363).

Sociotherapy Redesigned: Functional Analysis (Geopsychiatry)

Sociotherapy is only possible when therapy is organized around the social morphology or the forms of sociability and individual personalities. The sociodiagnostic questions Fanon employed were:

- What are the biological, moral, aesthetic, cognitive, and religious values of Muslim society?
- How do Muslims react from an affective point of view?
- What forms of sociability "rendered possible the attitudes of the Muslim"?

(Fanon, 2018, p. 363)

Fanon concluded that a "functional analysis had to be performed in order to facilitate [the] task" of reorienting sociotherapy for Muslim wards (Fanon, 2018, p. 364). He mentions a work-in-progress that will "demonstrate the complexity of North African society (which today is subject to extremely profound structural modifications)" (Fanon, 2018, p. 364). This work-in-progress would culminate in *Studies in a Dying Colonialism* (1959). What then followed was an analysis of "a few elements characteristic of this society" (Fanon, 2018, p. 364):

- Its theocratic spirit, wherein religion is a way of life, strictly regulates group and individual relations, as well as erstwhile secular institutions and ideologies.
- Muslim society is "gerontocratic" where the father directs family life.
- Families are extended, often to include whole villages, and tend to identify themselves with a clan, which is "the genuine social group in Muslim Algeria."

(Fanon, 2018, p. 364)

- Decision-making at the village and community level is made by a *Djemâ* or municipal council.
- In the ethnic complexity of North Africa, the Kabyle form a significant minority with their own language and culture but share Islamic religion amid a majority Arab population. The Kabyle inhabit mountainous areas, whereas Arabs inhabit the plains and cities. Out of the 220 patients on the Muslim men's ward, 148 were Arab and 66 were Kabyle.
- Land tenure, before French occupation, meant that land was a communal possession and wealth was connected to usufruct or land-use with yoke and plow. The possessors of such instruments of production were the real landowners.
- French land allotment policy impoverished most North African social strata, created a few Muslim owners (along with French colonialists, of course), formed a North African proletariat, a mass of small Muslim

land proprietors or *fellahs* who cultivated small plots of land with primitive means of production, and strata of day-laborers (*khammes*) who sold their labor.

Fanonian-Marxian Analysis

Fanon and Azoulay concluded their functional analysis with a Marxian turn, one which only seems "stretched" (Fanon, 1966, p. 32) because it was articulated prior to the discovery of Marx's writings on pre-capitalist societies in the *Grundrisse* and his *Ethnological Notebooks*, in the 1970s (Dunayevskaya, 1989, 1991; Krader, 1975; Marx, 1973). The breath of Fanon's Marxian analysis is almost disconcerting given the debates on the question of whether Fanon was a Marxist or not. All of this, moreover, was in the service of the kind of functional analysis required to reorient Tosquelles' sociotherapy within a North African context. In a unique recovery of the Marxian concept of Asiatic mode of production (AMP), Fanon's generalization of the new mode of life imposed on North African societies by French colonialism extended his Marxian analysis further with his observation that the French breakup of traditional Maghreb social relations regressed North African society back to ancient sedentarism and nomadism (Cf. Krader, 1975). In fact, he observed a bifurcated development, one branch of which resorted to archaic sedentarism and nomadism and the other to modern proletarianism.

The consequences of this split development are a set of anomalies that would appear later in Fanon's analysis in *Wretched*, viz., (1) seasonal laborers remained outside of the sedentary groups that they came to aid (this is consistent with the social labor phenomenon observed in South Africa's Bantustans), (2) the new nomadism broke down the traditional structures of authority and cohesion that prevailed in the old tribal nomadism, which would have such profound effect on women and young men, (3) with the breakdown of tribalization came proletarianization, and (4) with the breakdown of tribal-village structures came the development of new urban phenomena like the formation of "Bidonvilles" (shantytowns) "at the edge of large cities which constitute not only a defiance of aesthetics and [urban] planning but also a grave danger (from a sanitary and moral point of view)" (Fanon, 2018, p. 366).

Considering his functional Marxian analysis, Fanon enumerated the following social composition of the Muslim's men's ward: 35 fellahs (i.e., small land cultivators), 75 agricultural workers, sharecroppers, or day-laborers, 78 urban workers (bakers, painters, etc.), 5 intellectuals, and 26 without professions. The assumption that there were skilled workers in this cohort is sketchy because the urban workers were uprooted workers from the countryside who found work in the city. Only about a quarter of the urban workers could be said to have any specialization. The five intellectuals were native schoolteachers with little more than an elementary school education.

Fanon made an explicit social category of what he called "uprooted workers" because of the far-reaching consequences for (a) the breakup and fragmentation of traditional societies under colonialism, (b) the exponential growth in these strata of uprooted individuals, and (c) the inadequate analysis of this phenomenon by contemporary social science. His conclusion is at odds with the prevailing views of existentialists like Sartre and Camus, sociologists like Bourdieu, and orthodox Marxists, viz., that "traditional society, though often seen as fixed, is fermenting at its base" (Fanon, 2018, p. 367). Thus, Fanon's new point of view and his notion of the transformation of the socio-logical structure of Algerian society, though brief and in need of further devel-opment, "illustrate[s] the specificities of Algerian Muslim society which must be taken into account in order to create a basis for sociotherapy amongst Mus-lim patients" (Fanon, 2018, p. 367). In short, Fanon's sociotherapy *is* Marxian.

Failure Assessment: The Negative Dialectic of Language & Interpretation

The praxis and process of sociotherapy on the Muslim men's ward was not fruitful, in part, because Fanon and his colleagues did not speak Arabic and Kabyle and, instead, had to resort to interpreters. This vitiated the physician–patient relationship because in their social settings patients encountered inter-preters as agents of the colonial government and the criminal justice system.

Use of interpreters in the hospital setting provoked distrust, impairing the communication necessary for therapy. Patients grew agitated in the presence of the physician because they didn't think the interpreter could convey the feel-ing that they wished to express. The problem of interpretative communication represented a serious disturbance in the psychotherapeutic encounter.

Interpretation is potentially traumatic for the patient because the therapist arrives at a diagnosis through language and dialogue. Translation vitiates the gestural and verbal content of language. Communication is not experienced as one-to-one reciprocity because the expressive gestures of the patient, which cannot be interpreted until the end of the discourse, get reduced to a few words by the interpreter. The interpreter often translates the words of the patient according to stereotyped formulas that strip communication of its content. For example, there is no way to determine whether the patient's delirium is real or induced. Dialogue is the primary way to overcome the patient's reticence to trust the therapist or to expose/present abnormal behaviors. Not knowing Ara-bic or Kabyle meant that Fanon and his interns had no way of knowing "which cultural or affective elements of their patrimony were capable of availing their interest" (Fanon, 2018, p. 368).

Failure Assessment: Cultural Alienation

Attempts to organize festivals and festivities for European women was secu-lar in nature, whereas outside of familial or religious contexts, such festivities for Muslim men were "quite abstract" (Fanon, 2018, p. 368). From Fanon's and Azoulay's research, collective celebration among Muslims was different from Western festivities; for instance, Muslim men dislike singing in groups and singing is not done in Muslim households out of respect for the father or elder brother. Theatre did not elicit Muslim patients' participation because in North Africa, theatre, as performed in the West, did not exist. Although Arabic theatre was performed in large cities, it was a recent urban phenomenon of modernizing cosmopolitanism. In Arab villages or *douars*, itinerant storytellers wandered from place to place bringing news stories and folktales accompanied by rudimentary musical instruments. Fanon deployed another iteration of his analysis of North African storytellers in *Wretched* through an African modernist, anti-colonial, theatrical poetic piece, *African Dawn*, by Guinean poet, dancer, and founder of Les Ballet Africains, Fodeba Keita (Fanon, 1966, p. 183).

Failure Assessment: Group and Game Therapy, Cinema, the Journal, and Work

Game therapy relies on the teamwork of patients; the problem was that Muslim men rarely played such games at school in their youth. At ages 10–12, the Arab youth was a shepherd or helped his father in various tasks. Evening sociotherapeutic activities for Muslim men "had to be inspired by reality and in reality, Muslim men gathered in Moorish coffeehouses after work" (Fanon, 2018, p. 369). The coffeehouse was the cultural meeting place of Muslim men where they talked about current events, smoked, drank coffee and tea, and importantly listened to the *radio*. Listening to the radio was part of the sociotherapy that was successful, and Fanon would analyze its cultural utility and radical mutations, in depth, in *A Dying Colonialism*.

Cinema was of continuing interest to Fanon, dating back to *Black Skin*, where Fanon discussed the 1949 American war film *Home of the Brave*, which takes place in a military psychiatric ward (Fanon, 1967). Cinema showings were considered "diversions" by the hospital and did not hold much interest for Muslim patients and provoked no emotional engagement. Only action films aroused some interest. Fanon believed Muslims' disinterest stemmed from the improbable reactions of the Western characters to their situation in the films. More than likely the Muslim men could not identify with the plots and action of Western films, even when the settings were North African.

The ward journal reflected the social life of the hospital but was of no interest to those who felt excluded from that life, which is why even literate patients never contributed to it. However, illiteracy was the main barrier to Muslim patients contributing to the journal. Out of 220 Muslim patients only five could read and write Arabic, two read and wrote French. The attempt to have nurses write articles for the patients also failed. More importantly, from a cultural point of view, Algerian culture was oral and education was principally oral. Literacy was a specialized skill in North African culture in which those who possess it were charged with reading and writing as a social service of public scribes who wrote letters for people. Moreover, storytellers carried news and recounted historic events, folktales, and epics, which sustain "cultural linkages between different regions" (Fanon, 2018, p. 371).

Industrial society permits re-adaptation therapy that departs from existing social relations; however, the semi-feudal character of North African society made re-adaptation therapy difficult. At that time, in North Africa men worked the land and did not specialize in particular skills, except a few artisanal pursuits. Men did not do the kind of wool, raffia, and pottery work organized as ergotherapy on the ward because it was considered "women's work." Fanon concluded that

> For men, we must take our point of departure from the most general and firmly anchored dispositions of the personality of the patient. . . . It will suffice to give them a pick and a shovel which they will use to break the earth (and without which one will have to force them to work).
>
> (Fanon, 2018, p. 371)

Coming from a peasant culture, Muslim men derived their worth and identity from close relationship to the land. Ergotherapy meant assigning them a plot of land for cultivation for purposes of their rehabilitation. "Ergotherapy can only insert itself within a socially specific activity" (Fanon, 2018, p. 371).

Conclusion: Creative Failure (Negation of the Negation)

In the end, Fanon states that his and Azoulay's assessment has "definitively shown why our first attempt at implementing sociotherapy among Muslim patients was repaid in failure" (Fanon, 2018, p. 371). The experiment was not in vain because he understood the reasons for the failure and "modified the focus of our efforts" with "tangible results" (Fanon, 2018, p. 371): Creation of a Moorish coffeehouse in the hospital; holding regular celebrations of traditional Muslim festivals, and arranging for periodic visits by Arab and Kabyle storytellers. Redesigned sociotherapy increased participation by Muslim patients in the life of the wards, triggering Fanon's belief that his and Azoulay's "methodological errors" (Fanon, 2018, p. 371) were behind them.

Testimony: Decolonizing Forensic Psychiatry

In this section we will unpack Fanon's second clinical paper, coauthored with Raymond Lacaton, a section director at Blida, and a subsequent lecture he gave on the same subject of confession. These deal with one of several areas of Fanon's work that extended beyond the clinic walls, in this case, as a forensic psychiatrist evaluating the mental competency of Algerian defendants in judicial proceedings (Fanon, 2018). As is apparent from the case studies collected at the end of *The Wretched of the Earth*, another area of Fanon's work extending beyond the formal clinic setting involved his practice of psychotherapy for both victims and perpetrators of torture, as well as for militants who committed terrorist acts (Turner, 2011a). The multiple forms of testimonials in Fanon's psychotherapeutic practices has remained relatively unexplored terrain until the current encounter with his clinical papers and other formerly unavailable writings. As we will see, the Confessions paper was for colonial law what Fanon's analysis of the North African syndrome was for colonial medicine.

In their paper, Fanon and Lacaton (1955) assessed the cultural dissonance apparent in the confessions and recantations of Muslim offenders in colonial criminal justice proceedings. The Confessions paper and lecture treats the existential dilemma of the "truth" of self-confession in the Manichean context that the accused faces in a colonial society in which his social contract with his own cultural milieu comes into conflict with that demanded by the colonial system. The self-confession that formed the social solidarity with the former is recanted in recognition of the latter, as a form of resistance.

The forensic psychiatrist must attempt to discern the "truth" of the alleged criminal act, which is "fundamentally the truth of its author" (Fanon, 2018, p. 413). According to Sartre, for the accused author ("hero") of his act to deny it is to descend into alienation, whereas to embrace it is to resort to the absurd and attempt to make sense of it. Sartre's and Fanon's existentialist evaluation of the criminal act is made more manifest in the colonial context. The internal coherence of the act and the confession as the "truth" of the individual involves self-condemnation as the content of conscience, which ransoms his reintegration into his community (*gemeinschaft*) *contra* society (*gesellschaft*). The conduct of conscience and confession operates at the intersection of the colonized community and the larger colonial society, producing "a veritable segregation" (Fanon, 2018, p. 410). The accused's confession ransoms his reinsertion into his community while standing in defiance of the dominant colonizing society, producing an *intercultural conflict of laws*.

The ransom of a favorable resolution for a criminal act is not achievable without preexisting reciprocal recognition between the colonized individual and the group. Colonial society only recognizes the authenticity of the colonized at the moment of the latter's self-incrimination, or, properly, when the state's legitimacy hangs on the success of its procedures of compulsory, though spurious, incrimination of the subaltern. Fanon, as had Richard Wright before him through the persona of Bigger Thomas in *Native Son*, found that colonial society is also compelled to recognize black human authenticity when the colonized resists by recanting his confession. As a rule, the accused confesses before the trial, presenting the forensic psychiatrist with a defendant who totally denies his guilt and any knowledge of why he is being detained.

Berber customary law of the Kabyle rigidly prescribes rationales for various categories of crime (e.g., murder or attempted murder over inheritance, sale or exchange of land, or marital infidelity). Although Berber customary law elicits and permits strong denial of criminal guilt, the French criminal justice system ascribes criminal guilt for such acts governed by customary law. Karl Marx makes a similar argument on the conflict between customary and statutory law in his 1842 articles on the "Peasants Theft of Wood" (Marx, 1975). Once again, this shows Fanon employing the politics of psychiatry (in this case, evaluation of criminally accused Algerians—here, Kabyle) to spell out the

Manichean distinction between Algerian and French culture *contra* the French assertion that Algeria *is* France.

The Dossier

The dossier of preliminary investigations of such "criminal acts" elaborates the contradictory phenomena of confession and denial as a result of the lack of transparency in the investigation, which is unmindful of the ethno-legal duality at play. The psychiatric evaluator is summoned to clarify or explain the so-called confused mental state of the accused for the purpose of elaborating a dossier that will rationalize French legal action as an indispensable function of its colonial footprint.

Colonial Intercultural Dualism: The Denial

Although denial is sometimes established from the beginning, it is more often the case that the accused, in the context of customary Berber law, confesses. Preliminary investigation by colonial officials employing the interrogatories of Western law may elicit denials deposed according to Berber understanding of Western law. The preliminary investigation may include motives, narrative of events, and descriptions of the scene of the crime. Although the dossier may not change while the accused is imprisoned for several months, as the case proceeds to trial the accused retracts his confession. On the one hand, the accused's denial is intractable, on the other, he does not try to prove his innocence.

The accused appears to put his faith in the hands of the blind justice of the Western judicial system, but in fact he has decided to accept his fate in the name of Allah. This intercultural dualism, not to be confused with colonial Manicheism, reinforces the colonizer's social perception and insistence that Algeria's Muslims see themselves as "French." In fact, two fundamentally opposed structures of feeling and reference coincide to produce conduct that draws its meaning and legitimacy from two conflicting models of law—statutory and customary.

The Problem for the Forensic Psychiatrist

The psychiatrist is asked to evaluate the mental state of the accused "deprived of the diagnostic value of the type of confession spoken of by the respondent (who has shown the great difficulties that follow from a retraction)" (Fanon, 2018, p. 411). The absolute denial by the accused leaves the psychiatrist with an act (crime) without an agent or author. Since this makes criminological comprehension impossible, the psychiatrist is left only with the "dossier," the content of which contains the charges brought by the state *sans* any rationale provided by customary law. The dossier weighs heavily against the accused because it is the only actant that reconstitutes the crime. In comparison to the profile of a criminal offender that the dossier gives, the psychiatrist, on the day of his forensic psychological examination, encounters "a lucid, coherent, man who proclaims his innocence" (Fanon, 2018, p. 411). The ethics of Western law is suspended: the assumption of ownership of the criminal act (culpability) and thus acceptance of the penalty (condemnation) are totally suspended by the accused Muslim. Thus, "[t]he truth of the criminal cannot be found by the psychiatric evaluator" (Fanon, 2018, p. 411). Faced with a subject who has no assumptions of Western ethical law, Fanon asks whether the psychiatrist should not instead reconcile himself to an ontological explanation in which it is likely that the native Muslim has instead "made a contract against the group which henceforth holds him under its power" (Fanon, 2018, p. 411).

Do Muslim men and women feel bound by a social contract, and if so, to which group—European or Muslim? The question of "guilt" raises a further social contract question, viz., from which group does his guilt exclude him, European or Muslim? The question of the social contract in a colonized society *situates* criminal justice procedures such as trials and sentencing, and conversely, trials and sentencing situate questions of social contracts in colonized societies, in a *sui generis* light. To fail to address this question makes it possible to conclude that North Africans or other colonized peoples are pathological liars, lazy, underhanded, etc., for which the agents of the criminal justice system, the media, and employers readily provide numerous examples.

Orchestration of Falsehood: Confession and Reinstatement

The colonial accused's orchestration of falsehood requires an existential explanation, inasmuch as "the liar is someone who constantly poses the question of 'truth' to himself" (Fanon, 2018, p. 412). At the biopolitical level of ethnoracial bias, the assumption that a race or ethnicity has a natural propensity for lying and dissimulation because its individuals are incapable of distinguishing true from false because of an alleged phylogenetic deficiency is another evasion of the problem of confession and retraction.

Crime and punishment are existential fundaments of the ethical order of society (i.e., they reinforce the sustainability of the status quo). Therefore, any deviation or distortion in the operation of the ethical-social processes of criminal justice represents a departure from the social order. The ethical order of society requires for its maintenance, or resumption of its order following the disorder caused by a criminal act, that the offender confess his crime either explicitly or in the form of being found guilty and punished for the purpose of his reinstatement in society. Fanon resorts to Hegelian recognition as the mode of situating the reinstatement of the offender into society. In this sense, he maintains that reentry depends on recognition of the group by the individual, with the caveat that there cannot be reinstatement if the individual had not formerly been integrated in society before commission of the crime. The coexistence of different ethical-social processes, as happens in pluralist or colonialist societies, means that social solidarity is weak or absent. Nothing exposes this more powerfully than criminal justice systems. Thus, "[t]he subjective assent of the criminal which grounds and valorizes the sanction will not be accorded under such conditions" (Fanon, 2018, p. 412).

The offender's acceptance of his condemnation presupposes the coherent ensemble of collective consciousness of a specific ethical universe; that is, for an offender to recognize his act as criminal before a judge is to disapprove of the act and to negate his rupture of the public sphere by his private conduct. The North African refuses this ethical lobotomy by denial and retraction of his confession. The Manichean separation of two coexisting groups appears because the integration of one group by the other has not happened. The North African offender's refusal to confess to his crime negates the social contract's authenticity despite his apparent submission before the legal authority of the court. What Fanon finds inapparent is that the appearance of the colonized before colonial state power signifies acceptance of the social contract of colonialism.

Institutional Assessment of Colonial Mental Healthcare Is Political

Fanon's third clinical paper in the series is an assessment of hospital care (Fanon, Dequeker, Lacaton, Micucci, & Ramée, 1955). In this collaborative paper, Fanon strategically organized a team of psychiatric interns and physicians to author an assessment of Blida, albeit within the larger context of assessing the psychiatric services of French colonial mental health facilities. Fanon's selection of his assessment co-authors was purposeful, i.e., *political*. Fanon and his colleagues identified the challenges arising from colonial disinvestment, patient overcrowding, and the proliferation of mental health disparities produced by the dissonance between Western administrative practices and the cultural *habitus* of Muslim communities. The problems of mental health hospitalization, as in each of Fanon's clinical papers, were strategically seized as opportunities to initiate a program of institutional reforms and changes in therapeutic applications that have today become commonplace practices, but were often pioneered in the colonial periphery of Western medicine by innovative clinicians like Frantz Fanon and his team of psychiatric professionals (Keller, 2007a, 2007b).

Fanon was not the only black reformer of colonial mental healthcare delivery in Africa. Thomas Adeoye Lambo, a Nigerian psychiatrist, in 1954, after studying and working as a surgeon in Britain, returned to Nigeria where he was put in charge of the newly built Aro psychiatric hospital in Abeokuta, Ogun State. The outpatient treatment services Lambo initiated blended modern psychotherapy with traditional religion and indigenous medicine. He also secured the support of local farmers in employing some patients as laborers while undergoing treatment; their wages going toward payment of their mental health services. Like Fanon, Lambo sought the re-adaptation of patients into the cultural milieu of their community as part of their treatment (Heaton, 2013). Innovations were also pioneered by European colonial physicians, sometime from a humane perspective but often as agents of an imperialist "civilizing mission."

Demographic and Administrative Problems of Colonial Psychiatric Care

Colonies presented unique problems for psychiatric care from the point of view of the impact of state policies on hospital administration. The authors provided a brief chronology of relevant decrees passed to address the problems of colonial psychiatry and hospital administration, and they evaluated the persistent neglect in implementing reforms. A 1934 decree regulated the operations of psychiatric facilities in Algeria, creating a two-tier system of first- and second-line hospitals for acute care and non-acute care, respectively. Overcrowding was the first problem addressed in the assessment:

> Algeria had 10 million inhabitants in 1954, 8.5 million Muslims and 1.5 million Europeans.
> There were only 8 psychiatrists for a population of 10 million and only a little over 2500 beds in psychiatric facilities.
> There was only 1 bed for every 4000 inhabitants.
> Blida Hospital as a second-line facility was designed for 1200 patients but was severely overcrowded.

Problems of Hospital Admissions

The obligation to admit psychiatric patients in French hospitals did not apply in Algeria; instead, patients were admitted based on vacancies arising from discharges or deaths. The admissions problems because of overcrowding, which delayed patient admissions from a few months to a year, had the frequent result that "by the time a vacancy opens up, the patient is already cured" (Fanon, 2018, p. 398). Prolonged delays in admitting patients led to a range of negative unintended consequences, including:

- Patient aggression once hospitalized.
- Family abuse of patients because family members could no longer handle care.
- Family frustration and hospital malfeasance led to scandals of patient abandonment.
- Imprisoned patients had their prison release delayed on "medical grounds" as they awaited hospitalization.

Although there were two modes of hospital placement, PO (ordered placement) and PV (voluntary placement), the overwhelming number of placements were PO, mostly supported by the state. Hospital costs were fundamental to the problems of admissions. Indigent care costs determined the mode of placement, from PO to PVG (free voluntary placement), because of domestic monetary issues. Admissions problems also involved the missing identities of patients, especially for patients from rural areas or neighboring countries.

Hospitalization

Acute overcrowding at Blida led to repurposing of hospital wards and facilities like cafeterias and washrooms. Appeals to the colonial administration to construct and extend hospital facilities went unanswered. Hospital facilities were also multi-purposed. For example, the chapel doubled as an ergotherapy shop, a nursing classroom as a movie theater, the hospital mosque as a weaving workshop. Where there were no lounges or common areas for patients, they were deposited in the courtyard. The full complement of hospital staff (kitchen, electrical, linen, painting, carpentry, masonry, laundry, plumbing, and office) allowed the hospital to function without outside assistance. Blida Hospital's self-reliance was important for the sociotherapy Fanon sought to implement in constructing a clinical "neo-society." The assessment by Fanon and his team found: (a) Economic services needed improvement; (b) administrative services needed to be augmented; (c) general services needed improvement; and (d) medical services were "quite satisfactory." The neo-society of the clinic was formed by resolving these problems.

Total medical staff at Blida Psychiatric Hospital was approximately 820, which amounted to 1 staff person for every 15 patients in calmer wards; 1 staff person for every 10 patients in wards with agitated patients. In 1954, a nursing school was established at Blida, with 120 staff members enrolled in 1955 and preparing to take qualifying exams. Literacy problems among staff members were compensated by goodwill in responding to appeals for extra effort. Despite lack of literacy proficiency, these staff were "an essential resource to the wards on which they serve" (Fanon, 2018, p. 400), no doubt because of the cultural proficiency they brought to the care of Muslim patients. Nevertheless, a minimum requirement of a certificate of study or equivalent examination was required for staff.

The certification required at Blida for various categories of medical staff forms part of the criteria required to make the case for Fanonian psychological pedagogy and curriculum development today, especially for psychiatric nursing. What would a Fanonian certification exam look like? Local or indigenous mental health workers provided psychocultural proficiency when supported by professional staff by bringing their goodwill and enthusiasm for care to the "lived conditions of [the] patients" (Fanon, 2018, p. 400), thus making up with the cultural competency of their care what they lacked "from an intellectual point of view" (Fanon, 2018, p. 400).

The work of general services staff in building and arranging social events in the hospital was augmented by patients. Similarly, the contributions of economic and administrative services in funding social events supported collaboration between staff, patients, and local communities, e.g., opening a Moorish coffeehouse in the hospital. This collaboration between local and professional levels "rapidly improved the lived conditions of . . . patients" (Fanon, 2018, p. 400). Collaboration between local communities and professional hospital staff led to other collaborations.

Discharge

Problems of patient release were particularly concerning for Muslim patients because of their geographic distance from the hospital, which delayed release and added to overpopulation of the facility. Transfer of patients from first-line acute care facilities to second-line non-acute care hospitals like Blida, which were expected to serve as hospice care for the incurable, added to overcrowding. The following spectrum of cultural safety problems associated with caring for a Muslim population of the mentally ill was identified by the team's institutional assessment:

- Because of cultural constraints, Muslim patients also suffered delays in being admitted, allowing their conditions to advance to a dangerous state.
- Muslim men restricted the admittance of Muslim women for hospital care.
- Muslim law allowed for instantaneous divorce on the part of the husband, which meant that the discharge of women patients was often delayed, problematizing reintegration into their communities and families (presenting difficulties for hospital social services).
- Release into a Muslim environment for unmarried or divorced women was impossible and release into European sectors posed formidable problems.
(Fanon, 2018, p. 402)

- Contacting families far removed from the clinic was difficult when processing the release of patients, requiring the cultural competence of local Muslim intermediaries on staff.
- Release of the aged, the disabled, and epileptics from hospitalization was problematic given the sacred view that indigenous Algerians have of madness.
- For Muslims, release was precarious without an after-care infrastructure to track, follow-up, and help reintegrate patients into their communities ("social re-adaptation").
- Problems associated with the release of patients from distant provinces were particularly difficult because they had no way to return to the hospital to attend to problems associated with their release or with a relapse in their condition.

Fanon's assessment team recommended a number of policies and provisions to address release problems, including: (a) providing dispensaries for preventative and post-hospitalization psychiatric care; (b) creating a social service annex in the hospital; and (c) forming a benevolent society to aid discharged and relapsed patients.

Psychiatric Annexes (Fanon Centers)

Annex care represents one kind of solution to patient overcrowding. Annex care is the post-hospitalization extension of Fanon's sociotherapy and, as such, is part of his construction of the mental health infrastructure needed to accomplish the objective of "social re-adaptation." Psychiatric annex infrastructure met the demand for mental health services and the challenges of overcrowding at the primary hospital facility at Blida. The clinical directors at Blida were tasked with making monthly visits to the psychiatric annexes where they were "required to take total responsibility for the operation of the annexes" (Fanon, 2018, p. 403). During the rest of year, the annexes were directed by former section chiefs from Blida who employed local personnel whose cultural competency made up for their lack of psychiatric training. The description of clinical directors at Blida having to make monthly visits to the annexes was similar to the post-independence prescription Fanon issued in *The Wretched of the Earth*, namely that political leaders should be required to make monthly visits to rural outposts of the national revolution, as well as his description of the use of local personnel recruited from the indigenous population by annex directors. Later, Fanon recreated and extended the Blida annex model in Tunisia.

Conclusion: The Fanonian Clinic

Finally, Fanon's report was a policy rationale for construction of psychiatric hospitals in two other Algerian departments, Oran and Constantine, to relieve congestion at Blida. The assessment was another one of Fanon's strategic interventions into French colonial healthcare policy. The assessment of clinical problems also served the strategic purpose of providing an after-care and social re-adaptation framework for Fanon's sociotherapeutic practices and applications, which he developed across three clinical care platforms: (1) psychiatric (general) hospital care, (2) psychiatric annex after-care, and (3) day-hospitalization in Tunis.

Thematic Apperception Test (TAT): Sociology of Perception and Imagination

Fanon's fourth clinical paper, co-authored with Charles Geronimi, came at the end of Fanon's tenure at BPH, in 1956, when he submitted his famous "Letter of Resignation" (Fanon & Geronimi, 1956). It is essential to recognize that Fanon's letter of resignation was situated at the end of the series of Blida clinical papers, which formed the backdrop for his exit document and summary evaluation of French psychiatric services in the political environment of the French–Algerian revolutionary war. The paper deals with the lesser known cousin of the Rorschach test, the TAT, a projective test designed to elicit the underlying motives of respondents' reactions to ambiguous pictures of people's conduct and behavior in order to analyze respondents' social construction of the world through imaginary narration based on their perception of the situation projected on the TAT cards. Once again, Fanon's assessment functioned as a critique of the application and analytical instruments of Western social science in the colonial milieu and as an opportunity to pursue an ethnopsychological analysis of Muslim women.

As in the Confessions paper, an existentialist subtext runs through the TAT paper that is indebted to two of Fanon's intellectual influences, Maurice Merleau-Ponty's *Phenomenology of Perception* (1945) and Jean-Paul Sartre's *Psychology of Imagination* (1940). There are two other potential lines of inquiry that space does not allow us to trace. First, the TAT paper exemplifies the interdisciplinary vision of psychiatric psychoanalysis of Tosquelles' mentor, Emilio Mira y Lopez, a founder of Spanish psychoanalysis. Second, the sociological scope of the paper puts in question Fanon's difference with Bourdieu's sociology of North African society.

Fanon's finding from the failed TAT experiment that Muslim women adhered to the Islamic temporal proscription against foreseeing the future that only Allah knows may have originated in his reading of André Ombrédane's (1954) *L'exploration de la mentalité des Noirs congolais au moyen d'une épreuve projective: le Congo T.A.T.* Fanon's unmodified and Ombrédane's modified TAT test revealed a temporal dissonance among respondents. Importantly, Fanon reported that he and his colleagues were "developing a projection [test] intended for Maghribi Muslims (after cultural research is conducted)" (Fanon, 2018, p. 432). Although there is no extant record of Fanon's modified TAT, the efficacy of TAT for psychological analysis of the personalities of subjects led psychometric testers like Charles E. Thompson to modify TAT for African American respondents in 1948–49. Such modified personality testing is suggestive of the famous dolls study of Kenneth and Mamie Clark in the same period. A reviewer of the 1969 reprint of André Ombrédane's (1954) Congo TAT study lists more examples of modifications of TAT for non-white cohorts:

> adaptations of TAT to Hopi and Navaho children [Henry, 1947], to American blacks [Thompson, 1949], to the Zulu [Lee, 1953], to populations of Micronesia [Lessa & Spiegelman, 1954], to the Zwazi [Sherwood, 1957], the Congo TAT appears to be a useful instrument for ethnologists and psychologists who wish to understand the Congolese mentality and its actual modes of acculturation.
>
> [Laroche, 1971]

Madness and Colonialism

The fifth clinical paper, which Fanon coauthored with François Sanchez, "The Maghribi Muslim Attitude towards Madness," is foundational for Fanonian ethnopsychiatry, inasmuch as discernment of the ethical-cultural attitudes toward madness is concomitant of culturally competent mental health interventions (Fanon & Sanchez, 1956). Contrasting Western and Maghribi attitudes towards madness, Fanon and Sanchez not only unpacked the cosmological framework of Muslim cultural views but the logical inconsistency of Western medical ethics when confronting mental illness. There could not be a greater ethical-cultural dissonance between the two attitudes toward madness, which was once again taken as an opportunity to advocate for psychiatric retraining in cultural competency. Fanon returned to the question of the Maghrebi attitude to madness in his 1959–60 lectures at the University of Tunis. Gibson and Beneduce (2017) provide background context for the Fanon–Sanchez paper and the unpublished companion paper, "The Introduction to Sexual Disorders among North Africans".

The Tunis Papers (1957–60): Toward the Fanonian Clinic

Pathology of the Asylum

Western psychiatric hospitalization, which Fanon often referred to as "internment," came in for criticism in the sixth clinical paper in the series he coauthored with Slimane Asselah (Fanon & Asselah, 1957). They wrote the paper in Tunisia, where Fanon escaped into exile from French colonial authorities and paramilitary forces in Algeria. The phenomenon of patient agitation encountered in hospital settings, especially at Manouba Razi Hospital, Fanon's first residency in Tunisia on the outskirts of Tunis, was shown to have originated in hospitalization. His advocacy of the "open clinic" model, although not unique, was a logical and organic outcome of his analysis of the institutional provocation of neurological agitation in patients subjected to the practices of the asylum. Agitation reflected the internment structures of the asylum that alienated the agency and freedom of the individual from their lived experience of the external world. "Agitation may, thus, be seen as the gangrene of the asylum" (Fanon, 2018, p. 444). The open clinic Fanon prescribed was an "open institution" transformed through the "rigorous competency [of] flexible staff," which, in turn, evinced the "withering away of the organo-clinic" and promoted creation of the "hospital-village" (Fanon, 2018, p. 446). The theoretical conclusions of the Agitation paper were preparatory to the two-part analysis Fanon initially single-authored (Fanon, 1959), then coauthored with Geronimi (Fanon & Geronimi, 1959), on the value and limits of day-hospitalization as a socio-psychotherapeutic approach to the mental health challenges of poor, underserved, non-Western communities (the seventh and eighth papers).

Day Hospitalization

The two-part treatment of the Tunis Center for Day-Neuropsychiatry attached to the Charles-Nicolle Hospital (Day-Hospitalization in Psychiatry: Its Value and Limits. II. Doctrinal Considerations) is a detailed account of a specific set of therapeutic practices that were originally developed in England and, until Fanon's retooling of them for application in Tunis, only instituted in developed Western countries. Whether or not Fanon was aware of Thomas Lambo's innovations along similar lines in Nigeria, they both shared the same critical attitude toward the Anglo-South African psychologist J.C. Carothers, "an expert from the World Health Organization [who] put forward the idea that the normal African is a 'lobotomized European,'" in his *Normal and Pathological Psychology of the African: Ethno-psychiatric Studies* published by the World Health Organization in 1954 (quoted in Fanon,1966, pp. 244–245). According to Khalfa, Fanon rehearses his assessment of Carothers and his ideological relation to the Algiers School of ethnopsychiatry in a journal edited by Andre Mandouze, *Consciences Maghribines*, in the summer of 1955 (Fanon, 2018, pp. 405–412).

Day-hospitalization was the fourth in the typology of psychotherapeutic institutional approaches Fanon practiced in the North African milieu, viz., (a) the application of sociotherapy with Maghribi cultural proficiencies at BPH, (b) setting up psychiatric auxiliaries and annexes in outlying regions distant from the general hospital for underserved communities in Algeria's Oran and Constantine provinces, (c) the open clinic model he practiced at Manouba and Charles-Nicolle (including night therapy), and (d) neuropsychiatric day-hospitalization at Charles-Nicolle Hospital, in Tunis. The day-hospitalization project represented Fanon's most far-reaching application of existential psychology to psychotherapy by transgressing the boundaries between the clinic and the external world of the communities from which patients derived their meaning and lived their mental illness and healthcare within the authenticity of their cultural existence. It is in this final instance of Fanon's application of his unique therapeutic approach to mental health that he reached the dialectical turning point whence psychiatry becomes political, giving us a glimpse of the contours of the liberated reality of once colonized (occupied) peoples and nations. Fanon's Tunisian period represented his immersion in the postcolony, just as the Algerian period represented his immersion in and emersion from the colony as Algeria underwent decolonization. Algiers (Blida-Joinville) and Tunis constituted two fields of study for Fanon's psychotherapeutic practice and institutional reforms, fields that were as congruent as they were divergent.

The Encounter of Society and Psychiatry: Fanonian Social Psychology

This penultimate step in the development of a psychotherapy that transgressed the boundaries between the world and the asylum, between individual and society, between the mental health practitioner and the administrative apparatus of the mental health system, is a fitting segue to his final (ninth) paper, a set of lecture notes for a series of lectures Fanon gave at the University of Tunis, 1959–60, entitled "The Encounter of Society and Psychiatry" (Fanon,

1959–60). In these lecture notes, as in his other papers, Fanon's background in sociology contributed to his approach to psychotherapy.

As we saw in Fanon's third clinical paper, the multi-authored assessment of psychiatric hospitalization in Algeria, Fanonian social psychology is situated within our own contemporary concerns about mental health delivery systems for underserved communities. The report discloses how a Fanonian assessment of mental health administration exposes lacunae in the mental health-care infrastructure that his sociotherapeutic practice was uniquely qualified to address. Despite its administrative orientation, the assessment's identification of problems associated with the cultural dissonance between Western institutional structures and the *habitus* of non-Western colonial populations made Fanon's cultural competency/politicopsychiatric approach an effective means of addressing them. Problems of post-hospitalization "social re-adaptation" posed a range of challenges for psychiatric aftercare that Fanon's team assessed and for which they prescribed reforms that included auxiliary annexes in remote areas. A recent iteration of distance medical care is e-diagnostics and e-delivery of medical care. Another case of distance mental health delivery is the use of community radio programming for underserved communities. Such a mental health radio project was on the air for several years in Champaign, Illinois. ACCESS Live was the community education and engagement arm of the ACCESS Initiative, produced and hosted by Imani Bazzell. ACCESS Live aimed to communicate mental health information, messages, and psychopolitical understanding of the racialized social, political, and economic structures to the African American communities of Champaign-Urbana, Illinois and was pursued from an expressly Fanonian perspective. (See Chapter 9 interview with ACCESS Live producer and host, Imani Bazzell, in this book.)

We observe repeatedly in Fanon's clinical papers issues associated with psychiatric nursing, staff training, and certification, raising questions of what a Fanonian skillset and pedagogy for these professions and occupations would look like. (See Chapter 7 by Luke Molloy in this volume.) For Fanon, this involved the role of indigenous mental healthcare workers and staff in sociotherapy. In short, the clinical papers map the contours of a Fanonian mental health infrastructure suited to the global South and underserved communities in the global North. Importantly, the clinical papers authored by Fanon and his collaborators reveal much of the terrain he would cover in his final works, *A Dying Colonialism* and *The Wretched of the Earth*. The clinical papers intimate that Fanon's psychotherapeutic approach operated as an analogy for the anti-colonial revolution and that the humanization of the clinic was his analogue for the "new reality of the nation" (Fanon, 1967) gestating in the dissolution of the old colonial regime. This seemed to be the case in the clinical papers assessing the Tunis Center for Day-Neuropsychiatry, and his 1959–60 University of Tunis lecture notes for *Rencontre de la société et de la psychiatrie* (*The Meeting of Society and Psychiatry*). Nicholas Mirzoeff's description of these lectures puts another unexplored dimension of the afterlife of Fanon's thought in question:

These lectures are known only from notes taken by Lilia Bensalem as a student, which were transcribed and published in Tunis twenty years after Fanon's death (Bensalem, 1984). One question left hanging is whether Michel Foucault was aware of Fanon's ideas. While there are no references to Fanon in the multi-volume collection *Dits et Ecrits*, Foucault taught in Tunis from 1966 to 1968, where he taught a course on "Madness and Civilization": "it's hard to believe that seven years after Fanon's lectures, someone did not make the connection. It was in Tunis that Foucault experienced a student uprising—in March 1968. Although Fanon was associated with Sartre, whom Foucault opposed, some critics have recently identified some clear affinities in their thought."

(Mirzeoff, 2011)

Fanon's Detour

The lecture notes from Fanon's University of Tunis lectures are significant for the thematic formulations that they anticipate of early discursive formations of Michel Foucault, viz., the role of surveillance, breaking of bodies, and the extension of carceral instrumentalities to embedded regimens of social control. Fanon's treatment, however, is distinguished from Foucault's (as his ethnopsychiatric approach was distinguished from Bourdieu's ethnosociology). First, Fanon did not accept the no-win scenario programmed in colonial subjugation because, as he noted, "we have watched men [and women] being created by revolutionary beginnings" (Fanon, 1966, p. 153). Second, there was nothing inescapable about the trauma of colonial subjugation in Fanon's sociodiagnostics. Because the trauma was deeply racialized, it posited a sharper, deeper dialectic of liberation. Thirdly, the themes of the lecture notes from Fanon's University of Tunis lectures are grounded on the hypothesis of his 1951 dissertation, viz., "to approach the problem of history from a psychoanalytic and ontological angle . . . , history is nothing but the systematic valorization of collective complexes" (Fanon, 2018, p. 257).

Finally, in line with this hypothesis, the 1959–60 lecture notes disclose the affective and psychopathological forms of alienation that the material, architectural, electronic, and physically coercive design of colonial subjugation instilled in and elicited from "colonial subjects"—both the colonized and the colonizers. Although the broader frame for this thematic in Fanon's thought owes its origin to his intellectual inheritance from Tosquelles's institutional psychology and the existential psychology of Merleau-Ponty and Sartre, it was his reworking and repurposing these in the colonizing/decolonizing context of North Africa that was determinative. A key text in the clinical papers was the Confessions paper where the contours of what Gibson and Beneduce call critical ethnopsychiatry of the carcerality of society emerges along lines that predate Foucault, including, as we saw previously, the disciplining power of the "dossier."

The nodal point that the 1959–60 lecture notes represents in this genealogy is Fanon's extension of this thematic to a generalized examination of modes of surveillance ubiquitous throughout modern capitalist society: repetitive motion and surveillance (supervision) of factory labor, electronic monitoring, technological automation of production processes. As Simone Browne observes in her treatment of Fanon's University of Tunis lecture notes, he not only exposed the perpetual surveillance that closed-circuit monitoring afforded capitalist supervisors, but he

> also noted that workers displayed microresistances to managerial control in the way of sick leave, expressing boredom on the job, arriving late, and sometimes not arriving at work at all. Rather than being thought of as unproductive, such acts must be understood as disalienating, as they are strategic means of contesting surveillance in the workplace.
>
> (Browne, 2015, p. 6)

Along with Fanon's Confessions paper anticipating the Foucauldian "dossier" in *Discipline and Punish* (1975), it is evident from the psychiatric evaluation of criminal justice procedures he co-authored with Lacaton that a nascent criminological theory is embedded in Fanon's thought, which gets further developed in his published works. The Confessions paper anticipates Foucault's discourse on the "subject-to-subject cycle," i.e., the process by which an individual endowed by nature with rights, capacities, and talents must *become* a subject by virtue of her agency, i.e., subjectivized *vis-a-viz* the power relations of her society. In other words, a person becomes subjectivized face-to-face with the power relations of her society; a person attains legitimacy as a subject (e.g., citizen) in accordance with the laws of that society. What makes the subject-to-subject cycle really a cycle of legitimacy is that the legitimacy of the agency of the subject has to be recognized and respected. Just as Steve Biko employed Fanon's theory of recognition and self-consciousness to frame a range of psychopolitical formations (Turner, 2008), so Helen A. Neville's research on the function of recognition and respect in the identity formation of African-descended people is indebted to this thematic in Fanon's thought.

More broadly in the context of the relationship of social movements to the individual life narratives of counseling psychology, black individuals and/or social groups subjectivized in the power relations of white-dominated society either have the legitimacy of their right to occupy a place in the power relations of their society respected or such rights are disrespected for which they behave accordingly, viz., the pattern of their behavior corresponds to the experience of their legitimacy being respected or disrespected. The behavioral responses to white disrespect of black social legitimacy run the gamut from de-legitimation of the racialized power relations, which was the strategic approach of the Civil Rights, Black Power, and Black Consciousness movements, to the behavioral strategies at the interpersonal level of individualized micro-resistance or assimilation. Fanonian psychopolitics recognizes, indeed, privileges the importance of the power relations in which processes of social recognition and respect operate in the subject-to-subject cycle.

As a therapeutic paradigm, Fanon's trauma psychology is also an area in which his therapeutic approach intersects present-day concerns about post-trauma stress disorder, whether in the case of military veterans or residents of violence-torn inner-city communities, as well as critical studies of the use of PTSD (post-traumatic stress disorder) to pathologize the vulnerable populations of conflict zones. As apparent from Vanessa Pupavac's analysis (2001), "therapeutic governance" has become a new terrain in which Fanon's approach has relevance for understanding the globalization of mental health interventions in the global South and marginalized communities in the global North. Referencing the ambivalent attitude toward Fanon in NGO (non-governmental organizations) aid circles, Pupavac levels an indictment against global health agencies and their practice of "therapy governance" in disaster and conflict zones (2001).

Fanon's clinical papers map the préterrain he traversed to his political writings, *A Dying Colonialism* and *The Wretched of the Earth*. They are scripts of his ethnopsychiatric fieldwork even as they double as his practicum of mental health researches, pedagogy, and therapy that would have otherwise attained their logical ends in academic formalism were it not for his political engagements and revolutionary commitments to the anti-colonial movement and African unity. Fanon's detour around disciplinary normativity and academic careerism was, nevertheless, by way of direct and deep theoretical engagement with the human geography of colonialism and its decolonial transformation. In this book's chapters, the writers map the human geography of *Fanon's detour*. It is, in part, a detour around the academic and professional landscape that Fanon's "critical ethnopsychiatry," as Roberto Beneduce calls it, took through revolutionary decolonization. It is a detour whereby Fanon disavowed the psychotherapeutic ends of reintegrating the colonized back into the very alienating and subjugating structures of society whence the colonized sought disoccupation (Robcis). The revolutionary ends he sought through his ethnopsychiatry were instead expressed at the end of his 1959–60 University of Tunis lectures, "The colonized who resists is right" (Fanon, 2018, p. 530).

Bibliography

Allen, M. (2011). *Frantz Fanon's clinical studies (1954–1960)*. Retrieved from http:// gateway.proquest.com/openurl?url_ver=Z39.88-2004&res_dat=xri:pqdiss&rft_val_ fmt=info:ofi/fmt:kev:mtx:dissertation&rft_dat=xri:pqdiss:3465741.

American Psychiatric Association website on current uses of ECT. Retrieved from www.psychiatry. org/patients-families/ect.

Belmont Report. (1978). *Issued by the national commission for the protection of human subjects of biomedical and behavioral research*. Retrieved from www.hhs.gov/ohrp/sites/default/files/ the-belmont-report-508c_FINAL.pdf.

Baugh, B. (2003). *French Hegel: From surrealism to postmodernism*. London: Routledge.

Benjamin, A. (1993). *The Plural Event: Descartes, Hegel, Heidegger*. London: Routledge.

Bensalem, L. (Ed.). (1984). *Etudes et recherches sur la psychologie en Algerie*. Oran, Algeria: CRIDSSH.

Bourdieu, P. (1958). *Sociologie de l'Algérie*. Paris: Presses Universitaire de France.

Browne, S. (2015). *Dark matters: On the surveillance of Blackness*. Durham, NC: Duke University Press.

Bulhan, H. (1985). *Frantz Fanon and the psychology of oppression*. New York: Plenum Press.

Burawoy, M., & Holdt, K. (2012). Colonialism and revolution. In *Conversations with Bourdieu: The Johannesburg moment* (pp. 74–102). Johannesberg: Wits University Press.

Burman, E. (2017). Fanon's other children: Psychopolitical and pedagogical implications. *Race Ethnicity and Education, 20*(1), 42–56.

Burman, E. (2018). *Fanon, education, action: Child as method*. London: Taylor & Francis.

Carothers, J. C. (1954). *Normal and pathological psychology of the African: Ethno-psychiatric studies*. Paris: Masson and World Health Organization.

Carrigan, M. (2014). *Bourdieu meets Marx, Gramsci, Fanon, Freire, Beauvoir and Mills (in Burawoy's imagination)*. Sociological Imagination. Retrieved from http://sociologicalimagination.org/archives/15311.

Centre National de Recherches Préhistoriques, Anthropologiques et Historiques. Retrieved from www.cnrpah.org/data/fonds_frantz_fanon.pdf.

Cherki, A. (2006). *Frantz Fanon: A portrait*. Ithaca: Cornell University Press.

Clifford, J. (1989). Notes on travel and theory. *Inscriptions, 5*. Retrieved from https://culturalstudies.ucsc.edu/inscriptions/volume-5/james-clifford/.

Cross, W. E., Jr. (1971). Discovering the Black referent: The psychology of Black liberation. In V. J. Dixon & B. G. Foster (Eds.), *Beyond Black or White: An alternate America*. Boston: Little, Brown and Company.

Dalzell, T. (2011/2018). *Freud's Schreber between psychiatry and psychoanalysis: On subjective disposition to psychoses*. New York: Routledge.

Damon, L. (2017). Note on translating Frantz Fanon. In N. Gibson & R. Beneduce (Eds.), *Frantz Fanon, psychiatry and politics* (pp. 263–267). Johannesburg, South Africa: Wits University Press.

Deleuze, G., & Guattari, F. (2009). *Anti-Oedipus: Capitalism and schizophrenia* (R. Hurley, M. Seem, and H. Lane, Trans.). New York: Penguin Books.

Desai, M. U. (2014). Psychology, the psychological, and critical praxis: A phenomenologist reads Frantz Fanon. *Theory & Psychology, 24*(1), 58–75.

Dunayevskaya, R. (1989). *Philosophy and revolution, from Hegel to Sartre and from Marx to Mao*. New York: Columbia University Press.

Dunayevskaya, R. (1991). *Rosa Luxemburg, women's liberation, and Marx's philosophy of revolution*. Urbana: University of Illinois Press.

Fanon, F. (1951/2018). Mental alterations, character modifications, psychic disorders and intellectual deficit in spinocerebellar heredodegeneration: A case of Friedrich's ataxia with delusions of possession. In J. Khalfa & R. Young (Eds.), *Frantz Fanon, alienation and freedom* (S. Corcoran, Trans.) (pp. 203–275). London: Bloomsbury.

Fanon, F. (1959). L'Hospitalisation de jour en psychiatrie, valeur et limites. I. Introduction Générale. [Day-hospitalization in psychiatry: Its value and limits: I. General introduction]. *La Tunisie médicale, 47*(10), 689–712.

Fanon, F. (1959–1960/1984). Rencontre de la société et de la psychiatrie (notes de course, Tunis, 1959–60). [The encounter of society and psychiatry (Lecture notes, Tunis, 1959–1960)]. In L. Bensalem (Ed.), *Etudes et Recherches sur la psychologie en Algerie*. Oran, Algeria: CRIDSSH.

Fanon, F. (1966). *The wretched of the earth* (C. Farrington, Trans). New York: Grove Press.

Fanon, F. (1967a). *Black skin, white masks* (C. Markmann, Trans.). New York: Grove Press, (fifth printing).

Fanon, F. (1967b). *A dying colonialism* (H. Chevalier, Trans.). New York: Grove Press.

Fanon, F. (1967). *Toward the African revolution* (H. Chevalier, Trans.). New York: Grove Press.

Fanon, F. (2015). *Frantz Fanon, Écrits sur l'aliénation et la liberté* (J. Khalfa & R. Young, Trans.). Paris: La Découverte.

Fanon, F. (2018). *Frantz Fanon, alienation and freedom* (J. Khalfa & R. Young, Eds., S. Corcoran, Trans.). London: Bloomsbury.

Fanon, F., & Asselah, S. (1957). Le Phénomène de l'agitation en milieu psychiatrique considerations générales – signification psychopathologique. [The phenomenon of agitation in the psychiatric milieu: General considerations-psychopathological significance]. *Maroc médicale, 36*, 21–24.

Fanon, F., & Azoulay, J. (1954). La socialthérapie dans un service d'homme musulmans: difficultés méthodologiques. [Sociotherapy on a Muslim men's ward: Methodological difficulties]. *Information psychiatrique, 30*(9), 1095–1106.

Fanon, F., Dequeker, J., Lacaton, R., Micucci, M., & Ramée, F. (1955). Aspects actuels de l'assistance mentale en Afrique du nord. [Current aspects of psychiatric care in Algeria]. *Information Psychiatrique, 31*(11), 1107–1113.

Fanon, F., & Geronimi, C. (1956). Le TAT chez le femme musulmane: sociologie de la perception et de l'imagination. [The T.A.T. amongst Muslim women: Sociology of perception and imagination]. *Comptes Rendus Congrés des medicins alienistes et neurologists de France et des pays de langue française.* Bordeaux, 364–368.

Fanon, F., & Geronimi, C. (1959). L'Hospitalisation de jour en psychiatrie, valeur et limites. II. Considerations doctrinales. [Day-hospitalization in psychiatry: Its value and limits: II. Doctrinal considerations]. *La Tunisie médicale, 47*(10), 713–732.

Fanon, F., & Lacaton, R. (1955). Conduites d'aveuxen Afrique du Nord. [The conduct of confession in North Africa]. *Comptes Rendus Congrés des medicins alienistes et neurologists de France et des pays de langue française.* Nice, 657–660.

Fanon, F., & Sanchez, F. (1956). L'attitude du musulman devant la folie. [The Maghribi Muslim attitude towards madness]. *Revue pratique de psychologie de la vie sociale et d'hygiène mentale, 1*, 24–27.

Fanon, J. (2014). *Frantz Fanon, my brother: Doctor, playwright, revolutionary* (D. Nethery, Trans.). Lanham, MD: Lexington Books.

Fanon Research & Development Center. (1976). *Fanon research & development center: An overview* [an informational brochure]. Los Angeles: Frantz Fanon Research & Development Center.

Gendzier, I. (1974). *Frantz Fanon: Critical study.* New York: Vintage Books.

Gibson, N. (2011). *Fanonian practices in South Africa: From Steve Biko to Abahlali baseMjondolo.* New York: Palgrave Macmillan.

Gibson, N. (2013). Unpacking Fanon's books and putting them back again. . . . In *The Frantz Fanon Blog.* Algiers. Retrieved from http://readingfanon.blogspot.com/2013/06/unpacking-fanons-books-and-putting-them.html.

Gibson, N., & Beneduce, R. (2017). *Frantz Fanon, psychiatry and politics.* Johannesburg, South Africa: Wits University Press.

Gordon, L., Sharpley-Whiting, T. D., & White, R. (1996). Introduction: Five stages of Fanon studies. In L. Gordon, T. Sharpley-Whiting, & R. White (Eds.), *Fanon: A critical reader* (pp. 1–10). Oxford, England: Blackwell Publishers.

Gramsci, A. (1971). *Problems of Marxism: Selections from the prison notebooks of Antonio Gramsci.* New York: International Publishers.

Heaton, M. (2013). *Black skin, white coats: Nigerian psychiatrists, decolonization, and the globalization of psychiatry.* Athens, OH: Ohio University Press.

Hegel, G. W. F. (1874). *The logic of Hegel.* Translated from the *Encyclopedia of Philosophical Sciences* (W. Wallace, Trans.). Oxford: Clarendon Press.

Hegel, G. W. F. (1969). *Science of logic* (A. V. Miller, Trans.). Atlantic Highlands, NJ: Prometheus Books.

Hegel, G. W. F. (1977). *The Phenomenology of spirit* (A. V. Miller, Trans.). Analysis of the text and foreword J.N. Finlay. Oxford: Oxford University Press.

Henry, W. E. (1947). The thematic apperception technique in the study of culture-personality relations. *Genetic Psychology Monographs, 35,* 3–315.

Horton, R. (2018). Offline: Frantz Fanon and the origins of global health. *The Lancet, 392*(10149), 720.

Keller, R. C. (2007a). *Colonial madness: Psychiatry in French North Africa.* Chicago: University of Chicago Press.

Keller, R. C. (2007b). Clinician and revolutionary: Frantz Fanon, biography, and the history of colonial medicine. *Bulletin of the History of Medicine, 81*(4), 823–841.

Khalfa, J. (2015). Fanon and psychiatry. *Nottingham French Studies, 54*(1), 52–71.

Krader, L. (1975). *Asiatic mode of production: Sources, development and critique in the writings of Karl Marx.* Assen: van Gorcum.

Laroche, J. L. (1971). Review of L' exploration de la mentalite des noirs: Le "Congo T.A.T." (Congo T.A.T.: Exploration of Congolese mentality) by A. Ombredane. Paris: Presses Universitaires de France, 1969. (In French.) *Transcultural Psychiatry, 8*(2), 171–172.

Lazreg, M. (2007). Battling for the new man: Fanon and French counter-revolutionaries. *Human Achitecture: Journal of the Sociology of Self-Knowledge, 5*(3). Retrieved from http://scholarworks.umb.edu/humanarchitecture/vol5/iss3/4.

Lee, S. G. (1953). *Manual of a thematic apperception test for African subjects: Set of 22 pictures.* Pietermaritzburg, South Africa: University of Natal Press.

Lessa, W. A., & Spiegelman, M. (1954). *Ulithian personality as seen through ethnological materials and thematic test analysis.* Los Angeles: University of California Press.

Le Sueur, J. (2005). *Pierre Bourdieu Interview in Uncivil War: Intellectuals and identity politics during the decolonization of Algeria.* Lincoln, NE: University of Nebraska Press.

Macey, D. (1972). *The ethnological notebooks of Karl Marx* (Studies of Morgan, Phear, Maine and Lubbock). (L. Krader, Trans.). Assen: Van Gorcum.

Macey, D. (2000). *Frantz Fanon: A biography.* New York: Picador.

Marx, K. (1973). *Grundrisse* (M. Nicolaus, Trans.). New York: Penguin Books.

Marx, K. (1975). Debates on the law on thefts of wood: Proceedings of the sixth province assembly: Third article. In *Marx-Engels collected works* (Vol. 1). New York: International Publishers.

McCulloch, J. (1983). *Black soul, white artifact: Fanon's clinical psychology and social theory.* Cambridge: Cambridge University Press.

Merleau-Ponty, M. (1945/2014). *Phenomenology of perception* (D. Landes, Trans.). New York: Routledge.

Meyers, T. (2014). Jean Oury and Clinique de La Borde: A conversation with Camille Robcis. *Somatosphere, Science, Medicine, and Anthropology.* Retrieved from http://somatosphere.net/2014/06/jean-oury-and-clinique-de-la-borde-a-conversation-with-camille-robcis.html.

Mirzeoff, N. (2011). *"We are all children of Algeria," Visuality and counter-visuality, 1954–2011* (Vol. 3). Frantz Fanon. Retrieved from http://scalar.usc.edu/nehvectors/mirzoeff/jai-huit-ans-analysis.

Mokhtefi, E. (2018). *Algiers, Third World capital: Freedom fighters, revolutionaries, Black Panthers.* London: Verso.

Mudimbe, V. Y. & Bohm, A. (1994). Hegel's reception in France. *Journal of French and Francophone Philosophy*, 6(3), 5–33. Retrieved from http://www.jffp.org/ojs/index.php/jffp/article/view/86.

Neville, H. A., Viard, B., & Turner, L. (2014). Race and recognition: Pathways to an affirmative black identity. *Journal of Black Psychology*, *41*(3), 247–271.

Ombrédane. A. (1954/1969). *L'exploration de la mentalité des Noirs congolais au moyen d'une épreuve projective: le Congo T.A.T.* Paris: Presses Universitaires de France.

Pels, P. & Salemink, O. (2000). *Colonial subjects: Essays on the practical history of anthropology.* Ann Arbor: University of Michigan Press.

Pirelli, G. (1962). *Racconti di bambini d'Algeria: testimonianze e disegni di bambini profughi in Tunisia, Libia e Marocco* [Stories of children in Algeria: Testimonials of refugee children in Tunisia, Libia and Morocco]. Turin: Einaudi.

Pirelli, G., & Aruffo, A. (1994). *Fanon o l'eversione anticoloniale.* Rome: Massari.

Pupavac, V. (2001). Therapeutic governance: The politics of psychosocial intervention and trauma risk management. *Disasters*, *25*(4), 358–372.

Quercy, P. (1930). *L'Hallucination* (Vol. 1). Les Philosophes: Théorie de la perception, de l'image et de l'hallucination chez Spinoza, Leibniz, Bergson. Les Mystiques: Sainte Thérèse, ses misères, sa perception de Dieu, ses visions. Paris: F. Alcan.

Robcis, C. (2016). François Tosquelles and the psychiatric revolution in postwar France. *Constellations*, *23*, 212–222. https://doi.org/10.1111/1467-8675.12223.

Sabbatini, R. (2019). *The history of shock therapy in psychiatry.* Retrieved from www.cerebromente.org.br/n04/historia/shock_i.htm.

Sartre, J. P. (1940/2001). *Psychology of imagination.* London: Routledge.

Sartre, J. P. (1960/1991). Racism and colonialism as praxis and process. In *Critique of dialectical reason, volume 1: Theory of practical ensembles* (A. Sheridan, Trans.). London: Verso.

Sherwood, E. T. (1957). On the designing of T.A.T. pictures, with special reference to a set for an African people assimilating Western culture. *Journal of Social Psychology*, *45*, 161–190.

Sobott, G. (2016). *Dignity is essential: It means we are viewed by the other as a human being: An interview with Alice Cherki.* Retrieved from https://gaelesobott.wordpress.com/2016/11/23/dignity-is-essential-dignity-means-we-are-viewed-by-the-other-as-a-human-being-an-interview-with-alice-cherki/.

Srivastava, N. (2015). Frantz Fanon in Italy. *Interventions*, *17*(3), 309–328.

Srivastava, N. (2018). The Italian Fanon: Unearthing a hidden editorial history. In F. Fanon, J. Khalfa, & R. Young (Eds.), *Alienation and freedom* (S. Corcoran, Trans.). London: Bloomsbury.

Thompson, C. E. (1949). *Thompson modification of the thematic apperception test: Set of 18 cards and manual.* Cambridge, MA: Harvard University Press.

Tosquelles, F. (2017). Frantz Fanon in Saint-Alban, a rough translation of a 1975 interview with François Tosquelles that appeared. *Theory and Critique of Psychology*, *9*, 223–229. Retrieved from www.teocripsi.com/ojs.

Turner, L. (1996). On the difference between the Hegelian and Fanonian dialectic of lordship and bondage. In L. Gordon, T. D. Sharpley-Whiting, & R. White (Eds.), *Fanon: A critical reader.* Oxford, England: Blackwell Publishers.

Turner, L. (1999). Fanon and the FLN: Dialectics of organization and the Algerian revolution. In N. Gibson (Ed.), *Rethinking Fanon: The continuing dialogue.* Amherst, NY: Humanities Books.

Turner, L. (2002). Demythologizing the authoritarian personality: Reconnoitering Adorno's retreat from Marx. In N. Gibson & A. Rubin (Eds.), *Adorno: A critical reader.* Malden, MA: Blackwell.

Turner, L. (2003). Fanon reading (W)right, the (W)right reading of Fanon: Race, modernity, and the fate of humanism. In R. Bernasconi (Ed.), *Race and racism in continental philosophy*. Bloomington, IN: Indiana University Press.

Turner, L. (2008). Self-consciousness as force and reason of revolution in the thought of Steve Biko. In A. Mgnxitama, A. Alexander, & N. Gibson (Eds.), *Biko lives! Contesting the legacies of Steve Biko*. New York: Palgrave Macmillan.

Turner, L. (2011a). Fanon and the biopolitics of torture: Contextualizing psychological practices as tools of war. In N. Gibson (Ed.), *Living Fanon: Global perspectives*. New York: Palgrave Macmillan.

Turner, L. (2011b). *Rage and reason: Specters of Fanon in African American radicalism*. Paper presented at the National Council of Black Studies' Annual Conference, Cincinnati, OH, March 19.

Turner, L. (2018). *Fanon in question: Destructuring the possibility of race*. Paper presented at two-day symposium at Penn State University's Rock Ethics Institute, University Park, Pennsylvania, January 12–14.

Turner, L., & Alan, J. (1978/1986). *Frantz Fanon, Soweto and American Black thought*. Detroit: News & Letters.

Wikipedia. (2019). Nigel Gibson. *Wikipedia*. Retrieved from https://en.wikipedia.org/wiki/Nigel_Gibson.

3 History of the Fanon Research and Development Center in Los Angeles

A Narrative of Dr. Lewis M. King

Lewis M. King, Lou Turner, and Helen A. Neville

The chapters in the first section of Frantz Fanon's Psychotherapeutic Approaches to Clinical Work: Practicing Internationally with Marginalized Communities set Fanonian psychotherapy within multiple sociohistorical settings. Its origin in the French psychiatric movement centered in the radical environment of Saint-Alban Hospital at Loz'ere, a small town in central France, and traveled with Fanon's transfer of sociotherapy to the North African milieu undergoing revolutionary decolonization. As a traveling theory, Fanonian psychotherapy made multiple transnational voyages, the most consequential one being to the radical African American context of the Black Power Movement of the early 1970s with the creation of the first Fanon Center, in South Los Angeles. As an outgrowth of the National Institute of Mental Health and its Center for the Study of Minority Group Mental Health Programs, established in 1970, the Fanon Center was affiliated with the Department of Psychiatry of the Charles R. Drew Postgraduate Medical School affiliated with the Martin Luther King, Jr. General Hospital, in Compton, California, beginning in September 1974.[1]

When we (Lou Turner and Helen A. Neville) sat down to discuss the Fanon Center with its founding Director, Dr. Lewis M. King, in a series of interviews in September and October 2018, our first task was to situate the significance of the Fanon Center in the context of the research that Dr. King and his colleagues were pursuing in the years following the 1965 Watts Rebellion, in South Los Angeles. As one of the co-founders of the Fanon Center for Research and Development, the first set of questions we posed to Dr. Lewis M. King was:

> *What was the impetus for the Fanon Center?*
> *Why establish the Center at Martin Luther King General Hospital—Drew Post Graduate Medical School?*
> *In what way did you and your collaborators see Frantz Fanon's theory and practice contributing to the psychotherapeutic research and practices needed to meet the mental health needs of African American communities, especially in Los Angeles?*

This chapter consists of excerpts from the over 3-hour conversation, e-mail exchanges between Dr. King and us, and substantive rewrites from Dr. King.

After the interview was transcribed and edited, Dr. King provided additional detailed information, points of clarification, and new information to describe the development and operations of the Center. We organized the chapter to outline Dr. King's formation as a Fanonian scholar before his discussion of the history of the Fanon Center and the detailed outline of the three stages of its development. Information about the Fanon Center Restoration Model is included as well as the identification of various scholars in residence at the Center. The chapter concludes with an analysis of the successes, lessons learned, and new iterations of the Center.

Preamble: A Revolutionary Scholar-Activist in the Making

The Fanon Research and Development Center grew out of world history and more particularly Black world history. It would be a tragic mistake not to accurately report this as we undertake an understanding the social-psychological reality of the Fanon Center, 'West'—an extension of the original creation. The center on the west coast, in the name of Fanon, emerged from a highly action-oriented period of growth in Black life in the US—1963–1974. Imperial violence in the European colonies unleashed a dynamic of violent and racist extremism which directly contributed to the catastrophes of World Wars I and II and created millions of victims. These victims were finally ready to respond.

The actual use of the name Fanon began on the grounds of the Howard University campus, in 1965, at the height of the Civil Rights Movement. The Watts Rebellion of 1965 was not lost on the group. We named our study group—Fanon Student Group. Ours was an effort of five young Caribbean scholars attending Howard University to forge some solidarity with the student activism at that time. It was 1965–66 and the Caribbean student group, which I formed, began a study of Fanon's 1961 book—*The Wretched of the Earth*. In the Spring of 1965 we were in almost daily discourse on campus concerning both colonialism and 'Black Power' with students like Stokely Carmichael (from Trinidad and in my class) and professors like Nathan Hare, Sociology Professor—just to name two, as we anticipated our eventual return to our colonized island homes that were emerging from colonialism into independence. We sought to embrace a Pan-African perspective in our efforts to participate. We were quite fortunate to have world leaders as they visited Washington, DC, interacting with us—in particular, Eric Williams, Kwame Nkrumah—key figures out of the Pan-African freedom movement as well as other key liberation activists such as James Baldwin and the great Dr. M.L. King to name a few. This first Fanon group was focused on reading the text and trying to fully understand the actions we would undertake to 'speed-up' the emancipation efforts 'when we returned home'. This was the embarrassing truth . . . but we were soon to learn.

In 1967, I was awarded a scholarship to UCLA [University of California Los Angeles]—maybe not the first Black student in Psychology but certainly the first to graduate with a PhD, in 1971. While at UCLA, in 1969 I recreated a study group in L.A., working with two community-based Black psychiatrists and one student psychologist, but now focused on building a critical mass of progressive faculty and young scholars to impact UCLA and to serve the emerging Community Mental Health Centers. The group of four scholars became incorporated under the name *Progressive Psych Associates.* Our focus was on UCLA's Black faculty recruitment (UCLA had none), student recruitment (UCLA had only one), corrections to scientific literature on the Black child (UCLA had no courses at any level), program development and proposal writing support for Central City Community Mental Health Center. What we accomplished in two years was major—UCLA provided funding for four new Black faculty in Psychology, five new Black graduate students, and one new course on the Black Child.

In 1971, the Psychology Department created a Community Psychology Subdivision and asked me to head up this Division on a faculty appointment. We were also instrumental in developing all of the programs and grant awards for Central City CMH to include $3millon annually for Children MH services (known as Part-F); $1.8 million over 3 years for the Bricks–Kick Program for Drug Abuse intervention which used the Synanon model; $800,000 for a pre-adolescent reading program. As a young scholar, the building of this new, decolonized reality in real-life working relationships with other human beings meant that I took charge, began to write and critically think as we built capacity. Our group worked anywhere we were needed in the Black community. We became consultants in helping to develop programs, solve problems and write grants for organizations to acquire funding. In the course of doing this we built credibility in the community, we built influence, and we began to talk about issues central to emancipation and freedom.

These early efforts are being detailed to address the organic emergence of what was to become the Fanon R&D [research and development] Center in 1974. For me personally, in joining with African American colleagues, there was the recognition that I was already home and it was colonized. I did not have to wait 'to get home'. Second, that I had to be clear that I could not 'copy' a revolution—like a tourist appropriation—and take it back anywhere. I had to fully participate and build a revolution but now one consistent with Fanon's admonition—not to recolonize the masses (neo-colonization) but with the urgency and 'the necessity for each generation to discover its mission and to fight for it'. I thought long and hard about what this meant.

By December 1971, I was in this very unique place, the first Black psychologist with a PhD from UCLA and wanting to extend the work on the way, but now anchored in the community. I accepted an invitation from a Black psychiatrist—Dr. Alfred Cannon at the time Professor of Psychiatry at UCLA. I attended his 1-year seminar on the Tavistock[2] method. Dr. Cannon was a man with a vision and a mission of building a world-class teaching medical center in the heart of Watts, one of the outcomes demanded by the community out of the Watts Rebellion of 1965. An immediate response in 1966, out of the rebellion that must be noted was the chartering of a new Medical School—named after Dr. Charles Drew—The Charles Drew Postgraduate Medical School. This school later in 1972 became affiliated with the new hospital and

jointly became the King/Drew Medical Center. In 1972 Dr. Cannon became
the first Chairman/Professor of Psychiatry at the Postgraduate Medical School
and Chief of Psychiatry of the hospital. Services to the public commenced
in March 1972. I accepted the invitation from Dr. Cannon to serve as faculty
and Chief Psychologist (the first) for the new teaching hospital. It was I who
formally introduced the Fanon Center into the life of the King/Drew Medical
Center, in October 1974, and I need to explain how this evolved.

Stage 1: History of the Fanon Center in South Los Angeles

Dr. Al Cannon had become a close friend and mentor over the two years
(1971–73) of interactions and working. He was the founder of the Central
City Community MH Center where I did my community work and knew
of my contribution. The King/Drew Medical Center was in many ways a
cultural restoration vision of Dr. Cannon (a man more closely aligned with
Marcus Garvey). His great vision and firm support (as well as, leverage in a
medical setting) led me to significant discussions concerning Africa, the Caribbean and eventually to Frantz Fanon. I, with great respect and deep sensitiv-
ity in support of a realistic need to build a reality, told him that the critical
support of scholars to engage community in the work he envisioned for the
Watts community was not there; that we needed a 'Black scholars context' as
a buffer for the development of new paradigms and actions to allow a community which had just rebelled against oppression to move forward. He was
quite receptive and fully prepared for such a critique. He immediately recommended and provided funding for me to visit the National Institute of Mental
Health in Washington, DC to seek funding for the very idea that the Black
Psychiatrists of America (led by Dr. Chester Pierce) had argued with NIMH
was necessary to support.

My visit was timely. NIMH had just developed a new initiative to fund five
ethnic R&D centers to focus on mental health of the various ethnic communities (2 African American Centers, 2 Hispanic Centers and 1 American Indian).
Suffice it to say that my visit was successful and in six months we had the funding to initiate action on a Research and Development Center. I asked Dr. Cannon to allow the name Fanon to be attached to the new center. I resigned as
Chief Psychologist of the hospital and set out to forge a new set of relationships
to build the first Research and Development Center in the Black Community,
at a major Black university.

At the very outset in discussions primarily with Dr. Cannon, we set out that
the major focus of this new R&D center on '*person in socio-cultural context*'—
facing four prime life battles—*racism, colonialism, meaninglessness and struggle for
emancipation*. Dr. Cannon lamented the absence of 'belonging' and at one
point suggested, as Garvey, that we all migrate to Africa, which he eventually did three years later. We were both very clear that we certainly did not
want this catalytic funding from government to promote deviant constructions

concerning our community or preserve colonial narratives of addictions and poor mental health thus providing yet another level of accounts undermining our community.

The funding from NIMH was quite limited and restrictive in its demands. The strategic model imposed by the funding was copied straight out of the previously successful models on the materials development side of R&D. So, here was I faced with a dilemma. I'm a new kid on the block, taking leadership in creating a center whose operational structure was predefined by NIMH which also placed a demand that we undertake studies of 'Mental Illness in the Black community', find scientifically defined solutions and disseminate the results nationally. We had to push back given the false presumptions of the compelling challenge facing us—building a culturally viable and grounded vehicle as an instrument of the community to drive mental health preservation and promotion.

It's important for all to understand at this point what I am trying to convey. NIMH's R&D model grew out of the military, and the military struck upon a model growing out of World War II, when they had to quickly respond to Japan's attack on Pearl Harbor. They said, "How do we respond?" So, the military set up an operation in Albuquerque, New Mexico; in the hills, using a strategy of research and frequent verification through testing, the military built an atomic bomb. The R&D effort led to a specific outcome; they rushed it into production. The process was called 'research'; you engage in the product research, and then you develop it. So, R&D became a model, on the side, obviously, of a material world, and particularly effective in developing tangible products. That has always been the downfall of psychology, and all social sciences in America, and around the world. the attempt to mimic physics; in the misdirected emphasis on products we destroy what a person like Fanon was addressing—human consciousness and behavior—because fundamentally, you leave out two major issues. You leave out the human being, as a human being with *consciousness*, and you leave out the human being as having a *spirit essence*. If we ever forget those two, we are departing from anything Fanon tried to represent or that we were trying to address when addressing the needs of the historically oppressed.

TURNER: "You have something called the Fanon Center Restoration Model. Could you explain what that is? Was that specific to the Center? What was its impetus?"

That's an excellent question. This leads me to talk about the first major human development challenge of the Center—reinstating the person at the center of the discourse and why this became the first order of action.

We were trying to work with an 'imposed' funding structure, R&D; trying to remove ourselves from an entrapment; trying to figure out how to utilize the funding to move forward and humanize our efforts in communities that were suspicious of any further researching on or of them. The core funding provided only for the director's salary and another three staff members and space;

we had no money for doing research. The assumption was that we already had a critical mass of scholars ready to move forward. In fact, given hundreds of years of racism, it was just the opposite—we had to first build scholars. Initially we had to seek funding that met the needs of the community rather than any one scholar researcher.

We began to craft a response to the award that was responsive to its R&D general intent that gave respect to the community but in particular was sensitive to the deep-seated need of historically oppressed people. That theme of '*belonging*' introduced by Dr. Cannon, remained in my head and informed much of what emerged in what we later called The Fanon Model. So, the question for this new team was tied to creating a '*Context of Belonging*'. How do we restore a sense of Belonging—or a sense of Place in the geography of human reality. We have been excluded, deluded, discounted, and muted—where do we go from here?

So, in response to your critical question, we forged what we called—The Restoration Model—with its core *methodology* of Primary Inclusion out of our first major 3-year grant funding effort and our intensive scholars discourse internal to our daily workings in community. All of this work has been well documented and published [see King, 1977 publication Education for Emancipation: An Alternative to Compensatory Education].

In 1974, we applied and received 3-year funding from the then existing National Institute of Education, Washington, DC to address strategies for re- education of the Black Child. I saw this as an opportunity to do something good to promote the interests of the community. Central to the grant award was the formation of a Community-based Scholars Advisory Board of five people or more. Community in this case implied both geographic and disciplinary.

At the first assembly of the Scholars Advisory Board I shared our approach to undertaking the award. Our position was that Black children in the US were *marginalized* by their context of education. They came into a context of schooling that was deficient in its capacity to fully embrace them or include them—give them a sense of belonging. It was this failure to afford them a sense of belonging and inclusion that had to be overcome. The school context promoted an extended colonization. What the child needed was a context for an '*emancipatory education*', the prime method of which is '*Primary Inclusion*' (King, 1976). The Scholars Advisory Board, led by three professors, Dr. Leonard Duhl (Stanford University), Dr Antonia Pantoja (San Diego State University), and Dr David Seeley (University of California, Los Angeles), was unanimous in the approval of this approach and encouraged the successful execution of this award. The critical concepts emerging from this study was the launching pad for the work we undertook in Phase 1 and 2 of the Fanon Center.

What began to emerge from this study was a constant and consistent focus on a Fanonian vision in all our actions, explained as, placing the 'person' or Life World, in 'context' or System World—historical, cultural, social. In the internal workings of the Center this emerged as the *Fanon Model* (King, 1980,

1983a)—an overall conceptual vision that guided our work for the next ten years. The concept places the 'subject' of investigation [person, couple, family, community etc.,] in relationship [historical or social, or cultural]. Each—Life World and System World—is represented as a line. The lines are drawn in an 'orthogonal' relationship to each other thus forming a cross. [Why orthogonal? Is explained in the model]. The lines each have 'valence' represented as polarities on a continuum. The intersection of the two lines create four quadrants. Each quadrant is conceptually a 'socio-cultural context'—or dominant condition from which to begin to understand the person (in that context). What is central and primary to that understanding, particularly for a Black person, is the level of belonging (conscious and spiritual) that the person experiences. Thus, in our conceptual modeling we are able to link a definitive set of Principles with a clear methodology of 'Inclusion' in creating a unique theory concerning the lives of Black people. As an aside and a painful reality, this work is there and published since 1976—but deep and persistent racism has prevented mainstream Psychology from embracing it.

As we struggled to represent ourselves and still be responsive to the funding sources what began to emerge was a greater understanding of what was possible and what the Center could become—in fact it became a 'place' of belonging for Black students and faculty from adjacent California Universities. One of the first (1976) such formal arrangements was the placement of twelve graduate students in Urban Education from the University of Southern California (USC) at the Center; in addition students and faculty came from University of California, Pepperdine University and the California State system to work as research assistants or to participate in our weekly seminars on issues of the Mental Health of the Black community.

We began to boldly confront the issues raised by the community—Violence, Alcoholism, Substance Abuse, Suicide, Child Mortality, overwhelming stress—as well as to listen to the people who claimed to have solutions for the problems. Two such engagements were with the Black people practicing Transcendental Meditation and with the Nation of Islam. In the latter case we hosted a major conference between the Center scholars and the top five Nation of Islam scholars—resulting in a major book publication: *African Philosophy: Assumptions and Paradigms in Research on Black Persons* [see King, Nobles, & Dixon, 1977].

We challenged ourselves to ensure that our work in research and development was grounded in community and in our Fanon Model. We still got the usual pressurized inquiry from our Grant Officer in DC concerning whether we had published anything in depression or schizophrenia or bipolar disorders? Did we go to interview the folks who were left from the Tuskegee Syphilis experiment? Did we interview the families of folk who died in Jones Town, Guyana? This was quite a period in my personal development—how to operate under such stress and allow the precious possibilities to flourish into glorious realities to serve our community.

We were beginning to be successful in creating a place (Belonging), a center where there was a critical mass of scholars (four), four funded grants, 16 young scholars as research assistants and a host of excited community supporters. We met in an open public forum once a month; we talked about Black issues, so as to attract the attention of Black youth and Black folk in the community. We generously supported Black students who were now emerging from the University of Southern California, UCLA, the Cal State system. After five years (1974–79), we had succeeded in exciting the imagination of the community, college students from far and wide (we had dissertation students from states outside California), and major scholars both national and international. We had become the leading research group on five issues affecting the Black community—Mental Health, Suicide, Violence, Alcoholism and Stress. We were invited by the mainstream *Annual Review of Psychology* to undertake a review which was published in 1978 [see King, 1978].

Two years later (1980) we developed and published our own peer reviewed Journal—*The Fanon Journal*. Fanon Center became in the minds of young scholars and students alike—The Place to be, to study and be inspired. In this 'place' of belonging we were creating, grounded in community-based research, there was a new vision for faculty and students of a 'meaningful future' in their personal development. They benefitted from seeing organized and disciplined Black scholars in action; they gained a new sense of coherence and above all began to understand the need for a commitment to service. Now we faced a new challenge—with limited funding and great expectations from all, we had taken on much more than we were capable of adequately or competently completing. We had to now find a way to narrow our focus and to streamline the research process. By looking at these issues differently we were able to structure processes to complement our research model and meet with populations that were experiencing the problems. So, when the Compton Police approached us concerning the problem of Alcoholism in Compton (which is adjacent to Watts), we were well equipped to consult with them on an intervention and education model and how to utilize the services of the Dept. of Psychiatry at the local hospital to develop an intervention program. Incidentally, the program developed from this intervention in 1978 still exists today as one of the most viable in the Watts-Compton area [See King, 1981].

In this manner we developed a Suicide Prevention Hotline for the local community. The Center, in 1978, completed its first major review in conjunction with its Advisory Board. One major outcome of this review was a request from the Board to narrow our core research focus and studies. The general consensus from the review led us to the generic *Problems of Oppression* as a core focus; and its *wider small studies* of action-evaluation largely driven by community needs and requests from schools and community-based organizations. The latter grew from the sheer necessity of the community as well as the trust and respect of the Fanon-based network of young scholars who were now gaining greater insight into understanding of problems in the Black community. The community was able to call upon us for help—to lend our expertise, in the absence of funding, to 'do something about their problems' to include development of their base funding, providing guidance to staff and to student interns and conducting staff development workshops. We were able to use the good-will generated to later engage in major research efforts in all aspects of the mental health well-being of the Black population. The new core research focus on the *Problems of Oppression* did not exclude attention to mental illness constructions, but the lens through which we now viewed these issues had changed. We saw oppression as persistent disturbances of the social environment (particularly early relationships) exerting profound and lasting impacts on brain development, gene expression, neuroendocrine systems regulating stress responsivity, anxiety and affective disorders.

For the first time (1976) we entertained a traditional R&D approach by funding a scholar (Dr. Hector Myers) to focus exclusively on stress as a focus. In the narrow framework we adapted our Problems of Oppression to fit a cognitive-relational approach, the individual and their environment were seen as coexisting in a dynamic relationship, where stress is the psychological and emotional state that is internally represented as part of a stressful transaction. The research focused on two key concepts in this interaction—the subject appraisal (based on attribution of meaning the person gives to the events) and coping (in coping support network).

This work 'satisfied' the NIMH requirements and gave us some breathing room to build on the larger issues of the Fanon Model—framed as belonging and inclusion.

Stage 2: Exploration of Restoration through Local and International Connections

By 1979 we had received 5-year funding for the second grant cycle—and thus began simultaneously with the second stage efforts of the work of the Center. The language of the application was dominated by issues of 'stress' impact on the Black community in keeping with the direction of the funders; but with the support of our Advisory Board we pushed ahead with developing the core issue of exploring the nature and impact of oppression in its many forms. At this point I wish to give high praise to Dr. Wade Nobles and his research team from the Center of Advanced Studies of Black Family Life and Culture, for his enormous contribution to this entire process of Fanon Center's research effort. In particular, our rich and compelling conversations and exchanges over three years on issues of culture constructs and paradigms applied to Black children, families and populations, deepened our understanding of the core issues facing the Black population. In fact, we were both so amazed by the parallel nature of our formulations that we ended up forging an alliance that was to last over 20 years.

Dr. Nobles pointed out that what we were definitively stating in our Fanon Center Restoration approach appeared to be limited to restoration of 'place' and had to be more than restoration of 'place'; in fact, it had to be the restoration of African cultural history and reality—space, time and organization. We had been stolen from Africa, beaten and raped—abandoned and left for dead.

We survived slavery but were now totally marginalized in the 'master's' effort at genocide. We were not fighting a battle just for a place [inclusion] at the table. We must fully understand and embrace that the struggle is one of being fully 'restored'—a re-grounding into our culture and history, not a history framed in deliberately distorted Western time, but in continuous time, a place and time in which Africa is returned once more to be part of human geography. The question must become, given over 400 years of oppression: what must we restore in our efforts at gaining optimum health?

This question led me to engage in a series of in-depth conversations with major scholars in the US and the Caribbean—in and outside the Mental Health profession—Anthropologists, Economists, Social Scientists, Historians, revolutionaries and political leaders. Some of them are identified because they shaped the next iteration in my thinking concerning the Center's direction. One person in particular, Dr. Chester Pierce, a leading Psychiatrist and Professor, Harvard University and adviser to The National Aeronautics and Space Administration (NASA). In fact, he was one of the leading Black Psychiatrists who suggested to NIMH the R&D approach to Black and minority mental health. Dr. Pierce suggested that we had moved into a compelling new challenge, one that may require the resources of an institution such as Harvard University. He invited me to join him there. Chester Pierce was a very big supporter of the work of the Center and of my work personally. The Center in 1980 dedicated one of its Fanon Journal issues which I edited to the life and works of Dr. Chester Pierce. He is the only Black psychiatrist who has consistently written and published works on Black people since 1956. He is major as a scholar. He has over 50 publications, 1956–1980, including four publications on micro- and mini-aggressions of whites on Black folk. This concept only recently has gotten attention in the literature (without acknowledging him). He was the first to suggest that racism is a mental illness and wrote extensively about this.

One of the efforts of the Center was to write about and archive the works of Black scholars. We did this for several scholars. We still have an audio tape collection of complete speeches of seven of the top Black psychiatrists at the time (1973–1980). Dr. Chester Pierce's encouragement only reinforced the bold new move we were about to undertake in a new journey of understanding the condition of Black people in the US. The conversations with scholars led me in my role as the Center's director to one conclusion—to revisit as much as we could the original African civilization. We launched an exploration into the diaspora—the passage from Africa through the Caribbean to America.

The central idea of the visit was a search for spiritual rebirth, a deeper understanding of African culture and of ourselves as African scholars and people in the Western space. How crippling was this negated deeper 'belonging' that now left us a people vulnerable and with distorted identities; amazingly susceptible to mimicking our captors and thus disoriented, undermining our efficacy and indeed blunting our emancipatory will. Why is it that in the Western space we emerged at the bottom of every negative statistic—health and well-being, educational outcomes like test scores or graduation rates and health mortality and morbidity outcomes like—violence, crime, homicide, infant mortality, cancer, obesity, cardiovascular diseases, cerebrovascular diseases, diabetes, addictions (smoking, drug, alcohol) and serious mental illness to name a few. These statistics were (and are) not only alarming but depressing and disconcerting. Why? Why was (is) this the state of Black health and why were (are) the findings so persistent and why do the solutions seem so inaccessible? We were on a quest to fully explore this—the most fundamental question of our time . . . and we were in for a lifetime.

Here was our approach to what can be called the Cultural Recovery Quest. The Center, four years into its operation, had attracted young scholars from the African and Caribbean diaspora who were faculty or students in the United States. In our strategy we wished, as a first step, to develop a genuine relationship concerning issues of human development with such young scholars, share our vision of trying to understand and recover cultural elements of the scholars' home country; as a second step, visit the home countries to try to establish a dialogue with scholars and leaders, including the government officials. Our goal was to structure a formal study conference visit with a delegation of at least 10 Fanon scholars after the initial visit. I want to make it clear (although nobody ever questioned it) we accomplished this with funding we developed, not with grant funds.

In one of the first such visits, I flew into Surinam with a young Surinamese scholar to meet with the Poet Laurate of Surinam, Dobru. He was from the Saramaka people one of six original African groups that 460 years ago jumped in the Caribbean Sea and escaped inland into the country of Dutch Guyana (now Surinam) in South America, to escape slavery and were never recaptured. This was one group that the literature calls Maroons. There are groups in Jamaica as well. They can claim 'original African' status because they were never enslaved. At every turn they fought and won against their captors for over 300 years, eventually signing treaties to keep and live on the land they had occupied. There is a recent court case on this: Case of the Saramaka People *v.* Suriname; Judgment of November 28, 2007.

I had come to Surinam to arrange for a visit to three of the six groups (The Saramaka, the Ndyuka and the Aluku) all of whom lived deep in the interior 300-miles up rivers filled with Piranha fish in tropical jungle territory. On this first visit I met as a courtesy with the University of Surinam to seek their participation and then went on into the interior to meet the tribal Chiefs to seek their permission for a return visit of ten scholars. Dobru provided the translation necessary. We returned in 10 months with a delegation of 10 scholars—including well known national experts in human behavior (Dr. Wade Nobles), education (Dr. Asa Hilliard), neurosurgery (Dr. Yonas Zegeye) and one anthropologist (Dr. Lance Young)—to live among the people for two weeks to set up a health clinic and provide any needed health care services. The encounters with the villages were spectacular—observing their customs and listening to the chiefs concerning their lived history, rituals and practices.

We repeated this process of first and second visits, meeting with local scholars and then conferencing on issues of Culture and Human Development in:

- **Somalia,** where in addition to the 10 primary scholars we were joined by 117 Americans who wished to travel with us, in an intensive one week of conferencing.
- **Egypt,** where we were hosted by Egyptian scholars and a tour of the Pyramids.
- **Kenya,** where we met with the original freedom support group of Jomo Kenyatta and his chief archivist Mr. McKenon.
- **Trinidad and Tobago,** where we hosted a conference in conjunction with the President of the World Health Organization's Mental Health actions—Dr. Michael Beaubrun—who was a psychiatrist from Trinidad. In addition to our 10 scholars we had a contingent of an additional 156 people who were housed in homes of Trinidadians and stayed after the two-day conference to witness the enormously popular Trinidad Carnival.
- **Brazil,** into the spiritual essence of Bahia, to conference with the artist communities and the spiritualists. One of the scholars on this visit was the well-known Hon. Maxine Waters from the US Congress—a State Legislator at the time.

I'm trying to point out to you where Fanon was going with his work. We were not abandoning the quite successful first five years of action. We now were developing a very critical Black stress model. We were still concerned about issues of psychosis and neurosis but not in the traditional sense as they were represented in the DSM. We felt very strongly that those would be addressed if we could restore the context of how people live and understand what forces undermined their 'rhythms of belonging'. This became our expanded position. If people got an opportunity to be restored, they will be poised to be healthy again. They could truly begin the 'process of overcoming' the challenges faced in the Western context and not be left as earlier indicated 'always at the bottom'.

The culture question: We undertook this 'diaspora journey' not as a romantic exercise. I was born and lived overseas for 22 years. I was looking at the larger contextual issue of how we grow the Black community. How do we return the health of the Black community? How do we enrich the Black community? What do we need to do? Is it fundamentally an economic question? Is it simply a social question? Is it an employment question? Is it family question? Is it? So many issues. You're an egg, you know; it's Humpty Dumpty. And after you get crushed, where do you begin to rebuild? Do you start with the shell and build out and then pour the rest of it into the shell? Or do you start with the yoke? Or do you start with the egg white? I mean, where do you begin? We needed help. We called on our African scholars spread far and wide in the diaspora to the rescue. Many of them had captured the imagination at least of significant populations of Black people in their writings and work. That was good enough for us to begin our explorations of the problems of our people in the European contexts—colonial or as US or Canadian citizens.

Note, as we considered the issues, the confirmation of our history and culture was central. African culture was constituted in a space where Africa was the center of cultural values, whereas today we exist as a culture in a space in which Europe is the center of such values. African culture, as one author puts it— the primary generic skeleton, as a germinative structure which gives cultural specificity its corporeality—has been blunted and negated as a nucleus. So, we attempt to add to this negated 'generic skeleton' a European extension—a completely imposed incomprehensible distortion. There is no connection between the nucleus (the historic or traditional) and the imposed (European). The African nuclear reality had a way of mediating the individual's way toward divinity and spirituality; time was continuous through order and harmony (Maat). The new imposed reality presupposes a strictly empirical world, a world of successive experiences as experiments leading to a 'concrete becoming'. We wrote about this in two publications [see King, 1983a, 1983b].

In response to Neville's invitation to mention other scholars affiliated with the Center, King noted not only an extensive list of people but also the following.

Yes, I was giving a backdrop to this. The reason for identifying some of the scholars was to talk about the type of work and research work in which they were engaged in the name of Fanon. The very intent of the Fanon Center was not to participate in the clinical practices or one-on-one psychotherapy, but to understand how to promote significantly improved actions, including where necessary, clinical practices, to promote the quality of life for our people. Our work focused on the issue of colonialism, and in particular decolonization, and what that implies; racism and the impact of racism; we took these ideas and expanded them. We were aware that Fanon was just about 36-plus when he died, and it was left for people like us and beyond to build upon and utilize what he initiated concerning our own emancipation—what he called 'setting afoot a new man'.

We did not see ourselves as replicas of the Brookings Institute in Washington or the Stanford Institute in Palo Alto where we study something, produce a paper, and write a book. We were able to undertake this action also; but we rather saw ourselves as agents of community change. So we called upon scholars to be in residence to join with us in this community change effort as we structured, refined and pursued our research directions in the second five years. One of the requirements of the Center was to work with or through scholars-in-residence as leads in our critical research actions. We obviously had to modify this given the history of racist exclusion of Black researchers from R&D systems. Scholars had to be developed. We created five types of scholars and over the next eight years hosted and welcomed over 42 Black scholars and one white (Epidemiologist from John Hopkins) to our Center. Here is an explanation of the types of scholars-in-residence we welcomed and a partial listing of some of the people who occupied the role and their contribution to the life of the Center as well as the Center's work in the community (1974–1984):

1. Dissertation Scholars (15 scholars)—young scholars in the final years of completing dissertation and in need of guidance as well as a research base from which to do their work. One in particular stands out—Dr. Donna Blackwell, Psychology, University of Washington, St Louis. She spent two years at the Center and later became a Director of the effort with Lou Rawls to raise funds for United Negro College Fund. After this she was instrumental in developing The Desmond Tutu Peace Foundation, SA.
2. Developmental Scholars (10 scholars)—recent graduates in the field of Psychiatry or Social Sciences, who were interested in topics consistent with our Center direction. One such scholar was Dr. Richard King, Psychiatry, University of California. He spent 5 years at the Center pursuing research on the role of the Pineal Gland and Melanin in Psychosis, particularly schizophrenia. To buffer this biological approach, we also accepted Dr. Ntongela Masilela, a Marxist scholar and a recent graduate from UCLA. His outstanding critical thinking and writing over 4 years at the Center eventually led to an appointment as a Professor at the Claremont Colleges.
3. Research Scholars (8 scholars)—scholars who fit the original intent of the grant award—seasoned researchers who were attracted by the research questions being pursued by the Center and wished to take a sabbatical leave to work with us or our population. One such scholar was Dr. Vernon Dixon, Professor of Economics, Princeton University and author of the popular—*Beyond Black and White*. He joined us in residence for two years and made enormous contributions to our understanding of the issues of poverty in our overall agenda of the Problems of Oppression. Others fitting this category, each spending over 3-months, included:

    -   Dr. Walter Rodney—Professor of Social and Economic History, University of Uganda, Africa
    -   Dr. Hollis Lynch—Professor, Columbia University, History, expert on Slavery
    -   Dr. Andrew Billingsley—Professor, University of Maryland, Sociology, expert on the Black population
    -   Dr. Robert Staples—Professor of Sociology, Howard University, Washington, DC—expert on the Black Family
    -   Dr. Mervyn Dymally—Lt Gov. State of California, Health policy expert
    -   Dr. Yonas Zegeye, Neurosurgeon and Neurologist—expert on the human brain
    -   Oscar Brown Jr., world renown Jazz Artist,—expert on 'edutainment'—using the arts to educate the community
    -   Dr. Anita DeFrantz—a leading Psychologist and mother of Anita DeFrantz of the US Olympics. She was instrumental in community education and Black family development

4. Visiting Scholars (12 scholars)—persons who wished to spend one or two weeks exploring our approach or methods with some particular set of issues in the Black community or who we brought into the conversation base on critical issues facing the Black community. As one major example— We brought in Dr. Asa Hilliard to work with Pediatrics on issues of Black Child Development. We had for instance developed some expertise on the issue of youth violence and had played a major role in intervention efforts in the Rodney King riots (1992). The students of Atlanta in their annual Spring Fest had caused major damage in the Atlanta community. The community of Atlanta championed by Ms. Coretta Scott-King, led a delegation from Atlanta (including Betty Shabazz wife of Malcolm X) to visit with us to discern our strategies. Both Coretta Scott-King and Betty Shabazz spent two, two-week cycles with us in discovery. Other notable visiting scholars—Dr. Vincent Harding (Historian), Dr. Bill Strickland (Historian), Dr. Howard Dodson (Director, Schomburg Center, New York).

5. Consultant Scholars (5 scholars)—world experts in their field with whom I consulted concerning the progress and direction of the Center. They were both national and international and were not necessarily tied to a mental health agenda: for instance, I met quarterly (over 4 years) with the three Directors of other Centers in the Hispanic and American Indian communities; I met with Dr. Chester Pierce at Harvard University twice a year; I met with Dr. Wade Nobles monthly; I met with Dr. Al Haynes, a world expert in Primary Care and International Health, once monthly; I met with Robert Hill (Professor of History, UCLA), the world expert authority on Marcus Garvey and Rastafarians once monthly.

Women's Contribution to the Center

NEVILLE: "I'm wondering if you can tell me a little bit more about women's contributions to the Center."

That is an excellent question. Women have always played a significant role in the life of the Center and the women who served as scholars in any capacity were nothing short of spectacular. We named the Center after Frantz Fanon. He had long since died when we named the Center in 1974. The naming for us was primarily an acknowledgement of the idea of 'setting afoot a new person' if we were going to make headway in changing the mental health status of our people. We were delighted and overwhelmed that when Josie Fanon visited the United States on November 16, 1978, at Howard University's African American Center, she identified us as doing the kind of work that Fanon would have welcomed. She made it her business to come to Los Angeles when she left Washington to meet with us. We perhaps stand in a special place—the only place—where the wives of three world revolutionary leaders have spent some critical time—these were Josie Fanon, Coretta Scott-King and Betty Shabazz.

The most bold and far reaching of our scholars were women. We encouraged women scholars at every turn of the work of the Center. We had about 20 such scholars from 1974 to 1988. They addressed the human essence in unique human ways, very important work in American life. I already mentioned Donna Blackwell and how she applied her scholarship in fund development for young Black scholars at UNCF. She later worked to develop for South Africa the Desmond Tutu Center.

Our first developmental scholar funding award was given to Beverly Coleman, a community health activist working in the area of Women's health. She actually brought to my attention the first book she had written on remedies for a range of common health problems faced by our community. We funded her to build an alternative woman's health institution which still exists today. She had the first alternative center on healthcare, South Los Angeles. I funded her, to study acupuncture. She got an acupuncture degree in Arizona paid for by the Fanon Center. Dr. Coleman created N-A-C-H-E-S, a women's center for health and wellness in California, Arizona and Colorado. They all exist today, and women swear by her healthcare methods. We are proud of this.

Another visiting scholar (three months in residence) was Toni Cade Bambara, an outstanding American poet and writer. She used her deep passion for life for finding and elevating the divine in our culture, [as evident in revered classics like *The Black Woman: An Anthology*, which Bambara organized and edited in 1970] to inspire our students and community during her time with us.

At the core of the Center's infrastructure development was Dorothy Williams. What her contribution was cannot be overestimated. She came to us straight from NIH [National Institutes of Health] as an administrator. She met me and said, "I want to help you because I like what you're doing." Now, what she did was to put the Center's administrative realities down in concrete, and what you call the boiler plate stuff. We had a streamlined center. Mrs. Williams was like a joy to my heart . . . When I walked in, I knew the Center was in good hands. That's what you need, and that wasn't taken lightly. If somebody walked through the Center, they had to go through her. Sexism would not be tolerated in any form. Just a class person. Another young woman at the heart of the Center's work was a UCLA dissertation scholar—Donna Davis. Out of the Center she developed unique and national models for health care education for chronic illnesses—AIDS and Cancer. Her leadership led to models for churches and use of barber shops in education campaigns. She became the first Director of the Drew Medical School's Cancer Prevention Center.

We funded Brenda Shockley, a lawyer who spent a year with us in 1977–78 as a Developmental Scholar focused on Black youth gangs and violence. Ms. Shockley worked on this very important issue addressing youth violence and the media and developed a full-length feature film on the subject to be shown in high schools to talk to kids about issues of violence. The visual image became powerful.

Dr. Sylvia Wynter, a long term and outstanding Professor of Stanford University was a 2-week visiting professor. Her work focused on colonialism and issues of human oppression.

Once scholars were identified with the Center they continued to be in communication, received support from the Center and were able to provide young students with internship support or guidance as an extension of the Center's efforts.

Stage 3: The Fanon Center, It's Successes, and Its Changing Form

Let me go to this elephant in the room, which is what has happened to the Fanon Center.

I know you're waiting for it. In its glorious form in the first 10 years (1973–1983), it was really a place to be. And, all I've iterated and represented to you were those first 10 years. Our reputation as a Center world-wide was beginning to outstrip the name and work of the science and medical center that was the home of the Center—i.e., The Martin Luther King Jr-Charles R. Drew Medical Center. There was some sense that key emerging issues, compelling enough in the life of the community were not to be ignored. Thus began the third five-year cycle of the Center.

I was summoned by the President/Dean Dr. Al Haynes of the medical school in 1983 to help host a conference on the State of Black Health in the Black community served by the Martin Luther King Hospital. In their seminal article [McCord C, Freeman HP. Excess mortality in Harlem. New England J Med. 1990;322(3):173–177], McCord and Freeman estimated that in 1980 Black male youths in Harlem, New York City, were less likely to survive to the age of 65 years than were male youths in Bangladesh. Mortality rates in 1980 were approximately 6 times greater among Harlem women aged 25 to 34 years and Harlem men aged 35 to 44 years than among White women and men in the same age groups nationwide. This statistic had persisted through 1983 and the mortality indicators for the black population required immediate attention.

Dr. Haynes, [also a highly respected member of the Institute of Medicine in Washington, DC], at the time a Consulting Scholar of the Center around emerging work in International Health, hosted the conference of all 12 Department Chairs when he was Dean of the Medical College. What emerged was a consensus paper identifying the priority research emphasis of the medical center for the next decade and a concerted effort to develop joint funding to address each of the nine (9) identified problems: Violence, Infant Mortality, Cardiovascular and Cerebrovascular Diseases, Cancer, Diabetes, Addictions (smoking, alcohol, drugs), Mental Health, and Unintentional Accidents.

I was being called upon to use the expertise I had developed over the 10-year Center success to help the research agenda of a medical school. The Center was the only place in the University with both the greatest funding as well as publications. In fact, no department outside of Emergency Medicine had generated research.

In 1984, I perhaps made the first mistake—I delayed the fundamental cultural agenda we were pursuing as a Center to turn our assistance to helping the University. We made a major decision to place the Center's core research staff into a restructured Medical Center Research Institute to undertake the challenge defined by the Dean's conference. I was appointed as Dean for Research in 1984, without relinquishing my role as Director of the Fanon Center. I was planning to hold the Center in waiting to 'jump start' the University's effort. My task was to restructure the entire Medical Center to be a legitimate research enterprise, consistent with a primary care agenda, not consistent with a biomedical research agenda. I saw the Medical Center as vital to the life of the Black community.

So, for a year and a half, I approached the Fanon staff as well as the Department Chairs with two hats. It was killing me. I went to each department. I'll give you the names of the department because it's important for you to know the specificity: Family Medicine, Pediatrics, Psychiatry, Dermatology, ENT, Emergency Medicine, Radiology, Neurosurgery, Pathology, Internal Medicine, OBGYN, Surgery. I went to each department systematically in the first year. I began to help them restructure their department, consistent with a research approach in order to generate research in a primary care frame. You say what is primary care with surgery? Well, it is the most elegant primary care model you can think of. The primary care model in surgery was based upon the emphasis on violence. We were seeing 17 gunshot wounds on a Saturday night, and half of them were penetrating wounds that affected two or more organ systems. It was a high-powered ballistic weapon caused injury.

So, we were seeing the worst of the worst, and they were coming like gangbusters. The surgeons were telling me, "Man, we can't be wasting time on primary care. We don't want primary care. We need to be surgeons. We need to be doing our thing, cutting, and we're the best at it." I said, "Yeah, but if you could do an autopsy of each person coming in, you could know where the violence is coming, we can perhaps stop it." That's primary care.

TURNER: "Okay, let me stop you here. This is a very important moment. Because we have the intersection of a major moment in American political history that intersects the Black community. That is the role of the government in infusing crack cocaine into South LA. That's what you're talking about. That's huge. I don't think anybody has made that connection to what was going on with the Medical Center, let alone the Fanon Center. That's where Maxine Waters really came out on that. Right?"

This was the source issue of the mistake I earlier identified. I missed the early signs that a drug (crack cocaine) epidemic was about to sweep the community, partly because the US was complicit with the drug trade to allow the CIA to ship large quantities of cocaine from Nicaragua to EL Salvador and on to LA. Gary Webb sparked national controversy with his 1998 *Dark Alliance* series which alleged that the influx of Nicaraguan cocaine started and significantly fueled the 1980s crack epidemic. Investigating the lives and connections of Los Angeles crack dealers Ricky Ross and Norwin Meneses, Webb alleged that profits from these crack sales were funneled to the CIA-supported Contras.

While I was busy crafting a primary care research agenda in my new role, the community was entering into full blown crisis mode because of the Drug Wars—every department was affected, but in particular Emergency Medicine, Psychiatry and Surgery—crisis after crisis. At the time we had no way of knowing what was affecting us. We stayed the course on all fronts, dug deeper, rolled up our sleeves and worked. By the end of 1986–87, at midyear, June, [I'll give you concrete data and documentation for NIH], our effort coming out of the 1984 strategic plan, we had at least 16 new research awards to nine departments; generated $17 million a year, from $3.5 million in the prior year, in 1985. So, what happened to Fanon Center? Its model became the tool for funding the Medical Center and development of data to serve the entire community. This was the first step.

I took a personal second step. I moved the agenda, with the support of Dr. Haynes, the President/Dean to the other three Black medical schools [Morehouse [Medical College], Meharry, and Howard], taking on one problem (cancer prevention), not all the problems, as a working model. After careful education and preparation, working with [Congressman] Lou Stokes in Congress, we generated the legislation and the grant funding for the research centers for minority institutions, which awarded each of these schools $5 million a year in perpetuity. So, if you start in 1987, the year that legislation was finally approved, and multiply $20 million by the number of years to date, that is how I made a contribution. If I am going to claim success, this is one that I claim. This has done more for Black researchers than any other legislation in the history of America—this is mental health.

And it didn't stop there. Other People of Color said, "What about me?" They wrote the legislation agreement to include what's called Hispanic-serving institutions. And they added, in addition to the four original institutions, 64 new institutions. Wherever there was 30% or more Hispanics in an institution, the institution qualified. So, schools, the colleges here [California], the state colleges here get money like water. They don't know how to do research, but they get the money. I don't know if Illinois gets any money. We should check it out. Okay, so I did this, and Drew got the money and flourished. But, in some sense, I regretted having taken on the task. As much as I'm boasting about the success, because it was enormously successful in generating money. I was going down the wrong pathway for my own personal career. The original funding for Fanon had ended in 1984.

Fanon continued to develop grant awards and continued its work largely in Youth Violence in conjunction with Probation Departments and school-based problems. Three of our Developmental Scholars became connected to departments as primary researchers—Family Medicine, Psychiatry and Pediatrics and one became the Director of the Cancer Prevention effort. The entire group of research statisticians and research technicians continued to serve the Office of Research for the Medical school. No one lost a job. We lost the vibrant working atmosphere of a Center—no more scholars-in-residence or visiting; no more students; no more monthly seminars.

So successful was I as the Dean of Research, that by unanimous vote of the faculty in 1987, I was asked to serve as Dean of the Medical School. I served in that role for seven years- '87 to '94, and I enjoyed great personal respect. But the fundamental change I hoped for never came; so my work as a Dean was largely custodial—ensuring Medical School Accreditation, boosting recruitment of the best faculty and students and making gains in funding. My creative model on EcoPrimary Care won a major award from the National Institute of Medicine in 1991. In retrospect, given the assault on our community by our own government, I now understand. I resigned in 1984, took a leave of absence for one year and returned in 1996. I put Fanon on hold and went into serious studies while focused on culture and psychopathology for a postgraduate seminar in psychiatry with 3rd year residents. Now the task became 'restoration of Lew King'.

The idea and work of the Fanon Center continues quietly as I contemplate its new form. The scholar groups we assembled still meet to undertake major work. In 1994–1998 Dr. Nobles and I worked with on invitation for National Council of Black Churches and NIH to produce a diabetes prevention model for African American women [See King & Nobles, 1996].

I was called upon in 1998 by Dr. Walter Fluker of Harvard Divinity School to help form a Center for Ethical Studies at Morehouse College, Atlanta. We completed this task in 2002. Then 2004, I was called upon by Ms. Ethel Bradley, wife of the long-standing Mayor Tom Bradley of Los Angeles, 1973–93, to develop a Bradley Center. This I completed in 2008 and forged a model of Intentional Civility (King, 2008) to accompany the work of the Bradley Center. This model later blossomed into the latest contribution of the Center—The Intentional Critical Civility model which fully picks up on the cultural theme that was briefly suspended when I took on the task of the Medical School. It is now being used by our current Fanon Group of Scholars in several applications. The most compelling work is now being engaged by what I call a virtual Fanon Center. I have five scholars in the US and Caribbean working on the model. The group's primary focus is on decolonization. We recently won a major contract award to work within the Caribbean Community to address the major problems of violence and low work productivity. We are three months into a very exciting project working directly with governments of the various nation states.

The success of the Fanon Center is unquestionable however one chooses to look at it. I would have wished for more, but it was a wonderful experiment. I'd do it again. The central lesson learned—be vigilant about how racism disguises itself to undermine the Black agenda. We have a long way to go. I am at this time one of three scholars in the virtual Fanon. My work in the form of an upcoming new book, is focused on critical steps at every stage—in building this 'new person' of which Fanon spoke. It will be a practical compendium of all the lessons learned in my work as Director of the Fanon Center. I will not rest. There will be no silence on this—for as Fanon wrote, there comes a time when silence is dishonest. In the words of Fanon (1966): *"what matters is not [only] to know the world but to change it."*

Notes

1. *Fanon Research and Development Center: An Overview* [an informational brochure], May 1976.
2. The Tavistock Institute of Human Relations is a British not-for-profit organization which applies social science to contemporary issues and problems. It was initiated in 1946, when it developed from the Tavistock Clinic, and was formally established as a separate entity in September 1947. The journal *Human Relations* is published on behalf of the Tavistock Institute by Sage Publications. https://en.wikipedia.org/wiki/Tavistock_Institute. The Tavistock Trust and Clinic is a specialist mental health trust based in north London. The Trust specializes in talking therapies. The education and training department caters to 2,000 students a year from the United Kingdom and abroad. The Trust is based at the Tavistock Centre in Swiss Cottage. The founding organization was the Tavistock Institute of medical psychology founded in 1920 by Dr. Hugh Crichton-Miller. It has long been regarded as a professional center of excellence of international renown in its application of psychoanalytic ideas to the study and treatment of mental health and interpersonal dynamics. https://en.wikipedia.org/wiki/Tavistock_and_Portman_NHS_Foundation_Trust.

References

Fanon, F. (1966). *The wretched of the earth* (C. Farrington, Trans.). New York: Grove Press.

King, L. M. (1976). *Primary inclusion: A model for an emancipatory education agenda.* Fanon R&D Center, Los Angeles, CA.

King, L. M. (1977). Education for emancipation: An alternative to compensatory education. In *National institute of education research reports.* Washington: ERIC Publications.

King, L. M. (1978). Social and cultural influences in psychopathology. *Annual Review of Psychology, 29,* 405–433.

King, L. M. (1981). Alcoholism research among Black Americans. In J. DeLuca (Ed.), *Alcohol & health: 4th report to congress.* Washington, DC: NIAAA-HHS.

King, L. M. (1983a). *Two myths, one mythology: Cross-cultural research models and mental health.* Columbia University, Teachers College, New York, NY: Monograph.

King, L. M. (1983b). Psychology of Blacks reconsidered. In J. C. Chunn, P. J. Dunston, & F. Ross-Sheriff (Eds.), *Mental health and People of Color: Curriculum development and change.* Washington, DC: Howard University Press.

King, L. M. (2008). *Intentional critical civility: An education and training model.* Tom and Ethel Bradley Center, Los Angeles, CA.

King, L. M., & Nobles, W. (1996). *Science, culture, church, and community: An authentic prevention model for non-insulin dependent diabetes in African American Women.* Atlanta, GA: Center for Disease Control, USDHHS, October.

King, L. M., Nobles, W., & Dixon, V. (Eds.). (1977). *African philosophy: Assumptions and paradigms in research on Black persons.* Los Angeles, CA: Fanon Center Publications.

Webb, G. (1998). Dark alliance. *San Jose Mercury News,* 18–20.

Section 2

History, Theory and Fanonian Praxis

4 Therapy of/for the Oppressed

Frantz Fanon's Psychopolitical Pedagogy of Transformation

Erica Burman

It is through the effort to recapture the self and to scrutinize the self, it is through the lasting tension of their freedom, that men will be able to create the ideal conditions of existence for a human world.

(Fanon, 1970, p. 165)

This chapter aims to offer an appreciative—if also critical—reading of Fanon's contribution that encapsulates his distinctive psychopolitical perspective on therapy, and the necessary and constitutive role of personal questioning, healing and transformation for political mobilisation and change. I structure my discussion around three key issues: the conceptualisation and role Fanon accorded violence; how this and his other analyses help resituate and redefine the clinic; and how this reflects Fanon's psychoaffective pedagogy of transformation. Along the way, I consider corresponding implications for our understanding of therapy and the work of therapists.

Notwithstanding its controversial status, rather than shying away from Fanon's position on violence, I instead revisit its meanings and functions within his account, as a central guiding and—in its intrapsychic reading—humanizing, restorative and vital force for therapeutic change and relationship. This leads to a reconsideration of the status of the clinic and clinical work in Fanon's work and writing, from which we can derive further insights into his pedagogical approach to bringing about change. It is no accident that my title engages discussions of critical pedagogies, transposing Freire's (1972) famous title, *Pedagogy of the Oppressed*, to highlight Fanon's equivalent, and arguably equivalently pedagogical, contribution to therapy. In addition, this account juxtaposes aspects of Fanon's therapeutic practice both with educational literatures and other contemporary discussions of groupwork, indicating both convergences and divergences. The domain of the political, however, remains in the foreground: both the politics of therapy, and how politics enters into—in the sense of producing but also structuring the contexts for and of—distress.

Violence: Preexisting, Oppressive, Reparative or Creative?

Fanon's position on violence is typically regarded as one of the most uncomfortable aspects of his work. Fanon eventually supported armed struggle—indeed it is said he applied his professional psychiatric knowledge to help train Front Libération National fighters to deal with combat stress (Gendzier, 1973). Yet his position has been much misunderstood. This arises partly from Sartre's (1961/1963) Preface to *The Wretched of the Earth* (hereafter *WE*), a double-edged contribution that both significantly oversimplified Fanon's position and advanced Sartre's own agenda addressed to the French white left. Kuby (2015) argues that 'Sartre was not simply interested in "supporting" Fanon rhetorically. From the start of the Preface, he signalled that he was interested in the use of violence to heal metropolitan France'. So, although Fanon primarily addressed the colonised, Sartre took the opportunity to mobilise the power of, but an oversimplified version of, Fanon's call to resistance to fuel his particular political arguments addressed to the Parisian Left. Although Sartre characterised Fanon as advocating a cathartic, even murderous, violence to help throw off colonialism's shackles, Fanon's formulations were both less polarised and more nuanced. The outcome was that, as well as helping secure a wide audience for the book, Sartre's (mis)characterisation, as much as Fanon's own account, prompted it to be banned on publication in France. (Nevertheless, it still had a wide underground circulation—in France as elsewhere). Although Sartre depicted a zero-sum relationship between the 'child of violence' and those at whose expense 'he' was denied humanity, for Fanon the question of violence was a matter for concern and for action, rather than uncritical celebration. He understood the violence as already there, structured into the colonial context of inequality, such that any action on the part of the oppressed could be seen as violent in struggling to oppose or change this. As he indicated in his first book: 'It is understandable that the first action of the black man is a *reaction*' (*Black skin, White masks*, p. 27—emphasis in original).

A relevant interpretive point here is that we must avoid reading Fanon's statements ahistorically. Not to do so, abstracts his comments not only from their political context of formulation but also from later events affecting the way we might view the conditions in which he was writing. In an early critical evaluation, written proximal to Fanon's own, Gendzier (1973) pointed out:

> The objective, in Fanon's terms, of the cathartic effect of violence was not only to transform men, it was to make them capable of creating a better society. In retrospect, it is hardly possible to claim it is the absence of adequate illumination by violence that is responsible for the political tragedies of post-independence nations. It is the prohibition of politics and the inadequacy of political organization that have robbed yesterday's partisans of their rewards. That Fanon knew this himself is clear from *WE*.
>
> (202)

Indeed, far from asserting polarisation, as early as *Black Skin, White Masks* (hereafter *BSWM*) Fanon repudiated essentialist racialised positions: 'The Negro is not. Any more than the white man.' (*BSWM*, p. 165). But this was, of course, a future world he was struggling to envisage, thereby to promote—and, performatively, to invoke—its conditions of possibility. His focus on time and being in time, as well as owing so much to his reading of phenomenological philosophy, worked precisely to emphasise the historical, contingent *and so changeable*, character of oppressor–oppressed relationships: 'The architecture of this work is rooted in the temporal. Every human problem must be considered from the standpoint of time' (*BSWM*, p. 11). Yet to get to this point of being able to 'touch the other, to feel the other, to explain the other to myself' which Fanon poetically invoked as a future project, alongside the 'open door of every consciousness' (*BSWM*, p. 165), there is work to be done. This openness and preparedness 'to discover and to love man, whatever he may be' (*BSWM*, p. 165) is only possible when injustice has been recognized and redressed.

Action and Reaction

Fanon's radical humanism envisaged a postracialised world where personal and institutional histories have been transformed. This process of transformation is an active one: Fanon writes many times in *BSWM* of 'effort'. This is the effort to be 'actional' (p. 157), rather than 'only reactional' (p. 157), since 'there is always resentment in a reaction' (p. 157). This effort to transcend mere reaction is what is needed to 'recapture the self and to scrutinise the self' (*BSWM*, p. 165), just as much as it will take effort on both sides 'to persuade my brother, whether black or white, to tear off with all his strength the shameful livery put together by centuries of incomprehension' (*BSWM*, p. 11).

Two key points arise here. Firstly, the call to action (rather than reaction) is relational, as well as individual. But, secondly, Fanon also acknowledges that alongside the 'yes, to life. Yes, to love. Yes, to generosity', there is also '*no. No* to scorn of man. *No* to degradation of man. *No* to exploitation of man. *No* to the butchery of what is most human in man: freedom' (*BSWM*, 158). What makes the Fanon of *BSWM* a radical, rather than a liberal humanist, then is his rooting of humanist authentic communication within a vision of a potential future of changed societal relationships and organisation (see Hallward, 2011; Hudis, 2015).

Commentators have identified discontinuities or seeming contradictions in Fanon's position on violence or understand his changes of orientation as a development arising from his greater political experience that resulted in a hardening and closing down of that 'openness'. However, like Gibson (2011) and Gordon (2015), I read a shift of focus according to the compelling and urgent work at hand. Included in *Alienation and Freedom*, the recent collection of Fanon's (2018) previously untranslated writings, the text of Fanon's address to the Accra Positive Action Conference, held in April 1960, at which key anticolonial political leaders were present. Khalfa and Young, the editors of Fanon's (2018) writing mark this text, entitled 'Why we use violence', as offering a significant counterpoint to dominant readings of 'Concerning Violence', the infamous first chapter of *WE*. Although 'Why we use violence' was addressed to a clearly political, rather than clinical or therapeutic, arena, he acknowledges the ways the colonized is driven to violent means as a form of 'just anger' through being 'caught in a web of three-dimensional violence, a meeting point of multiple, diverse, repeated, cumulative violences' (Fanon, 1960/2018, p. 654). Significantly, he highlights how such violence is not only encountered daily, but it also obliterates the memory of a pre-enslaved history and renders unthinkable a free future 'for the colonial regime presents itself as necessarily eternal' (p. 654).

However, far from celebrating this violence, he argued that it was the role of the party, of political leadership, to manage this internal violence:

> The role of the political party that takes the destinies of the people into its hands is to curtail this violence and to channel it by providing it with a peaceful platform and a constructive basis, since for the human spirit which contemplates the unfolding of history and which tries to stay on the ground of the universal, violence must first be fought with the language of truth and of reason.
>
> (p. 655)

Fanon, then, advocated the use of violence in the sense of armed struggle only as the last strategy available within the bitter, protracted and brutal struggle for independence in Algeria, where, as he starkly put it: 'finally, it was no longer a question for the Algerian of giving a meaning to his life but rather of giving one to his death' (p. 655). Thus, Fanon focused on colonial violence as creating the unequal playing field, resistance to which may eventually require violent means. But even here he embeds his analysis within an elaborated picture of the de-subjectifying and alienating impacts on the 'soul', that eventually finds its way into embodied experience, or as he put it, into 'muscles' and the 'blood' (p. 655), that is, it has bodily as well as psychological effects.

Clinical Interventions

> This book is a clinical study. Those who recognize themselves in it, I think, will have made a step forward.
>
> (*BSWM*, p. 11)

The clinical project—for Fanon and for us—must be considered both individual and sociopolitical. Fanon's naming of *BSWM* as a 'clinical study' invites its readers to render themselves subjects of investigation, in the service of political if not also therapeutic change. Fanon's arrival in 1953 in Algeria as clinical director of the psychiatric hospital of Blida-Joinville, outside Algiers, coincided with the violent escalation of anticolonial struggle and the French forces' brutal efforts to suppress this. He soon became directly politically involved, as well as challenging the physical and symbolic violence of colonial psychiatry meted upon the native population.

Whatever his preexisting political sympathies, it was primarily through his commitment to supporting his patients' mental health that he became politicised. In an early assessment of his contribution, Irene Gendzier (1973, p. 90) noted:

> As Fanon watched French troops coming in and out of the Blida-Joinville hospital to remove suspected nationalists, as he watched others carry in men who had been tortured and lay dying under the hand of doctors who preferred not to risk themselves by doing anything, Fanon began to turn towards Algeria.

What Fanon saw, then, was that doing nothing can be an act of culpable violence. As is well-known, he resigned his post in December 1956, on the grounds that "If psychiatry is the medical technique that sets out to enable individuals no longer to be foreign to their environment, I owe it to myself to state that the Arab permanently alienated in his own country, lives in a state of absolute depersonalization. . . . [T]he troubles in Algeria are the logical consequence of an abortive attempt to decerebralize a people' (Fanon, 1956/2018, p. 434). That is, he declared as unethical and impossible the attempt to 'treat' as mental health issues what were political matters requiring political, rather than psychiatric or psychotherapeutic, responses of restoration and restitution.

However, Fanon's personal trajectory, from clinical practitioner to political revolutionary, indicates continuities of commitment that reciprocally redefine the domain of politics and therapy. His was no crude social reductionism of psychological problems to political conditions, nor would his political analysis— indeed denunciation—of colonial and other forms of oppression allow for their psychologization or individualization. As early as *BSWM*, Fanon opposed the ways colonial psychiatry, especially that formulated by the Algerian school of ethnopsychiatry, functioned to legitimise and apologise for colonial domination, with its tropes of biological and mental inferiority, primitivism and criminality.

But his practice shows much more than this. Fanon redefined dominant understandings of the 'clinic'. Far from being a rarefied arena, set away from sociopolitical material realities, Fanon shows the importance of understanding the clinical as integral to these. Not only did his actions reflect how those realities impact the responsibilities of the clinician, but they also highlight key connections between clinical, political and educational practice. I will suggest that these contributions deserve equal recognition, and also how understandings of their mutual relations were deepened by Fanon. The 'clinic' was transformed from a quasi-medical concern with the individual 'bedside' to a social arena concerned with reconnecting the suffering subject to his agentic capacities. (Indeed, it is worth noting that, according to the Oxford English Dictionary, the origin of the term 'clinic' is from klinē or 'bed', a point that emphasises the double aspects of passivity inscribed in the position of the 'patient'.) His writings in *A Dying Colonialism* and *WE* further his analysis of the narcissistic psychic insults wrought by racialisation and marginalisation, including hopelessness, boredom, despair and rage—usually meted out to other equally powerless parties. We must not forget, however, that Fanon worked at the practical level with such alienation.

Restoration of Subjective Agentic Capacities: A Psychopolitical Project

A key effect of colonial oppression described by Fanon in *BSWM* is how the white world orients the Negro (as a 'sensitising action') to limit subjective possibilities. Situating the (capacity for) 'action' outside the black subject has devastating effects: 'If his psychic structure is weak, one observes a collapse of the ego. The black man stops behaving as an *actional* person. The goal of his behaviour will be The Other (in the guise of the white man), for The Other alone can give him worth' (p. 109, emphasis in original). Fanon therefore contrasted 'being actional' with being 'reactive'. For Fanon, the impact of this orientation to 'The Other (in the guise of the white man)' produces a challenge '. . . on the ethical level of self-esteem. But there is something else' (p. 109). That 'something else' is what takes Fanon's ideas beyond compensatory or therapeutic discourse into political action. Butler (2015, p. 191) takes a similar view, tracing continuities between *BSWM* and *WE* in her reading of the status of violence in both Sartre's Preface and Fanon's account in that book, to suggest: 'Violence here is not defended as a way of life, and certainly not as a way of imagining the normative goal of a social movement. It is an instrumentality in the service of invention'.

Thus, Fanon's engagement with the question of subjectivity was concerned with undoing the negative 'reactions' created by historical and current everyday oppressive insults, to enable the (re)joining of reflection, affection and action. He therefore recognised that, once installed, even oppression can be hard to give up: shedding the known discomfort of being marginalised demands a subjective, decisive, agentic transformation, a necessary violence perhaps, to transform the psychic effects of alienation, dehumanisation and desubjectification into something else. Whereas Sartre (1961/1963) appealed to a 'full-grown' or mature humanity ('And when one day our human kind becomes full-grown, it will not define itself as the sum total of the whole world's inhabitants, but as the infinite unity of their mutual need' (p. 23)), Fanon can be read as less masculinist and prescriptive in orientation, rather offering a model of relational co-constitution in the service of forging a different future.

Fanon as Therapist

Although some of his medical psychiatric papers are now available (Fanon, 2018), aside from some early joint papers recording treatments, there are few accounts of his specifically therapeutic practice. The only complete therapy we see in *WE* is the account of B-, in what is a damning catalogue of the psychic as well as physical damage wrought by colonial violence (Burman, 2016a, 2019). Fanon's psychoanalytically attuned interventions indicate B-'s symptoms as structured neither as only the effect of political repression (so avoiding a crude sociopolitical reductionism), nor are they only matters of individual pathology/predisposition. Rather, the therapy shows his symptoms as shaped by, and through, *his own reactions to* and complex relationships with historically and socially structured affiliations, including gendered and familial as well as colonial relations. That is, the conflict was internal as well as external; both external and internal conflicts must be addressed for resolution, or resumption of subjective agentic capacities, to be restored.

Unlike other radical psychiatrists and psychoanalysts of his time such as Deleuze, Fanon does not romanticise madness as an escape from societal oppressions or conventions. Rather, even in his resignation letter, he expounds his model of madness is a form of unfreedom: 'Madness is one of the ways that humans have of losing their freedom. And I can say that, placed at this junction, I have measured with terror the extent of the alienation of this country's inhabitants' (Letter to the Resident Minister, Fanon, 1956/2018, p. 434). Madness or distress may therefore arise from, or parallel, other oppressions but it also imports its own impairment of being, such as being subject to compulsions or obsessions, or of being isolated and separated from the social.

At Blida, beyond modernizing the hospital from its brutal carceral regime of chaining patients, Fanon applied the institutional psychotherapy model learnt at Saint-Alban from his mentor Tosquelles (Keller, 2007; Khalfa, 2015). Tosquelles, it should be recalled, was also both a psychoanalyst and a political exile, from Fascist Spain and, like Fanon, he had been active in antifascist struggles. Recall that Fanon had fought for France in the antifascist struggle of the Second World War, and it was because of his military prowess in this that he was funded to study in France. What emerges from their shared political understanding is a commitment to social psychoanalysis, that takes as the central therapeutic project the re-engagement of the sufferer into a social system. In an Editorial, 27 May 1954, no. 23, entitled 'Patients' relations with the outside world of *Notre Journal*, the patient magazine he founded, Fanon emphasised the need to resocialise patients to ward off their isolation and indifference:

> for the entire duration of hospitalization, we must strive to keep intact the links that unite the patient with the outside world. We must insist that patients write to their family and friends as often as possible. We must insist that the patients receive visits as often as possible.
>
> The patient's place in society, in his or her family, must be maintained. This is why the patient has to have a social attitude: writing, receiving news and narrating are some of the most important social activities. It must be seen to that the incoming patient is not desocialized.
>
> (Fanon, 1953–56/2018, pp. 320–321)

As is now well known, Fanon's re-socializing interventions included various cultural activities, including a film club, theatre productions and sewing groups, as well as the hospital magazine (*Notre Journal*). Equally well documented is how these interventions worked well with the European women, but not the Muslim men. This precipitated some reflections on cultural appropriateness of prevailing practices and transformations of provision (Fanon & Azoulay, 1954/2018). Fanon introduced a café for the men, and football groups; he also arranged for the celebration of Muslim festivals and visits of Muslim clerics to hold services. Beyond questions of cultural settings, he also reflected critically on the appropriateness of psychological assessment materials, presenting papers at professional conferences highlighting the meaninglessness of Thematic Apperception personality tests for Muslim women patients, and instigated (though was unable to complete) a process of reformulating a more culturally appropriate set of test materials (see Fanon & Geronimi, 1956/2018). As clinical director, he not only agitated for proper resources (in a context of chronic and massive overcrowding) (Dequeker et al., 1955/2018), but he also opposed the siting of asylums/mental hospitals in isolated, remote places that prevented patients from maintaining contact with their families and their daily lives. He was able to recognize the coercive and isolating aspects of institutionalisation, that psychiatric hospitals are typically experienced as prisons. In particular, he emphasised the role of writing as a means to restore the sense of one's own identity and address to others: 'The discovery of writing is certainly the most beautiful one, since it allows you to recall yourself, to present things that have happened in order and above all to communicate with others, even when they are absent' (Fanon, 1953–65/2018, p. 315). Although Gendzier (1973), among others, suggests that writing was an activity where he felt most at home, nevertheless this is a particularly humanising recommendation that is remarkably prescient of the recent revival of interest in narrative approaches and therapies.

Groups as Therapeutic

Fanon's interventions should be read alongside other contemporary developments in social psychiatry. There are key similarities with Group Analysis, but although Fanon acknowledges Anglo-Saxon models, he shows no evidence of knowledge of the work of Foulkes, the founder of Group Analysis. Perhaps this knowledge was in part through Jacques Lacan, a clear influence on both Tosquelles and Fanon. As I discuss elsewhere (Burman, 2012), Lacan clearly knew about Rickman and Bion's work in the British military hospital, Northfield (described by Harrison, 2000). But, notwithstanding his social account of psychic formation, Lacan's psychoanalytic practice was individual. Perhaps more likely (according to Khalfa (2018) in his editorial framing) is Fanon's awareness of Deleuze and Guattari's groupwork interventions, through the work of Jean Oury.

In terms of clinical implications, it is worth noting that the founder of group analysis, S.H. Foulkes, who like many British psychoanalysts was a refugee, also subscribed to a social model of distress. 'What is inside is outside, the social is not external but very much internal too and penetrates the innermost being of the individual personality' (Foulkes, 1990, p. 227). In Foulkes' (1975) model, like Fanon's, distress is individual, yet its individual features must also be addressed such that 'neurosis itself must be seen as a multipersonal phenomenon' (Foulkes, 1990, p. 206). He too understood distress as a question of isolation, with therapy a process of enabling exchange and communication:

> The language of the symptom, although already a form of communication, is autistic. It mumbles to itself secretly, hoping to be overheard; its equivalent meaning conveyed in words is social. This process of communication is the medium of all other therapeutic agencies. . . . Thus there is a move from symptom to problem, from dream to the conflict underlying the dream.
>
> (Foulkes & Anthony, 1957, pp. 259–260)

One key implication might be to bring British group analysis into closer conversation with Fanon's more explicitly sociopolitical insights. Such groundwork can be seen as underway in accounts that highlight the contribution of Norbert Elias (2000) to group analysis (Burman, 2012; Dalal, 1998), and also use it to interrogate the constitutive cultural role played by structures of racialisation (Dalal, 2001). In summary, it is worth connecting Fanon's practice, especially in its later form when in Tunisia he shifted from institutional psychotherapy to community psychiatry, with both contemporaneous and more recent developments in democratic therapeutic community models.

Groups and the Social Contract, Inside and Outside the Clinic

Many of Fanon's papers, including joint conference papers and publications, were clearly interventions to promote progressive interventions within his professional community. Yet some specific features arising from Fanon's context of practice, and the insights he brought to this, are worthy of attention. For example, his comments on low discharge rates recognise the subjugated position of (usually divorced) Muslim women (Fanon & Azoulay, 1954–5/2018; Fanon & Sanchez, 1956/2018). So, although he clearly understood and changed psychiatric practice to recognise its cultural context, further questions were posed when the social system to which the patient is being encouraged to restore their relation was not benign.

Fanon also indicated he could be critical of the norms of the group, as well as of the conditions that produced the distress—so maintaining an understanding of the psychiatric organisation as a political space. This can be seen in his commitment to engage people as social-cultural beings (as in the adaptations to Blida to work with Muslim male patients)—with the modifications not merely technical (such as the characteristics of the film for a film club, for example) but prompted by the need for their recognition *as persons*. Secondly, as we have seen, he understood (and indeed mobilised) the power of psychological/psychiatric discourse—as indicated by his testimony *as* a psychiatrist in documenting the psychological fallout from the colonial struggle in *WE*. Third, as we see next, he repudiated claims of Muslim 'primitivism' in relation to not confessing their 'crimes', reinterpreting this as a strategy of withholding submission to the colonial social contract. This also therefore indicates as a key political responsibility of the psychological practitioner to attend to and not simply reproduce those dominant norms; a point very relevant to the use of milieu therapy and Therapeutic Communities now, especially in closed institutional environments, such as prisons.

Noteworthy for his analysis of the contested political space in which psychiatric practice occurs is a joint paper (Fanon & Lacaton, 1955/2018) which discussed alternative ways of interpreting anomalies encountered in medico-legal assessments of Algerians in the context of determining responsibility for criminal activities. They argued that, rather than being an indication of 'primitive' thinking, retraction of confessions instead expressed a withholding or refusal of recognition of an exclusionary social system:

> For the criminal to recognize his act before a judge is to disapprove of it, to legitimize the irruption of the public into the private. By denying, by retracting, does the North African not refuse this? What we probably see concretized in this way is the total separation between two social groups that co-exist—alas tragically!—but where the integration of one by the other has not begun. The accused Muslim's refusal to authenticate, by confessing his act, the social contract proposed to him, means that his often profound submission to the powers-that-be (in this instance, the power of the judiciary), which we have noted, cannot be confounded with an acceptance of this power.
>
> (Fanon & Lacaton, 1955/2018, p. 412)

Groups and Psychiatry as Reiterating Oppression

However, some aspects of Fanon's practice should not be emulated. Khalfa and Young attempt to rehabilitate Fanon's apparently more organicist subscription to neurological models (that were prevalent at that time). They suggest that his medical thesis (the one that he wrote in place of his original submission, *BSWM*) in fact intervenes in that reductionist and asocial discourse by highlighting the necessity to see social and relational features structure the experience and prognosis of even a neurologically-generated condition. From this, they propose that Fanon was demonstrating how even the apparently most 'biological' conditions cannot entirely be understood, and certainly not treated, without taking account of how psychological and social issues enter into the historical and embodied subjective experience of the sufferer.

Moreover, Fanon did not only practice psychotherapy. Even if both Tosquelles and Fanon were political revolutionaries, they also practised the dominant psychiatry of their time. Their joint papers, addressed to the professional community and designed to advocate for Tosquelles' institutional therapy model, nevertheless include case histories describing intensive electro-shock and insulin 'therapies' of significant duration, offered to bolster their claims that these were enhanced by their new group and individual therapeutic approaches. Even in his account of the day hospital he established at Tunis, Fanon emphasises how this can still accommodate drug-induced comas and electro-shock sessions, known as either the Bini method or annihilation therapy, explicitly so named on the basis that the maladaptive aspects of the patient's personality should be obliterated and so that more appropriate behaviours and characteristics could be imprinted. Khalfa and Young note: 'The Bini method or electroconvulsive shock therapy is named after Professor Lucio Bini, who delivered the first ever report on the use of electricity to induce a seizure for therapeutic purposes in psychotic patients in . . . 1939' (p. 435). In fact, Bini first noticed this effect in pigs who were stunned before slaughter (Bollorino, Valdrè, & Giannelli, 2012). The invention of this 'method' under political conditions of fascism should be noted. These, then, are aspects of Fanon's psychiatric practice that—true to his own practice of speaking truth to power, we should not shy away from condemning as complicit with an abusive psychiatric system.

Nevertheless, Fanon's psychotherapeutic practice and leadership as a clinical director of a major psychiatric institution highlighted what ethical-political commitments mean in professional practice—including giving refuge to dissidents, providing clinical support to revolutionaries, and resigning a senior professional post when its practice became untenable. This is so, even if some might hesitate to apply their professional knowledge to train guerrillas to cope with their own fear/distress; albeit that the American Psychological Association, like some South African psychologists and psychiatrists during apartheid, have clearly endorsed and practically aided torture, so once again we could see such interventions as simply redressing an already existing imbalance (see also Turner, 2011).

Taking psychotherapeutic issues seriously has implications for political practice, as does attending to bodily experience. The practice of politics should not be at the expense of our mental health; nor should it be a way of dealing with our mental health difficulties (even if ultimately working for a better world must, hopefully, help to repair societal alienation). As with the feminist tenet that 'the personal is political', how we interact with each other in the process of undertaking political activity is itself as political as what we do (Rowbotham, Segal, & Wainwright, 2013).

Yet notwithstanding his political sympathies, we should note Fanon's psychiatric professional commitments were non-partisan, in the sense that he recognised the suffering and distress of the oppressor as well as the oppressed (even the torturer), as indicated by *WE*. This links to his wider educational/ pedagogical orientation.

Education and/Through Therapy

In philosophy, Fanon has been hailed as being better than Foucault (Macherey, 2012) for situating his account of the social construction of identity within a specific material field of social relations (i.e., of colonialism). In education, it has been suggested that Fanon offers a more adequate account of emancipation through decolonisation than Paolo Freire because he engages in less individualising/psychologising (Tuck & Wang, 2012). But important as educational engagements with Fanon have been for illuminating the dynamics of disaffection and exclusion underlying minority students' educational under-attainment (Pellegrini, 2008; Phoenix, 2009), or even the ways globalisation and internationalism of schooling and universities re-insert neo-colonialism and marginalise indigenous knowledges, the full spectrum of Fanon's ideas have yet to be addressed.

At the end of the substantive text of *BSWM*, before his final chapter entitled 'By way of conclusion', Fanon states: 'To educate man to be *actional*, preserving in all his relations his respect for the basic values that constitute a human world, is the prime task of him who, having taken thought, prepares to act' (*BSWM*, p. 158). The notion of 'action' at play traverses the intrapsychic, interpersonal and the political, while Fanon is here foregrounding the question of education and pedagogy. Applying Fanon's ideas to teaching and learning contexts, Leonardo and Porter (2010) take seriously Fanon's conceptualisation of the role of violence as a 'productive force that can be life affirming through its ability to promote mutual recognition' (p. 149). They suggest that 'Fanon leaves us with a dialectical definition of violence, one that accounts for its potential for brutality, but also its power to destroy, create, and unify' (Leonardo & Porter, p. 144). Becoming agentic, restoring a sense of subjective capacity in the context of previous deprivations, is not only a political and therapeutic act. It takes 'effort' on the part of the patient that demands activity, even what might feel to the self as violent activity to shift from inertia, lethargy, resignation or depression into engagement. (This, if it could be regarded as having any legitimacy, was the rationale for Fanon's use of the Bini method.)

Aside from such political 'grandstanding', in his everyday practice as a psychiatrist and psychotherapist, Fanon was an educator. His practice inspired the nurses and doctors he worked with at Blida and then he taught a course at Tunis University for students of social psychology, sociology, psychiatry and philosophy. Understanding the clinic as also a political space meant challenging abusive aspects of his own profession, too. Hence his phenomenological and pedagogical commitments extended to his methods of engaging colleagues/ staff, as well as patients, at Blida. Khalfa (2018) suggest Fanon's first attempts to introduce institutional psychotherapy at Blida, which worked well with European women patients but were a dismal failure with the Muslim men, in fact were a ploy to enlist, inspire and unify staff to back the changes he wanted to introduce. They suggest that this initial failure helped to mobilise the staff to support further, more far-reaching, changes that included controversial (because they were culturally and indigenously sensitive) adaptations to the organisation and daily life of the hospital (including creating a café for the Muslim men, a radio station, and the celebration of Muslim festivals).

Applications to Antiracist Pedagogies

Fanon has a key place in the recent interest connecting educational with therapeutic development and the role of psychological well-being in enabling or impeding learning, albeit that we might draw from his analyses some caution about where the debilitating aspects reside. Indeed, violence is a theme that has characterised much discussion in educational research, typically mobilising Bourdieusian accounts of symbolic violence, as well as other post-colonial-inspired accounts of epistemic violence (Spivak, 1988). Spivak is of course recognised as a key figure in the postcolonial revival of interest in Fanon (Gates, 1991). Given the relative importance accorded Bourdieu rather than Fanon in educational theory, it is worth noting that Bourdieu is known to have read and drawn upon Fanon's work (Calhoun, 2006; Galloway, 2015; Go, 2013; Haddour, 2010; von Holdt, 2013), even if he disagreed with Fanon's conclusions. Indeed, Fanon and Bourdieu were working (as part of the French colonial administration) in Algeria at the same time.

Elsewhere (Burman, 2019), I suggest that antiracist pedagogical strategies can be illuminated by close reading of Fanon's narrative structuring and strategies. I explore the significance of Chapter 5 of *BSWM*, 'The fact of blackness', in which the famous 'Look, a Negro!' incident takes place, as the middle chapter of the book. This is the place where Fanon describes the trauma, the 'amputation' from the social, the nausea induced by becoming racialised as other and his body abjected and 'epidermalized'. The graphic and extended stream of associations violently evoked fills the page between a child's racist hailing and the mother's intervention (and much before and after this, too). I consider the significance and status of the child in apparently precipitating all this, as well as that of the mother. But here I want to emphasise how his account performatively highlights not only how and why Fanon, as the now black/ened man, fails to hear what is said, but also how he also supplies more around it. In so doing, Fanon offers a powerful narrative illustration of how traumatic experiences work to fix or paralyse the subject, such that they are prevented from being open and receptive to new relational possibilities.

Even in this famous rendering of the narcissistic injury of racialisation, a pedagogy of (opposing) violence can be seen at work. Closer reading of the text indicates how, in the space of one and a half pages, Fanon moves from a position of absolute abjection, or rejection from the intersubjective field, to one of agency. Further, Fanon's narrative suggests that it is the mother's (albeit woefully inadequate) attempt at engagement that shifts him from abjection to the domain of possible relationship. This shift detaches him enough from absorption in the torrent of collective traumas that comprise racism to enable him to be 'set free from those ruminations' (p. 81), restoring his position as subject, albeit an angry one. He is ready to fight back: 'The field of battle having been marked out . . . I had incisors to test. I was sure they were strong' (*BSWM*, p. 81). What Fanon demonstrates in the structure of his text is, literally, the narrative space of the 'rumination', a rumination (of the chain of insulting associations set in motion or rekindled by the child's utterance) that is finally broken by his response to the mother. From being alienated from his own body and excluded from the social field by the 'othering' of 'Look, a Negro!', he is at least restored to the interpersonal field by the mother.

Moreover, it is the 'shame' flooding her face that frees Fanon/the narrator 'from my ruminations. At the same time I accomplished two things: I identi-fied my enemies and I made a scene. A grand slam. Now one would be able to laugh' (*BSWM*, p. 81). That is, the mother's attempt at least enabled him to respond, to act; in this case, to oppose and resist, to name her as 'enemy'. The mother's shame, it must be noted, was generated not at the boy's racist hail-ing but at Fanon's rejection of her racialised 'compliment' on his appearance. This at least acknowledges some level of reciprocal impact so that they coexist within a relational, intersubjective field. It is surely an improvement from hav-ing been excised from this. The mother's embarrassing attempt was productive in at least enabling the racialised subject to respond, to act; in this case, to oppose and resist, to name her as 'enemy'.

Revisiting the Narrative Arc of 'Look, a Negro!'

As with his clinical case histories in *WE*, I suggest that Fanon's narrative indicates a therapeutic pedagogy that can be read from the structure of his account. Fanon traces other emotional transitions that follow from the trau-matic encounter: from expulsion/exclusion (and its nausea) to rage/outrage (and the desire to resist/fight back). He describes the anguish of abjection and exploration of strategies available to the subject of dealing with this, including affirming the very qualities that are the source of the rejection. But by the end of *BSWM*, even of the chapter, Fanon offers other ways of proceeding, reflect-ing his radical humanist commitments that foresee a time when black and white are no longer functioning as defining, or even meaningful, categorisations.

What makes his model psychosocial is the way that Fanon's humanist commitments—demanding recognition and relationship—coexist with both his psychoanalytic and political engagements. It is psychoaffective in linking the body and emotions with lived history and relationships. Finally, across his writ-ings, Fanon's model of the subject is psychoanalytic in that it is as much internally conflicted as externally driven and constrained, albeit that the internal conflicts arise through the external events and current relational encounters. Hence the 'ruminations' arise from experience but also interfere with them. Fanon's depic-tions of the various stages of processing and the role of particular responses (or lack of responses) highlight the need to engage external constraints to enable new conditions of possibility to liberate the individual from those conflicts, to be bet-ter able to forge relationships with others that can support joint action.

This is where we can see connections with postcolonial (psycho-)educational discussions of pedagogies of dissensus, discomfort, dissolution (Andreotti, 2011). The dissolution advocated here, as a project of subjective destabilisation in the service of the building of new positions, might in some circumstances be intrusive, paternalistic, even violent (Burman, 2016b). Benign interventions may indeed be experienced as such, even as the insertion of therapeutic approaches into education (in the name of 'soft skills' considered necessary for neoliberal knowledge-based economies) can work to import socioeconomic agendas into educational and mental health concerns to further subjective regulation and (self)surveillance (Burman, 2009, 2019; Ecclestone & Hayes, 2009; Irisdotter Aldenmyr & Olson, 2016). But even if they address current perversions of a therapeutic agenda into an adaptive pedagogy for neoliberal citizens, these analyses perhaps risk oversimplifying the complex subjective inter-relations that Fanon was able to discern in the formulation of symptoms. Similarly, even well-intentioned 'social justice'-oriented educational interventions risk performing aspects of the violence they seek to redress, by instigating encounters that are potentially retraumatising for the victims of oppression and so anxiety-provoking for participants that the kind of openness and self-questioning that Fanon gestured towards as necessary for genuine communication and (self-) transformation becomes impossible. This is in part what Worsham (1998) cautions against, whereas Britzman (2003) counters the omnipotence of the educator by highlighting how the work of educational transformation is in part a matter of individual working through. Nevertheless, as Bailey (2017) also acknowledges, some discomfort may be necessary to learning and change.

Psychotherapists know these dilemmas. Any therapy has to provide a balance between support and exploration; too much exploration and the client may become too destabilised to tolerate the process; too little and their maladaptive defences are simply being shored up. Fanon offers an account of thwarting the patient's desire to be told what to do as thereby enabling him to authorise himself. This is surely ethical-political practice in action, and Fanon does indeed depict this action as occurring in the anticipation of an 'independence' that links the individual and the social.

Clinical Conclusions?

Fanon's radical humanism prefigured the possibility of mutuality and reciprocity across racialised divisions. His pedagogy of perpetual questioning, at the end of *BSWM*, envisaged and performatively invoked this not on the basis of reconciliation but on just recognition, narratively attempting to prefigure the conditions of possibility for such transformed relations and the sense of healing and benefit this could bring.

Yet to single Fanon out would be to desocialise and essentialise, even to psychologise, him in ways that his analyses directly oppose. Rather, his life and work exemplify why and how the domains of therapy and politics, the personal and the political, must be linked together. Similarly, we have seen how the question of violence comes to the fore, as the condition of distress but also—at the level of the subject—as a vital component in resisting it.

Other examples can be found of psychoanalysts, psychotherapists and even psychiatrists who were politicised through and alongside their therapeutic practice. The South African psychoanalyst, Wulf Sachs, was led by his psychoanalytic inquiry into the mental life of an ordinary black man into not only supporting his family and community, but into other political forms of solidarity and action (Sachs, 1996). There are other subjugated histories of radical engagement of mental health practice, especially psychoanalytic practice, as in Marie Langer's work in Nicaragua (Langer, 1989), or even the psychoanalytic clinics that were established in Berlin and Vienna, offering free therapy to men, women and children, including groupwork, that flourished until they were shut down with the rise of Nazism (Danto, 2005). Hence while clearly Fanon was an exceptional and inspirational figure, this does not prevent us from learning from his practice, in relation both to what we might also be able to do, as therapists and educators, but also what not to do.

References

Andreotti, V. (2011). *Actionable postcolonial theory in education*. Basingstoke: Palgrave Macmillan.

Bailey, A. (2017). Tracking privilege-preserving epistemic pushback in feminist and critical race philosophy classes. *Hypatia, 32*(4), 876–892.

Bollorino, F., Valdrè, R., & Giannelli, M. V. (2012). Ugo Cerletti and the discovery of electroshock: An imaginary interview. *Psychiatry Online, Italia*. Retrieved from www.psychiatryonline.it/node/2094.

Britzman, D. (2003). *After-education: Anna Freud, Melanie Klein, and psycho-analytic histories of learning*. Albany: SUNY Press.

Burman, E. (2009). Beyond emotional literacy in feminist and educational research. *British Education Research Journal*, (35:1): 137–156.

Burman, E. (2012). Group acts and missed encounters: Lacan and Foulkes. *Lacunae, 1*(2), 23–42.

Burman, E. (2016a). Fanon, Foucault, feminisms: Psychoeducation, theoretical psychology, and political change. *Theory & Psychology, 26*(6), 706–730.

Burman, E. (2016b). Fanon's Lacan and the traumatogenic child: Psychoanalytic reflections on the dynamics of colonialism and racism. *Theory, Culture & Society, 33*(4), 77–101.

Burman, E. (2019). *Fanon, education, action: Child as method*. Abingdon: Brunner Routledge.

Butler, J. (2015). *Senses of the subject*. New York: Fordham University Press.

Calhoun, C. (2006). Pierre Bourdieu and social transformation: Lessons from Algeria. *Development and Change, 37*(6), 1403–1415.

Dalal, F. (1998). *Taking the group seriously: Towards a post-Foulkesian group analytic theory*. London: Jessica Kingsley.

Dalal, F. (2001). *Race, colour and the processes of racialisation: New perspectives from psychoanalysis, group analysis and sociology*. London: Routledge.

Danto, E. A. (2005). *Freud's free clinics: Psychoanalysis & social justice, 1918–1938*. New York: Columbia University Press.

Dequeker, J., Fanon, F., Lacaton, R., Micucci, M., & Ramée, F. (1955/2018). Current aspects of mental assistance in Algeria. In F. Fanon (Ed.), *Alienation and freedom* (pp. 395–404). London: Bloomsbury.

Ecclestone, K., & Hayes, D. (2009). *The dangerous rise of therapeutic education.* London: Routledge.

Elias, N. (2000). *The civilising process* (revised ed.). London: Blackwell, originally published (in German) in 1939, first published in English in 1973.

Fanon, F. (1952/1970). *Black skin, white masks* (C. L. Markmann, Trans.). London: Paladin.

Fanon, F. (1953–1965/2018) Our journal. In *Alienation and freedom.* (pp. 311–349). London: Bloomsbury.

Fanon, F. (1955/2018). Ethnopsychiatric considerations. In F. Fanon (Ed.), *Alienation and freedom* (pp. 405–408). London: Bloomsbury.

Fanon, F. (1956/2018). Letter to resident minister. In *Alienation and freedom* (pp. 433–436). London: Bloomsbury.

Fanon, F. (1959/1965). *A dying colonialism* (H. Chevalier, Trans.). New York: Grove Press.

Fanon, F. (1960/2018). Why we use violence (address to the Accra positive action conference, April 1960). In F. Fanon (Ed.), *Alienation and freedom* (pp. 653–660). London: Bloomsbury.

Fanon, F. (1961/1963). *The wretched of the earth* (C. Farrington, Trans.). London: Penguin.

Fanon, F. (1964/1967). *Toward the African revolution: Political essays* (H. Chevalier, Trans.). New York: Grove Press.

Fanon, F. (2018). *Alienation and freedom* (J. Khalfa & R. J. C. Young, Eds., S. Corcoran, Trans.). London: Bloomsbury.

Fanon, F., & Azoulay, J. (1954/2018). Social therapy in a ward of Muslim men: Methodological difficulties. In F. Fanon (Ed.), *Alienation and freedom* (pp. 353–372). London: Bloomsbury.

Fanon, F., & Azoulay, J. (1954–1955/2018). Daily life in the douars. In F. Fanon (Ed.), *Alienation and freedom* (pp. 373–374). London: Bloomsbury.

Fanon, F., & Geronimi, C. (1956/2018). TAT with Muslim women, sociology of perception and imagination. In *Alienation and freedom* (pp. 427–432). London: Bloomsbury.

Fanon, F., & Lacaton, R. (1955/2018). Conducts of confession in North Africa. In F. Fanon (Ed.), *Alienation and freedom* (pp. 409–412). London: Bloomsbury.

Fanon, F., & Sanchez, F. (1956/2018). Maghrebin Muslims and their attitudes towards madness. In F. Fanon (Ed.), *Alienation and freedom* (pp. 421–426). London: Bloomsbury.

Foulkes, S. H. (1975). *Group analytic psychotherapy: Methods and principles.* London: Maresfield.

Foulkes, S. H. (1990). *Selected papers: Psychoanalysis and group analysis.* London: Karnac.

Foulkes, S. H., & Anthony, E. (1957). *Group psychotherapy: The psychoanalytic approach.* Harmondsworth: Pelican.

Freire, P. (1972). *Pedagogy of the oppressed* (M. B. Ramos, Trans.). New York: Herder and Herder.

Galloway, S. (2015). What's missing when empowerment is a purpose for adult literacies education? Bourdieu, Gee and the problem of accounting for power. *Studies in the Education of Adults, 47*(1), 49–63.

Gates, H. L. (1991). Critical Fanonism. *Critical Inquiry, 17*(3), 457–470.

Gendzier, I. (1973). *Frantz Fanon: A critical study.* London: Wildwood House.

Gibson, N. C. (2011). Living Fanon? In N. C. Gibson (Ed.), *Living Fanon: Global perspectives* (pp. 1–10). New York: Palgrave Macmillan.

Go, J. (2013). Decolonizing Bourdieu: Colonial and postcolonial theory in Pierre Bourdieu's early work. *Sociological Theory*, *31*(1), 49–74.

Gordon, L. R. (2015). *What Fanon said: A philosophical introduction to his life and thought*. New
York: Fordham University Press.

Haddour, A. (2010). Torture unveiled: Rereading Fanon and Bourdieu in the context of
May 1958. *Theory, Culture & Society*, *27*(7–8), 66–90.

Hallward, P. (2011). Fanon and political will. *Cosmos and History: The Journal of Natural and
Social Philosophy*, *7*(1), 104–127.

Harrison, T. (2000). *Bion, Rickman, Foulkes and the Northfield experiments: Advancing on a different front*. London: Jessica Kingsley.

Hudis, P. (2015). *Frantz Fanon: Philosopher of the barricades*. London: Pluto Press.

Irisdotter Aldenmyr, S., & Olson, M. (2016). The inward turn in therapeutic education:
An individual enterprise promoted in the name of the common good. *Pedagogy, Culture &
Society*, *24*(3), 387–400.

Keller, R. (2007). Clinician and revolutionary: Frantz Fanon, biography, and the history
of colonial medicine. *Bulletin of the History of Medicine*, *81*(4), 823–841.

Khalfa, J. (2015). Fanon and psychiatry. *Nottingham French Studies*, *54*(1), 52–71.

Khalfa, J. (2018). 'Fanon, revolutionary psychiatrist'. In *Alienation and freedom*. (pp.167–
202). London: Bloomsbury.

Kuby, E. (2015). "Our Actions Never Cease to Haunt Us": Frantz Fanon, Jean-Paul
Sartre, and the violence of the Algerian War. *Historical Reflections / Reflexions Historiques*,
41(3), 59–78.

Langer, M. (1989). *From Vienna to Managua: Journey of a psychoanalyst*. London: Free Association Books.

Leonardo, Z., & Porter, R. K. (2010). Pedagogy of fear: Toward a Fanonian theory of
"safety" in race dialogue. *Race Ethnicity and Education*, *13*(2), 139–157.

Macherey, P. (2012). Figures of interpellation in Althusser and Fanon. *Radical Philosophy*,
173: 9–20.

Pellegrini, A. (2008). What do children learn at school? Necropedagogy and the future
of the dead child. *Social Text*, *26*(4), 97–105.

Phoenix, A. (2009). De-colonising practices: Negotiating narratives from racialised and
gendered experiences of education. *Race, Ethnicity & Education*, *12*(1), 101–114.

Rowbotham, S., Segal, L., & Wainwright, H. (2013). *Beyond the fragments: Feminism and the
making of socialism*. London: Merlin Press.

Sachs, W. (1996). *Black Hamlet*. Originally published in 1937. New introduction by Saul
Dubow and Jacqueline Rose. Baltimore: Johns Hopkins University Press.

Sartre, J. P. (1961/1963). Preface to Fanon. F. *The Wretched of the Earth* (C. Farrington,
Trans.). London: Penguin.

Spivak, G. C. (1988). Can the subaltern speak? In C. Nelson & L. Grossman (Eds.), *Marxism and the interpretation of culture* (pp. 217–313). Urbana: University of Illinois Press.

Tuck, E., & Wang, K. W. (2012). Decolonization is not a metaphor. *Decolonization: Indige-
neity, Education & Society*, *1*(1), 1–40.

Turner, L. (2011). Fanon and the bio-politics of torture: Contextualising psychological practices as tools of war. In N. C. Gibson (Ed.), *Living Fanon: Global perspectives*
(pp. 117–130). New York: Palgrave.

von Holdt, K. (2013). The violence of order, orders of violence: Between Fanon and
Bourdieu. *Current Sociology*, *61*(2), 112–131.

Worsham, L. (1998). Going postal: Pedagogic violence and the schooling of emotion.
JAC, 213–245.

5 The Psychic Life of History

Migration, Critical Ethno-Psychiatry, and the Archives of the Future

Roberto Beneduce

In recent years the debate on ethnopsychiatry and how to cure immigrant patients has raised questions and conflicts on the role of cultural belonging in the forms of symptoms, in the experience of suffering, and in the choice between different types of treatment. Reflections on the need to resort to interpretative models deriving from the universe of supposedly "traditional" therapies (Nathan, 1994), or criticism of the risks of reproducing through this return to cultures concealed forms of "ghettoizing the outskirts"[1] and reproducing a colonial psychiatry (Fassin, 2000, p. 238), have given rise to not a few polemics, particularly in France, where ethnopsychiatry actually seemed to call into question the principles of the republican state to the advantage of "communities" and "cultural" or "identitarian isolationism."

Thus, against a background of questions originally limited to anthropological theory or cultural psychiatry (how do symbols work during therapeutic rituals? are traditional cures effective or do they only achieve provisional changes? and so on), a series of cruxes and questions have been emerging that concern not only clinical work, but are essentially political, regarding both the anxieties of the host societies and the immigrants themselves, their demand for cures, their loyalty to the values of the welcoming countries, and their own cultural belonging.

Research in the colonial archives has brought to light other questions, including the long-lasting effects of historical traumas like slavery, the colonization and violence that marked them, as well as the specific forms of suffering connected to forms of "cultural genocide" (or, by contrast, the therapeutic value of interventions that are moored to a society's own symbolic horizons and effective when they can refresh a shared memory and a degree of sovereignty and political subjectivity) (Anderson & Kowal, 2012; Chandler & Lalonde, 1998).

Another underlying question in the debate is that of the limits of psychiatric knowledge, which is complicit—given the proliferation of its diagnostic categories, which have passed from 106 in the 1952 edition of the DSM to 374 in the 2013 edition (Cohen, 2016, pp. 2–3)—with a widespread medicalization of suffering (Hacking, 1995), particularly in marginal groups and minorities. In its incapacity to handle other idioms of suffering and other ontologies of experience, silent in the face of the threat of institutional racism (or "cryptoracism;" Beneduce & Martelli, 2005, p. 367), Western psychiatry has sometimes ended up reproducing styles adopted in the colonial era toward alterity. Very often, however, when it has wanted to recognize the importance of a cultural framework in which to situate symptoms and experiences, it has forgotten the social and political reasons for suffering.

An approach that seeks to resist this spiral should be able to articulate a political analysis of alienation with a theory that can decipher the effects of historical traumas in the incrustations of the post-colonial unconscious (Nandy, 1983) and at the same time construct an idea of culture that is adequate to what is at stake, one that entails curing suffering in the immigrant population.

The critical and radical ethnosychiatry dealt with here aims to combine consideration of the world of subalterns and their demand for recognition with a rigorous analysis of those "minor" forms of knowledge (to paraphrase Deleuze & Guattari, 1986) that have often been too easily labeled as "beliefs" or "traditional etiologies." The project that has taken shape in this horizon of ideas is one that draws on Fanon's work on colonial alienation, and Gramsci's and de Martino's on the cultural world of the subaltern classes, to try and imagine a different alliance among ethnography, ethnopsychiatry and psychoanalysis, centered on listening to the other, and the words and ravings of the other: listening to their "truth" rather than simply "understanding" them (Lacan, 1993, pp. 21–49).

The work dealt with here, which originated in the analysis of the narratives and traumatic memories of immigrant patients, seeks, in the end, to explore and interrogate the historical and political significance of their cultural past, suggesting an idea of "culture" that is freed of the false alternative between cultural tyranny on the one hand and the reproduction of universal categories on the other (the latter being a risk that has been reproduced in many famous ethnographies).[2]

Fanon, a "Symptomatic Reading" of Alienation

In his last book, *The Wretched of the Earth*, Fanon devoted an entire chapter to the mental disturbances that had arisen during the colonial war, and once again formulated a radical criticism of colonial psychiatry and of one principle, above all: the supposed criminality of Algerians ("The Algerian is an habitual killer [. . .] The Algerian is a savage killer [. . .] The Algerian is a senseless killer") (Fanon, 2004, p. 222). His analysis of the relation between violence, the liberation struggle and psychological suffering suggests a specific correlation between colonial war, psychiatric knowledge and the difficulties of curing *this* suffering. It also liberates the problem of social violence from the potential banality of cultural interpretations. His suggestions offered guidelines for a clinical approach anchored in history and the political; the foundation of that critical and radical ethno-psychiatry will be discussed in the following.

Faced with a history that continued to agonize and oppress those whom de Martino called "the last" (de Martino, 1949), and living at a period that was poisoned by racism and injustice, Fanon explored the darkest recesses of racial prejudice in the Antilles, the ambivalent feelings and imaginary of a nervous society and the complicity of the social and psychological sciences. He also set out his project to try and escape the determinism of the past.[3]

Fanon knew, of course, that the struggle against racial alienation is an unending duel: an *impossible* task, one that constantly returns to the beginning, not unlike the anti-colonial struggle which, immediately after independence, found itself having to cope with the selfishness and interests of the national élites. And the memory of past humiliations, losses and terror, even when transformed into myths or forgotten in the archives of history, would continue to cause pain, would become a symptom—"affective erethism" or "delusional intuition" (Fanon, 2008, pp. 42–43).[4]

The contempt and violence inflicted upon the colonized set off an infinite autoscopic process, generating the impulse to wonder constantly *where* one's humanity was, *what* one desired: "Because it is a systematized negation of the other, a frenzied determination to deny the other any attribute of humanity, colonialism forces the colonized to constantly ask the question: 'Who am I in reality?'" (Fanon, 2004, p. 182).[5]

It is a radical question, and one which seeds the premises of a subversive anthropology, designed to think of a *historical subject*, and to always connect the subject's position to the specific relations of power and meaning that have at different times molded, classified, excluded or subjugated them. Kelly Oliver (2004) reformulates the question in these terms: "What happens to someone's sense of herself as a subject and her sense of her subjectivity or agency when she is objectified through discrimination, domination, oppression, enslavement, or torture?" (p. 4).

Ultimately, Fanon's inquiry is a question about the historical consciousness of the oppressed, the morality of the dominated and the perception of the world by those who have seen their humanity measured, animalized and negated, experiencing the mutation of their body and their life into a tamed means of production.

Similar questions would also be posed by writers like Ashis Nandy (1983) in relation to colonial and post-colonial India, by Rita Laura Segato (2006) in Brazil, and by Cedric Robinson (1983) who, recalling the relation between African laborers, slavery and the production requirements of the European empires, wrote:

> the more authentic question was not whether the slaves (and the ex-slaves and their descendants) were human. It was, rather, just *what sort of people they were . . . and could be.* Slavery altered the conditions of their being, but it could not negate their being. Long before the troubled American republic of the nineteenth century even became a possibility, a part of the answer began its unfolding. As we shall soon see, its *historical imprint is still clear.*
>
> (p. 166; italics mine)

These contributions, which I return to below, are decisive for imagining a clinical psychiatry or a critical, "litigant" (Segato, 2015) anthropology able to articulate the formation of the (postcolonial) subject *with* the formation of the nation state; subjectivity, desire and the Oedipal *with* the racial origins of the modern state and its institutions—and equally so in both the colonial and post-colonial context. Fanon's interest in the literary work of Richard Wright in fact offers the outline of a coherent project that aims to combine sociology, literature, politics and psychoanalysis: a project that he pursued untiringly and first articulated in *"La plainte du Noir"*, an article published in the journal *Esprit* in 1951 and reprinted in *Black Skin, White Masks*.

Fanon would later make a fundamental contribution to thinking in America where, from the 1930s on, psychologists and psychiatrists made the racial question central to their practice. The experiments of Kenneth and Mamie Clark on the consequences of racism in the processes of racial identification in black children (i.e., the Doll Test and the Coloring Test) (Clark & Clark, 1939, 1940, 1950),[6] or the Lafargue clinic in Harlem, opened by Frederick Wertham in 1946 to respond to the care needs of the black population of Harlem, had already clearly suggested that only a psychology and a psychiatry able to consider the psychic effects of racism would be able to understand and cure the suffering of minorities and the effects on psychological development and mental health of a racist society.[7]

Fanon would examine the consequences of an internalization of racial prejudices mediated by laws, speeches, bans and representations, whose effect would be a self-alienating identification, a corporeal schema determined not by somatic experiences but by the gaze of the other (Marriott, 2010):

> Below the corporeal schema I had sketched a historical-racial schema. The elements that I used had been provided for me not by "residual sensations and perceptions primarily of a tactile, vestibular, kinesthetic, and visual character," but by the other, the white man, who had woven me out of a thousand details, anecdotes, stories.
>
> (Fanon, 2008, p. 84)

This was an extraordinary intuition, one which conceives history and symptoms as *palimpsests* (Beneduce, 2016, 2017; Gordon, 2008), and suggests a "symptomatic reading" of literary texts, alienation violence as well as of history itself.[8]

Fanon set himself a goal that shifted and expanded in the various locations of his activities and his meetings, bringing to light unexpected problems, hidden connections and new theoretical objects: in Martinique with Césaire, in France with Tosquelles or Sartre, in Blida and Tunisia with the militants of the FLN who had been tortured by the French army. He explored the enigmas of suffering in a different and new way; a *symptomatic* reading that would not spare himself or his choices, and that showed how the spasmodic search for recognition and the need to be seen could become the mark of a pathology characteristic of the oppressed (Oliver, 2001). The effect would be to finally bring to the surface what had been timidly emerging in the writings of psychoanalysts like Wulf Sachs and Octave Mannoni, and in the novels of Mayotte Capécia, Abdoulaye Sadji and Richard Wright: the link between colonialism, psychoanalysis and social sciences, between "colonial situation" and alienation, between experience of slavery and its protracted psychological consequences.[9] But what Fanon witnessed in Algeria imposed a different rhythm on reading history and on his idea of psychiatry and psychological curing.

Fanon was aware that the pages devoted to mental disorders—in a work till then consisting of analysis of the colonial city, scenes of massacres, or of the contradictions in the national culture—might surprise the reader, appear "untimely" and extraneous. He argued, however, that those reflections are nevertheless inevitable.[10]

The criticism of colonial psychiatry or of the silence of psychoanalysis now takes on darker tones, and the limits of psychiatry or of its diagnostic categories, once attributed essentially to methodological errors or racial prejudices, are here placed in direct relation to the very nature of the suffering generated by the colonial war, to the "countless and sometimes indelible wounds" (Fanon, 2004, p. 8) inflicted on the Algerian people. Fanon's argument is, once again, developed with scalpel-like precision.

The mental disturbances that arose during the early phases of colonization, when the collapse of the resistance and the triumph of colonial oppression fomented "a constant and considerable stream of mental symptoms" (Fanon, 2004) were overlaid by those caused by seven years of war, but classical psychiatry proved inadequate in dealing with these latter, for at least two reasons. First, Fanon (2004) questioned the very notion of "psychotic reaction," which was used by war psychiatry, as it was unable to take account of an immense tragedy: "We believe that in the cases presented here the triggering factor is principally the bloody, *pitiless atmosphere*, the generalization of inhuman practices, of people's lasting impression that they are witnessing a *veritable apocalypse*" (p. 183; my italics). In addition, faced with a war that had all the characteristics of genocide, even the physiognomy of the symptoms was *new*; the benign prognoses suggested for the mental disturbances observed during the two world wars did not apply to the war in Algeria, where disturbances tended to be "frequently malignant [. . . .] In all evidence *the future of these patients is compromised*" (Ibid., pp. 183–84; my italics). As he had noted a few years earlier in another work,[11] the legacy of a war with the features of an apocalypse would be painful and deep: the personality of Algerians and Algerian society as a whole would for a long time be "compromised" (*hypothéquées*).

What theoretical project arises from these reflections? Why do I insist on defining Fanon's work as a critical, dynamic and radical ethno-psychiatry? And above all: why do I not hesitate to find in his writings and practice the indispensable premises for a clinical approach to migration today? The reflections that follow try to answer these questions, mixing heterogeneous theoretical contributions and thoughts deriving from my clinical ethnography at the Fanon Centre.[12]

An Unsleeping History

I met Majid, a young North African man 17 years old, and his parents many years ago. It was at the Fanon Centre with Alla Lahcen, a Moroccan mediator. Our small group (as well as Lahcen and myself, there were two psychologists and two interns) began to talk to the family (Majid's parents and his sister), following what was our standard procedure.

A psychotherapeutic group is often the first step toward the patient finding a voice, which reconstitutes the dignity and attention necessary for one to be able to recount and remember one's experience. It is a time-space that has been constructed for speaking what has long been shut away, thrust back into oblivion, made secret, and at the same time rejecting the illusory reassurance of readymade diagnoses like "Antisocial Behaviour," "Oppositional Defiant Disorder" or "Disruptive mood dysregulation disorder"—diagnoses that had been made by the health services and that had done nothing to increase the understanding that Majid and his family had of their problems. The paternal grandfather—an Algerian—had enlisted in the French army in the colonial period, and later moved with his family to Morocco after independence to flee the retaliation against those who had collaborated with the occupying army. Majid's father found work there and married a Moroccan woman (who would become Majid's mother). Following the Algerian-Moroccan conflict, the Sands War of 1963, the two governments decided to expel each other's workers from their countries. Majid's father, however, could not return to Algeria, where the son of a *harki* would encounter hostility and reprisals, but nor could he remain in Morocco. He then took the decision to emigrate to Europe—first to Spain and then to Italy, where he tried to start a new life.

Algeria no longer appears in the memories and words of this man. Forced to abandon Morocco because he was an Algerian citizen, at first he left on his own. His wife joined him some years later. However, Majid's childhood and the life of the whole family was marked by a tragic event: a maternal uncle, who had also emigrated to Turin a few years earlier and to whom Majid was very close, was murdered in obscure circumstances. This marked the beginning of a slow spiral of decline.

During a meeting Majid mentioned his mother's constant references to the possibility that he too might repeat his uncle's tragic destiny: it was a prophecy that obsessed him. Described as an intelligent but feckless lad (at one meeting his sister, who was a year older, said: "If I had just half his intelligence! But he wastes it."), Majid gradually became more and more withdrawn, inaccessible and aggressive. He stole money at home, often got into fights with neighbours, and ran away from his family countless times. One day, at one of our meetings, no sooner had he sat down than he shouted at me, "What do you know about Sétif?"[13]

Majid's question was the echo of an inaccessible past (how often must his father have remained silent about his memories?), a disputed memory. This silence, this mutilated time, is a widely common experience in migrant families coming from countries that knew massacres and violence (as in the case of civil war in Nigeria, or in 1990s in Congo). In the same way, Algerian colonial history, its massacres, the fratricide that characterized colonial war, are rarely remembered between parents and children. That past remains an amputee past. Its wounds continue to generate painful conflicts, like a phantom limb (Lazali, 2018, p. 107).

The violence of numbers forces us to reflect in this case too on the meaning and effects of a quantitative difference: what does it mean that the French sources have spoken of *only* 1000 dead, while the Egyptian and Algerian sources of the period put the figure at 45,000 dead? Where did those dead end up, who seem to have left no trace in the registers and the archives?

When remembering becomes a dangerous act, the only possible testimony becomes silence—as with his father and grandfather—or symptom. Majid often went out secretly at night, sometimes climbing out of a window, and was found the next morning by his father or friends of the family, still half asleep inside a car he had forced open to sleep in. What are these "escapes" a metaphor of? His grandfather's escape from Algeria? Or his father's? His gesture was that of an exile and it was repeated incessantly as if to escape the "curse of being nothing" (I am borrowing here a formula from Wacquant, cited by Jewsiewicki, 1988). It was a wandering among the ruins of a present that did not belong to him, as happened to many Algerians whose land and language and culture were segregated and humiliated.

Though the family had achieved relative economic stability in Italy, Majid's problems began to ruffle their calm and serenity. During one of his stays in Morocco, his mother convinced Majid to go with her to a *fkih* (a traditional healer), despite his father's scepticism. His response was negative: there was nothing wrong with him, his problems were not caused by the presence of a *jinn*, he only needed a psychiatrist. During the sitting (*hādra*), however, his mother fell into a trance and experienced a fit of possession.[14] Upon awaking, she claimed to remember nothing, yet the episode in itself brought to the surface the woman's past suffering, her contact with an alterity (possession by spirits) that, like the sleeping relics de Certeau (1997) speaks of, seemed suddenly to reawaken painfully.

On returning to Italy, Majid stopped studying and became more and more surly with his family. There were suspicions he was mixing with young Moroccans involved in drug-dealing. His mother regarded him as "abnormal, crazy," his father's gaze betrayed profound solitude and the traces of a deception that he had never been able to share. To escape a situation of intolerable uncertainty, the family decided to ask for Italian citizenship. At one meeting we were speaking with Majid about this and the need to help the family, particularly now, after an accident at the workplace had seriously limited his father's use of his right hand. Majid, however, seemed distant and indifferent to the concerns of the family.

Majid, thinner and more tense than usual, returned on his own: he remained stubbornly silent when Lahcen spoke to him, and insisted he needed nothing, wanted nothing, asking aggressively before leaving the room, why he was in a centre for immigrants: just another form of racism. A few weeks later, his mother convinced him to meet another *fkih*, for whom Majid's flights and behaviour had a specific cause: that he was possessed by a "tourist *jinn*" who was making him restless and driving him to run away and go on a journey.

The family was on the point of receiving Italian citizenship when Majid committed a crime, putting an end to all hope for him on this score. It was another laceration for the family: all of them, except for Majid, had become Italian citizens. As with his grandfather before him, as with his father in Morocco, a political decree, an *act of law*, had severed the link between members of the family and changed its destiny.

A few months later we lost track of Majid, until one day we received a call from Algeria: the Algerian police had arrested a young man without documents, who claimed to have entered the country via Morocco and to be seeing a psychiatrist in Italy. The authorities wanted to check his identity and the truth of his claims.

What Does This Story Suggest?

Three generations continue to be caught in the mesh of the colonial tragedy, of memories still awaiting redemption. The condition of the *harki* is a still open wound for France as for Algeria: taken in at the end of the war, they long lived in wretched, precarious conditions; a significant percentage (around 70,000) were abandoned in Algeria, where their fate was often terrible. This too was part of the colonial situation: a scalpel that cut into the colonized societies, fomenting ambivalence and turning it into suspicion and hatred and pitting the Algerians against each other.[15]

After being frozen for thirty years, there was a new upsurge in the violence of the colonial war in 1992, when the civil war caused more than 70,000 deaths. Stora has no hesitation in using the clinical formula "acting out" to describe the explosion of this violence (Stora, 1998, p. II). As in Balandier (1951), the language of psychopathology seems, strangely, to be the only one able to give a name to the social conflicts and violence of colonial times as well as to the "colonial racism" that is re-emerging in present-day Europe with the parties of the extreme right.

The way that anthropologists like Balandier or historians like Stora indulge in expressions taken from clinical psychiatry to discuss the consequences of the colonial situation on family and social ties is similar to what Fanon had suggested in his chapter on colonial war and mental distress, when speaking of the compromised future of his patients. But, beyond the patients, it is the whole of Algerian society that will be "compromised," haunted by the ghosts of an *obliterated* past, in the etymological sense of the term (cancelled, made illegible because it has been written over, but is still present). A past that has been *foreclosed*: how else can we define the dead of Sétif that the statistics do not mention?

The use of the Lacanian term *forclusion*, originally introduced by Pichon with a different sense, should here be taken literally, in its Freudian meaning of "verdict," *and* in the sense it has in legal language: something that can no longer be demanded beyond a certain term.[16] The law adds something that psychoanalysis seems to have done little with, but which to me seems decisive in a Fanonian clinical perspective ("The problem considered here is one of time," Fanon, 2008, p. 176). That is the rule by which the responsibility for the foreclosure falls on the "victims" themselves (the creditors, in civil law): though they may know of the time limit when the procedure lapses, they have not filed the documents required within the necessary time limit. So, they lose their rights, they are responsible for this *forclusion*.

This double dimension—psychoanalytical and juridical—of *forclusion* (what cannot be assimilated and returns in the real in the hallucinatory form of having been excluded from the process of symbolization, along with the responsibility for letting it lapse), is useful for understanding the intimate and enduring resonance of collective catastrophes (Lazali, 2018). The traumatic memory is this too: the siege of an unattainable past, the responsibility for whose *forclusion* rests with the vanquished. What could be done about Majid's haphazard peregrinations and his family's sense of helplessness? In what sense can we "cure" the ruins of the past?[17]

Abdallah Laroui writes that during the French colonization of North Africa, the local system was suppressed and replaced with French laws, the Muslim schools were closed or deprived of funds, leaving no alternative to the French schools, and the populations were driven into the desert areas, repressing "in their soul whatever had been acquired of their history, religion and language" (Laroui, 1975, p. 117). The aim was to fabricate a population to be civilized.

Rather than settling for a diagnostic label, we accompanied the family in re-examining a past that was submerged by silence, pain and shame, trying to decipher their "distant gaze."[18] Constructing a fragment of shared memory is the premise for any therapeutic bond. Majid's symptoms contain recognizable traces of a history marked by violence and by the humiliation of an entire culture. His flights are the expression of the displacements (metonyms, according to Lacan) marking a past that cannot be mentioned, and a society that was divided between two orders of loyalty: to the French government (the *harki*) and to the Algerian Liberation Front. This divide, the crisis of imaginary (national) unity, continues to haunt the present, to oppose, in the form of symptoms, suspicion or violence, the traitors to the loyalists, not unlike what happened in the Basque country, where Aretxaga has brilliantly described a similar metonymy:

> Unlike the invader, or the stranger, the traitor retains a trace of us and his/her betrayal has separated us. But this separation is not complete [. . . .] The betrayal itself ties us together, it makes the betrayal part of me, a wounded part to be sure, *but still a part that cannot be extricated* until the betrayal itself has disappeared, forgotten.
>
> (Aretxaga, 2008, p. 59; my emphasis)

In this sense, the family as a whole is trying to build a unity that history has made impossible; the conflict between Morocco and Algeria made new "traitors," new suspects and enemies, breaking again the imaginary unity of Maghrebi people. And that Majid's mother tries to find an answer in a ritual healing is another illuminating image of the struggle to recompose an absent unity. After all, the *fquih* is a perfect metonym of loyalty to the culture, identification with the tradition, and belonging.[19] Is it not the case that curing is the fundamental aspect of a culture (de Rosny, 1981)?

Resorting repeatedly to the *fquih*, despite its ineffectiveness, is a search for a meaning for what seems to have no meaning in the modern nation's order of things. A meaning that it is hoped to be found in that humiliated knowledge, in the rituals of one's culture. "Culture" is a lifestyle, but also a form and language of resistance (Nandy, 2003). In listening to the story of a therapeutic ritual or the diagnosis of a healer, our work is not tempted by what has been described as cultural absolutism; our work does not settle for adhering to one or another of the so-called "traditional aetiologies." Our work involves questioning, using the words of patients or their families, and with *their epistemology*,[20] that feeling of "being acted on" that Ernesto de Martino explored among the oppressed and the labourers of Southern Italy. After everything, the spirits sometimes *speak* of history, giving voice to a critique of the present.[21]

For Majid the verdict is, in one case, severe in that he needs psychiatric care. The other is designed to restrain his suffering inside the principles of tradition; in this frame, he is under the influence of a jinn who only wants to drive him to do what in those places seems negated: to be a tourist. The second response tries to name a modern anxiety, just a further example of the ability of religious (or "traditional") aetiologies to capture and to tame new conflicts and re-enclose them within familiar categories. We need not underline the political value of cultures that have "begun to return, like Freud's unconscious, to haunt the modern system of nation states" (Nandy, 2003, p. 2). Nevertheless, we may recognize in this "return" another aspect, whose role is not insignificant for the theoretical project of a critical ethnopsychiatry, and about which not enough may have been said: it is the role that those areas of consciousness that were not colonized and domesticated continue to play in the experience and writing about themselves of the post-colonial subject, in the aesthetics the subject continues to create, and in the interpretation of the world and the form of their suffering.

If Majid's clinical history is partly the story of a failure, we may be able to glimpse another meaning too in his choice to abandon Italy. After all, Majid did not simply flee from his family, which had at last gained its Italian citizenship. Majid ceased to be in exile, he returned to the land of his paternal grandparents, to a country that is certainly still tormented by the memory of unjust deaths and ancient lacerations, but also by the strong desire to construct new relations with its past. In Algeria, Majid may be able to find a place for himself: "All water has a perfect memory and is forever trying to get back to where it was" (Morrison, 1998, p. 199).

Bamboozled. Affect, Race, Myths, and Social Memory in the Life of a Migrant Woman

In recent years Italy has become the country of choice for female migrants from Nigeria. While in the past the growing demand for care work for old people living alone or for domestic help had attracted female migrants from Peru, the Philippines and the Horn of Africa, since the 1990s another kind of migration has appeared on the scene: the sex trafficking of women, often from Nigeria, and particularly from Benin City.[22] So far there have been few studies of this in Italy (Taliani, 2017, 2018). Often the process has become a battleground between the institutions and social services on the one side, and individual idioms of suffering and unfamiliar moral horizons on the other.

The roots of the phenomenon go back to the colonial period when prostitution developed in the Gulf of Guinea. It was seemingly an almost "inevitable" process determined by the profound changes in trade, work and family and social ties. As the Nigerian historian Aderinto (2007) suggests, "prostitution is one of the long neglected social legacies of colonialism in Nigeria" (p. 4).[23] Aderinto recalls that concern over the spread of venereal disease and the idea that prostitutes were the main vehicle of it drove the colonial administration to promulgate laws preventing women from visiting some regions and obliging them to submit to health controls for sexually transmitted diseases. In the document cited, Aderinto brings out the "spiritual perspective on the sex trade" provided by one of Dickinson's informants (Theo Ashife):

> One week before the departure of the girls to the Gold Coast they have to go to a place called Ono-Ago to a Native Doctor who gives them medicine to drink known as Calabar beans or sash wood. It is the common belief amongst these people that when they drink this medicine, they are immune from the attack of venereal disease. After three or four years' stay in the Gold Coast and after they have had sufficient money and personal effects, they return home to their native land, and before they reunite with their husbands, they go back to the native medicine man who prescribes for them a course of retreat and ablution after which they go back to their husbands when other wives will have to migrate to replace those at home.
>
> (Aderinto, 2012, p. 11)

The circulation of goods and people, the disorderly processes of urbanization, the implosion of social hierarchies, and the chaos that affected the whole symbolic-cultural horizons of these societies, constituted genuine "social surgery" (Chancelé, cit. in Balandier, 1951). The reduced demand for slaves on the Atlantic route made available a larger workforce that could now be used in the war economy, agriculture or in the plantations, while continuing to provide sexual services. Other forms of dependence flowered during the colonial period, such as the loaning of money on the basis of pawnage. The term "pawn" designates a person who guarantees the reimbursement of a loan and must serve her creditor till the debt has been paid or cancelled. It epitomizes this social and commercial scenario well, along with its psychological and sociological effects. The term was commonly translated as *iwofa* in Yoruba area, *iyoha* in the region of Benin City, *awowa* in the Ashanti region. Taking up Moran's work from the 1930s, commissioned by the colonial government in French West Africa, Lydon recalls:

> This may well be an indication that her assignment was prompted by concern with the incidence of pawning in the aftermath of the 1930s Depression. Henri Ortoli [. . .], the joint-administrator to the French colonial office, defined pawning in 1939 as *"une convention orale par laquelle un débiteur remet à son créancier pour garantir le paiement une dette une ou plusieurs personnes de sa famille ou engage lui-même."* The pawn was therefore a guarantee for the creditor, and the pawn's labour was in lieu of the interest on the loan. However, never was a pawn substituted for an actual loan [. . . .] Most of Moran's regional reports contain cases of women and mainly girls forced into slavery as pawns. For instance, in Ouagadougou early in 1938, a man volunteered his daughter to someone who had given him a loan. The girl was entirely at the disposal of the creditor and was in turn loaned to his brother. In another case which took place in the courthouse of Pita, a town in Guinea, an owner sued to obtain possession of the child of a slave he had pawned. This, as well as other similar examples, caused Moran to declare that "ni l'esclavage ni la mise en gage ont entièrement disparu du Pouta comme certains commandants et chefs le prétendent."
>
> (Lydon, 1997, pp. 573–574)[24]

It is only in the "long duration" (Braudel) of these processes, these imbued images of bodies, debts, forms of subjugation and power relationships, then, that we can understand the phenomenon of Nigerian prostitution as it is today, its genealogy and its contradictory social and psychological profiles. And it is only when we look at the heterogeneous cultural memories, the knitting together of different "durations," that we can fathom the vocabulary of these women, which constantly combine references to slavery and witchcraft, fetish and money, experience of subjection and a desire for autonomy.

I want to quickly consider these aspects, starting from the case of Mercy, a Nigerian woman who arrived in Italy many years ago within this trafficking of women. I shall be considering just some of the events in her life and some of the significant moments in her relationship with our centre. A few months after her arrival in Italy, Mercy met an Italian, with whom, as often happens between these women and their clients, she began a relationship. The relationship was marked in her case by uncertainty and violence. During the following months her symptoms became more and more serious. She had episodes of confusion, headaches, paraesthesia and anxiety attacks and she was eventually admitted to hospital. On being discharged, she was advised to contact the Fanon Centre.

As with other similar cases, the clinical intervention sought to situate the origin of her symptoms in the context of her condition, but also to enable her to recount her experiences in her own language—which is the only effective way of working on metaphors, and their memories and sense of belonging. Overcoming her initial reluctance, Mercy described her childhood in Benin City. She talked about her father, who was the priest of a local cult and an expert in the art of divination. He had five wives, the last of whom was her mother. As a child, she was entrusted to the first of her father's wives when her mother left. At first she did not suffer much, but when her father's first wife died, things deteriorated, and she was left to herself, wandering about alone, often asking for food from friends. Her father demanded that Mercy's mother give back her "bride-wealth" for leaving the family, but only after several years did her mother return to do so. When this took place, Mercy remembered being shut up in a room so as not to see her mother. It was only much later that she was able to meet her again. During this time, she was isolated, did not like speaking to anyone else and was often ill. When they were together again, her mother organized a ceremony to free Mercy from these problems: a ritual in honour of Olokun, the divinity of fertility and wellbeing.[25]

Mercy remembered dancing until she fell down exhausted, whereupon she was possessed by a spirit. Actually—she added at once—she had not been "wholly" possessed. She had remained partly conscious, but had not dared to say so, to please those present. Her relation with Olokun and the spirit that had possessed her would always remain profoundly ambivalent. When she talks about it, even today, she sounds elusive, seemingly afraid of "invoking it" simply by uttering its name, only to laugh it off and insist that she "does not believe in these things," as she's a Christian (adding: "when you don't believe in these things, nothing happens to you"). Yet she admitted to being particularly worried after her mother told her on the phone that she had met people who insistently reminded her that her daughter had to complete the ceremony of affiliation to the confraternity, which had been interrupted by her conversion to a Pentecostal church.

As is often related in the literature, the Pentecostal churches are particularly active in combatting these cults and their ties with fetishes, shrines or divinities like Olokun or Shangó, not because they are seen as survivals of the past or mere superstitions, but because they are regarded as a place where demonic forces may act dangerously. In fact, by confirming the threat represented by the spirits in the life of its adepts, the discourse of the Pentecostal churches only contributes to distressing and bamboozling them.

Mercy gradually became more and more worried because she had no money to carry out the ceremony her mother had mentioned. And in any case the pastor of her church told her to "throw away everything." Her words have more recently been dominated by a new worry: her mother's poor health and her own recurrent nightmares. In one of them her brother attacks her; in another he steals one of her shoes and she is unable to get it back. The Nigerian mediator suggested that Mercy is distraught because she met the madam who accompanied her to Italy and ordered her to pay back the remaining part of her debt. When Mercy made it clear she did not have the means to pay, the woman threatened her, hinting at what might happen both to her and to her mother.

At one meeting, Mercy described in her uncertain Italian, flavoured with pidgin and Edo, the dreams she had had the night before. In one of them, some women climb on top of her chest, almost preventing her from breathing. In another, she hears the phone ring: it is her Italian partner, but sitting on her shoulders is a black man-child, naked, who gives her an orgasm. But Mercy becomes angry with him as it is his fault that she could not reply to the phone call. In a later dream, which again featured her "spiritual husband,"[26] Mercy said she tried to bite his penis. She found this extremely troubling as she believed these dreams presaged misfortunes.

In the following months, her arguments with the madam—whom she suspects of casting a spell on her—and with another Nigerian woman gave further cause for anxiety, attenuated only by the birth of her son, from the fruit of her relationship with her Italian partner. This relationship was marked by increasing conflicts and became impossible, finally breaking down after much uncertainty. Despite her economic problems and the difficulties arising from her disturbances, Mercy continued to bring up her child as a loving single parent with the help of the social services. Her relationship with her child expressed the strength of an intense maternal bond, indifferent to bureaucratic problems, the conflicts with her partner, her precarious legal position and the spiritual threats of the madam—at least until the disturbances became more serious. When the world became hostile again, she fell into states of confusion more frequently and her prescription drugs began to have no effect.

Mercy closed up on herself again, just as when she was young. She stopped opening the windows in her home, she lost her job and started talking more and more often to herself in her mother tongue, frightening her child who couldn't understand her. The child had to be fostered by an Italian family, which Mercy reacted strongly against at first. She saw it as no less than "robbery" and interpreted the decision of the social services—like other African mothers whose children are fostered or adopted by other families—as the expression of a hostile plan by the Italian state to "steal African children because women in Italy are no longer able to have children."[27] In the end, Mercy accepted giving up her child, admitting, after much resistance, that she could no longer handle it.

During this period the Fanon Centre was a place where Mercy felt able to go whenever she was in distress, besieged by the phantoms of the past, or unable to understand incomprehensible or threatening facts: as in the case of her name not appearing on her child's identity card—which, for her, was just further evidence that people wanted to "steal her child."[28]

Mercy's account reveals the mixture of directly experienced violence and the echo of collective traumas (slavery), the state of subjection that gave rise to her journey (the ritual, the construction of a fetish containing fragments of her body) and the memory of the subjection of other women who have had the same experience of being "pawned persons." Her grief, expressed in the form of intrusive persecutionary thoughts and mania contains within it a whole history of glances, humiliations, racial prejudice and ambivalent desires. And, she may seem to *see* in her condition of mother—black—immigrant, whose child is being fostered by an Italian family, the repetition of another theft—that which saw so many Africans removed from their families and their mothers, sold as slaves and disappearing forever. Everything seems to remind her that she is still inside the nightmare of a dark past.

What Does Cure or Psychotherapy Mean Here?

In the face of the tale of night-time visits from a "spiritual husband" or her uncertainty as to the nature of these other beings, we must recognize that we are dealing with other epistemologies. Though we can repeat with Zempléni that, like most of those possessed by spirits in Senegal (Zempléni, 1966, p. 5), they are "neither mad nor abnormal." Even in the case of those who host spirits such as Abiku or Mami Wata, these are people who are neither mad nor abnormal. Yet, in the case of immigrants, if this principle is often confirmed, it is no less important to admit that, even when we are faced with authentic distress, as in the case of Mercy, there is *something else* in the symptom that appeals to our knowledge and the meaning of cure.

Mercy's anxiety and the ambivalent desires she experienced, the painful memories of a precarious childhood, and with a debt once again in the background, may well be captured in a specific ontology of the body, cultivated by the idea of spirit possession and the fear of a threatening fetish. However, the challenge she throws down to the models of Western psychology and psychoanalysis originates not only from the fact that the particular ontology embodied in her discourse constitutes a genuine "philosophical war machine" (Viveiros de Castro, 2015, p. 9), but also from the fact that this ontology, this embodied archive,[29] is itself mixed with a specific historicity and economy,[30] of a relentless *law of debt*, so to speak.[31]

Her experiences question psychiatric categories, her body interpellates our notions of person, her morality outlines another kind of motherhood. Mercy's story is an authentic *mother-child counter-narrative*, placing the desire of a black, immigrant mother at the heart of the nation state's institutions. Her cure, then, must, among other things, construct the conditions for bringing to light a non-subaltern representation of herself[32]—which becomes possible when we learn to recognize, in the dismembered memories of a patient, "history's forgotten doubles" (Nandy, 1995) that have been marginalized in the dominant discourse, but still remain decisive in the existence of the oppressed. The critical ethnopsychiatry discussed here tries to mingle the dull sound of the dependence economies in which the existence of immigrants is immersed with the sounds of resistance that emerge from other poetics of experience, from different perceptions of the body and the world. And to imagine an aesthetic of care that can *cure* these wounded consciousnesses, these places of the Self that are "dominated, but not domesticated" (Fanon, 2004, p. 16).[33]

The "Others" of the Nation State, and a Fanonian Aporia

The stories of Majid and Mercy, and of the countries they come from, may be regarded as eloquent metaphors of what colonialism was and the legacy it left in the lives of individual immigrants and in the questions that assail their genealogies and their bodies. Their migration is a chaotic mixture of heterogeneous historicities, the reflection of societies that are tense and divided, and the sum of infinite ambivalences (Bhabha, 1994). As Wright Mills wrote, "Seldom aware of the *intricate connection between the patterns of their own lives and the course of world history*, ordinary men do not usually know what this connection means for the kinds of men they are becoming and for the kinds of history-making in which they might take part".

(1959, pp. 3–4; italics added for emphasis)

The figure of the refugee adds another feature. It literally makes the national borders bleed; it questions their *raison d'être* and their legitimacy (Malkki, 1995, 1996). A clinical account of their restless destinies must necessarily anchor our interpretations and our attempts at cure to the complex and often obscure articulations that exist between symptom, history, myth and law (i.e., to the bureaucratic systems that regulate the right of asylum, the new forms of citizenship, and so on). It must listen carefully to these languages of uncertainty, these scattered memories, and try to reconstruct networks of meaning and sociality in the face of suffering that de Martino has magnificently described as a "crisis of presence" (de Martino, 2012).

The ethno-psychiatry that began in the late 1950s in Haiti with Louis Mars, in Brazil with Bastide and his psychology of "resentment," in Nigeria with Lambo, in Dakar with Collomb, Collignon, Zempléni and others, succeeded in casting off its heavy colonial inheritance, with its tendency to pathologize the culture of the colonized peoples (Mahone & Vaughan, 2007; Sadowsky, 1999; Vaughan, 1991) and trivialize local knowledge and curing techniques (de Rosny, 1981). A decisive step forward was made at the same time by Fanon in Algeria and Ernesto de Martino in Italy.[34] An interest in popular models of illness and cure would bring to the fore the state of the "damned" (Fanon) and the "last" (de Martino). Their approach would transform the theoretical perspectives of the preceding years, making relevant not only the politico-cultural and subjugated, "minor idioms" of suffering,[35] not only the symbolic networks within which illness was named and cured, but also, above all, the racial question, the radical policies of alienation, and the echo and metamorphosis of historical traumas (as in the case of the aetiologies of the Aymara shamans).[36]

The resigned gaze of the colonized would no longer be seen as mere fatalism or passivity, or the "serenity of stone," wrote Fanon (2004), but rather as a way of reacting that has a precise effect. In the face of fate, even the power of colonial administration is suspended—itself subject to a superior power (God, destiny, and so on).[37] That gaze became the impenetrable enclosure of the experience of the dominated, their incomprehensible language, which makes their thoughts invisible and marks out a space of sovereignty: a heterotopia in Foucault's sense of the term, one might say. Thanks to this break with the past, "culture," "folklore" and "traditional cures" would now reveal an aspect that had been hitherto disregarded—one that criticized the hegemonic discourse. Feierman (1995) would take up these topics, speaking of traditional medicine in colonial Congo as a social critique and a therapeutic insurgency.[38]

These new horizons of research led to a need to scan the symptoms, deliriums and discourse of a mental patient (like the one encountered by John and Jean Comaroff in South Africa; 1992) for another form of historical consciousness, and sometimes the attempt to re-appropriate a history that had been negated—of the kind that Taussig calls "forbidden images."[39]

We have already invoked this perspective in speaking of the flights of Majid or the oneiroid experiences of Mercy and the cultural archives she incorporates, implicitly suggesting an idea of cure as an act that can disinter the text hidden in a patient's situation.[40] What sub-text is this? I shall give an example that seems close to the symptomatic reading invoked earlier.

Starting from the debate in the last century between anthropology and psychoanalysis about Oedipus (Malinowski, Jones, Leach, Spiro), Rita Laura Segato has reconsidered the figures of maternity and the position of the black wet-nurse in the imaginary of Brazilian society—a society marked by racism,[41] where the closeness (affective and physical) between the black wet-nurses and the children of middle-class white families had to remain invisible, foreclosed. Only in a few rare portraits of the period—those by Debret, for example—does this proximity burst through, showing an affectionate black wet-nurse holding in her arms a calm child (probably because it was the only way to keep the child quiet for the time necessary to paint the portrait or, later, take the photograph). Behind this foreclosure and the profound ambivalence toward a figure that was both necessary and negated, there was also a late-nineteenth-century medico-hygienic insistence on the supposed risks of biological or linguistic contamination to children brought up by black women.[42]

Segato's research brings out in great detail the consequences of this process. The foreclosure toward the black subject, the refusal to accept the subject's desire for her difference to be recognized and accepted by society, and the profound racism of this country, are, for Segato (2015), connected with another foreclosure—that of the black wet-nurse. The racist of today, she writes,

> loved and—why not?—still loves his black wet-nurse. He simply cannot recognize her in her racial quality [. . . .] If she suddenly appeared on the scene, demanding the kinship due to her, he would react with uncontrollable violence. *We are speaking of what cannot be named, either as one's own or as alien.*
>
> (p. 205; italics in the original)

There is another consequence. The black wet-nurse— a slave or descendent of slaves—is contrasted with the figure of the white mother: the natural mother, the legitimate and *cold* mother, who effectively incorporates the function of educator, the function of the law. One of the effects of the dislocation of the paternal function was to dehumanize the wet-nurse, turning her into a mere object to be bought and sold, but another was to create a form of Oedipus that the author calls "black."

While, in the "African" Oedipus in Senegal (Ortigues & Ortigues, 1966), it was the family structure, the role attributed to ancestors and the importance of the phratry and age divisions that supported the different expressions of the Oedipus complex in the child, in Brazil, it was the *racial situation* that carved out the forms of a psychism, of *another* Oedipus, it was "what cannot be named, either as one's own or as alien" that wrote the law of Oedipus.[43] Kortenaar (2007, p. 182) remembers a further profile. With regards to the failure of democracy in Africa and what African literature says about this, he emphasizes the different trajectory of political struggle in postcolonial societies:

> The sons of independence in Africa were not successful in establishing the hegemony of the bourgeois state. The revolution described by Sembène in 1960 did not take place. Indeed, the trial of the father in *Les bouts de bois* was not, strictly speaking, an Oedipal scenario. Fathers are indeed obstacles in the progress of their sons, but they do not have a power that the sons can seize for themselves. The displacement of the father only results in the dissipation of his power. Real power, what Achille Mbembe calls *le commandement*, lies elsewhere, with the railway and the colonial administration. The colonizers, however, are not fathers, and it is almost impossible for the young rebel protagonists of African novels to inherit from them.[44]

I could never find a more effective example of what I have called elsewhere "the psychic life of history" (Beneduce, 2012). There is, however, a third effect, no less central to what I am saying. The silence of the archives, the medicalization of the black wet-nurse, her foreclosure, did not prevent this figure and the hostile or ambivalent feelings surrounding her from finding other ways of being thought, reproduced and narrated.

Segato (2015) recalls being led to discover these connections by listening to some songs during the rituals of the Candomblé, which featured a recurrent opposition between "salt" Mother (Yemanja) and loving Madre, associated with freshwater rivers. In the songs, the divinity Yemanja is identified with the legitimate mother, who is false and calculating, and who recognizes the king and protects her clever son (Xangó) who cunningly usurped the position of legitimate heir from Ogún, simply to save the formal order. "Culture" and myth (or the *strange* fragments of tales recounted by so many immigrants) are the place where the history of painful events that have been driven back into silence or denied is *thought* and tended, and where the lies of hegemonic discourse are revealed metaphorically. It is a "pragmatic psychology" that is almost in counterpoint to the scientific psychology of childhood, maternity and attachment. Myth

The Psychic Life of History145

indicates unfathomable complexities of the collective psyche in the perspective of a people that was forcibly incorporated in the nation through the slave trade, only to be economically and politically marginalized due to the complete lack of public policies able to offer appropriate forms of inclusion. Choosing the side of "illegitimacy," the people decided to speak through its myths [. . . .] In this way *the political discourse of the myth* becomes clear. Its cryptic utterance is related to the lie that is at the very foundation of the establishment and its laws [. . .] the intention of the mythic comment *is not to formulate an alternative ethical principle, but rather a sociology, a hermeneutics of the social environment.* This *pragmatic psychology* [. . .] *constitutes a survival manual* under an alien, authoritarian regime.

(Segato, 2015, pp. 189–90; my italics)

This is a valuable argument, which questions the sense and destiny of belonging and of the heterogeneous forms of loyalty that survive in the nation state and suggests that the figure of maternity had a pivotal role in the convulsive history of slavery, colonialism and the birth of the modern state.[45] Afro-Brazilian religious traditions are defined as a "monumental African codex containing the accumulated ethnic experiences and strategies of African descendants as part of a nation [. . . .] This codex tells us, in its own metaphoric language, *not only about religion but also about the relationships between blacks and the white state*" (Segato, 1998, p. 143; my italics).

In connecting the attitudes and racist laws of a society, the particular trajectory of a nation and the role of cultural traditions in the New World,[46] Segato also offers an important argument for rethinking the role of the symbolico-religious themes that immigrants often refer to: as a "reservoir of meaning," that code, those images, do not speak only of *alterity* or *tradition* but also, above all, of dispossessed memories, and of the relation these minorities have built and continue to build with the institutions of the nation states and the knowledge that claims to assign a name to their experiences, their needs and their conflicts.[47]

Turning to the lies of the modern state and the hypocrisies of human rights and "integration," these recall—continues Segato—the "point zero of racial truth"—segregation and violence as the expression of a "dystopian conviviality" (Segato, 1998, p. 131). Only a clinical-political semiotics can grasp the subterranean effects of these acts of violence and recognize the link between racism and symptom, and between institutional racism, exclusion and alienation[48] in "raced subjects" (on "racial melancholy" and the moral impossibility of forgetting, see Cheng, 2001).[49]

But the War Goes On . . .

The title of this section refers to one of Fanon's aporias, alluding to the contradiction he expresses between his firm intention not to allow himself to be enclosed in the "Tower of the Past"[50] and his equally strong awareness that a past marked by alienation and violence will cast its shadow for a long time on the life and times of the colonized societies. "But the war goes on. And for many years to come we shall be bandaging the countless and sometimes *indelible wounds* inflicted on our people by the colonialist onslaught" (Fanon, 2004, p. 181; my italics).[51]

It sounds like a prophecy of the malaise of post-colonial "disorders,"[52] of nights lit up by flashes of violence and death that go on igniting our present: from Gaza to Afghanistan, from Syria to Mali, from the Mexican border to Libya or Europe. . . . Immigrants and asylum-seekers, too, seem to interminably reiterate *but the war goes on*, in the face of the militarized borders, the massacres in the Mediterranean and hypocrisies of humanitarian law.

Fanon's aporia—the tension between the need to free oneself of a traumatic past and the awareness of its persistent influence on individuals and collectivities—is, in any case, at the heart of any therapeutic project, which, in curing the consequences of violence, is faced with the piercing question of how much should be remembered, witnessed, translated, and how much pushed back down into oblivion, with the awareness that this tension is indelible. "Excess memory or excess oblivion—and nothing else," Maren and Marcelo Viñar wrote incisively in recounting the "hurricane of history" during the dictatorship in Uruguay and the stories of the victims of a meaningless violence (Viñar & Viñar, 1993, p. 14).[53] Fanon's aporia—the nagging tension between what one would like to leave behind one and what cannot be forgotten—increases the sensation in curing the effects of terrible acts of violence like torture. That is, a technique specifically aimed at dismembering the connection between speech, body and memory, the "ability to respond,"[54] the clinician is carrying out an "impossible profession" (Freud), but one which he cannot give up.

When Fanon acknowledges that only time can cure the psychological pain of an act of violence like that of the colonial war, or when Viñar draws on the experience of extermination camp survivors (2005), they both seem to be suggesting that a cure necessarily involves facing up to the past and its spectres, even the horror that shaped it, but without remaining enslaved and crushed by it to the point of becoming no more than a victim, and without being surprised that the horrors of the past may be repeated today with monotonous ferocity. Remember, yes—remember everything—but in such a way that the memory of the horrors is not destructive. In any case, the oppressed, the victims of the horror, are fully aware that the "emergency situation" is the rule.[55] We need, to paraphrase Benjamin, *a concept of curing that corresponds to this fact.*

In the final pages of *Beloved*, Morrison traces with unique delicacy the uncertainties and the pain of the survivors, the pain and the needs of bodies branded by history, and the dilemma of a past that is not worth handing down, but which one cannot abandon or forget. Her words suggest almost a model of cure for my ethno-psychiatry and for my anthropology of memory, a path that Fanon too might have followed:

> There is a loneliness that can be rocked. Arms crossed, knees drawn up; holding, holding on, this motion, unlike a ship's, smooths and contains the rocker. It's an inside kind—wrapped tight like skin. Then there is a loneliness

that roams. No rocking can hold it down. It is alive, on its own. A dry and spreading thing that makes the sound of one's own feet going seem to come from a far-off place. Everybody knew what she was called, but nobody anywhere knew her name. Disremembered and unaccounted for, she cannot be lost because no one is looking for her, and even if they were, how can they call her if they don't know her name? Although she has claim, she is not claimed. In the place where long grass opens, the girl who waited to be loved and cry shame erupts into her separate parts, to make it easy for the chewing laughter to swallow her all away. It was not a story to pass on [. . . .] By and by all trace is gone, and what is forgotten is not only the footprints but the water too and what it is down there. The rest is weather. Not the breath of the disremembered and unaccounted for, but wind in the eaves, or spring ice thawing too quickly. Just weather. Certainly no clamor for a kiss.

(Morrison, 1987, p. 275)

Conclusions: Another Step in the Construction of a Critical Medical Anthropology and Ethnopsychiatry

By analyzing the clinical history of two immigrants, I have sought to retrace the story-lines of a history that has been humiliated, of cultural memories that have been repressed but not tamed, and which often emerge in the form of symptoms: perhaps just another expression of what Bovenschen called "experiential appropriation of the past."

> This experiential appropriation of the past differs qualitatively from that of the scholar in the archive—at least with respect to its everyday manifestation. It deals with something other than what traditional sources, data and commentary have to offer. In it are incorporated elements of historical and social fantasy which are sensitive to the underground existence of forbidden images; it is anarchical and rebellious in its *rejection of chronology and historical accuracy*.
>
> (Bovenschen, 1978, p. 84; my italics)

Recent anthropological and historical studies that have brought out these dimensions are essential in clinical work if we are to escape interpretations that squash complex meanings and symbols into universal principles or underestimate the way in which historical traumas (like colonization) may return today in the form of a symptom in the present existence of a young immigrant. The critical ethnopsychiatry that I have presented in these notes, operating in the framework of a historical ethnography, aims to heed these shades and these forgotten figures: retracing, for example, the history of prostitution in colonial Nigeria down to the controversial negotiation of forms of sexuality in the postcolonial state (Aderinto, 2015) so as to listen to the truth and cure the suffering of a dispossessed body—that of Mercy, a prisoner of an infinite debt, besieged by the echoes of a vocabulary that has gradually become alien to her (that of the *juju*, of *Mami Wata*, etc.), but that still has the effect of keeping her in subjugation.

Within these territories it is possible to capture the metamorphoses by which the violence of history and racial violence are transformed into myths, experiences and attitudes (such as "racial melancholia").[56] This is what is suggested by the works already cited by Rita Laura Segato (2015), and research such as Platt's (2002, 2013) and Weismantel's (2001). Fanon's lesson—the analysis of colonial alienation—has kept all its value intact, in particular when it examines the ambivalence and uncertainty of those who are at the same time *dominated* and *sick*.[57] Clinical treatment of immigrants should be particularly alert to the "long-forgotten message" (Jameson, 1981, p. 19) that emerges today from their bodies, between new forms of violence and exclusion. Ethnopsychiatrist, like the anthropologist-messenger Crapanzano writes of (1992, p. 3), becomes the archive of confiscated memories and voices, and with its work reactivates[58] forms of historical consciousness that, although they combine in the course of time with other historicities, memories or cultures, never see their differences wholly saturated.

Notes

1. Here Fassin makes reference to a sentence by Nathan (1994, p. 216) on the need of "encouraging ghettos" to prevent immigrant families from being forced to abandon their cultural systems.
2. In this connection, see Apter's analysis of Griaule's research and its obsession with the idea of "secret" in Dogon society, an attitude that has been described by Mudimbe as "iconic of colonial imagination" (Apter, 2005, p. 95). Or, again, Manfredi's critique of Ottenberg's Oedipal interpretation of an Igbo initiation ritual and its symbols, showing—on the basis of a rigorous semantic analysis of oral texts—that the ritual is less concerned with solving Oedipal conflict than preventing the failure of the process of reincarnation (Manfredi, 1997).
3. "The problem considered here is one of time. Those Negroes and white men will be disalienated who refuse to let themselves be sealed away in the materialized Tower of the Past. In no way should I derive my basic purpose from the past of the peoples of color. In no way should I dedicate myself to the revival of an unjustly unrecognized Negro civilization. I will not make myself the man of any past. *I do not want to exalt the past at the expense of my present and of my future*" (2008, p. 176; my italics).
4. The English translation ("fantasy intuition", Fanon, 2008, p. 43), however, completely misrepresents the sense of Dublineau's work, cited by Fanon.
5. Out of a population of 9 million, French sources estimate that 300,000 to 500,000 died in the French–Algerian war. Bourdieu and Abdelmalek Sayad, in *Le déracinement* (1964), estimate that over 2 million Algerians (one-quarter of the pop.) were displaced and herded into concentration camps, causing the final colonial collapse of indigenous agriculture.
6. "It is clear that the Negro child, by the age of five is aware of the fact that to be colored in contemporary American society is a mark of inferior status. The negation of the color, brown, exists in the same complexity of attitudes in which there also exists knowledge of the fact that the child himself must be identified with that which he rejects. This apparently introduces *a fundamental conflict at the very foundations of the ego structure*" (Clark & Clark, 1950, p. 50). The small child Pecola, who is the central figure in Toni Morrison's novel *The Bluest Eye* published in 1970 (Morrison

2007), is obsessed by the desire to have blue eyes like Shirley Temple's, and this is a particularly effective and painful expression of the racial alienation analyzed by the Clarks in America and by Fanon in Martinique. I shall return later to Toni Morrison's fiction for the unique blend of history, myth, psychology and traumatic social memory that shapes her novels.

7. See Gibson and Beneduce (2017) and Mendes (2015). On these questions Oliver writes: "Without a psychoanalytic theory for and revolving around those othered by the Freudian model subject, we continue to base our theories of subjectivity on the very norm that we are trying to overcome; in this way, our theories collaborate with the oppressive values that we are working against. A psychoanalytic theory of oppression must consider *the role of subject position in subject formation*, that is, the relationships between subject position and subjectivity [. . .] *Theories that level suffering by proposing that all subjectivity is born from subjection and exclusion, however, cover over the suffering specific to oppression.* In so doing, they risk complicity with values and institutions that abject those othered to fortify the privilege of the beneficiaries of oppressive values" (Oliver, 2004, p. xvi; my italics).

8. The idea of "symptomatic reading" was suggested by Althusser. In taking up Marx's criticism of Smith for not having seen what was in front of him—the difference between constant capital and variable capital ("he did not grasp what was, however, in his hands") (Althusser & Balibar)—Althusser reads Marx and *Capital* from a similar critical perspective. The concept arises from an awareness of how what is visible can often escape the observer: "What classical political economy does not see, is not what it does not see, *it is what it sees*; it is not what it lacks, on the contrary, *it is what it does not lack*; it is not what it misses, on the contrary, *it is what it does not miss*. The oversight, then, is not to see what one sees, *the oversight no longer concerns the object, but the sight itself*. The oversight is an oversight that concerns vision" (Ibid.: my italics). In underlining how Marx's work has disclosed a new theoretical strategy, Althusser recognizes his debt to Freud and Lacan, and still more to Spinoza ("The first man ever to have posed the problem of reading, and in consequence, of writing, was Spinoza, and he was also the first man in the world to have proposed both a theory of history and a philosophy of *the opacity of the immediate*.") (Ibid., p. 16; my italics). On these issues, see also Assiter (1984) and Jean-Marie, who observes: "La lecture symptômale doit en quelque sorte produire un *autre texte* qui éclaire et déplace le premier, rend lisible ce qui autrement aurait été illisible [. . .] *Elle fait apparaître de nouvelles problématiques et de nouveaux objets à travailler*" (www. multitudes.net/La-lecture-symptomale-chez/; my italics).

9. As Eyerman recalls, Fanon's reading was to have a decisive role too in rethinking the narrative of slavery, contributing to determining the "shift from an emphasis on the economic to the psychological effects of slavery" (Eyerman, 2003, p. 182).

10. "Perhaps the reader will find these notes on psychiatry out of place or untimely in a book like this. There is absolutely nothing we can do about that" (Fanon, 2004, p. 181). An interest in the question of time is constant in Fanon and had already been expressed in the form of the theoretical project in *Black Skin, White Masks*: "The architecture of this work is rooted in the temporal. Every human problem must be considered from the standpoint of time" (2008, p. 5).

11. "In the unpublished introduction of the first two editions of *L'an V de la révolution algérienne* (Studies in a Dying Colonialism), we already indicated that an entire generation of Algerians, steeped in collective, gratuitous homicide with all the psychosomatic consequences this entails, *would be France's human legacy in Algeria*" (Fanon, 2004, p. 184, note 22, my italics). Fanon's symptomatic reading of the historicity of Algeria's embeddedness in our present is France's 21st century shameful/shameless "disclosure" of its documentary history and dossier of its Algerian atrocities which mirror darkly Fanon's reading and indictment of Western civilization, not differently from what Foreign and Commonwealth Office recently made with its

"migrated archives" (on colonial Kenya and the difficult disclosure of its colonial archives, see Elkin, 2005, 2015). "The lesion of the historic trauma is never allowed to close, leaving Fanon's diagnosis the only one worth considering. The Western Allies' post-Holocaust apocalypse is as much the blood of our times as fascism; indeed, they are indistinguishable. It's what George Jackson called 'blood in my eye', when he theorized U.S. corporativist-fascism, from San Quentin Prison" (Lou Turner and Helen A. Neville, personal communication). I am grateful to Lou Turner and Helen A. Neville for their suggestion about this issue.

12. I founded the Fanon Centre in the early 1990s, together with a group of psychiatrists, psychologists, sociologists, psychotherapists and, above all, cultural mediators from various countries (Argentina, Brazil, Morocco, Peru, Senegal, Somalia, and so on). The aim of the project, which was originally part of the public health service, was to guarantee patients who were immigrants, refugees or victims of violence the possibility of free psychotherapeutic treatment. Its principles would be those of a clinical approach guided by anthropology and free of any diagnostic obsession or constraints of time (psychotherapies would be constructed merely on the basis of the clinical needs of each individual patient or family, with flexible hours); an environment without bureaucratic restrictions (patients with or without a proper residence permit could have access to it, irrespective of their place of residence); psychotherapy usually adopted the mother tongue of the patients and was directed at enabling a deep exploration of the symbolic-metaphoric universes underlying the symptoms, but, above all, to cure the *political anxieties* of patients, and to correct the effects (whether visible or not) of institutional violence. In many respects it was a project inspired by the same premises as the Lafargue Clinic. For some aspects of this experience, see Beneduce (2010), Beneduce and Martelli (2005), and Beneduce andTaliani (2016).

13. Sétif is an Algerian town where the French air force harshly put down a revolt of the Algerian people, killing thousands, including civilians. What can one say of a question that invades the space of the conversation, the linear time of a case history, imposing another rhythm, another geography of personal attachments and events, and that seems incomprehensible to the point of raving? Deleuze and Guattari wrote: "All delirium possesses a world-historical, political, and racial content, mixing and sweeping along races, cultures, continents, and kingdoms" (1983, p. 88).

14. On possession cults in Morocco, and that of Aisha Qandisha in particular, see Crapanzano (1973).

15. "We have demonstrated that in the colonial situation the colonized are confronted with themselves. They tend to use each other as a screen [. . .] Yes, during the colonial period in Algeria and elsewhere a lot of things can be committed for a few pounds of semolina. One can kill. You need to use your imagination to understand these things. Or your memory. In the concentration camps men killed each other for a morsel of bread" (Fanon, 2004, pp. 230–231). It was only in September 2018 that the French presidency wanted to "reconcile memories", set aside funds for the *harki* and their descendants, grant them the Legion d'Honneur, and admit the responsibility of the French army in the torture, assassination and disappearance of the young mathematician Maurice Audin, a communist, arrested in Algiers in June 1957. Only sixty years later was there public recognition of what had been fully documented by the historians (Branche, 2016; Stora, 1998; Vidal-Naquet, 1975): that torture was a current practice (Kessel & Pirelli, 1962), that Algerian society had been poisoned by 130 years of occupation, colonized down to its nerve endings.

16. Giacinto Mosca, an Italian lawyer makes this point in a work on civil law procedure (1840, p. 343).

17. I think here of the ruins invoked in Kateb Yacine's *Nedjima* ("Not the remains of the Romans. Not that kind of ruins, where the soul of the multitudes has only time

to waste away, engraving their farewell in the rock, but the watermarked ruins of all times, the ruins steeped in the blood of our veins, the ruins we carry in secret, without ever finding the place or the time suitable for seeing them: the inestimable ruins of the present" (1991, p. 232).

18. Laroui writes on French colonization in North Africa: "Who can deny that at a certain point this repression seemed to have succeeded? The North African, impoverished and 'deculturated,' no longer left his hearth and, if he went out, *his empty, distant gaze*—that gaze that has struck travellers so much and that one sometimes sees again even today in the waiting rooms of France or the Maghreb—fell on a land that was no longer his" (Laroui, 1975, p. 117).

19. Our reading tries to repeat Aretxgaga's gesture: tracking the "hidden metonymic associations" (2008, p. 54) at the basis of madness and violence. Pandolfo adopts a similar strategy and her work is enlightening in that it illustrates the ambivalent process of identification in contemporary Morocco (as in the case of Reda, a young man the author encounters in a psychiatric hospital; Pandolfo, 2018, p. 107).

20. On the strategic need to "choose" the epistemology of the dominated, Nandy writes that "The essential reasoning is simple. Between the modern master and the non-modern slave, one must choose the slave not because one should choose voluntary poverty or admit the superiority of suffering, not only because the slave is oppressed [. . . .] One must choose the slave also because he represents a *higher-order cognition which perforce includes the master as a human, whereas the master's cognition has to exclude the slave except as a 'thing.'* Ultimately, modern oppression, as opposed to the traditional oppression, is not an encounter between the self and the enemy, the rulers and the ruled, or the gods and the demons. It is a battle between dehumanized self and the objectified enemy, the technologized bureaucrat and his reified victim, pseudo-rulers and their fearsome other selves projected on to their 'subjects'" (Nandy, 1983, p. xvi).

21. In her specialization thesis, Suzanne Taïeb, an Algerian psychiatrist from the time of the school of Antoine Porot, has a short note ("observation no. 6—depressive states") on a patient diagnosed as affected by "melancholic depression with active hallucinatory elements, suicide attempts, ideas of influence that have partly continued after healing (witchcraft)". The case is eloquent when the patient tells the psychiatrist that "she cannot sleep at night: the fusiliers [*author's note:* a division of the French army consisting of African soldiers] persecute her, France hates her, the doctor is trying to poison her" and, referring to the impulse to cut her throat, adds that a jinn appeared to her and ordered her to do it, telling her: "If you don't, the French will" (Taïeb, 1939, p. 90). Unfortunately, Taïeb adds no more and practically refrains from any interpretation, for, though it is written in the symbolic and cultural vocabulary of the jinn, she fails to see in these references a precise, detailed expression of a present that is ravaged by the oppressive presence of the colonial army and by violence, with the despair and desire for death of those who experienced on a daily basis misery, expropriation of their land, the ban on teaching Arabic in school. Like the classical economists Marx criticized, she too cannot see (and cannot hear) what she has in front of her, what is in her hands. Along with Michèle Chappert, Taïeb was the only female psychiatrist working at the hospital of Blida, in Algeria, at the time of Porot (Studer, 2015, p. 251).

22. The economic and social reasons behind this process are complex and cannot be analyzed here in detail for reasons of space. Those involved tend to be young women, often minors. They take the risk of unauthorized emigration, driven by poverty and the desire for independence. Women who are usually older or have for some reason a dominant role over these "social cadets" (Taliani, 2012, 2017) exploit their desires and subjugate them in a relation of economic and psychological dependence (Ellis, 2016). Advancing their travel costs, they effectively bind

them to an exorbitant debt (up to 50–60,000 euros), which many of them manage to pay off after a few years. The ritual that ratifies the agreement is described as "voodoo" by the women as a way of *translating it* into more familiar categories for those working in Western institutions (Taliani, 2012; van Djik, 2001). It culminates in the production of a "fetish" composed of the woman's nails, hair, pubic or arm-pit hair and menstrual blood and also, at times, the blood of a sacrificed animal (a chicken or a pigeon). The fetish incarnates the most obscure aspect of the depen-dence between the "victim" and the madam, who can exercise her power over this "fetish-body" (in which fragments of victim's body have been *imprisoned*) even from far away, should the woman not meet her obligations to pay the debt or refuse to work as a prostitute. It is a *literal metonymy*, as it is the whole of the person that is subjugated through those fragments that have remained imprisoned in the fetish possessed by the madam, reducing her to a slave. As well as the threats of disease, madness or death if the pact is violated, there is also that of harming members of the woman's family who have remained behind in Nigeria (as none of this excludes the use of forms of real coercion and violence). This is the source of the anxiety originating from the most banal negative events, which are interpreted as confir-mation of the madam's inexorable power. In this state fear of death, persecution mania, and what Warnier (2017) calls *"crises sorcellaires"* can arise. Warnier does not, however, do full justice to the complexity of this crisis and, above all, he understates how widespread it is. See the works of Simona Taliani (2018) for an analysis of these aspects. We cannot analyze here another no less dramatic question: the com-plicity of the family in supporting these migrations, accepting that their daughters and sisters prostitute themselves, demanding that they send them money, no matter what their condition and suffering. There have been many Nigerian films on these family conflicts and the economic conditions that encourage the phenomenon. See for instance *Ebuwa* (2009), by Lancelot Oduwa Imasuen.

23. "It would appear that by 1920 a well-organized prostitution ring connecting south-ern Nigeria with the Gold Coast had emerged" (Aderinto, 2012, p. 10). The work, written in 1939 by Dickinson, Gold Coast Labor Chief Inspector, was not, how-ever, made public as it was classified as "confidential."

24. On this topic, see also Brühwiler Amani (2015) and Cammaert (2014). See also See Buchi Emecheta's novel, *Slave Girl*.

25. Olokun is an androgynous divinity with various names, sometimes confused with Mami Wata. The role of these divinities in Nigerian migration is no less complex: the Mami Wata spirit epitomizes the desire for riches, success and autonomy, and its iconic representation, as well as its history, is the perfect metaphor of these multiple and intricate imaginaries. See Beneduce and Taliani (2006) and Taliani (2017).

26. This is how Mercy describes the male figure who disturbs her dreams. On this idea, widespread throughout sub-Saharan Africa from Senegal to Mozambique, with similar definitions (*"mari spirituel"*, "night lover", etc.), see Bastian (1997, 2002) with regards to Nigeria, and Tonda (2015). According to Tonda, it is a figure that emerges from the breakdown of moral and social order in the colonial period, the epitome of ambivalence and betrayal.

27. These fantasies of child-snatching, which are extremely widespread among immi-grant women from Africa, deserve more space, which cannot be given here, but are a reminder of the need to explore the power relations, the political value of "per-secutory ideas" and the spectres of racial violence in the experience of immigrant mothers (Beneduce, 2018; Beneduce & Taliani, 2013). Writing about melancholic agency and politics of loss, Judith Butler makes clear a key issue of this experience: "What results is a melancholic agency who cannot know its history as the past, cannot capture its history through chronology, and does not know who it is except as the survival, the persistence of a certain unavowability that haunts the present.

Places are lost—destroyed, vacated, barred—but then there is some new place, and it is not the first, never can be the first.

And so there is an impossibility housed at the site of this new place. What is new, newness itself, is founded upon the loss of original place, and so it is a newness that has within it a sense of belatedness, of coming after, and of being thus fundamentally determined by a past that continues to inform it. And so this past is not actually past in the sense of "over," since it continues as an animating absence in the presence, one that makes itself known precisely in and through the survival of anachronism itself. We could say, with well-deserved pathos and in the voice of traditional modernism, that this new place is one of no belonging, where subjectivity becomes untethered from its collective fabric, where individuation becomes a historical necessity." (Butler, 2003, p. 468)

28. The document gives only the child's first name and the surname received from the Italian father who acknowledged him, but there is no *trace* of the mother, nor does the child appear on Mercy's certificate of family status. For her, this means a desire to cancel all proof of the relation between her and the child. It is no accident that compliments to African children are interpreted as expressing a desire to appropriate them and often generate anxiety and hostility in mothers.

29. "What is remembered in the body is well remembered." (Scarry, 1995, p. 110).

30. On the issue of body, ontology, and experience, see Jackson (2013, pp. 93–113).

31. In the history of psychopathology and cultural psychiatry Western man, with his "sense of guilt", has often been contrasted with African man, dominated by a "sense of shame". I have long been convinced that in the African context the dominant feeling is that of debt, not that of shame. This theme is the centre of my current research, that would articulate the psychology of debt (toward ancestors, the dead, chiefs, and so on) with the specific history of slave trade, colonization, and dependence. We should again recall another question: as Taliani reminds us (2012, 2018, 2019), the right to citizenship of these women is often suspended and revocable, often mediated by their very condition as mothers: paradoxically, while the adoption of her children confers a new status and permanent guarantee of citizenship upon the minor, the woman, *no longer a mother*, is often worn down by psychological suffering, loss of rights and marginalization. It marks the start of a *dual spiral*, which removes both the child, and the possibility of renewing her residence permit (realising the spectre of expulsion or, alternatively, that of a permanent underground existence).

32. Though coined by Muellen in another context (the "slaves' narratives"; Muellen, in Gordon, 2008, p. 221), the formula "resistant orality" is particularly appropriate to recall the value of heterological narratives that resist any classification.

33. "There are certain areas of the African consciousness which will remain inviolate" (Okri, quoted in Fulford, 2009, p. 234). Writing on Ben Okri, Fulford sums up in this way the most original feature of his narrative and poetics (and that of African literature in general): "Okri undermines the tacit idea of much post-colonial criticism, which is that colonialism has an all-pervasive impact on the colonized culture. By challenging the importance of colonialism within 'the African consciousness,' Okri also questions the most Marxist of Marxist thought as he imagines an uncolonized cultural space within the spirit of the people that can be both reached and confirmed by the aesthetic." (Fulford, 2009, p. 234). See also Fulford (2008) on "spiritual realism" of Ben Okri's novels; moreover, see Appiah's criticism (1992) and McCabe (2005).

34. On the similarities between Fanon and de Martino, see Beneduce (2017). De Martino was the pioneer of ethno-psychiatry in Italy: his approach to the religious feeling and folklore of peasants and subalterns was profoundly influenced by Gramsci's thinking, and his ethno-psychiatry certainly did not tend toward cultural relativism. The Fanon Centre draws extensively on his contributions and concepts,

and hence there is no foundation in what Giordano (2008) wrote on the use of the symbolico-cultural universe of immigrant patients in the care systems, describing the Fanon Centre's strategy as a form of "cultural emancipation".

35. Here I paraphrase the title of Deleuze & Guattari's book (1986) as well as the Foucauldian concept of "subjugated knowledges" (Foucault, 2003). On Fann-Dakar's experience and its "impossible experience" in postcolonial Senegal, see Kilroy-Malrac (2014, 2019).

36. "Most notions of illness held by Aymara shamans find their equivalents in notions of Colonialism [. . . .] They are notions of loss, imposition, and incompleteness [. . . .] Contemporary Aymara notions of illness and contemporary Aymara notions of Colonialism [. . .] share, to a noteworthy degree, the same dynamic frame of interpretation. They depart from the same social and cosmic order, and they acquire meaning and are articulated from within shared, but by no means static, cosmological dimensions of significance" (Burman, 2009, pp. 20–21).

37. "The colonized subject also manages to lose sight of the colonist through religion. Fatalism relieves the oppressor of the responsibility of being the cause of wrongdoing, poverty, and the inevitable can be attributed to God. The individual thus accepts the devastation decreed by God, grovels in front of the colonist, bows to the hand of fate, and mentally readjusts to acquire the serenity of stone" (Fanon, 2004, p. 18).

38. Once this set of historico-political arguments has been recognized, we can turn to Nandy's suggestion ("culture as form and language of resistance") and apply it to other contexts. Yet this perspective is only legitimate if we remember that acts of resistance—individual or collective—are always contradictory and ambivalent (Ortner, 1995), and that the understanding of other imaginaries and vocabularies of resistance only becomes possible when we stop using "the basic tropes of Western historiography (biography and event)" (Comaroff & Comaroff, 1992).

39. "In turning to such images, people are reflecting on their symbolic potential to fulfill hopes for release from suffering" (Taussig, 1984, p. 88).

40. I think in particular of those patients who remember being "Ogbanje children," having contact with spirits like Mami Wata, or hosting animal "doubles" in their bodies. The idea of *Ogbanje* among the Igbo, and similar ones (*Igbakhuan* among the Edo or *Abiku* among the Yoruba in Nigeria, etc.) indicate a spirit-child destined to an eternal cycle of birth, death and rebirth. A central figure in contemporary African and African-American literature (Soyinka, Achebe, Morrison, Okri, etc.), the Ogbanje child *recalls* the slave trade, the trauma associated with the disappearance of millions of human beings scattered, felled or abused, but also the vicissitudes of the diaspora and migration, and the invincible desire for autonomy (Ogunyemi, 2002).

41. In similar tones to those of Fanon in Martinique or of the Clarks in the USA, Freire Costa claims that the black subject in Brazil "establishes a persecutory relation" with their body, which subjects them to constant mental tension and drives them to "destroy the signs of color on their bodies and in their offspring" (cit. in Segato, 2015, p. 204). The film *Pelo Malo*, made in Venezuela, is another subtle description of these processes, describing a child's attempts to eliminate the frizziness of his hair in a society that is chauvinistic as well as racist. I am grateful to Simona Taliani for introducing me to Segato's work.

42. Designed to discourage a practice that was regarded as dangerous, this insistence was possible thanks to the availability of wet-nurses from Europe, and from Portugal in particular, reducing the need for black wet-nurses. On wet-nursing in the antebellum South of the USA, see among others Cowling, Pereira Toledo Machado, Paton, and West (2017), Jones-Rogers (2017), and West and Knight (2017).

43. In her analysis of the black Oedipus, Segato restores Oedipus to the context from which it had been removed, that of history, and also avoids the traps of a cultural interpretation of the different expressions of Oedipus complex, something

even Fanon had been tempted by (Fanon, 2008, p. 117). See also Beneduce (2010, pp. 87–110) on this issue.

44. "Authors of *Oedipe africain* [Marie-Cécile and Edmond Ortigues] explain that ancestor worship makes parricide logically impossible: the ancestors are already dead and therefore can be supplanted. The application of psychoanalysis to uncover African difference is also proven problematic when not disastrous. Those European scholars sought Oedipus in Africa, such as Wulf Sachs, Octave Mannoni, and Edmond Ortigues, either ignored colonization or made it seem inevitable. Jonathan Crewe argues that we must read Sachs's *Black Hamlet* not for the psychology of an African but for what it reveals of the self-deceptions, and complicity of European psychoanalysis" (Kortenaar, 2007, p. 183).

45. In Toni Morrison's novel *Beloved*, the image of the slave Sethe's milk being stolen by her master's nephews sucking it from her breasts is a tightly-packed metaphor for how slavery and colonialism stole people's lives (Morrison, 1987).

46. A no less decisive contribution to our thinking on the intricate relations between ethnicity, racism, violence, poverty and maternity, which also avoids the traps of a naïve ethno-psychiatry, is the research in Venezuela by Briggs and Mantini-Briggs (2000) on an alleged case of infanticide.

47. "This codex operates as a stable reservoir of meaning from which flows a capillary, informal, and fragmentary impregnation of the whole of society. At certain corners of society, its presence becomes diffuse and tenuous, *but it is there*" (Segato, 1998, p. 143). On psychiatry and racism in UK, see Littlewood and Lipsedge (1982). On the role of this "reservoir of meaning" in the asylum seekers' narratives, see Beneduce (2018).

48. Toni Morrison writes that her first novel, *The Bluest Eye*, "was interested in racism as a cause, consequence, and manifestation of individual and social psychosis" (Morrison, 1997, p. 9).

49. "Racial melancholia affects both dominant white culture and racial others; indeed, racial melancholia describes the dynamics that constitute their mutual definition through exclusion. The terms thus denote a complex process of racial rejection and desire on the parts of whites and nonwhites that expresses itself in abject and manic forms. On the one side, white American identity and its authority is secured through the melancholic introjection of racial others that it can neither fully relinquish nor accommodate and whose ghostly presence nonetheless guarantees its centrality. On the other side, the racial other (the so-called melancholic object) also suffers from racial melancholia whereby his or her racial identity is imaginatively reinforced through the introjection of a lost, never-possible perfection, an inarticulable loss that comes to inform the individual's sense of his or her own subjectivity. Already we see that these two 'sides' are in fact implicated by one another [. . . .] The model of melancholic incorporation, far from prescribing or reifying the conditions of the racial other, reveals an intricate world of psychical negotiation that unsettles the simplistic division between power and powerlessness." (Cheng, 2001, p. xi)

50. "Those Negroes and white men will be disalienated who refuse to let themselves be sealed away in the materialized Tower of the Past. For many other Negroes, in other ways, disalienation will come into being through their refusal to accept the present as definitive [. . . .] In no way should I derive my basic purpose from the past of the peoples of color. In no way should I dedicate myself to the revival of an unjustly unrecognized Negro civilization. I will not make myself the man of any past. I do not want to exalt the past at the expense of my present and of my future" (Fanon, 2008, p. 176).

51. In the original, Fanon uses the term "sore" (*plaie*), not "wound" (*blessure*), and any doctor will be familiar with the difference.

52. On "postcolonial disorders," see Del Vecchio Good, Hyde, Pinto, and Good (2008).

53. See also Viñar (2005, p. 314): "The lack of any reason or explanation for torture, the infinite and inescapable bodily pain combined with the arbitrariness and

cruelty as central motives of psychic causality configure a traumatic nucleus of horrifying specificity".

54. "To conceive of oneself as a subject is to have the ability to address oneself to another, real or imaginary, actual or potential. Subjectivity is the result of, and depends on, the process of witnessing—address-ability and response-ability. Oppression, domination, enslavement, and torture work to undermine and destroy the ability to respond and thereby undermine and destroy subjectivity" (Oliver, 2001, p. 17).

55. "The tradition of the oppressed teaches us that the 'emergency situation' in which we live is the rule. We must arrive at a concept of history which corresponds to this [. . . .] The astonishment that the things we are experiencing in the 20th century are 'still' possible is by no means philosophical. It is not the beginning of knowledge, unless it would be the knowledge that the conception of history on which it rests is untenable" (Benjamin, 2006, p. 392).

56. "In the work of racial melancholia there, too, lies a nascent ethical and political project [. . .] Racial melancholia thus delineates one psychic process in which the loved object is so overwhelmingly important to and beloved by the ego that the ego is willing to preserve it even at the cost of its own self [. . . .] Hence, the melancholic process is one way in which socially disparaged objects—racially and sexually deprivileged others—live on in the psychic realm. This behavior, Freud remarks, proceeds from an attitude of 'revolt' on the part of the ego. It displays the ego's *melancholic yet militant refusal to allow certain objects to disappear into oblivion* [. . . .] This preservation of the threatened object might be seen, then, as a type of ethical hold on the part of the melancholic ego. The mourner, in contrast, has no such ethics. The mourner is perfectly content with killing off the lost object, declaring it to be dead yet again within the domain of the psyche. While the ambivalence, anger, and rage that characterize this preservation of the lost object threaten the ego's stability, we do not imagine that this threat is the result of some ontological tendency on the part of the melancholic; it is a social threat. Ambivalence, rage, and anger are the internalized refractions of an ecology of whiteness bent on the obliteration of cherished minority subjectivities. If the loved object is not going to live out there, the melancholic emphatically avers, then it is going to live here inside me" (Eng & Han, 2018, pp. 364–365).

57. "Racial melancholia affects both dominant white culture and racial others; indeed, racial melancholia describes the dynamics that constitute their mutual definition through exclusion. The terms thus denote a complex process of racial rejection and desire on the parts of whites and nonwhites that expresses itself in abject and manic forms. On the one side, white American identity and its authority is secured through the melancholic introjection of racial others that it can neither fully relinquish nor accommodate and whose ghostly presence nonetheless guarantees its centrality. On the other side, the racial other (the so-called melancholic object) also suffers from racial melancholia whereby his or her racial identity is imaginatively reinforced through the introjection of a lost, never-possible perfection, an inarticulable loss that comes to inform the individual's sense of his or her own subjectivity. Already we see that these two 'sides' are in fact implicated by one another [. . . .] The model of melancholic incorporation, far from prescribing or reifying the conditions of the racial other, reveals an intricate world of psychical negotiation that unsettles the simplistic division between power and powerlessness" (Cheng, 2001, p. xi).

58. I am borrowing this expression from the title of an anthology edited by Apter and Derby (2010): the role that the contributions to this volume recognize in religious rituals, masquerades, scarifications or altars in activating the past is recognized by my ethnopsychiatry in the symptoms of immigrant patients from what were once colonies.

Bibliography

Aderinto, S. (2007). The girls in moral danger: Child prostitution and sexuality in colonial Lagos, Nigeria, 1930s to 1950. *Journal of Humanities and Social Sciences, 1*(2), 1–22.

Aderinto, S. (2012). "The problem of Nigeria is slavery, not white slave traffic": Globalization and the politicization of prostitution in Southern Nigeria, 1921–1955. *Canadian Journal of African Studies, 46*(1), 1–22.

Aderinto, S. (2015). *When sex threatened the State: Illicit sexuality, nationalism, and politics in colonial Nigeria, 1900–1958*. Urbana, IL: University of Illinois Press.

Althusser, L., & Balibar, E. (1968). *Lire le capital*. Paris: Maspero.

Anderson, H., & Kowal, E. (2012). Culture, history, and health in an Australian Aboriginal community: The case of utopia. *Medical Anthropology, 31*(5), 438–457.

Appiah, A. K. (1992). Spiritual realism. Rev. of *Famished Road* by Ben Okri. *The Nation*, 146–148.

Apter, A. (2005). Griaule's Legacy: Rethinking "la parole claire" in Dogon studies. *Cahiers d'Études Africaines, 45*(177), 95–130.

Apter, A. (2012). Matrilineal motives: kinship, witchcraft, and repatriation among Congolese refugees. *The Journal of the Royal Anthropological Institute, 18*(1), 22–44.

Apter, A., & Derby, L. (Eds.). (2010). *Activating the past: History and memory in the Black Atlantic world*. Newcastle upon Tyne: Cambridge Scholar Publishing.

Aretxaga, B. (2008). Madness and the political real: Reflections on violence in postdictatorial Spain. In M. Del Vecchio Good, T. S. Hyde, S. Pinto, & B. J. Good (Eds.), *Postcolonial disorders* (pp. 43–61). Berkeley, CA: California University Press.

Assiter, A. (1984). Althusser and structuralism. *The British Journal of Sociology, 35*(2), 272–296.

Balandier, G. (1951). La situation coloniale: Approche théorique. *Cahiers Internationaux de Sociologie, 11*, 44–79.

Bastian, M. (1997). Married in the water: Spirit kin and other afflictions of modernity in Southeastern Nigeria. *Journal of Religion in Africa, 27*(2), 116–134.

Bastian, M. (2002). Irregular visitors: Narratives of Ogbanje (spirit children) in Southern Nigerian popular writing. In S. Newell (Ed.), *Readings in African popular fiction*. Bloomington: Indiana University Press.

Beneduce, R. (2010). *Archeologie del trauma. Un'antropologia del sottosuolo*. Laterza: Roma-Bari.

Beneduce, R. (2012). La vie psychique de l'Histoire. Fanon et le temps fracturé de la mémoire. *L'Autre, 13*(3), 273–284.

Beneduce, R. (2015). The moral economy of lying: Subjectcraft, narrative capital, and uncertainty in the politics of asylum. *Medical Anthropology: Cross-Cultural Studies in Health and Healing, 34*(6), 551–571.

Beneduce, R. (2016). Traumatic pasts and the historical imagination: Symptoms of loss, postcolonial suffering, and counter-memories among African migrants. *Transcultural Psychiatry, 53*(3), 1–25.

Beneduce, R. (2017). History as Palimpsest: Notes on subalternity, alienation, and domination in Gramsci, de Martino, and Fanon. *International Gramsci Journal, 2*(3), 134–173.

Beneduce, R. (2018). Une nouvelle bataille de vérité. Discours sorcellaires, cicatrices corporelles et régimes de crédibilité dans les droits d'asile. *Cahiers d'Études Africaines, 231/232*(3), 763–792.

Beneduce, R., & Martelli, P. (2005). Politics of healing and politics of culture, ethnopsychiatry, identities and migration. *Transcultural Psychiatry, 42*(3), 367–393.

Beneduce, R., & Taliani, S. (2006). Embodied powers, deconstructed bodies: Spirit possession, sickness, and the search for wealth in Nigerian migrant women. *Anthropos, 2*, 429–449.

Beneduce, R., & Taliani, S. (2013). Les archives introuvables. Technologie de la citoyenneté, bureaucratie et migration. In B. Hibou (Ed.), *Bureaucratisation néolibérale* (pp. 231–261). Paris: La Découverte.

Benjamin, W. (2006). *Selected writings, 4: 1938–1940*. Harvard, MA: Belknap Press.

Bhabha, H. (1994). *The location of culture*. London: Routledge.

Bourdieu, P., & Sayad, A. (1964). *Le déracinement. La crise de l'agriculture traditionnelle en Algérie*. Paris, Minuit.

Bovenschen, S. (1978). The contemporary witch, the historical witch and the witch myth: The witch, subjectof the appropriation of nature and object of the domination of nature. *New German Critique, 15*, 82–119.

Branche, R. (2016). *La torture et l'armée pendant la guerre d'Algérie (1954–1962)*. Paris: La Découverte.

Briggs, C. L., & Mantini-Briggs, C. (2000). "Bad mothers" and the threat to civil society: Race, cultural reasoning, and the institutionalization of social inequality in a venezuelan infanticide trial. *Law & Social Inquiry, 25*(2), 299–354.

Brüwhile, A. B. (2015). *Moralities of owing and lending: Credit, Debt, and Urban Living in Kariakoo, Dar el Salaam*. Dissertation Submitted to Michigan State University in partial fulfillment of the requirements for the degree of History-Doctor of Philosophy, Ann Arbor, ProQuest.

Burman, A. (2009). Colonialism in context an aymara reassessment of "colonialism", "coloniality" and the "postcolonial world". *Kult, 6*, 117–129.

Butler, J. (2003). Afterword: After loss, what then?. In D. L. Eng & D. Kazanjian (Eds.), *Loss: The politics of mourning* (pp. 467–474). Berkeley, CA: The University of California Press.

Cammaert, V. J. (2014). *"Undesirable practices": Women, children and the politics of development in Northern Ghana, 1930–1972*. A thesis submitted to the Department of History. In conformity with the requirements for the degree of Doctorate of Philosophy Queen's University Kingston, Ontario: Canada.

Chandler, M. J., & Lalonde, C. (1998). Cultural continuity as a hedge against suicide in Canada's First Nations. *Transcultural Psychiatry, 35*(2), 191–219.

Cheng, A. A. (2001). *The melancholy of race: Psychoanalysis, assimilation, and hidden grief*. New York: Oxford university Press.

Clark, K. B., & Clark, M. P. (1939). The development of consciousness of self and the emergence of racial identification in Negro preschool children. *Journal Social Psychology, 10*, 591–599.

Clark, K. B., & Clark, M. P. (1940). Skin color as a factor in racial identification of Negro preschool children. *Journal of Social Psychology, 11*, 159–169.

Clark, K. B., & Clark, M. P. (1950). Emotional factors in racial identification and preference in negro children. *The Journal of Negro Education, 19*(3), 41–350.

Cohen, B. M. Z. (2016). *Psychiatric hegemony: A Marxist theory of mental illness*. New York, NY: Palgrave Macmillan.

Comaroff, J., & Comaroff, J. (1992). *Ethnography and historical imagination*. Boulder, CO: Westview Press.

Cowling, C., Pereira Toledo Machado, M. H., Paton, D., & West, E. (2017). Mothering slaves: Comparative perspectives on motherhood, childlessness, and the care of children in Atlantic slave societies. *Slavery & Abolition: A Journal of Slave and Post-Slave Studies, 38*(2), 223–231.

Crapanzano, V. (1973). *Hamadsha: A study in Moroccan ethnopsychiatry.* Berkeley, CA: University of California Press.

Crapanzano, V. (1992). *Hermes' dilemma & Hamlet's desire: On the epistemology of interpretation.* Cambridge, MA: Harvard University Press.

De Certeau, M. (1997). *The capture of speeches and other political writings.* Minneapolis, MN: University of Minnesota Press.

Deleuze, G., & Guattari, F. (1983). *AntiOedipus: Capitalism and schizophrenia.* Minneapolis, MN: University of Minnesota Press.

Deleuze, G., & Guattari, F. (1986). *Kafka: Toward a minor literature.* Minneapolis, MN: University of Minnesota Press.

Del Vecchio Good, M.-J., Hyde, S. T., Pinto, S., & Good, B. J. (2008). *Postcolonial disorders.* Berkeley, CA: University of California Press.

De Martino, E. (1949). Intorno a una storia del mondo popolare subalterno. [About a history of subaltern popular world]. *Società, 5*(3), 411–435.

De Martino, E. (2012). Crisis of presence and the religious integration. *HAU: Journal of Ethnographic Theory, 2*(2), 434–450.

De Rosny, E. (1981). *Les yeux de ma chèvre. Sur les pas des maîtres de la nuit en pays douala (Cameroun).* Paris: Plon.

Douglas, M. (1964). Matrilinearity and pawnship in Central Africa. *Africa, 34*(4), 310–313.

Elkins, C. (2005). *Imperial reckoning: The untold story of Britain Gulag in Kenya.* New York, NY: Henry Holt and Company.

Elkins, C. (2015). Looking beyond Mau Mau: Archiving violence in the era of decolonization. *American Historical Review, 120*(3), 852–868.

Ellis, S. (2016). *This present darkness: A history of Nigerian organised crime.* New York, NY: Oxford University Press.

Eng, L. D., & Han, S. (2018). *Racial melancholia, racial dissociation: On the social and psychic lives of Asian Americans.* Durham, NC: Duke University Press.

Eyerman, R. (2003). *Cultural trauma slavery and the formation of African American identity.* Cambridge: Cambridge University Press.

Fanon, F. (2004). *The Wretched of the earth.* New York, NY: Grove.

Fanon, F. (2008). *Black skin, White masks.* London: Pluto Press.

Fassin, D. (2000). Les politiques de l'ethnopsychiatrie. La psyche africaine, des colonies africaines aux banlieues parisisiennes. *L'Homme, 153,* 231–250.

Feierman, S. (1995). Healing as social criticism in the time of colonial conquest. *African History, 54*(1), 73–88.

Foucault, M. (2003). *Society must be defended. Lectures at the Collège de France, 1975–1976.* New York, NY: Picador.

Fulford, S. (2008). Points of enchantment: An interview with Ben Okri. *Resurgence, 251,* 48–50.

Fulford, S. (2009). Ben Okri, the aesthetic, and the problem with theory. *Comparative Literature Studies, 46*(2), 233–260.

Gibson, C. N., & Beneduce, R. (2017). *Frantz Fanon: Psychiatry and politics.* New York, NY: Rowman and Littlefield & Johannesburg: Wits University Press.

Giordano, C. (2008). Practices of translation and the making of migrant subjectivities in contemporary Italy. *American Ethnologist, 35*(4), 588–606.

Gordon, A. (2008). *Ghostly matters: Haunting and the sociological imagination.* Minneapolis, MN: University of Minnesota Press.

Hacking, I. (1995). *Rewriting of the soul: Multiple personality and the science of memory.* Princeton, NJ: Princeton University Press.

Jackson, M. (2013). *Lifeworlds: Essays in existential anthropology.* Chicago, IL: The Chicago University Press.

Jameson, F. (1981). *The political unconscious: Narrative as a socially symbolic act.* Ithaca, NY: Cornell University Press.

Jewsiewicki, B. (1998). Les traumatismes des affirmations identitaires, ou la malédiction de n'être rien. *Cahiers d'études africaines, 38,* 150–152, 627–637.

Jones-Rogers, S. (2017). "[S]he could . . . spare one ample breast for the profit of her owner": White mothers and enslaved wet nurses' invisible labor in American slave markets. *Slavery & Abolition: A Journal of Slave and Post-Slave Studies, 38*(2), 337–352.

Kessel, P., & Pirelli, G. (1962). *Le peuple algérien et la guerre: Lettres et témoignages 1954–1962.* Paris: Maspero and Enaudi, Turin.

Kilroy-Malrac K. (2014). Speaking with revenants: Haunting and the ethnographic enterprise, *Ethnography, 15*(2): 255–276.

Kilroy-Malrac, K. (2019). *An impossible inheritance. Postcolonial psychiatry and the work of memory in a West African clinic.* Berkeley, CA: University of California Press.

Kortenaar, N. T. (2007). Oedipus, Ogbanje, and the sons of independence. *Research in African Literatures, 38*(2), 181–205.

Lacan, J. (1993). *The psychosis: The seminar of Jacques Lacan* (J.-A. Miller, Ed.). Book III 1955–1956. London: Routledge.

Laroui, A. (1975). *Histoire du Maghreb. Un essaye de synthèse* (Vol. 2). Paris: Maspéro.

Lazali, K. (2018). *Le trauma colonial. Une enquête sur les effets psychiques et politiques contemporains de l'oppression coloniale en Algérie.* Paris: La Découverte.

Lipsitz, G. (1990). *Time passages: Collective memory and American popular culture.* Minneapolis, MN: Minnesota University Press.

Littlewood, R., & Lipsedge, R. (1982). *Aliens and alienists: Psychiatry and ethnic minorites.* London: Unwin Hyman.

Lydon, G. (1997). The unraveling of a neglected source: A report on women in Francophone West Africa in the 1930s. *Cahiers d'études africaines, 37*(147), 555–584.

Mahone, S., & Vaughan, M. (Eds.). (2007). *Psychiatry and empire.* Cambridge, MA: Cambridge University Press.

Malkki , L. H. (1995). Refugees and exile: From "Refugee Studies" to the national order of things. *Annual Review of Anthropology,* 24, 495–523.

Malkki , L. H. (1996). Speechless emissaries: Refugees, humanitarianism, and dehistoricization. *Cultural Anthropology, 11*(3), 377–404.

Manfredi, V. (1997). Ìgbo initiation: Phallus vs umbilicus? *Cahiers d'études africaines, 37*(145), 157–211.

Marriott, D. (2010). On racial fetishism. *Qui Parle: Critical Humanities and Social Sciences, 18*(2), 215–248.

McCabe, D. (2005). "Higher realities": New age spirituality in Ben Okri's the Famished road. *Research in African Literatures, 36*(4), 1–21.

Mendes, C. G. (2015). *Under the strain of color: Harlem's Lafargue Clinic and the promise of an antiracist psychiatry.* Ithaca, NY: Cornell University Press.

Morrison, T. (1987). *Beloved.* London, UK: Vintage.

Morrison, T. (1997). Home. In W. Lubiano (Ed.), *The house that race built* (pp. 3–12). New York, NY: Vintage.

Morrison, T. (1998). The site of memory. In W. Zinsser (Ed.), *Inventing the truth: The art and craft of memoir* (pp. 183–199). Boston and New York: Houghton Mifflin Company.

Morrison, T. (2007). *The bluest eye.* New York, NY: Vintage.

Mosca, G. (1840). *Commentario su le leggi di procedura ne' giudizi civili e commerciali.* Napoli: Stamperia Mosca.

Nandy, A. (1983). *The intimate enemy: Loss and recovery of self under colonialism.* New Delhi: Oxford University Press.

Nandy, A. (1995). History's forgotten doubles. *History and Theory, 34*(2), 44–66.

Nandy, A. (2003). *The romance of the state and the fate of dissent in the tropics.* Oxford: Oxford University Press.

Nathan, T. (1994). *L'influence qui guérit.* Paris: Odile Jacob.

Ogunyemi, C. O. (2002). An Abiku-Ogbanje atlas: A pre-text for rereading Soyinka's *Aké* and Morrison's *Beloved. African American Review, 36*(4), 663–678.

Oliver, K. (2001). *Witnessing beyond recognition.* Minneapolis, MN: University of Minnesota Press.

Oliver, K. (2004). *The colonization of psychic space: A psychoanalytic social theory of oppression.* Minneapolis, MN: University of Minnesota Press.

Ortigues, M.-C., & Ortigues, E. (1966). *L'Œdipe africain.* Paris: L'Harmattan.

Ortner, B. S. (1995). Resistance and the problem of ethnographic refusal. *Comparative Study of Society and History, 37*(1), 173–193.

Pandolfo, S. (2018). *Knot of the soul madness, psychoanalysis, Islam.* Chicago, IL: The University of Chicago Press.

Platt, T. (2002). El feto agresivo. Parto, Formación de la persona y Mito-Historia en los Andes. *Estudios Atacameños, 22,* 127–155.

Platt, T. (2013). Care and carelessness in rural Bolivia: Silence and emotion in Quechua childbirth testimonies. *Bulletin de l'Institut français d'études andines, 42*(3), 333–351.

Robinson, C. J. (1983). *Black Marxism.* London: Zed Press.

Sadowsky, J. (1999). *Imperial Bedlam: Institutions of madness in colonial Southwest Nigeria.* Berkeley, CA: California University Press.

Scarry, E. (1995). *The body in pain: The making and unmaking of the world.* New York, NY: Oxford University Press.

Segato, R. L. (1998). The color-blind subject of myth or, where to find Africa in the Nation. *Annual Review of Anthropology, 27,* 129–151.

Segato, R. L. (2006). Antropologia e Direitos Humanos: Alteridade e ética no movimento de expansão dos direitos universais. *Mana, 12*(1), 207–236.

Segato, R. L. (2015). *La crítica de la colonialidad en ocho ensayos: y una antropología por demanda.* Buenos Aires: Prometeo libros.

Stora, B. (1998). *La gangrène et l'oubli.* Paris: la Découverte.

Studer, N. S. (2015). *The hidden patients: North African women in French colonial psychiatry.* Wien: Böhlau Verlag GmbH & Cie.

Taïeb, S. (1939). *Les idées d'influence dans la pathologie mentale de l'indigène Nord-Africain. Le rôle des superstizions.* Algier: Ancienne Imprimerie Victor Hentz.

Taliani, S. (2012). Coercion, fetishes and suffering in the daily lives of young Nigerian women in Italy. *Africa, 82*(4), 579–608.

Taliani, S. (2016). Calembour de choses dans le vaudou italien: Corps-fétiche et principes d'inégalité devant les dieux. *Social Compass, 63*(2), 163–180.

Taliani, S. (2017). Femmes nigérianes déplacées, filles à la merci. Sur les usages de l'ethno psychiatrie. In A. Ceriana Mayneri (Ed.), *Entre errances et silences. Ethnographier des souffrances et des violences ordinaires* (pp. 65–98). Louvain-la-Neuve: Academia-L'Harmattan.

Taliani, S. (2018). Du dilemme des filles et de leurs réserves de vie. La crise sorcellaire dans la migration nigériane. *Cahiers d'Études africaines, 58*(3–4), 231–232, 737–761.

Taliani, S. (2019). *Il tempo della disobbedienza. Per un'antropologia genetica.* Verona: ombre corte.

Taussig, M. (1984). History as sorcery. *Representations, 7,* 87–109.

Tonda, J. (2015). *L'impérialisme postcolonial. Critique de la société des éblouissements.* Paris: Karthala.

van Djik, R. (2001). "Voodoo" on the doorstep: Young Nigerian prostitutes and magic policing in the Netherlands. *Africa: Journal of the International African Institute, 71*(4), 558–586.

Vaughan, M. (1991). *Curing their Ills: Colonial power and African illness.* Cambridge: Polity Press.

Vidal-Naquet, P. (1975). *Les crimes de l'armée française. Algérie 1954–1962.* Paris: Maspero.

Viñar, N. M. (2005). The specificity of torture as trauma: The human wilderness when words fail. *International Journal of Psychoanalysis, 86,* 311–333.

Viñar, N. M., & Viñar, M. (1993). *Fracturas de la memoria. Crónicas para una memoria por venir.* Montevideo: Trilce Ed.

Viveiros de Castro, E. (2015). Who is afraid of the ontological wolf? Some comments on an ongoing anthropological debate. *The Cambridge Journal of Anthropology, 33*(1), 2–17.

Warnier, J.-P. (2017). Ceci n'est pas un sorcier. De l'effet Magritte en sorcellerie. *Politique africaine, 146*(2), 125–141.

Weismantel, M. (2001). *Cholas and pishtacos: Stories of race and sex in the Andes.* Chicago, IL: The Chicago University Press.

West, E., & Knight, R. J. (2017). Mothers' milk: Slavery, wetnursing, and black and white women in the Antebellum South. *Journal of Southern History, 83*(1), 37–68.

Wright Mills, C. (1959). *The sociological imagination.* New York, NY: Oxford University Press.

Yacine, K. (1991). *Nedjma.* Charlottesville, VA: University of Virginia Press.

Zempléni, A. (1966). La dimension thérapeutique du culte des rab. Ndöp, tuuru et Samp, rites de possession chez les Lebou et les Wolof. *Psychopathologie africaine, 2*(3), 295–439.

Section 3

Fanon in Clinical Action

Psychotherapeutic and Community Applications

6 Subversive Healing

Fanon and the Radical Intent of Surviving Torture

Hawthorne E. Smith and Joseph Gonkapieu Gueu

In a real sense, this chapter willed itself into being. The subject matter, so vital at this historical moment, seemed to track the authors down and compel us to write. It prodded and nipped at our heels, while serenely awaiting us at the crossroads—passing the time until we finally realized what we were meant to do. "All things in divine order," as the elders would say. Many vectors brought this particular point of realization to fruition: the steadfastness and persistence of this volume's editorial team; the groundbreaking humanism and brilliance of Dr. Fanon; and the courage and insights of torture survivors grappling with the poisoned blessing of survival. These displaced, wounded and "wretched" survivors, whose continued existence is based on a fragile sense of shared humanity, humbly manage to open eyes, ears and hearts to deeper truths. They have clearly underscored the importance and absolute imperative of this narrative. They manifest, as Fanon has traced, that healing from race-based, colonial and/or neo-colonial torture and human rights abuses is not a passive act. It reaches beyond simply being defined as an active endeavor. It is subversive. It is a purposeful, focalized and determined effort girded in a resistant posture.

In this chapter, we will endeavor to look through a Fanonian lens at the goals and objectives of torture and human rights abuses in the ongoing "asymmetrical warfare" (Turner, 2011, p. 126) experienced by oppressed peoples in long-existing colonial and neo-colonial systems. The impact of torture, in both personal and communal contexts will be detailed and examined, including the direct effects of torture itself, as well as the ongoing stressors of dislocation, deracination and violent marginalization. The role of medical and psychiatric "science" will be addressed, including the subsequent distrust or ambivalence that survivors may harbor toward practitioners, potentially standing in the way of creating adaptive and appropriate therapeutic interventions.

Lastly, we will focus on Fanon's notion of Liberation Psychology and how it relates to the experience of those who are fighting to retain their sense of humanity despite the ongoing violent attempts to render them sub-human. Their shared struggle and insights will be used to illustrate and buttress some of Fanon's ideas, and hopefully lead to a way of understanding their healing process from a more fundamental, anti-oppression framework.

"Why Me? Why Us?" The Benefits
of Intentional Horror

In the 1970s film, *Apocalypse Now*, one of the most powerful and disturbing scenes depicted the deranged Colonel Kurtz, a tragic Conradian character, describing how a local despotic ruler responded to an unsolved crime by hacking off the left hands of all the male villagers in his fiefdom. The crazed colonel described this abusive action as "genius," as it brought the subjugated population further under control. He emphasized the power of "the horror . . . the horror."

Decades of psychological work with survivors of torture from around the world have reinforced the same crucial lesson. The essential goal of torture, in addition to its sadistic antecedents and inclinations, is to break the spirit of the individual, so that the population can be further oppressed. It is understood that if one stands up for his or her rights, look what can, and likely will happen.

Fanon reflected upon these notions throughout his career. In *The Wretched of the Earth*, he wrote about how the colonial powers strive to create "pacified populations" (Fanon, 1963, p. 249) by assuring that the community's "indocile nature has been tamed" (Fanon, 1963, p. 250). He named the phenomenon the "philosophy of torture" in his treatises on the African political revolution (Fanon, 1964, pp. 75–76). Ajari (2014) expanded upon this idea in his doctoral dissertation, explaining that the philosophy of torture went beyond causing pain. It was used as a rationalization of the power dynamics at play. It was used to maximize the suffering inflicted upon native populations. It was used to uphold the social order that had been defined by oppressive, race-based societal structures. It was a tool to force the oppressed people to "give up their resistance and loyalty" (Ajari, 2014, p. 166), and to deprive them of their humanity. He describes the destruction of a survivor's life as creating a "mort-vivant"—a living cadaver (p. 168). To that point, he quoted Patrice Lumumba, who stated on the occasion of Congo's independence on June 30, 1960, "We have known atrocious suffering related to our political opinions or religious beliefs; exiled in their own homeland, their fate is truly worse than death itself" (reprinted in the San Francisco Bay View National Black Newspaper, 2009).

As such, personal and communal levels of suffering are toxically intertwined, and torturers will use all of the tools at their disposal—both physical and emotional—to attain their goals. The systematic efforts to achieve these goals are varied in their application, but singular in their intent. Turner describes the "breaking and disciplining of colored bodies" (Turner, 2011, p. 117), while Fanon expounds upon the "systematic negation of the person" (Fanon, 1962, p. 250). The abuses reverberate from the micro-level and have lasting, pernicious impact on the macro-sphere. Fanon noted how "depersonalization is felt in the collective sphere" (Fanon, 1963, p. 293).

These processes and techniques are well documented among the survivors we meet at the Bellevue/NYU Program for Survivors of Torture. Whether it is a Tibetan monk being abused with electric cattle prods in a Chinese prison;

a Camerounian human rights advocate being beaten on the soles of his feet (a.k.a. falanga) until he must crawl to his interrogation sessions; an opposition politician from Congo being raped in front of her husband; or a young Sierra Leonean boy being drugged, having a machete placed in his hand, and being ordered to mutilate his neighbor or be killed; the objectives are clear. Destroy a spirit. Set an example for others who would dare resist. Eliminate opposition. Sow hatred and distrust within communities. Uphold the hegemonic order. Extract maximum profit. "The horror . . . the horror."

The experiences recounted in our clinic are not new. Although Fanon's writings on torture took root during the colonial age, the insights are still apropos. People speak today of neo-colonial, oppressive and exploitative relations between the "metropole" and its former colonies. The tools of divide and conquer are on full display, and they pit community members against one another for the economic spoils available to them. Class divisions, religious schisms and ethnic animosity are fomented in a way that still benefits the extraction of African goods and resources for the metropole, while oppressed people turn on one another—impoverished gladiators in a struggle for survival, where the notion of human rights and mutual respect are challenged in such a harsh and forbidding context (Ajari, 2014; Haddab, 2007; Turner, 2011).

Today, these oppressive systems may have a "different face." Colonial and abusive tactics thrive within the corrupt political, military and law enforcement structures throughout Africa. The torrent of people fleeing these circumstances—including those who risk their lives in perilous pirogue journeys across the Mediterranean, give testimony to the horrors they are trying to escape. The dehumanizing processes of immigration and exclusion in western countries—including along the southern border of the United States—show that the tactics may have changed, but the oppressive hierarchy remains in effect.

Fanon describes electrocutions, beatings, isolation, forced positions, rape, disfigurement and extrajudicial killings as part of the reality of the Algerian War. As Haddab (2007) points out, part of the urgency and power of Fanon's writing is that it is so immediate to the events in question. In the novel *Fanon*, John Edgar Wideman (2008) notices that Fanon generally writes in the present tense, "as though it's happening as you speak" (p. 139). We've come to understand that this tendency goes beyond the professional convention of a clinician writing chart notes; rather, it is a both a precursor and an epilogue to an ongoing reality. His patients speak to ancient realities while presaging events to come, long after they have left the living stage. As an old street hustler once explained, "The game was ancient when you found it; and it will still be brand new when you put it down." Fanon's truths cut that deeply—and persistently; even in the "postcolonial" age.

Ongoing Impact: "Some Wounds Will Never Heal"

In the ongoing support group for French-speaking African survivors of torture that has run at the Bellevue/NYU Program for Survivors of Torture for the past 22 years, certain subjects come to the fore time and time again. One of them is a debate about the desirability of forgetting one's trauma. Many survivors desire such a blissful relief from the torment of ongoing nightmares, insomnia, anxiety and shame. There are others, however, who claim they would never want to forget, insisting that their experiences are part of who they are, and that the associated suffering is a painful price they have to pay. The debates may go back and forth, but one essential truth comes forth each time.

It is not possible to forget.

Group members counsel one another to focus on "overcoming, as opposed to forgetting." This is in line with Fanon's idea of "ineffaceable wounds" (Fanon, 1963, p. 250). In *The Wretched of the Earth*, he goes into great detail about many of the ways in which torture impacts a survivor's emotional, behavioral and biological functioning. His observations overlap greatly with much of the symptomatology captured in the DSM-5. Among his patients, he notes: headaches, heart palpitations, enuresis, atypical speech patterns, low mood, thought disorders, suicidal and homicidal ideation, tearfulness, sexual dysfunction, appetite disruptions, paresthesia, mood swings and agitation, substance abuse, dissociation, motor instability, hallucinations and trauma-related phobias. These overlap greatly with the presentation of survivors at our clinic. A mere recitation of symptoms does not capture the entirety of torture's impact, particularly when it is in combination with forced exile and concurrent levels of marginalization. Many factors do not make it into the diagnostic manuals, or may be treated as peripheral "culturally bound syndromes."

An example of a stressor that frequently escapes diagnostic categorization is guilt. Survivor guilt is reported with great frequency, especially with our population of survivors who have been able to make it safely out of their country, while others are still in harm's way. Fanon shared the story of one patient who decried his "hellish good luck" (Fanon, 1963, p. 261) in surviving the violence visited upon his community. Our clinical experience shows that feelings of guilt deepen when people feel dislocated from others and lack a sense of purpose in their lives. Wideman (2008) described Fanon's teachings on the subject as having "taught me how divided from myself and others I'd become" (p. 5).

Survivors may ask what good does it do to struggle in their new country and scrape together a meager living at a menial (often exploitative) job to gain their "daily bread," if they cannot be sure that their children back home ate sufficiently that day. Even if they are able to send money home to their families, perhaps they have lost the sense of connection that being a parent, a spouse, a family and community member brings. The rape survivor may see herself (or himself) as "dirty" and "damaged." The widower may see himself as a failed family protector. The "mort-vivant" struggles mightily with the debatable merits of survival.

Fanon examined the diagnostic label "reactionary psychoses" (Fanon, 1963, p. 251), which was used to encompass much of the clinical presentations he observed, but not without identifying some caveats. Similar to some of the debate regarding the diagnosis of post-traumatic stress disorder or PTSD (as currently defined), Fanon seems to caution against blaming the victim or judging the survivors as being feeble or defective by nature. If one has experienced the profound traumatic shocks that torture survivors have endured (as well as the ongoing stressors to be detailed later in this chapter), would it not be understandable (if not expected) to have some significant disturbances in functioning? Does placing the diagnostic label of reactive psychosis or PTSD place the onus on the survivor as somehow being responsible for their own symptomatology because of the inherent weakness of their character? We now explore the role that psychiatry has played in influencing social and political perceptions of this debate.

Is a Cigar Just a Cigar? The Role of Psychiatry in Torture and Oppression

Though the debate about differential diagnoses is treated by some as being purely clinical in nature, Fanon goes much further and examines the role of medical and behavioral health "science" to undergird oppressive structures and practices. "Scientific racism" (Turner, 2011, p. 120) has been utilized for many years to uphold hegemonic power structures. In the medical and behavioral health context, it has been used to provide cover to oppressive structures by presenting oppressed populations as inferior beings (sometimes classified as sub-human), who do not merit equal treatment, protection or opportunity.

Though the debate as to whether a torture survivor suffers from PTSD as a disorder, as opposed to suffering human responses to inhumane circumstances, may seem like an academic exercise; it can also be seen as part of a larger composite where oppressed people are seen as weak, faulty and sub-par regardless of their traumatic experiences. Haddab (2007) explains that Fanon did not deny the psychiatric consequences of the material and symbolic violence of colonialism; rather he attributed the effects to "causes that were totally different than the explanations imputed by the ideologues of colonial oppression" (p. 82). Turner (2011) also described "modern racial alienation" and that subsequent violent or anti-social behaviors stem from the "oppressive material conditions" of colonialism and neo-colonialism (p. 129).

Fanon takes time to detail the ways in which these processes were taken to an extreme in the Algerian context. In the academic Algerian biomedical community, it was widely believed and promoted that the Algerian character was synonymous with "appalling criminality" (Fanon, 1963, p. 296). This notion was purposely reinforced the more Algerians took active steps to resist the French domination. As young Algerians were trained to become medical and behavioral health professionals, they were indoctrinated into this belief system. Fanon (1963) writes "Algerian doctors were obliged to hear and learn that Algerians were born criminal" (p. 298).

These character assassinations went beyond social context and conditioning and were linked to biological explanations. Fanon (1963) speaks of the "Primitivism" that was assigned to Algerians because it was believed that they had "no cortex" in their brains, and how medical leaders of the day wrote that "Africans make little use of the frontal lobes" (pp. 301–302). As Haddab (2014) summarizes, "Classical psychiatric knowledge can be used as an instrument of domination, or as a means of justification of positions of dominance and widespread discrimination" (p. 81).

One way this can be achieved in a broader sociological sense is via "Identification by contrast" (Ajari, 2014, p. 45), which is a process by which colonial and neo-colonial powers have fortified their perceived and projected notion of being upstanding, righteous and superior to oppressed people of color by portraying themselves as the antithesis and antidote to the depravity of the colonized populations. In his classic *Black Skin, White Masks*, Fanon describes how depictions of people of color in literature and fiction serve as a subtext for how they are seen in reality. He remarks that "the wolf, the devil the evil genie, the bad guy, the savage, are always represented by a Black or Indian person" (Fanon, 1952, p. 110). Ajari (2014) writes about how these terrifying savages are then vanquished in dramatic and bloody fashion by the hard-charging White hero, giving a cathartic pleasure to both the tale-teller and the spectator (p. 46).

These images are not only potent in rationalizing and excusing the abuses of torture and oppression on the occupying population and the world at large, they begin to eat at the psyche of the oppressed peoples themselves, and begin the process of "internalized inferiority" (Ajari, 2014, p. 8), self-hatred and "fostered dependence" (Turner, 2011, p. 118) that afflict many under the yoke of tyranny.

I remember my father telling me of going to see "Gone with the Wind" as a young man when it first came to theaters in 1939. As segregation was still the law of the land in his home state of Maryland, he saw the movie in the company of dozens of other Black people. My dad recalled the scene arrived when the lazy, undependable, childlike Black character played by Butterfly McQueen was smacked hard across the face by her White mistress/owner (whose character was portrayed as put-upon, strong, mature and courageous), because the hapless slave "didn't know nothin' 'bout birthin' no babies." My dad was shocked, saddened (and haunted for decades) by the rapturous applause the Black movie patrons put forth at that pivotal moment. There were whoops and hollers, and declarations that "Niggers ain't shit!" It is clear from historical patterns and current struggles that, over time, the yoke of oppression becomes a poison that attacks the oppressed from within.

Again, Fanon writes in the present tense, as his insights carry unfortunate weight to this very day. Those who stand up against oppressive regimes or systems are easily identified and labeled as terrorists or criminal elements. Racial minorities, particularly Black people, are considered to be lazy or inept. Here in the US, the long-standing, dual narratives of Black men as dangerous and criminal goes hand-in-hand with "scientific" broadsides like the *Bell Curve* (Herrnstein & Murray, 1996) that portrayed Blacks as being less capable of learning and, therefore, not worthy of equal educational resources and opportunities. Not coincidently, we have a situation in the US, today, where more young

Black men are in prison than young Black men attending university. No matter how suspect the data, or how poorly grounded in theory the "science" might be, it can have a significant impact on policy—if it supports the colonial and oppressive narrative.

The additional danger is when oppressed individuals and populations begin to believe the negative aspersions cast upon them. In our ongoing therapeutic group for French-speaking African survivors, there are times when individuals may look back fondly to the "good days" when the colonizers were still in direct control of their countries. The ongoing misery that Africans and African nations currently face is frequently attributed to the frailty, criminality, corrupt nature and avariciousness of Africans themselves. Other group members will invariably push back regarding the ongoing neo-colonial structures that still impede true independence for African countries and people. They do not turn a blind eye to the transgressions of "brother against brother" in their home countries but will usually put it into the context of the structure of enforced poverty and "divide-and-conquer and separate-and-rule" that still holds sway to this day.

Again, they echo what Fanon insisted in his writings, that the colonial (oppressive) context was the construct that set community members against one another, enforced poverty and dislocation, and led to the destruction of familial and social structures. Context influences behavior and complicates the healing process as "the circumstances of the cured patients maintains and feeds these pathological kinks" (Fanon, 1963, p. 279).

As such, the voices of dignity and self-belief are in a constant uphill battle with the voices of those who would give into the ideas of self-loathing and inferiority—even within the same individual. Historically, it has been difficult for the oppressed to differentiate between what is inherent to their character and what is inherent to the situation of being materially and emotionally oppressed, much to the detriment of their emotional functioning and self-regard (Fanon, 1963; Turner, 2011). The "sciences" of psychiatry and sociology have played an ongoing and pernicious role in keeping this confused state all too essential and relevant for oppressed people and populations.

Medical and behavioral health professionals have also played a role in maintaining hegemonic domination by directly participating in the abuse and torture of subjugated people under their care. Fanon details the ways in which doctors may try to earn the trust of a captive, stating, "I am a doctor. I am not a policeman. I am here to help you" (Fanon, 1963, p. 284), while drugging them with Pentothal or preparing them for further torture by their captors.

This is still evident today, as many survivors are reticent or at least ambivalent about engaging in any sort of behavioral health assessment or treatment. Turner (2011) states, "The attitude of ambivalence of the colonized is inseparable from the colonial situation" (p. 122). Part of this may be culturally driven, where psychiatry and psychology are either unfamiliar or stigmatized, being seen as the realm of the "sick and crazy" (Smith, 2003). In addition, however, may be the notion that medical and behavioral health providers are not only complicit, but instrumental, to the mistreatment and ongoing domination of the people in their "care."

Clinicians (such as one of the authors of this chapter), who have engaged directly with survivors of the "Enhanced Interrogation" regimen of the United States government, have reported that through positive interactions and signs of genuine shared respect over time, these survivors/captives have occasionally begun to engage with the clinician on a humanistic level. Some have subsequently responded and explained that the clinician's apparent humanistic interest and civility is "exactly the same tactic" previous interrogators had used on them before, during, or after the period that other "enhanced techniques" were used. A friendly face and empathic bearing may no longer be reassuring, but will be signs of danger that intentionally inflicted pain may be forthcoming. Survivors may come to see the clinician and the torturer as the same, and the medical/psychiatric milieu as nothing more than another franchise within the oppressive neo-colonial system.

Trust is an essential, but fragile, element in the healing process. A clinical example from our program is that a young woman (we will call her Biba) was tortured in her Central African country because her father had been in an elite position in the government. When there was a coup d'état, it was Biba's bodyguards who first turned on her. The very people who had been charged with her protection since she was a young girl were the first (of many) to do her harm. When Biba finally made it to the US and came to us for treatment, we discussed the possibilities and parameters of engaging in a therapeutic relationship. When we spoke of openness and trust, she told her therapist, "There is absolutely nothing you can do to earn my trust. Even if you say all the right things. Even if you do all the right things. I mean, you could do all of that for 20 years, because that is what my bodyguards did. But in the end, they still betrayed me." After a prolonged silence, which seemed most appropriate with what she has shared, Biba continued, "Yeah, you cannot earn my trust—but perhaps it is something I can offer."

Biba's insightful courage has guided our clinical thinking for more than two decades. I now understand that as a Westerner, as an American, as a psychologist, as a man (my skin color notwithstanding), one can never earn the trust of the clients with whom we work. We can only understand the trust they may choose to share, as being a gift—a precious gift to be honored. Taking this attitude of allowing survivors to teach, to find their voice in a context that is foreign and surreal to them is the only way to find my footing and be of any use on their healing journey. It is the only way to bear witness to their vigorous grasping for humanity, belonging, connection and meaning.

Once asked how many people he thought he had healed in his career, the lead author of this chapter replied, "None." The truth is that I have never healed anyone, but I have been blessed and honored to see a great number of people get better over time. It is in this context of the proactive healing processes employed by survivors, and in deep conversation with the co-author of this chapter, that we endeavor to describe some of the ways that survivors work to heal themselves as a purposeful, anti-oppressive act.

As a point of reference, it should be mentioned that the Bellevue/NYU Program for Survivors of Torture has treated more than 5,000 men, women and children from more than 100 countries since its inception in 1995. We are an interdisciplinary program that utilizes primary care medicine and other medical specialties, psychiatry, psychology, social work and social services, educational and legal services in a humanistic, resilience-based approach to our survivor-clients (Smith, 2018). Many of the insights and anecdotes shared in this chapter come from the support group for French-speaking African survivors of torture that has been in continuous existence since 1996. Here, it seems that the historical and sociological processes upon which Fanon derived his insights are most pertinent, persistent and present.

"Do Not Give the Victory to Those Who Do Not Deserve It"

Suicidal ideation is a dangerous reality for many exiled survivors of torture in our program. Being able to explore these painful, yet understandable, impulses in a safe and supportive environment has played a part in many people being able to overcome these difficult moments.

Once, such occasion occurred in a group session when a man from Mauritania decried the fact that he had survived and had been able to make it to the US, but his family (who had escaped slavery as he had) were still living in hiding, in a tenuous existence deep in the Sahara. His guilt and longing were intolerable and he shared with the group his desire to put it all to an end. It was a woman from Cameroun who helped to support him and place his suffering in context. She spoke frankly, and from the heart; and as we reviewed the literature for this chapter, it became evident that she spoke from a shared perspective with Fanon. She said,

> My brother, do not give the victory to those who have oppressed you. You know that they torture us to break us. They try to make us think we are nothing—that we are less than human. They try to break us so they can continue to oppress our communities and enslave our families.

She asked if the Mauritanian survivor had experienced prison, and when he answered affirmatively, she continued:

> Then you know about the four walls, the darkness, the loneliness. But somehow you escaped from that. You made it out of your country. You crossed an ocean to try to start a life here. But if you give up now—if you agree with them that your life is not worth living. If you enter into their evil accord that your struggle, your family and your people are not worth the pain—then you give them the victory. They will smile. They will know that their poison killed you even when they could no longer lay hands on you. They do not deserve to smile! Do not give them this victory!

These words could not have come from a Western mental health practitioner without being paternalistic, patronizing and ineffective; but by allowing survivors to engage as healing instruments for one another, in addition to their own healing processes, it has a multi-directional, empowering effect. Survivors learn to see themselves as "needed, not just needy" (Smith, 2003), valued and valuable. Small steps in an improbable journey. As group member say, "Rien n'est facile, mais tout est possible"—"Nothing is easy, but everything is possible."

It is a matter of purposeful and proactive existence. Managing to live, and aspiring to thrive beyond mere survival. Practicing defiance by taking the next breath. Fanon (1952) accentuates the point, "When we revolt it's not for a particular culture. We revolt simply because, for many reasons, we can no longer breathe." (p. 226).

Who Am I? Character v. Circumstances

Fanon had identified one of the primordial struggles for survivors of torture and colonial oppression as one of identity (Fanon, 1952, 1963). Who am I really? Who are we? What is my role? What is my value? Ajari (2014) writes about the oppressive colonial processes as going beyond the mere appropriation of land or mineral resources—it is actually a "life appropriation" where identity is destroyed and boundaries are blurred beyond recognition.

It is in this context that group members have helped to support each other (and themselves) by insisting on the great difference between character and circumstance. The sudden, violent and purposeful abuses of human rights violations and societal oppression can cause the upheaval of one's notion of self in profound ways. We are often reminded by clients that "you never know who is driving your taxi or sweeping your floor" (Smith, 2018, p. 281). Many survivors are targeted precisely because they were community leaders and people of influence. Now things have shifted. Some clients will confide that they no longer recognize themselves in the mirror. Some complaints we hear are things like: "I gained (or lost) so much weight; I never wore clothes like this; I was once the head of my extended family, now I'm the 14th person in a one-bedroom apartment; I was once an intellectual, now I am semi-literate in this country;" and so on.

Fellow survivors help to make the point that if someone was an intelligent, humanistic, generous, caring person in their homeland, then they remain intelligent, humanistic, generous and caring now. The character remains firm; a survivor does not permit him or herself to let go of it—or have it ripped away from them. In addition, it is those very aspects of character that allow oppressed people to survive the change in circumstances and hold on until the day circumstances will change again—not to what they were before, but to the new reality they are involved in creating.

Reconnecting with a community that is experienced in being culturally syntonic is another way in which one can regain control of their internal narrative of how they define themselves. One senior member of the Francophone African group, a respected elder among his colleagues, once stated that there was a big difference between being "an old man, washing dishes and living in a shelter; who happens to attend a support group," as opposed to being "a respected community member, who happens to be washing dishes and living in a shelter until he can do better."

The notion of defining for ourselves who we are, and not buying into the colonial or "pseudo-science" screeds in which oppressed people of color are seen as inferior, is a key factor in the healing process. Being a survivor of torture can become a reference group identity that trumps all others. People may say that it doesn't matter what country they come from, what matters is that they are a rape survivor or a survivor of torture. It is the trauma that defines them. We work very hard in our program to honor the fact that the traumatic experiences are a significant part of someone's history, but that they were someone before the events happened; they were someone during the traumatic events; they are someone now; and they are still evolving into someone. It is not the trauma that defines us, we can still retain the ability to define for ourselves who we are and the role we will play in our societies (Smith, 2007).

Another issue for the colonized and tortured individual living in exile is the notion of acculturation. There is a sense of being betwixt and between, neither fish nor fowl, or a "beast of no nation," as Achebe (1958) once called it. For group members, the pull of adapting to one's new reality and norms in the US, as opposed to holding on to one's African norms and comportment, is a tenuous balancing act. Many approach it from a position of weakness. There is fear that cleaving too closely to one's African roots will foreclose the possibility of adapting and advancing in the metropole, as opposed to the fear of assimilating too much and being a "sell out" or the "petit-negre" that is used as a pawn and tool to keep the masses and the "true Africans" down (Ajari, 2014; Fanon, 1952, 1963).

Group members have counseled each other in terms of striding both the Western and African worlds, but from a position of strength in which they can not only walk in both worlds—but can be the best in both. Using the content and information they obtain from being in both worlds, as well as the abilities to be adaptive, multilingual, quick on their feet, multicultural, open and authentic, is a combination of traits that work well in any context if one can believe in one's own effectiveness.

The ongoing stressors and insults experienced by oppressed survivors living in exile necessitate ongoing interventions to help fortify their sense of self and purpose. To that end, we recently had a group meeting where only men happened to be in attendance. All of these men were fathers, separated from their families, and dealing with tenuous and long-standing immigration cases. Their shared sadness about being "bad, absent fathers" was palpable, and made evident when one shared his experience of his daughter saying that she had "no idea" if he was a good father or not, since he had been away from her for most of her young life. Tears were shed as the men recounted similar stories of being laid low by their circumstances and wondering if the aspersions were true. Were they just cowards who had run away? Were they weak? Had they abandoned their families?

Their efforts were reframed by the therapist as being examples of selfless sacrifice that a father would put forth for his family to help ensure a better future for his children and the generations to come. They were actually doing an immeasurable amount of work as fathers even though they were being disparaged by their loved ones (and themselves) for doing so. We did an exercise where the men were encouraged to look at one another and asked if they saw good fathers or cowards. They shared their positive regard for one another, and then asked that if several people they respected (who also understood what it is the others were going through) were able to see them as good fathers, could they see it in themselves? Group members hugged each other at the end of the session and left in a much less dysthymic mood, determined to continue their fight for their families. Their mutual assistance in holding on to their sense of manhood was akin to Fanon's notion of "authentic virility" (Fanon, 1963, p. 302). The lesson these men took from this exercise is that they hold the power to define for themselves who they are, what they aspire to, and how they understand their role and value. It can no longer be for others to control how they think about themselves.

What Impact Can I Have on the Future?

One of the most pernicious aspects of torture, colonialism/neo-colonialism, and oppression is that they compromise the victim's ability to have agency on creating a future for themselves or for their community (Ajari, 2014; Fanon, 1963). One may ask what is the purpose of the struggle, if it will have no impact on the future. Again, this is a way in which the community of survivors takes the lead in supporting one another and insisting on perseverance as a way of rectifying injustice.

Recently, there was a gentleman from Guinea in the Francophone African support group who had had enough. With recent changes to immigration policies under the Trump administration, he had finally come to a breaking point. He had already waited for almost three years for an asylum interview, and recent policy changes made it unclear when his interview would ever come. He announced that he was returning home, even though he was certain that he would be killed as soon as the authorities had discovered his return. When group members asked about this indirect suicidal intent, he responded, "They may not know I have returned for a few days; perhaps even a week or so. But at least I'll be able to go home and hug my babies. Right now, I can't even do that. It's been too long and they cry to me on the phone every night. I have no answers to give them about my immigration status. What can I do?"

It was at this point that group members intervened and shared their experiences of waiting for years, but eventually being able to reunite their families. Others talked about their ongoing hope to be able to do the same for their children so that they would have opportunities that they never had themselves. A man from the Democratic Republic of Congo then gave some very pertinent advice to his struggling comrade. He told him,

> You can no longer think of your family as the family you left behind you. You must think of them as the family you have waiting in front of you, so that you can find a reason to get through all of the merde ("shit") you must traverse in order to make this dream a reality. If you look back you will drown. If you look ahead, you have the chance to succeed; and they will never know again the misery that we have endured.

The elderly group member we mentioned earlier in this chapter was also a human rights crusader. He embarked on a journey that spanned over a quarter century to bring the dictator who imprisoned and tortured him to justice (Quirijns, 2007). He started by collecting testimonies from other survivors, orphans and widows. He hid the small pieces of paper with their stories under his house. Eventually he connected with an international human rights organization. He escaped to the US with his documentation. He came to our program for medical and psychological support. His struggle continued and he joined our Francophone African support group.

Over the years, he scored judicial victories and suffered setbacks. Whenever he had news of progress on his case, he would inform group members; but sometimes the response was pessimistic. "You know that an African dictator will never be judged on African soil, because the other dictators do not want to see it happen. It will make them vulnerable too." The gentleman took these comments in stride and explained that his critics may be right. "It may not happen in my lifetime. It is very likely that I will fail, but I have no choice but to try. Even if it is not for me, but for my children and their children. Africans must see that they can stand up and that justice can be served in our lands—if we just insist on it, and are willing to sacrifice, even our lives for it."

He persisted. He inspired many others in our group to raise their voices and to be "les voix des sans-voix"—"the voices of the voiceless." By accepting the possibility of failure within his lifetime, he set the stage to freely attempt the improbable. Three years ago, the dictator in question—Hissene Habre of Chad—was sentenced to life in prison by a Special African Tribunal in Dakar, Senegal. The old man living in the shelter is now living with his reunited family in a modest apartment in New York, watching his children and grandchildren aspire to things that were once beyond his grasp. He utilized his today to affect tomorrow. His healing is truly a subversive act, in the absolute sense.

Divide and Conquer? Let's Talk About Us

Irving Yalom (1995) taught that homogeneous groups will find variation while heterogeneous groups will find commonality. This has been particularly important to recognize in the Francophone group which is homogeneous in the sense that they are all French-speaking African torture survivors, but heterogeneous in the sense that there is diversity in terms of religion, country of origin, gender, social class, level of education, time in the US, etc. (Smith, 2003). They have taken on the mantle by recognizing that the divisions between them have been used to keep them oppressed for generations. "Divide and conquer— separate and rule."

Theorists have noted that these divisions, and the shared ignorance of one oppressed people regarding the oppression of another people, have been useful in joining people who espouse African unity from various places within the Diaspora. They are able to make connections regarding the painful experiences and disparate strategies by which their people are exploited and create links among marginalized people (Ajari, 2014; Benot, 1969). Similarly, group members speak to the opportunity to learn "the realities" of what is transpiring in other countries and how they relate to their lived experiences. A member from Cameroun may learn about what is transpiring in the Casamance region of Senegal. A Guinean survivor may explain the divisions between Peul and Malinke populations, while a Congolese expat talks about the history of extortion, mineral extraction and mercenaries in the Goma region. Members will point out that they are crossing the "gardes de feu," the firewalls that are usually used to keep people of the African Diaspora separated from one another, when they attend a session where there may be 10 participants from seven different countries. Not only is the sharing of information and insights something that helps with individual healing, it also helps to create and strengthen a community; despite being feared and purposefully marginalized by oppressive forces. Sharing, which connects and educates across politically enforced boundaries, may be viewed as treacherous by those who wish to enforce the status quo.

Ironically, the language utilized during group sessions, the colonial French language, has also been something that has been a tool of division and oppression. Fanon (1952) writes about how varying levels of French have long been used to separate the assimilated bourgeoisie from the "native villagers" and keep the population divided and weak. In the case of the Francophone group, French is also a minority language in the Anglo-dominant American context. As such, much of the mystique and power has been removed as group members work to master English and Spanish, which will serve them more effectively in their daily lives. This runs counter to Fanon's experience working in Blida Hospital where French wound up being a tool to squelch use of Arabic or the indigenous Kablye language because the clinicians lacked proficiency. French (and the needs of the clinicians) was prioritized above the clients' ability to fully engage in a therapeutic process. Though the situation is almost the dialectical opposite at Bellevue Hospital, the importance of considering the multiple meanings of language remain important.

In the Bellevue context, French is demystified, de-deified, and becomes a glue, as opposed to its usual wedge function, when people from so many countries come together and have a common language to discuss the imperatives of survival and resistance. Again, survivors take the power to define, in this case, the language that was habitually used to define them, in order to utilize the tools in hand to move ahead, reconnect and redefine who they are vis-à-vis their challenging reality.

Engagement and the Ongoing Nature of Struggle

The context in which our work takes place at the Bellevue/NYU Program for Survivors of Torture is similar to Fanon's context, but certain things have changed as well. The survivors are no longer under the yoke of direct colonial occupation, although the ongoing nature of torture and neo-colonial oppression is still powerful. As the initial trauma caused by torture is exacerbated by upheaval, displacement and marginalization, so too, the supports, interventions and healing energies must be persistent and ongoing. The bad news is that the challenges are numerous and pernicious. The good news is that there are so many different ways to intervene and for survivors to engage in their own healing processes (Smith, 2018).

Shared respect, coupled with the opportunity for authentic expression and mutual understanding, are vehicles survivors are using to foment a change of consciousness. Turner (2011) describes it as "an awakening" and a way of "winning hearts and minds" that the oppressors did not intend (p. 130). The shared insights help on a communal level, but also in the internal life of the survivor. Fanon (1963) states that the survivor must "pay attention to the liquidation of all the untruths implanted in his being by the oppressor" (p. 309).

It has been stated that "two watchdogs are ten times better than one." We understand this to mean that a single watchdog may be scared or ambivalent about checking out noises or investigating smells for fear of being vulnerable to attack. But when there is a second dog, and one feels confident now that there is someone to watch their back, to give support, or even just to be there during painful times, then the first dog howls at the moon. The partnership is powerful. Isolation is reduced. Fear and wariness are normalized and diminished. They may even approach comprehending what is incomprehensible and become better able to tolerate what has been purposely constructed to be intolerable.

Group members have explained that the healing process does not end when one is feeling a bit better or is secure in terms of their immigration status. The healing continues as one survivor helps another to traverse the daunting emotional and logistical terrain. Healing is not a discrete event. Rather, healing is an ongoing process that is both personal and communal. Innovative medical scholars now conceptualize health as "the ability to adapt and self-manage in the face of social, physical and emotional challenge" (Huber et al., 2011; Jadad & O'Grady, 2008). They posit that healing is not about the absence of sickness or challenge; it is more of a proactive comportment in terms of how one engages with life's challenges.

As such, attention must be paid to how one grapples with the stressors associated with daily life in addition to the ramifications of severe trauma. Recent research shows that paying attention to the post-trauma stressors (addressing housing, employment, and chronic pain issues) is associated with improved well-being above and beyond the benefits of treatment directly targeting the trauma itself (Kashyap & Joscelyne, 2018). Findings show that interdisciplinary treatment is effective, but in order to be so, a survivor must engage diligently in the process.

The capacity to engage in this ongoing effort to adapt and heal requires a great deal of effort. It is often easier to "give up and give the victory to those who oppress you," yet many survivors keep pushing forward. It may be surprising to some. One may recall the scene in the movie "Gladiator" when the evil usurper to Caesar's throne had failed yet again to assassinate his nemesis—the heroic gladiator Maximus. In desperation the despot exclaimed, "You just won't die!" One might say that Maximus' defiant glare was Fanonian in its intent and impact. I will not be broken. My existence sheds light on the shameful nature of your behavior.

When trying to understand how this subversive healing attitude takes root, it recalls a group session from a couple decades ago. Appropriately, the lesson came from the survivors' experiences as opposed to the psychiatric academy. A torture survivor from Mauritania was trying to cope with his tenuous existence. He asked the other group members, "What are the qualities we need to change the world—or at least to survive in this world?"

Members discussed and debated over the course of the session, and surprisingly, came to a consensus. Members identified "la sagesse, le courage et l'espoir"—"wisdom, courage and hope" as the essential ingredients (Smith, 2003). They went further and described how if a survivor possesses any two of these three qualities, it is insufficient. They explain that if you are courageous and hopeful, but lack wisdom, you will probably go about your activities in a way that is ineffective, and you will ultimately fail. Conversely, if you are wise and hopeful, but lack courage, you will remain trapped in a prison of inertia and will never act upon your needs and principles.

The main challenge facing these courageous and wise survivors, however, was holding on to hope. They explained in more detail, stating that hope is not so much something you have; rather, it is something you do. It is a capacity to hope in an active sense. It is an attitude, a comportment, a way of leaning into the realities of the world. Our research has shown that engagement in the group is linked to survivors utilizing more program resources in terms of behavioral health and associated services (Smith, Keatley, & Min, 2018). Perhaps it is the beginning of seeing ways in which hope can be operationalized.

The survivors went further and said that this capacity to hope, most importantly, is something that can be shared. That is now how we see the crux of our clinical endeavors—we help survivors to hold on to their capacity to hope, so that they are able to utilize the wisdom and courage they already possess.

Conclusion

The insights of the group members come full circle to the teachings of Fanon, and his notion of liberation psychology. Hope is subversive. It is a revolutionary act that flies in the face of the wishes of the oppressor. It also helps the survivor to fight "against the stereotype of himself" (Turner, 2011, p. 130) Like Maximus, these survivors simply refuse to die. They gird each other and refuse to hate themselves or to blame themselves for their suffering and ongoing challenges they face on the path to healing. They shed light where there had been obscurity. Their testimony shows an unwilling world the realities that they wish did not exist. They speak truth to power. They manifest the shared humanism and consciousness that Fanon identified as the beginning of a healing revolution.

These survivors move past victimhood. They defy the odds to begin their lives again at "less than zero," as one survivor phrased it. Their struggle goes beyond race, religion, or immigration status. If we take Fanon's words to heart that these survivors revolt because they cannot breathe, then we must see each breath as an act of defiance. This subversive insistence on existing then extends beyond the individual. They become part of one another's healing process. A survivor evolves into a healing force and a literal breath of fresh air for a compatriot. In the Fanonian sense, if surviving is a rebellious act, then helping others to heal is revolutionary.

References

Achebe, C. (1958). *Things fall apart*. London: Heinemann.

Ajari, I. M. (2014). *Race et violence: Frantz Fanon a l'éprouve du postcolonial* (Doctoral dissertation). L'Université de Toulouse Jean Jaurès, France.

Benot, Y. (1969). *Idéologies des indépendances africaines*. Paris, France: Maspero.

Fanon, F. (1952). *Peau noire, masques blanques*. Paris, France: Editions du Seuil.

Fanon, F. (1961/1963). *The wretched of the earth* (C. Farrington, Trans.). London: Penguin.

Fanon, F. (1964/2006). *Pour La Révolution africaine. Écrits politiques*. Paris: Reprint by La Découverte.

Haddab, M. (2007). La violence et l'histoire dans la pensée de Frantz Fanon. *Sud/Nord*, *22*(1), 79–87. doi:10.3917/sn.022.0079.

Herrnstein, R. J., & Murray, C. A. (1996). *The bell curve: Intelligence and class structure in American life*. New York: Simon & Schuster.

Huber, M., Knottnerus, J. A., Green, L., van der Horst, H., Jadad, A. R., Kromhout, D., Leonard, B., Lorig, K., Loureiro, M. I., van der Meer, J. W., Schnabel, P., Smith, R., van Weel, C., & Smid, H. (2011). How should we define health? *BMJ*, *343*, d4163.

Jadad, A. R., & O'Grady, L. (2008). How should health be defined? *BMJ*, *10*, 337, a2900.

Kashyap, S., & Joscelyne, A. (2018). Post-migration treatment targets associated with reductions in depression and PTSD among survivors of torture seeking asylum in the USA. *Psychiatry Research*, *271*, 565–572.

Quirijns, K. (2007). *The dictator hunter*. Documentary produced by Human Rights Watch; Netherlands.

Smith, H. (2003). Despair, resilience, and the meaning of family: Group therapy with French-speaking survivors of torture from Africa. In R. Carter & B. Wallace (Eds.), *Understanding and dealing with violence: Multicultural perspectives* (pp. 291–319). Thousand Oaks, CA: Sage Press, Inc.

Smith, H. (2007). Multicultural issues in the treatment of survivors of torture and refugee trauma: Toward an interactive model. In H. Smith, A. Keller, & D. Lhewa (Eds.),

Like a refugee camp on first avenue: Insights and experiences form the Bellevue/NYU Program for Survivors of Torture (pp. 38–64). New York: Jacob and Valeria Langeloth Foundation.

Smith, H., Keatley, E., & Min, M. (2018). Group treatment with French-speaking African survivors of torture and its effects on clinical engagement: Can hope be operationalized? *International Journal of Group Psychotherapy.* https://doi.org/10.1080/0020 7284.2018.1504295.

Turner, L. (2011). Fanon and the biopolitics of torture: Contextualizing psychological practices tools of war. In N. Gibson (Ed.), *Living Fanon: Global perspectives* (pp. 117–130). New York, NY: Palgrave Macmillan.

Wideman, J. E. (2008). *Fanon: A novel.* New York: Houghton Mifflin Company.

Yalom, I. D. (1995). *The theory and practice of group psychotherapy* (4th ed.). New York: Basic Books.

7 The Ideas of Frantz Fanon and Practices of Cultural Safety With Australia's First Peoples

Luke Molloy

Aboriginal and Torres Strait Islander peoples are the first inhabitants of Australia. Torres Strait Islander peoples come from the islands of the Torres Strait, situated between the north of Australia and Papua New Guinea. Aboriginal nations have historically lived on the mainland of Australia and in many of the country's offshore islands. According to the 2016 census, Aboriginal and Torres Strait Islander peoples represent 2.8 percent of the population of Australia, with 91 percent being of Aboriginal origin, 5 percent being of Torres Strait Islander origin, and 4.1 percent reporting being of both Aboriginal and Torres Strait Islander origin (Australian Bureau of Statistics, 2017a). To understand the current circumstances of Aboriginal and Torres Strait Islander peoples, historical background is imperative (Dudgeon, 2014). Archaeologists have identified that people lived in Australia for at least 50,000 years before the decision by the British to colonize the continent (Broome, 2010). From 1788 onwards, Indigenous communities were subjected to a violent invasion that subjected them to torture, rape and murder (Broome, 2010; Kidd, 2005; Reynolds, 2013). The initial period of colonization saw the devastating impact of introduced diseases, such as smallpox, measles and influenza (Eckermann et al., 2010). The settlers also introduced agricultural processes that excluded people from their sources of food, leading to widespread hunger and associated illnesses (Broome, 2010; Eckermann et al., 2010).

During the mid-Nineteenth Century, the settler population began systematically segregating the surviving Indigenous communities. Christian missions and government reserves were established throughout Australia (Kidd, 2005). A period of intensive government control of Aboriginal and Torres Strait Islander people had begun under the guise of protection. Legislation empowered "protection boards" to remove children from their families (Human Rights and Equal Opportunity Commission, 1997). The seizure of children would continue even as government policies towards Aboriginal and Torres Strait Islander peoples changed and between 1910 and 1970, it is estimated that somewhere between one in ten and one in three Indigenous children were forcibly taken from their families (Human Rights and Equal Opportunity Commission, 1997).

By the early 1960s, the Australian government introduced policy focused on the idea of assimilating Aboriginal and Torres Strait Islander peoples into non-Indigenous society. The government stated that:

> All Aborigines and part Aborigines are expected to eventually attain the same manner of living as other Australians . . . enjoying the same responsibility deserving the same customs and influenced by the same beliefs, hopes and loyalties as other Australians.
>
> (Hasluck, 1961, p. 1)

The policy was premised on the belief that the only way to achieve a harmonious coexistence in Australia between the Indigenous and non-Indigenous communities was by breeding out Aboriginality (Saggers & Gray, 1991). In 1967, over 90 percent of the electorate voted on amending the Australian constitution in favour of transferring legislative powers for Indigenous communities away from State governments to the Federal parliament and including Aboriginal and Torres Strait Islander people in the national census. The result and the changes it initiated provided a foundation for weakening the regime of control that had developed around Aboriginal and Torres Strait Islander peoples (Hunter, 1993).

Despite this paradigm shift, Aboriginal and Torres Strait Islander peoples continue to experience disadvantage and institutional racism in Australian society (Howard-Wagner, 2019). In this chapter, I will explore one area where disadvantage and discrimination converge, the public mental health services. There have been criticisms about the quality of mental health services provided to Indigenous communities since the 1990s (Swan & Raphael, 1995). Embedding the decolonizing model of practice, *cultural safety*, in mental health care has been identified as a key requirement to changing these circumstances (Congress of Aboriginal and Torres Strait Islander Nurses and Midwives, 2017). Critical reflexivity is fundamental in ensuring cultural safety; however, the form this reflection should take was unclear to me in my role as a mental health nurse. This chapter will describe how I used Frantz Fanon's in-depth analysis of colonialization as a conceptual strategy to support cultural safety in my own practice. I will discuss how Fanon's ideas can shape an approach to mental health care that can truly meet the needs of Aboriginal and Torres Strait Islander people.

Current Health Status of Aboriginal and Torres Strait Islander Peoples

An overview of Indigenous health status can provide an insight into how colonization continues to affect Aboriginal and Torres Strait Islander communities. These statistics should be viewed in the context of the tremendous strength and resilience that have been characteristic of Aboriginal and Torres Strait Islander communities in the face of extreme adversities (McNamara et al.,

2018). Currently, it is estimated that an Aboriginal and Torres Strait Islander person born between 2010 and 2012 is likely to live about ten years less than a non-Indigenous person born during the same period (Australian Bureau of Statistics, 2013). Some examples of Indigenous health disparities include long-term cardiac conditions which are around 1.2 times more common for Aboriginal and Torres Strait Islander people than for non-Indigenous people; cancer rates are 1.3 times higher; diabetes rates are 3 times higher; renal disease rates are 6.6 times higher; and the level of respiratory disease is 1.2 times higher (Australian Indigenous HealthInfoNet, 2017). There are also significant disparities seen in communicable diseases including pneumonia, tuberculous, sexually transmissible infections and hepatitis (A, B and C) (Quinn, Massey, & Speare, 2015). The overall disability rate for Aboriginal and Torres Strait Islander people is 1.7 times the rate for non-Indigenous people (Australian Indigenous HealthInfoNet, 2017). Colonization traumatically impacted Aboriginal and Torres Strait Islander communities with resulting intergenerational mental health impacts (Calma, Dudgeon, & Bray, 2017). Aboriginal and Torres Strait Islander people have reported experiencing psychological distress at a rate 3 times that of non-Indigenous people (Matthews, Bailie, Laycock, Nagel, & Bailie, 2016). Mental disorders are reported to be the leading cause of disease burden among Aboriginal and Torres Strait Islander peoples after cardiovascular disorders (Australian Institute of Health and Welfare, 2016a). According to the 2014–2015 National Aboriginal and Torres Strait Islander Social Survey, 29 percent of Aboriginal and Torres Strait Islander people ($n = 11,178$) reported having a diagnosed mental health condition (25 percent of males and 34 percent of females) (Australian Bureau of Statistics, 2016). Aboriginal and Torres Strait Islander people living in non-remote areas were twice as likely to report a diagnosed mental health condition than those living in remote areas (33 percent compared with 16 percent) (Australian Bureau of Statistics, 2016). The Australian Bureau of Statistics has estimated that 20% of the broader Australian population experience a diagnosed mental condition in any year (Australian Bureau of Statistics, 2008).

In the context of public mental health service provision, specialized community mental health service contacts for Aboriginal and Torres Strait Islander peoples were four times the rate for non-Indigenous Australians in 2014–2015 (Australian Health Ministers' Advisory Council, 2017). Between 2011 and 2013, the hospitalization rate for Indigenous women with mental health issues was 1.5 times the rate for non-Indigenous women, and the hospitalization rate for Indigenous men with mental health issues was 2.1 times the rate for non-Indigenous men (Australian Health Ministers' Advisory Council, 2017). Between 2013 and 2015, 5 percent of all emergency department presentations for Aboriginal and Torres Strait Islander people were mental health related, compared to 3 percent for non-Indigenous presentations (Australian Institute of Health and Welfare, 2016b). Once admitted to hospitals, the average length of stay for Indigenous inpatients was ten days, compared to twelve days for non-Indigenous inpatients (Australian Health Ministers' Advisory Council, 2017).

Suicide is believed to have been a rare occurrence among the Aboriginal and Torres Strait Islander people in precolonial times. However, it has become increasingly prevalent in communities since the 1980s (Australian Bureau of Statistics, 2012). In 2016, deaths from suicide accounted for a greater proportion of all Aboriginal and Torres Strait Islander deaths (5.5 percent) compared with deaths by suicide for non-Indigenous Australians (1.7 percent) (Australian Bureau of Statistic, 2017b). The median age for Aboriginal and Torres Strait Islander persons dying by suicide was 29, compared with 45 for non-Indigenous persons (Australian Bureau of Statistics, 2017b). Aboriginal and Torres Strait Islander people under 18 years of age accounted for approximately 30 percent of suicide deaths in that age group between 2007 and 2011, despite only representing 5.5 percent of the national population for the age group (Dudgeon & Holland, 2018).

Substance use, including illicit drug use and alcohol use, are associated with negative impacts on health and social harms that have been reported to disproportionately affect Aboriginal and Torres Strait Islander communities (Gray et al., 2017; MacRae & Hoareau, 2016). Aboriginal and Torres Strait Islander peoples are more likely to experience exposure to child neglect and abuse, violence, and contact with the criminal justice system than non-Indigenous Australians (Australian Health Ministers' Advisory Council, 2017; Gray et al., 2017; MacRae & Hoareau, 2016). Drug-related hospitalizations for mental/behavioral disorders for Aboriginal and Torres Strait Islander peoples were three times higher than the rate for non-Indigenous people (Steering Committee for the Review of Government Service Provision, 2014). Mental and behavioral disorders because of psychoactive substance use, including alcohol, represents approximately one-third of all mental health-related hospitalizations among Aboriginal and Torres Strait Islander women and 43.4 percent among Aboriginal and Torres Strait Islander men (Gray et al., 2017). High levels of alcohol and drug use have been noted in Indigenous suicide clusters (Dudgeon, Calma, & Holland, 2017).

Aboriginal and Torres Strait Islander Social and Emotional Well-being

For Aboriginal and Torres Strait Islander peoples, social and emotional well-being is the foundation for both physical and mental health (Commonwealth of Australia, 2017). This conceptualization of health recognises the importance of connection to family, community, culture, land, spirituality and ancestry, and how these affect the individual (Gee, Dudgeon, Schultz, Hart, & Kelly, 2014). Swan and Raphael (1995, p. 19) have noted this

> Aboriginal concept of health is holistic, encompassing mental health and physical, cultural and spiritual health. This holistic concept does not just refer to the whole body but is in fact steeped in harmonised interrelations which constitute cultural wellbeing. These interrelating factors can

be categorised largely into spiritual, environmental, ideological, political, social, economic, mental and physical. Crucially, it must be understood that when the harmony of these interrelations is disrupted, Aboriginal ill health will persist.

Aboriginal and Torres Strait Islander understandings of social and emotional well-being is found to vary between communities and individuals (Gee et al., 2014).

Hellsten (2015) notes that mental illness and social and emotional distress differ, with the latter resulting from the sociopolitical disadvantages experienced by Aboriginal and Torres Strait Islander peoples since the beginning of colonization. This distress is unlikely to be relieved by psychiatric interventions (Hellsten, 2015; Westerman, 2004). The concept of mental illness as a physiological disease within the biomedical paradigm fails to address Aboriginal and Torres Strait Islander health perspectives (Dudgeon, 2014; Saggers & Gray, 2007). Furthermore, this paradigm is based on an approach to illness and disease that is both inappropriate and irrelevant to the beliefs of most Aboriginal and Torres Strait Islander peoples (Westerman, 2004).

It is increasingly recognised that to improve social and emotional well-being in Indigenous communities, there needs to be a focus on increasing community capacity and community resilience (Parker & Milroy, 2014). Cultural healers also play a key role in maintaining social/emotional well-being and healing social and emotional distress in individuals (Commonwealth of Australia, 2017). Optimal health service provision should combine traditional healing-based treatments informed by the person's culture with clinical approaches focused on holistic well-being (Commonwealth of Australia, 2017).

Concerns about the quality of public mental health services provided to Aboriginal and Torres Strait Islander peoples have been identified since the 1990s (Human Rights and Equal Opportunity Commission, 1993; Royal Commission into Aboriginal Deaths in Custody,1991; Swan & Raphael, 1995). Both the Burdekin report and the Royal Commission report found that mental health professionals had minimal understanding of Indigenous culture and that this regularly resulted in inappropriate treatment. The reports outlined how the denial of human rights within a discriminatory mental health system placed a serious burden on Aboriginal and Torres Strait Islander people (Mental Health Commission of New South Wales, 2013; Calma et al., 2017). Despite the findings of the reports and later attempts at change through the National Strategic Framework (Commonwealth of Australia, 2004) and the National Mental Health Plan (Commonwealth of Australia, 2009), health professionals have continued to practice in exclusionary ways to the detriment and disadvantage of Indigenous service users (McGough, Wynaden, & Wright, 2018; Walker & Sonn, 2010; Trueman, 2017). Inflexible models of service delivery and inadequate cultural awareness have continued to present barriers for Aboriginal and Torres Strait Islander service users (Isaacs, Pyett, Oakley-Browne, Gruis, & Waples-Crowe, 2010; McGough et al., 2018; Walker, Schultz, & Sonn, 2014).

The health needs of Aboriginal and Torres Strait Islander people have continued to be marginalized by the mental health system (Calma et al., 2017).

Cultural Safety

Cultural safety (*kawa whakaruruhau*) was conceptualized by Maori nurses to address the poor health status and negative health care experiences of the Maori people in New Zealand/Aotearoa in the 1980s. Cultural safety involves an approach to nursing people:

> where there is no assault, challenge or denial of their identity, of who they are and what they need. It is about shared respect, shared meaning, shared knowledge and experience of learning, living and working together with dignity and truly listening.
>
> (Williams, 1999, p. 213)

The concept of cultural safety also promotes nursing practice that is guided by understandings of historical power differences and personal biases (Doutrich, Arcus, Dekker, Spuck, & Pollock-Robinson, 2012). By focusing on insights into the relationship between minority status and health status, cultural safety has been viewed as a way of changing nurses' attitudes that marginalize Indigenous service users (Doutrich et al., 2012, p. 143). To achieve this, cultural safety identifies the need for the development of a critical consciousness within nursing care (Smye, Josewski, & Kendall, 2010).

Cultural safety influences nursing practice through reflection; it requires nurses to explore and identify the assumptions surrounding their nursing care. This includes nurses reflecting on their own cultural perspective, and how it affects the nursing care they provide. Purdie, Dudgeon, & Walker (2010) suggest that "creat[ing] a culturally safe space requires a high level of critical reflexivity" (p. 162). Because cultural safety aims to empower the person receiving nursing care, only the recipient can assess its effectiveness. This gives the person the power to shape their nursing care through contributing to the nursing process. Cultural safety challenges nurses to look at their own practice and reflect on its consequences, and to question professional traditions, such as the ethic of treating everyone the same, regardless of their ethnicity or gender (Eckermann et al., 2010).

Cultural safety provides a decolonizing model of practice that is based on dialogue, negotiation and power sharing (Congress of Aboriginal and Torres Strait Islander Nurses and Midwives, 2017). Its importance for nursing practice with Aboriginal and Torres Strait Islander peoples has recently been identified by the Nursing and Midwifery Board of Australia, which identified the need for the regulations and codes establishing professional standards to clearly communicate the requirement for cultural safety (Nursing and Midwifery Board of Australia, 2018a). By using the concept to guide practice, the mental health nurse can provide care that is focused on the service user and is supportive of their personal recovery. Culturally safe nursing care demands a move beyond professional-controlled, myopic biomedical approaches to mental health, and promotes ways of caring that have the potential to promote personal liberation within the experience of mental health service use. With its clear focus on critical reflexivity, cultural safety can also challenge the assumptions of *Western* psychiatric traditions that limit the scope of mental health service delivery.

Migrant Experience

I emigrated from Ireland to Australia in 2004. I had qualified for a skilled migration visa because of my professional background as a registered psychiatric nurse and was sponsored to work in an acute inpatient ward in the inner city of Sydney. I regularly provided care to Aboriginal and Torres Strait Islander people in this setting. Before I came to Australia, my understanding of Aboriginal and Torres Strait Islander peoples was impersonal and limited. My knowledge was based on the history I had learnt in school about the settlement of Australia. Aboriginal people seemed to me to be there initially to observe the arrival of the British but then disappeared from the pictures that followed. I had vague memories about the film "Crocodile Dundee" having Aboriginal characters who lived in the desert. That was about it.

When I attempted to inform my practice with Aboriginal and Torres Strait Islander peoples, I found literature that made me uncomfortable (Molloy, 2017). I read about the Indigenous concept of social and emotional well-being that went beyond my understanding of mental health (Swan & Raphael, 1995). I read about the national reports that criticized mental health services and the health professionals who worked in them, going back over twenty years (Human Rights and Equal Opportunity Commission, 1993). I read about the horrors of the Indigenous experience of invasion and colonization (Broome, 2010; Kidd, 2005). Reading the authors Eckermann and colleagues (2006), I was struck by the statement "the implementation of strategies towards cultural safety would be powerful evidence that the process of reconciliation in Australia was being taken seriously by the health sector." (Eckermann et al., 2006, p. 174) When I read further about the concept of cultural safety, its importance was clear to me but I had questions. How could I create a meaningful personal strategy for reflection that could shape my own practice? Was there some knowledge that could guide me in my critical reflexivity to support cultural safety practice with the Aboriginal and Torres Strait Islander people I cared for? The literature on the area of cultural safety provided me with no clear answers.

I looked at the care provided by Australian colleagues, who appeared to have a sound knowledge about acute care in mental health inpatient settings. However, there was nothing different in the approach taken with people who were admitted to the ward. This was a "one size fits all" biomedically-inspired mental health nursing practice, focused on administering medication, observing behavior and reporting back to psychiatrists about the symptoms of illness. It was the same for Indigenous and non-Indigenous people. The nurses were

not talking about cultural safety in their care or documenting it in their notes or
care plans, so there were no practice behaviors that I could role model. Having
encountered the work of Frantz Fanon as a student, I thought it worthwhile to
revisit his ideas about colonization (Molloy & Grootjans, 2014). I saw a potential for them to focus my critical reflection to promote cultural safety in my
mental health nursing care in a way that was meaningful for me.

Fanon and Cultural Safety

Although Fanon's scholarship is drawn from his experiences of European colonization in the West Indies and North Africa and his time as a migrant in
France in the mid-Twentieth century, his theories have continuing relevance
and can serve as a framework for understanding the continuing inequality in
colonized countries, such as Australia. Fanon provides a theoretical analysis of
the nature of oppression, of how it is sustained and how it is reproduced, and
the effect it has on the oppressed and the oppressor (Hopton, 1995). While
practising psychiatry in Algeria in the 1950s, Fanon found his medical colleagues viewed the local Algerians as culturally inferior to the French settler
population (Keller, 2007). He observed how the psychiatric approach to mental illness he had learned in France was problematic when it was applied in
Algeria. In the psychiatric hospital at Blida-Joinville, he noticed that treatment
approaches that were effective with patients from settler backgrounds had
no significant impact on Algerian patients. According to McCulloch (1983,
p. 111), "This transposition of European expectations and methods was based
upon an implicit denial of any cultural differences between North Africa and
the metropole. More precisely, it assumed the absence of any semblance of
originality among the Muslim population." Recognising the effects of cultural
difference, Fanon's approach to psychiatric treatment evolved to become more
cognizant of his patient's social circumstances and how they affected mental
health (Butts, 1979).

Fanon undertook an in-depth analysis of the colonial experience and the
reverberations that it had on mental health (Fanon, 1963). A primary assumption in colonial society was that settlers were *good* and the indigenous population
were *bad*. Violence was fundamental to perpetuating this binary opposition.
Physical violence was used in the initial invasion to capture land and subjugate
the indigenous population, while psychological violence was used to keep the
indigenous population feeling worthless. Fanon explored how the experience
of this violence shattered the indigenous society, causing it to disintegrate, and
with it the personality of the individual (Fanon, 1963).

Now placed at the bottom of a colonial hierarchy which privileged settlers
in their country, the indigenous people found that the validity of their cultural
beliefs was denied; consequently, they became withdrawn (Fanon, 1965). The
disintegration within indigenous society led to the "the internalization or better,
the epidermalization of this inferiority" (Fanon, 1967, p. 299). For Fanon, the
objective of therapeutic approaches focused on the feelings of despair caused

by colonization should not be about ensuring adaptation to the status quo, but should promote choice between passivity and action in response to domination (Fanon, 1967). However, Fanon (1967) observed, in oppressive societies, the therapeutic relationship between therapist and service user is generally a microcosm of the power relationships that exist in the wider society.

Fanon (1967) described how colonization created a society where the oppressor and the oppressed were mutually dependent on one another. In such circumstances, it is only by understanding *the Other* that we can understand ourselves (Fanon, 1967). However, such understandings cannot be achieved if *the Other* is viewed through frames of inferiority or superiority. Improvements in the mental health of oppressed people begins with the demystifying of the oppressors and their hegemonic society, through the recognition that the oppressed are "victim[s] of a delusion" (Fanon, 1967, p. 255). For Fanon (1967, p. 299) the way forward was self-evident and presented in his suggestion that "I have one right alone: That of demanding human behavior from the other." The oppressed need to demand humanity; the oppressor needs to reflect on their actions that limit another's humanity.

The continuing marginalization of Aboriginal and Torres Strait Islander people by mental health services in Australia has persisted despite several national reports and policies that have attempted to ensure appropriate service provision. In revisiting the work of Frantz Fanon, I found an analysis of colonization that had relevance within the mental health settings I practiced in. Fanon's work reinforced the importance of my need to reflect not just my own practice but on the societal circumstances in which it was taking place. This critical reflection challenged me to question the ideology supporting my assumptions about *mental illness* and promoted an alternative consciousness about the impact of colonization in Australia, including insights into the ongoing failures of mental health services for Aboriginal and Torres Strait Islander peoples.

Using Fanon in Practice

The code of conduct for nurses in Australia requires that nurses "understand and acknowledge the historic factors, such as colonisation and its impact on Aboriginal and/or Torres Strait Islander peoples' health, which help to inform care" (Nursing and Midwifery Board of Australia, 2018b, p. 9). I have found the ideas of Frantz Fanon to be a powerful enabler of these understandings within my own practice. They gave me an insight into the processes of colonization that are absent in the narratives around the *settlement* of Australia. However, could Fanon's work be used to guide the profession? Putting Fanon's ideas into practice in a clinical setting where professional practice can often be biomedically-biased and *Western*-centric is a significant challenge. To begin, nurses need to be taught that colonization continues to affect Aboriginal and Torres Strait Islander peoples and that to practice nursing without critical reflection is to perpetrate the oppression of the Indigenous peoples of Australia. Culturally unsafe health organisations sustain health disparities and the poor health outcomes experienced by Aboriginal and Torres Strait Islander peoples.

Fanon's ideas about oppression can be used as a conceptual strategy that prompts reflection on both the relationships we have with the people we provide care to and the actions we take within those relationships. This can provide practitioners with a critical theoretical perspective that links power imbalances and inequitable social relationships in health care. Critical reflection can also be directed to the effects of cultural imposition and the denial of recognition of the Aboriginal and Torres Islander people's concept of health within nurses' practice. By embedding the concept of understanding *the Other* within nursing practice, nurses can be guided by Aboriginal and Torres Strait Islander people towards appropriate approaches to nursing care that provide cultural safety. Fanon's ideas prompt nurses to reflect on, and move beyond, the "delusions" of dominant cultural perspectives and the impact they have within practice to develop a true knowledge of the person they are providing care to. This knowledge is aware of the frames of cultural superiority and stereotyping of Aboriginal and Torres Strait Islander peoples that exist among non-Indigenous Australians.

In his focus on the dualistic world of the colonized society, Fanon gives us insights into the relationships between colonization, inequality and health status. Such understanding should be the basis of changing nurses' attitudes from those that continue to support current dominant practices and systems of health care to those that support the health of Aboriginal and Torres Strait Islander people. Fanon's ideas would seem to have great potential at the national level for guiding the nursing profession in Australia to realise cultural safety in all nursing practice and to take an active role in challenging endemic racism experienced by Aboriginal and Torres Strait Islander people in Australian society. Because Australian nurses reflect the prevailing conditions of the time in their care and attitudes, their movement toward addressing the impact that mental health services have on Aboriginal and Torres Strait Islander people's humanity would be a powerful indicator of a positive advance towards decolonization and reconciliation within Australian society.

Conclusions

The land of Australia was annexed by the British as Terra Nullius—an unoccupied land. This designation indicates that from the beginning of colonization, the settlers had no respect for the Aboriginal and Torres Strait Islander peoples that they encountered. The settlers' view of Indigenous society reflected the ethnocentric and xenophobic ideology of colonialism. The legal standing of Terra Nullius would have official designation until 1992. Since the arrival of European settlers, Aboriginal and Torres Strait Islander people have been subjected to hegemonic systems that have been imposed upon them because of conceptions of their inferiority. This belief in the inferiority of Aboriginal and

Torres Strait Islander peoples among non-Indigenous Australians shaped successive government policies and silenced public outcries from a tiny minority. Fanon explored the forms of racism and exploitation that provided the foundations of colonialism and the conscious and unconscious processes that sustain it. He described how indigenous people are dehumanised and devalued. He identified the denial of their reality and the imposition of hegemonic systems, both of which are reflected in the healthcare system. By using the ideas of Fanon as a framework for critical reflection, nurses are guided to reflect on and move beyond the delusions perpetuated by dominant cultural perspectives and develop a true knowledge of the needs of the persons they care for. For the nurses who work in mental health services, the real challenge in ensuring reconciliation and recovery is to develop mental health care that truly meets the needs of Aboriginal and Torres Strait Islander people. This care must ensure cultural safety.

References

Australian Bureau of Statistics. (2008). *National survey of mental health and wellbeing: Summary of results, Australia, 2007: ABS cat. no. 4326.0.* Canberra: ABS.

Australian Bureau of Statistics. (2012). *Suicides in Australia, 2010: Catalogue 3309.0.* Retrieved from http://abs.gov.au/AUSSTATS/abs@.nsf/mf/3309.0.

Australian Bureau of Statistics. (2013). *Life tables for Aboriginal and Torres Strait Islander Australians, 2010–2012.* Retrieved from www.abs.gov.au/ausstats/abs@.nsf/mf/3302.0.55.003.

Australian Bureau of Statistics. (2016). *Aboriginal and Torres Strait Islander people with a mental health condition.* Retrieved from www.abs.gov.au/ausstats/abs@.nsf/Lookup/by%20Subject/4714.0~2014-15~Feature%20Article~Aboriginal%20and%20Torres%20Strait%20Islander%20people%20with%20a%20mental%20health%20condition%20(Feature%20Article)~10.

Australian Bureau of Statistics. (2017a). *2016 Census shows growing Aboriginal and Torres Strait Islander population.* Retrieved from www.abs.gov.au/ausstats/abs@.nsf/MediaRealesesByCatalogue/02D50FAA987D6B7CA25814800087E03?OpenDocument.

Australian Bureau of Statistics. (2017b). *Causes of death, Australia 2016: Catalogue3303.0.* Retrieved from www.abs.gov.au/ausstats/abs@.nsf/mf/3303.0.

Australian Health Ministers' Advisory Council. (2017). *Aboriginal and Torres Strait Islander health performance framework 2017 Report.* Canberra: Australian Health Ministers' Advisory Council.

Australian Indigenous HealthInfoNet. (2017). *Overview of Aboriginal and Torres Strait Islander health status, 2016.* Perth, WA: Australian Indigenous HealthInfoNet.

Australian Institute of Health and Welfare. (2016a). *Australia's health 2016: Australia's health series no. 15: Cat. no. AUS 199.* Canberra: AIHW.

Australian Institute of Health and Welfare. (2016b). *Mental health services provided in emergency department, Table ED: Services provided in emergency departments.* Canberra: AIHW. Retrieved from https://mhsa.aihw.gov.au/services/emergencydepartments/.

Broome, R. (2010). *Aboriginal Australians.* Sydney: Allen and Unwin.

Butts, H. F. (1979). Frantz Fanon's contribution to psychiatry: The psychology of racism and colonialism. *Journal of the National Medical Association, 71*(10), 1015–1018.

Calma, T., Dudgeon, P., & Bray, A. (2017). Aboriginal and Torres Strait Islander social and emotional wellbeing and mental health. *Australian Psychologist, 52*(4), 255–260.

Commonwealth of Australia. (2004). *Social and emotional wellbeing framework: A national strategic framework for Aboriginal and Torres Strait Islander mental health and social and emotional wellbeing 2004–2009.* Canberra: Commonwealth of Australia.

Commonwealth of Australia. (2009). *Fourth national mental health plan: An agenda for collaborative government action in mental health 2009–2014.* Canberra: Commonwealth of Australia.

Commonwealth of Australia. (2017). *National strategic framework for Aboriginal and Torres Strait Islander Peoples' mental health and social and emotional wellbeing.* Canberra: Commonwealth of Australia.

Congress of Aboriginal and Torres Strait Islander Nurses and Midwives. (2017). *The Nursing and Midwifery Aboriginal and Torres Strait Islander Health Curriculum Framework: An adaptation of and complementary document to the 2014 Aboriginal and Torres Strait Islander Health Curriculum Framework.* Canberra: CATSINaM.

Doutrich, D., Arcus, K., Dekker, L., Spuck, J., & Pollock-Robinson, C. (2012). Cultural safety in New Zealand and the United States: Looking at a way forward together. *Journal of Transcultural Nursing, 23*(2), 143–150.

Dudgeon, P. (2014). Introduction. In P. Dudgeon, H. Milroy, & R. Walker (Eds.), *Working together: Aboriginal and Torres Strait Islander mental health and wellbeing principles and practice* (pp. xxi–xxviii). Canberra: Commonwealth of Australia.

Dudgeon, P., Calma, T., & Holland, C. (2017). The context and causes of the suicide of Indigenous people in Australia. *Journal of Indigenous Wellbeing, 2*(2), 5–15.

Dudgeon, P., & Holland, C. (2018). Recent developments in suicide prevention among the Indigenous peoples of Australia. *Australasian Psychiatry*, Online first. Retrieved from http://journals.sagepub.com/doi/abs/10.1177/1039856218757637.

Eckermann, A., Dowd, T., Chong, E., Nixon, L., Gray, R., & Johnson, S. (2006). *Binan Goonj: Bridging cultures in Aboriginal health* (2nd ed.). Sydney: Elsevier.

Eckermann, A., Dowd, T., Chong, E., Nixon, L., Gray, R., & Johnson, S. (2010). *Binan Goonj: Bridging cultures in Aboriginal health* (3rd ed.). Sydney: Elsevier.

Fanon, F. (1963). *The wretched of the earth.* New York: Grove Press.

Fanon, F. (1965). *A dying colonialism.* New York: Grove Press.

Fanon, F. (1967). *Black skin, white masks.* New York: Grove Press.

Gee, G., Dudgeon, P., Schultz, C., Hart, A., & Kelly, K. (2014). Aboriginal and Torres Strait Islander social and emotional wellbeing. In P. Dudgeon, H. Milroy, & R. Walker (Eds.), *Working together: Aboriginal and Torres Strait Islander mental health and wellbeing principles and practice* (pp. 55–68). Canberra: Commonwealth of Australia.

Gray, D., Cartwright, K., Stearne, A., Saggers, S., Wilkes, E., & Wilson, M. (2017). *Review of the harmful use of alcohol among Aboriginal and Torres Strait Islander people.* Retrieved from https://healthinfonet.ecu.edu.au/uploads/docs/alcohol-review-2017-revised.pdf.

Hasluck, P. (1961). *The policy of assimilation: Decisions of Commonwealth State Ministers at the Native Welfare Conference January 26th and 27th, 1961.* Canberra. Retrieved from https://aiatsis.gov.au/sites/default/files/catalogue_resources/18801.pdf.

Hellsten, D. (2015). Indigenous mental health nursing: The social and emotional wellbeing of Aboriginal and Torres Strait Islander Australians. In O. Best & B. Fredericks (Eds.), *Yatjuligin: Aboriginal and Torres Strait Islander nursing and midwifery care* (pp. 204–218). Port Melbourne: Cambridge University Press.

Hopton, J. (1995). The application of the ideas of Frantz Fanon to the practice of mental health nursing. *Journal of Advanced Nursing, 21*, 723–728.

Howard-Wagner, D. (2019). Success in closing the socio-economic gap, but still a long way to go: Urban aboriginal disadvantage, Trauma, and Racism in the Australian city of Newcastle. *The International Indigenous Policy Journal, 10*(1), 3.

Human Rights and Equal Opportunity Commission. (1993). *Human rights and mental illness: Report of the national inquiry into the human rights of people with mental illness (Burdekin report)*. Canberra: AGPS.

Human Rights and Equal Opportunity Commission. (1997). *Bringing them home: National inquiry into the separation of aboriginal and Torres Strait Islander children from their families*. Canberra: AGPS.

Hunter, E. (1993). *Aboriginal health and history: Power and prejudice in remote Australia*. Melbourne: Cambridge University Press.

Isaacs, A. N., Pyett, P., Oakley-Browne, M. A., Gruis, H., & Waples-Crowe, P. (2010). Barriers and facilitators to the utilization of adult mental health services by Australia's Indigenous people: seeking a way forward. *International journal of mental health nursing, 19*(2), 75–82.

Keller, R. C. (2007). Clinician and revolutionary: Frantz Fanon, biography and the history of colonial medicine. *Bulletin of the History of Medicine, 81*(4), 823–841.

Kidd, R. (2005). *The way we civilise*. St. Lucia: University of Queensland Press.

MacRae, A., & Hoareau, J. (2016). *Review of illicit drug use among Aboriginal and Torres Strait Islander people*. Retrieved from www.aodknowledgecentre.net.au/aodkc/illicitdrugs/illicit-drugs-general/reviews/illicit-drug-use-review.

Matthews, V., Bailie, J., Laycock, A., Nagel, T., & Bailie, R. (2016). *Priority evidence-practice gaps in Aboriginal and Torres Strait Islander mental health and wellbeing care: Final report*. Darwin: Menzies School of Health Research.

McCulloch, J. (1983). *Black soul, white artefact*. Cambridge: Cambridge University Press.

McGough, S., Wynaden, D., & Wright, M. (2018). Experience of providing cultural safety in mental health to Aboriginal patients: A grounded theory study. *International Journal of Mental Health Nursing, 27*(1), 204–213.

McNamara, B. J., Banks, E., Gubhaju, L., Joshy, G., Williamson, A., Raphael, B., & Eades, S. (2018). Factors relating to high psychological distress in Indigenous Australians and their contribution to Indigenous-non-Indigenous disparities. *Australian and New Zealand Journal of Public Health, 42*(2), 145–152.

Mental Health Commission of New South Wales. (2013). *Yarning honestly about Aboriginal mental health in NSW*. Retrieved from https://nswmentalhealthcommission.com.au/sites/default/files/assets/File/Yarning%20honestly%20about%20Aboriginal%20mental%20health%2020130925.pdf.

Molloy, L. (2017). Nursing care and Indigenous Australians: An autoethnography. *Collegian, 24*(5), 487–490.

Molloy, L., & Grootjans, J. (2014). The ideas of Frantz Fanon and culturally safe practices for Aboriginal and Torres Strait Islander people in Australia. *Issues in Mental Health Nursing, 35*(3), 207–211.

Nursing and Midwifery Board of Australia. (2018a). *Code of conduct for nurses*. Melbourne: NMBA.

Nursing and Midwifery Board of Australia. (2018b). *Cultural safety: Nurses and midwives leading the way for safer healthcare*. Retrieved from www.nursingmidwiferyboard.gov.au/documents/default.aspx?record=WD18%2F25108&dbid=AP&chksum=rUoevBUF2wIJy%2FkYRor4qw==.

Parker, R., & Milroy, H. (2014). Aboriginal and Torres Strait Islander mental health: An overview. In P. Dudgeon, H. Milroy, & R. Walker (Eds.), *Working together: Aboriginal and*

Torres Strait Islander mental health and wellbeing principles and practice (pp. 25–38). Canberra: Commonwealth of Australia.

Purdie, N., Dudgeon, P., & Walker, R. (2010). *Working together: Aboriginal and Torres Strait Islander mental health and wellbeing principles and practice*. Canberra: Commonwealth of Australia.

Quinn, E., Massey, P. D., & Speare, R. (2015). Communicable diseases in rural and remote Australia: The need for improved understanding and action. *Rural and Remote Health, 15*(3), 1–19.

Reynolds, H. (2013). *Forgotten war*. Sydney: New South Publishing.

Royal Commission into Aboriginal Deaths in Custody. (1991). *Royal commission into aboriginal deaths in custody: Overview and recommendations*. Canberra: ATSIC.

Saggers, S., & Gray, D. (1991). *Aboriginal health & society: The traditional and contemporary aboriginal struggle for better health*. Sydney: Allen & Unwin.

Saggers, S., & Gray, D. (2007). Defining what we mean. In B. Carson, T. Dunbar, & R. Chenall (Eds.), *Social Determinants of Indigenous Health* (pp. 1–18). Sydney: Allen and Unwin.

Smye, V., Josewski, V., & Kendall, E. (2010). *Cultural safety: An overview*. First Nation, Inuit, and Metis Advisory Committee. Calgary: Mental Health Commission of Canada.

Steering Committee for the Review of Government Service Provision. (2014). *Overcoming Indigenous disadvantage: Key indicators 2014*. Canberra: Productivity Commission.

Swan, P., & Raphael, B. (1995). *"Ways forward": National consultancy report on Aboriginal and Torres Strait mental health*. Canberra: Commonwealth of Australia.

Trueman, S. (2017). Indigenous clients intersecting with mainstream nursing: A reflection. *Rural and Remote Health, 17*(1), 1–17.

Walker, R., Schultz, C., & Sonn, C. (2014). Cultural competence: Transforming policy, services, programs and practice. In P. Dudgeon, H. Milroy, & R. Walker (Eds.), *Working together: Aboriginal and Torres Strait Islander mental health and wellbeing principles and practice* (pp. 95–221). Canberra: Commonwealth of Australia.

Walker, R., & Sonn, C. (2010). Working as a culturally competent mental health practitioner. In N. Purdie, N. P. Dudgeon, & R. Walker (Eds.), *Working together: Aboriginal and Torres Strait Islander mental health and wellbeing principles and practice* (pp. 157–180). Canberra: Commonwealth of Australia.

Westerman, T. (2004). Engagement of Indigenous clients in mental health services: What role do cultural differences play? *Australian E-Journal for the Advancement of Mental Health, 3*(1), 1–7. https://doi.org/10.5172/jamh.3.3.88.

Williams, R. (1999). Cultural safety: What does it mean for our work practice? *Australian and New Zealand Journal of Public Health, 23*(2), 213–214.

8 The Case of K

Looking to Frantz Fanon to Guide Cross-Racial Trauma-Informed Therapy

Maria Judith Valgoi

In this chapter I present a clinical case illustration based on the theory and work of Frantz Fanon. I strive to examine the complexities of using Fanon's ideas in a cross-racial therapeutic relationship. Specifically, Fanon's assertion that racist hierarchies place the oppressed and the oppressor into distinct social roles that maintain the racial order (Fanon, 1991) and that deconstruction of the social order requires a dismantling of these roles from a bottom up process whereby the oppressed, collectively, reclaim space, self-determine and create a "new man" (Fanon, 2004).

Fanon writes about "infusing a new rhythm" where liberation is enacted through an emotionally painful, interpersonal process that ends in the creation of two totally new beings and the creation of a "new humanity" (Fanon, 2004, p. 2). I believe that the process of cross-racial psychotherapy is fertile ground for this complex process of liberation. Because I identify as white, I am especially concerned with a cross-racial therapeutic alliance where a client of color has a white therapist. I believe in order to achieve Fanon's "new rhythm" within psychotherapy a white clinician would need to be aware of three specific dynamics of oppression and liberation. First, the therapist would need to recognize that social oppression is real and is maintained on many levels, including the interpersonal level. Second, the therapist would need to adopt Fanon's view that social oppression creates not only symptomology involved in many "mental disorders" but also a learned helplessness and internalized oppression that thwarts liberation and healing (Fanon, 1991). Finally, the therapist would acknowledge that liberation is a healing act and is derived not from a paternalistic process between expert healer and one that suffers but an active process on the part of sufferers. This process involves people taking agency over their own suffering, receiving validation for their attempts at self-liberation, and as Fanon (1991) outlines in his concept of "sociotherapy", being encouraged to channel their individual efforts toward community and societal liberation. As Fanon (2018) warns, this process can be unpleasant, as both parties are deconstructing their social roles and recreating "a neo-society" within the therapy room. It requires the therapist to exhibit expert emotional regulation, transparency in grieving the limitations race and whiteness put on their competency in counseling clients of color, and the courage to allow the self-derived boundaries and coping mechanisms of clients of color to redefine traditional therapeutic practices.

In addition to connecting Fanon's work to cross-racial therapeutic alliances, I also link his applied research and practice to trauma psychology. Much of my clinical training has been with and for traumatized populations. Yet, Fanon is not a familiar name incorporated into training material or theory. I find Fanon helpful in defining how racism is uniquely traumatic and, in his conceptualization, that liberation from the trauma of racism is often the only necessary intervention for clients of color. Fanon's definition of racism as traumatic includes the contention that the state of internalized racism, where a child of color is socialized to hate their blackness and encouraged to participate in the patronizing, self-defeating, and ultimately impossible quest of becoming white, is uniquely traumatic and that this socialization, even within the context of a loving home environment with no exposure to physical/sexual violence, is enough to create a post-traumatic response (Fanon, 1991). Because Fanon (2004) finds "mental symptoms [to be] direct sequels to oppression" (p. 182), he offers that resistance to oppression from the bottom up, where oppressed people unite to creatively cope with oppression and demand the right to their own humanity, is the only cure to the suffering under oppression.

First, I state my racial identity and explain the phase of preparation or consciousness building that I found helpful before and during my clinical practice. I then move to a specific case. This specific case is an amalgam of several different clinical situations I have encountered. This case will present a wide range of complexities that arise in cross-racial clinical work with survivors of trauma that is liberation focused.

Building My Consciousness

I identify as a white woman. Growing up in a predominantly black city, I was exposed to racial difference early, as well as the dramatic, stark boundaries created by racial segregation of neighborhood, school, and religious contexts. Growing up in multiracial settings did not inoculate me from socialization experiences grounded in white supremacy, racist cultural practices, and social benefits based on racial privilege that would ultimately separate and divide me further from members of communities of color who I had physically grown up alongside and come to love. This is the society of which Fanon (1991, 2004) writes. It is a racialized society that places both a person of color and me in our specific societal roles and social functions that are designed to reinforce the racial hierarchy we were born into. This "othering" process that Fanon (1991) identifies as being foundational to a racialized society, creates a social and psychological dynamic whereby a white person is defined by the inferiority of people of color.

Fanon offers that these roles and functions play out interpersonally as well as structurally and this interpersonal oppression brings a particularly devastating blow. Fanon (2004) calls specifically for liberation to take on a humanistic element. He writes, "It is through the effort to recapture the self and to scrutinize the self, it is through the lasting tension of their freedom that men will be able to create the ideal conditions of existence for a human world" (Fanon, 1991, p. 231). Because within a racialized society, the worth of white people is defined by the inferiority of people of color, it is often only through the interpersonal process of shared deconstruction and recreation of identity that the seeds of a truly humane society will be sown. My early experiences taught me that complete social liberation comes equally from the liberation of the oppressed as well as the liberation of the oppressor, a symbiotic process whereby we both play a part in the others process. I assert the white person's liberation comes from witnessing the power of the agency of the oppressed, recognizing this force as a basic, powerful, human right and realizing that this display does not detract from their own humanity but rather confirms and ensures it.

I am intensely grateful for my early experiences within multiracial contexts as they have allowed me to build a social consciousness I feel is required for all white clinicians. In order for me to witness and serve as an ally or co-conspirator in the social/psychological liberation of oppressed groups, I must develop awareness of my place in the racial context, grieve for the instances where I have been complicit in maintaining oppressive status quos, and have the strength to share my personal societal power, as well as work with other white people to build their social consciousness. I want to mention a few endeavors I found foundational to my development of a social consciousness as a practitioner and my ability to use liberation interventions in the therapeutic context. They include self-examination in the company of peers of color, investigation of the history of oppression committed by the field of psychology, and developing awareness of and possible partnerships with community healing efforts.

Because I grew up in a predominantly black city, I had the opportunity from a young age to undergo an intense examination of racial self in the company of people of color. As a very young child, black peers on the playground talked with me about race and my whiteness. These conversations were immature and painful, at times, but laid the groundwork for my understanding that social consciousness building in white people has to involve the oppressed as expert. White people must develop the strength to continue to focus on self with limited defensiveness during these exchanges in order to ensure a balance of emotional labor between themselves and their compatriots of color.

In my graduate school training, it was incredibly helpful to interrogate how racism functions in general in American society and specifically in psychology. Psychology, like many social institutions, has a history of oppressive tactics including misdiagnosis and over diagnosis of people of color, denying people of color's experiences of pain and emotion as valid, denying access to treatment, as well as using diagnosis and hospitalization as a form of social control (Guthrie, 2004). This history creates a sense of institutional mistrust on the part of many people of color toward the mental health field. The depth of this history is not built into most psychology training programs and often practitioners are blind to what they represent to clients of color.

As I began to practice during my pre-doctoral clinical internship and post-doctoral clinical fellowship, I found it extremely helpful to connect with local community efforts toward healing/liberation. The literature from these community groups/efforts is visible in my office and I know their leadership by name. This process does take time but it serves multiple purposes: it signals to people of color that I am connected with diverse communities outside of my institution and I consider multiple avenues toward healing; it provides me information on local healing movements for referral purposes; and it works to create partnerships between my home institution and community efforts. Along this same line, I try to make a thoughtful attempt to compile a referral list of clinicians of color in the event that a client requests a same race clinician and my institution cannot provide this at the time.

There have been many instances in my clinical practice where I have used my social consciousness to create trauma-informed, liberation-focused therapy. The case of K is an amalgam of several of these instances. I have broken down the case of K into four phases: Phase One: trust building; Phase Two: monitoring boundaries, sharing power, and creating corrective, liberating exchanges; Phase Three: attention to individual agency; and finally, Phase Four: bridging personal agency to group agency. For this case each phase took approximately a month but time frames for these phases can vary.

Case of K

K presented to her local rape crisis center, with her newborn baby, as a referral from a family friend, stating "I need to talk to someone about some things." K is a 26-year-old who identifies as a black, Christian, lesbian. She prefers the pronouns she/her.

Phase One: Trust Building (Month One)

Working in a rape crisis center comes with the advantage of being able to wear multiple hats: therapist, educator, and advocate. It also comes with the advantage of flexibility around session allotment and fees. Many community rape crisis centers offer unlimited sessions and require no fee for service. This flexible treatment model is aligned with thinking around traumatic stress that comes from feminist traditions in which sexual violence is specifically labeled as traumatic. Sexual violence experienced at a young age by trusted adults can make healing complex and lengthy (Herman, 1992). Because of the complexity and severity of chronic traumatic experiences, Herman (1992) in her groundbreaking work *Trauma and Recovery*, suggests that healing from "complex trauma" should happen in stages with the first being establishment of safety.

Fanon's work is built on concepts and ideas involving psychological trauma, primarily that the "colonial situation" or racial power structures are created and maintained not only through human violence against the bodies of people of color but in their minds as well. Fanon (2004) notes while presenting cases of those suffering under the French colonial occupation of Algeria, "Because it is a systemized negation of the other, a frenzied determination to deny the other any attribute of humanity, colonialism forces the colonized to constantly ask the question: 'Who am I in reality?'" (p. 182).

In order to justify this violence, a victim blaming occurs where myths about the psychology, mental worth, and physicality of the oppressed are presented as rationalizations for controlling them through violence. Racism, as Fanon outlined, fits well into thinking around complex trauma because the violence is chronic, instituted at a young age, and very interpersonal in nature. Part of liberation, according to Fanon, is preventing the oppressed from internalizing the mythology used to condone racial violence and maintain racist social structures. Without these internalized myths, a survivor is free to feel empowered to demand individual justice as well as the dismantling of the system or institution they suffered under. We see the victim blaming language used with survivors of sexual violence as well because gender stereotypes are often used to justify sexual violence against those identified as women, gender non-conforming or transgender.

While the recommendation of establishing safety as a first phase of treatment for complex trauma makes sense, it becomes complicated when the individual cannot easily escape their chronic torment and further when those attempting to aid in ending torment belong to or represent the structures of torment. This is the case of people of color living in a racist social structure. I, as a clinician, cannot simply focus on healing; I must aid the individual in ending their torment, to find safety. This is where I find the field of traumatic stress lacking. I found I needed to turn to theorists such as Frantz Fanon to assist me in not just aiding in healing those suffering from oppression, but in creating safety by providing experiences of personal and community liberation in the interactions I have with survivors.

When K initially came to the rape crisis center, she indicated she needed to talk but did not explicitly ask for therapy. I identified myself as a clinician; I also explained other roles that I could provide to her such as advocate or educator. I indicated our initial discussion was simply to address her needs and discuss her goals in general. I assured her she did not need to enter individual therapy if she was not interested. K revealed the following during this initial information gathering session.

> K's son was conceived as a result of rape and she wanted assistance in sorting out paperwork for the state around child support and state medical benefits for her son. She indicated she did not want to come in and ask for help but that every time she goes to try and figure out the paper work she "gets really emotional" and could never finish. The state could discontinue her and her son's medical benefits if she did not complete the form and send it in. She then mentioned that she has been feeling depressed and didn't want to sound racist but would prefer to talk to a black clinician about this.

As soon as K revealed more about herself and her trauma history, I relied heavily on active listening to achieve the common therapy factors of empathy, congruence, and unconditional positive regard (Wampold, 2015). I validated her courage to come in for assistance and her keen self-awareness of her emotional reaction to the forms. I also validated K's clarity around wanting to see a black clinician. Her apology for potentially being "racist" in her request gave me information around her complex reaction to her own agency over her healing process. K's comment inferred she may have felt she was being racist toward white people in her request for a black therapist. While seeking out safety in the company of same race community members has been found to be restorative and protective for people of color, this response is often shamed, stigmatized, and feared by white people (Tatum, 2017). K labeling her own pursuit for safety as racist and apologizing to me (a white person) is an example of the internalized racism Fanon warns against.

I informed her that our clinic has four clinicians, one of whom was black. However, this clinician was granted a three-month extended leave of absence. I reinforced K's agency toward her protective instincts by telling her I did not personally take her comment as racist. I refrained from lecturing K about the realities of racism in society because coming from a white person this was patronizing. I made an adamant statement that I understood I am a white person in a racist society and I believed that racism is a reality for people of color. The crux of modern-day racism is the myth that we have transcended race, that racism no longer exists and we now are free to just be "human" (Bonilla-Silva, 2010). The simplicity of the statement that I understand my whiteness and that racism exists takes on a more complex function and becomes an act of alliance with K. I checked in with K after I made my statement regarding racism and she indicated she appreciated that I did not find the request racist.

K elaborated a bit more about experiences she had in the past with therapy,

> She reported having received a range of diagnoses including schizophrenia, bipolar disorder, depression, and most recently post-partum depression. She indicated she never stayed with any therapist for very long and gave up on therapy after she graduated high school. She mentioned feeling disrespected and confused by doctors and therapists; she felt they never understood her and just tried to label her.

K's extrapolation allowed another area of complexity into the room in her report of her mistrust not just of white people but also people representing the mental health field. This meant that I represented two areas of mistrust for K, white people and people working in the mental health field. Because part of my own consciousness raising process was to investigate how the mental health field has historically and contemporarily participated in racism, I saw no need to interrogate K on her experience for accuracy or clarity at this point. I simply validated her experience and mentioned that I understood I represented white people and the field of mental health.

From a trauma-informed perspective, my presence as a white, mental health practitioner could potentially evoke not just discomfort in K, but fear in the form of a psychological or physiological cue or "trigger" that reminded her of past experiences where she felt afraid or victimized. If I was not thoughtful and vigilant, I could have easily recreated K's past experiences with the mental health field, reinforced any negative thoughts or feelings she had about the field, and potentially caused her to drop out from our interactions. If K were to leave therapy because I "triggered" or reminded her of past, painful interactions with the mental health field, she could have experienced this flight as empowering because it would be of her own choice. However, in her attempt to seek safety from being victimized yet again by the mental health institution, she will have been retraumatized in a basic process of seeking help, thinking her instincts were pointing her to a place where she would be safe and receive support, instead, she reexperienced a predictable pattern of abuse. The guilt/shame from thinking your healing instincts have led you astray and caused you further harm can be very detrimental and lead to a learned helplessness around one's individual agency to participate in one's own healing/liberation. Further, many clinicians perceive a client's early termination of therapy as a form of resistance or noncompliance with treatment. This viewpoint essentially blames the survivor for their own attempts to create safety as opposed to looking deeply into clinician factors in early termination rate.

Given all that K revealed, I queried about emotional safety. I prefaced my query with the understanding that K only wanted to talk on an "emotional level" with a black clinician, but I wanted to check in and see if she was feeling emotionally safe in the room, given her disclosure about past experiences with therapists and doctors. I asked a closed-ended question in an attempt to allow K to answer with a simple yes or no, which was more in line with her request to keep emotions out for the time being. K indicated with a short response that she felt safe.

I offered K some options in terms of moving forward. I showed K a list of other clinicians of color in the community and indicated I could help with a referral. I offered another option was that I could work with her around practical and advocacy issues, and she could wait for the emotional processing to begin when our black clinician returned. I also reminded her she was free to leave at any time she chose.

I elaborated briefly on what our relationship would look like if we continued to work together. I informed K that experiencing emotions in the room might be unavoidable, especially when actually filling out the forms. I indicated that we could create ground rules and boundaries for our relationship. These boundaries would specifically, clearly outline what emotional work or processing would look like. This discussion about boundaries included how she could signal to me she felt we needed to back off from a process or topic that was making her feel unsafe. I also offered that we could schedule a follow-up meeting to complete the forms in which she could bring in a trusted family member or friend to sit with her or wait in the waiting room for support. Additionally, I asked her if she felt comfortable receiving psychoeducation around psychological trauma from me.

K indicated she felt safe enough to work through practical issues with me and would like to receive psychoeducation about psychological trauma. She mentioned that she would like to use the rest of the time together for psycho-education and schedule a follow-up to fill out the forms with someone present with her. I used the remainder of the time to validate her experiences as traumatizing, clarify the trauma response in the mind and body, highlight her natural healing instincts, and suggest ways to support her healing instincts. All the literature and handouts on trauma I gave K included historical and social trauma as a valid traumatizing experience. Because the handouts reinforced this perspective, I spent less time reviewing the materials to reduce the risk of sounding patronizing. Finally, K indicated she would like to bring her son's Godmother to the appointment next week for support. K called her friend and asked for availability for next week to come to an appointment and we scheduled the follow-up at that time with the friend's schedule in mind.

The following week, K returned with her son and her friend to address the task of completing the forms. K indicated she would like her friend in the room. We started this session with introductions and moved to create boundaries and ground rules around emotional experiences. I summarized for K what I understood her boundary to be from the last session in which she preferred talking about "emotional topics" with a black clinician. I conveyed to her that I was more than willing to respect her boundary.

Allowing K to dictate emotional and interpersonal boundaries with me in therapy was extremely important from both a trauma informed and Fanonian perspective. Resetting racial boundaries is a fundamental act of individual liberation. Segregating races physically and psychologically has always been a significant tactic in maintaining oppressive structures. Further, this segregation is always structured by and benefits the white population (DuBois, 1982). By allowing K to initially set limits around much of our interaction, we created a corrective experience in which K had the power to structure the healing environment based on her instincts and needs. K's recognition of her own agency and my deference to this agency was an example of the painful, yet humanizing liberation process Fanon calls the "new rhythm" required for a creation of "a new humanity" (Fanon, 1991).

I started by asking K what she meant by "emotional level" and she responded that she means "talking about things that are personal, that you would only talk with a few people about or maybe no one about." I proposed that a ground rule for our relationship be for me to ask her if she's comfortable talking about topics before I ask information about it specifically. K agreed. I explained to K that post-traumatic stress makes it such that our emotions throw us off, come out of the blue, or seem out of control. I explained that I may do or say something that unintentionally causes a strong emotional reaction in her. K mentioned she has noticed this lately in regards to her emotions. I engaged K in exploring if there are any small signs in her mind or body that signal to her strong emotions may be present. This exploration allowed both of us to be prepared to slow down or back away in accordance with K's stated boundaries. K indicated she noticed her nose starts to itch and her tear ducts fill. She also noticed her mind gets "very scared someone will see me cry." I affirmed K's self-awareness and encouraged her to let me know we need to stop or take a break if she feels these things within her.

We briefly discussed crying in front of others. K attached shame to crying. She laughed when she said, "I hate thinking that anyone would see me cry, especially a white person, no offense." I laughed with her and reiterated I didn't take offense to the rules and boundaries she established when interacting with white people. I stated concisely to her that she is the best expert on herself and whatever rules she has in place are there for a purpose.

A hallmark of post-traumatic stress theory suggests people create rigid beliefs about self, others, and the world in order to exert the most control over one's environment, and thus maintain physical and emotional safety. These rigid beliefs often limit one's life and restrict one's ability to interact in the environment with others, and ultimately one's own psychological space (Resick & Schnicke, 1992). One could view K's rigid rules around "all white people" as limiting and restrictive; however, if safety is not reached one could not be expected to transform or alter beliefs and attitudes that keep them safe. Since racism is a social reality, people of color have not reached safety from it and rigid rules around race relations are necessary in many circumstances to avoid continued trauma. I could never expect K to stop using her protective rules for interacting with white people around me. After all, I was a stranger and represented not only whiteness but the mental health field.

K and I then turned to completing the form. The form requested information pertaining to her son's father in order for child support to be pursued and for the family's state benefits to continue. Because of the nature of her rape she had none of this information and needed to file a "just cause claim". A "just cause claim" alerts the state office that she could not comply with their process for a specific "just cause." K expressed distress at the end of the form where it required her to write in the "just cause."

K immediately began to look away from the form and drop her head. She reached for her friend and started taking deep breaths. I reminded K that she could leave the office and take a break if she wanted. K decided to walk with her friend in the hallway for a few minutes. When she returned, she said she was scared she would cry when answering the one remaining question. I validated K's fear, but I held off processing why she felt upset as a way of respecting her emotional boundary. Instead, I reminded her that there are creative alternatives to this process we could consider. I offered to talk out the answer and she could try and write it in at home. I offered she could go in the other room with her friend, try to answer the form, and check back with me after it was done. Finally, she could go home, I could call her and we could do it over the phone. Part of the debilitation of post-traumatic stress is that rigid, survivalist coping responses such as fear based self-isolation or dysregulated, aggressive self-harm stifles creative, expressive, liberating coping responses (Herman, 1992). In regards to the complexities of racial trauma, many successful attempts at creative coping, are often stigmatized or stereotyped in order to thwart the healing efforts of the practice (Cross, 1995). An example of this is the genre of hip-hop

206 *Maria Judith Valgoi*

music, a form of creativity in direct response to societal oppression that is often stereotyped as being violent, angry, and dangerous.

By offering K multiple possible responses to her anxiety, I modeled a creative approach to coping. I made suggestions only because the fear response made it difficult for K to initially access this creativity. Once K realized she could think creatively about how to answer the questions she adapted two of my offerings into one that made sense to her. She asked if she could go in another room with her friend and call me on her cell phone to fill out the form. I obliged her and we set this situation up. With me on the phone and in a separate room, K felt comfortable allowing herself to display emotions if they arose. K and I talked through her response to the question over the phone. She needed to write a few sentences about the "just cause," which was conception through rape. After writing the explanation, K indicated she needed to hang up the phone, but would return to my office in a few minutes.

K returned to my office a few minutes later with her friend. She thanked me for helping her. I asked K if we could talk for a few minutes about how the alternative solution went. K agreed and indicated she felt so much relief not having me in the room. She mentioned she could easily get away (hang up the phone) when she wanted to and not feel ashamed or guilty about leaving our encounter or hurting my feelings. She reflected that this experience made her realize that trying to hold back her emotions takes up a lot of energy and when she was allowed to display emotion while doing the task she could complete the task. With me in the room and all I represented (a stranger, a white person, a person from the mental health field), she was concentrating more on holding back her emotions. This made her anxious and prevented her from completing the form.

Before K left, she mentioned she had a question she wanted to ask me. The phone intervention gave her an idea of how she could deal with her anxiety in a few situations in her life in the next few weeks. She asked if I could be on the phone with her when she went to the state office to drop off the forms and when she talked to a case worker. We were able to schedule these phone meetings in advance. I invited K to return to the rape crisis center after these events so we could check in and talk about what happened. K indicated as long as we stuck to the ground rules and only discussed things that happened in the present, she would feel comfortable coming in and talking with me.

K's requests communicated a few things. First, I may have gained some trust. Second, she applied creative coping to other areas of her life, which meant she gained something from our simple process intervention of using the phone. Finally, her decision to ask me if I could play a role in her coping designed by her (phone call), and her willingness to consent to my ethical process for care (follow-up), was an example of a person of color using the mental health system in a way that fits her needs.

As planned, K. called me to bear witness and provide support to help her get through the events she mentioned. K returned for a follow-up after each event. In this phase, K and I have initiated Fanon's suggested "new rhythm" toward "a new humanity" where I viewed K as the expert of her identity and experience, yielded to her in the co-creation of therapeutic boundaries, and utilized non-traditional interventions so that K experienced her own agency in session. The process of establishing the "new rhythm" allowed me to gain additional trust from K and we moved into phase two: monitoring boundaries, sharing power, and creating corrective, liberating exchanges.

Phase Two: Monitoring Boundaries, Sharing Power, and Creating Corrective, Liberating Exchanges (Month 2)

As K began to feel safer with me as a clinician, she naturally offered more of her background and personal history. Using the body and mind signifiers from our initial ground rules discussion, K was able to label her own responses and shared with me what she wanted to talk about and when. I kept track of the changing nature of our boundaries and reflected these changes to K. K recognized she felt comfortable enough with me to "share many things from my past but not everything." Within a few weeks K shared her history with me

> K entered into the foster care system at birth and was placed and eventually adopted by relatives of her paternal grandmother. Growing up, she had little contact with her biological mother. Her biological father had sporadic contact with K, until he entered prison when she was approximately 7-years-old. He was recently released from prison and was currently living at K's grandmother's (his mother's house). K reported a contentious relationship with her adoptive mother, stating, "She never liked me. I think she hated me." K talked about her adoptive father extremely positively stating, "He was the only one that cared about me." Unfortunately, K's adoptive father died of cancer when she was 13. It was after the death of her father that K reported being sexually abused by a man related to her adoptive mother. In her teens, she began to display signs of depression, intense, overwhelming emotional experiences, self-harm through cutting, thoughts of suicide and perceptual experiences involving seeing angels at the foot of her bed and hearing her dead father's voice. School systems initiated mental health services for K and she received multiple diagnoses over a three-year span. K did not feel respected by these doctors and therapists and she has not sought out mental health treatment since being referred as a high schooler. Since high school, K struggled maintaining employment, stating "I'm always getting into it with someone on the job. This town is too small sometimes." K reported a string of intimate relationships that lasted at least 6 months, but usually ended in her partner disappointing her emotionally. K reported she felt she has struggled in her life but now lives for her son. She struggled to identify personal strengths but stated her goals are to be a "good mother" and "go to college." K did not report any substance use past or present. She denied head injury or history of physical illness.

I asked K if she felt comfortable enough to reflect on her history and try to construct a narrative that connects all the details in the story to her past and current psychological suffering. This collaborative approach to conceptualizing one's presenting concern was valuable in maintaining trust, congruence, and transparency as it shares power in knowledge gathering, knowledge organizing, and knowledge interpreting. During the session, we used visual aids to organize information. We created a genogram to keep track of important relationships, timelines of traumas and of symptoms that we compared against each other, and we generated lists of triggers and coping behaviors. K and I relied on her self-knowledge and the psychoeducation around post-traumatic stress I facilitated to co-create a life story.

K talked about the birth of her son but did not talk about his conception or her pregnancy. K avoided this topic completely. I reflected this detail back to K after we created visual aids and the narrative. K's tone and volume changed when she said, "I thought you said I didn't have to talk about things I don't want to." I told K that she still had control over what we talked about and I was reflecting an observation of mine. I assured her I was just reflecting and I had no ulterior motive to force or encourage her to talk about this topic. K continued, "I don't want to talk to you about that. I already told you so much stuff." I told K I heard her when she put up a boundary around that information and I would not push it further. I asked K if she was feeling any of her emotion signals in her body or mind. K responded, "No. I'm not feeling anything. Actually, I am feeling something. Anger."

I told K that I respect her anger and asked her how she wanted to proceed. K responded, "I don't know." She stepped out and returned a few minutes later. After K returned, she said,

> I thought about it and I remember how we agreed that you would ask before you brought up a topic. Even though you didn't ask me a question about it, I still felt thrown for a loop that you brought it up without asking. I'm not ready to talk to you about that. Can we make a ground rule that you don't bring it up and I will let you know when I'm ready?

I responded that I absolutely understood how my reflection was a violation of our original ground rules. I apologized to K and thanked her for letting me know how I made her feel and also for providing me with a way to make it better. This moment was a significant point in our therapeutic relationship because it represented a rupture and repair. My violation of the ground rule and K's direct response represented the rupture. The repair occurred through a respectful discussion and an agreement on how to move forward.

In general, using boundaries and ground rules is helpful language that allows survivors to voice concerns or grievances. Boundary language and the extended trust building phase allowed K and me to survive this rupture. This repair process with K was another example of her taking agency over her own healing as well as confronting me for a perceived wrong. Our baseline trust was what allowed this to be liberating for the both of us. K asserted not only her anger, but her needs going forward. I neither shamed nor patronized K for her expression of anger. By validating K's anger as rational, we were able to move

forward in our work together with a new understanding to support the maintenance of our relationship.

Phase Three: Attention Toward Individual Agency (Month Three)

Based on the narrative/conceptualization that K and I co-created we identified some target issues she felt comfortable working on. She mentioned that
the release of her biological father from prison shortly before her son was born
brought up a lot of confusion and anxiety. K attributed many positive qualities
to her biological father (smart, good with cars and numbers, loyal), but she also
mentioned her father was selfish and was constantly bothered by her baby's
crying. Additionally, he made rude remarks to her about identifying as a lesbian
and her son's future sexuality, "if you never bring a male role model around
that boy, he will grow up to be gay." K said she wanted to give her biological
father a chance to be a grandfather to her son but she felt resentful because he
abandoned her at birth. Furthering her resentment, he boldly told her how she
should raise her son. K said she gets emotional when her son's crying becomes
overwhelming, because she knows that if her adoptive father were still alive he
would help make her feel better and support her.

Once we established a trusting, strong therapeutic relationship, K discussed
aspects of her identity beyond race; the intersections of her multiple identities
created complexity in our work together. K's intersecting identities of black and
lesbian complicated her liberation process because these two distinct communities do not generally support the liberation of the other. There is homophobia
in the black community and racism in the LGBT community. Thus, K's course
to liberation was multiplexed.

K and I talked about how many of the symptoms that led to her past diagnoses of schizophrenia, bipolar, and most recently postpartum depression were
more aptly connected to symptoms of grief, loss, and childhood trauma. K
revealed the most disrespectful thing a doctor ever said to her was that he felt
her attraction to women was just a phase in response to her childhood trauma.
K said this confused her for years and induced profound shame and doubt
about her sexuality. This revelation illuminated K's mistrust of the medical and
mental health establishments.

I assured K that just as I considered her the best expert on her racial identity,
the same goes for her sexual orientation. K mentioned one of the most difficult
struggles she experienced was feeling like her paternal grandmother, whom she
loved and adored, did not completely accept her and often made comments
such as, "Did you find a nice man yet?" or "Don't worry. The right man will
come around." K said she did not come out directly to her grandmother, but
she suspected her grandmother knew the truth because of the rumors circling
in the community. K noted she did not see many people of color at the LGBT
groups in town that help people plan and talk through coming out. Through
our work together, K decided to talk to her grandmother, initially suggesting we

use the phone advocacy intervention. As she reflected, she thought it would be disrespectful to her grandmother. Her grandmother might have been embarrassed or ashamed if she knew K's white counselor was on the phone. After I validated K's protective instinct and her creative coping, I suggested we brainstorm how we could use our relationship, community resources, and her personal coping skills to work toward this goal of talking to her grandmother.

K ultimately decided her grandmother should meet me because the phone intervention might work someday if I form a relationship with her. When K came to appointments, her grandmother babysat her son. K suggested we FaceTime her the following week while we were in session. K also shared she considered attending an open mic event to read some poetry aloud she wrote about her pain and suffering. She felt like the open mic was a good substitute, at the moment, for talking to her grandmother because it allowed her to verbalize things in her own way and be listened to.

After careful preparation, the next session K and I FaceTimed with her grandmother. In the brief call, K identified me as "the lady who advocated for me on the phone when I had to go to the state offices." K's grandmother thanked me for helping K and made a comment about how she felt the state office was being ridiculous. I agreed and mentioned how it was a pleasure working with K. We concluded the call with invitations to stay in touch if needed. Connections made with K's grandmother, on K's terms, were an essential component to long-term work with K. Her grandmother was potentially the most pivotal person in her life, aside from her son. While connecting with family and community supports for K was a great strategy for long-term care, this case exemplifies how this could be complicated based on my whiteness. The fact that K was able to initiate this contact and create ground rules around our dialogue was imperative and another example of K guiding her own treatment.

K's performance at the open mic was greeted with applause and verbal praise. She mentioned that she connected with another woman who wrote about similar themes and that the two considered meeting up to write together. Although K felt a strong pull to speak at the mic, she felt depressed the next day. K and I processed how her healing journey has "felt up and down." She used the metaphor of "finding my voice" and stated that she felt the best when it felt like she was "using my real voice." However, many times she used code like the metaphors in her poem.

Liberation practice is often enacted in secret or in code because these attempts are shamed or squelched by the mainstream. Further, Fanon writes of the dual awareness the oppressed possess because of their need to understand not just their world, but the world of the oppressor in order to ensure physical and psychological survival (Fanon, 2004). This duality could lead to exhaustion, depression, anxiety, and identity confusion. So, as K increased awareness and knowledge about her capacity for liberation, she was also overwhelmed and experienced anxiety, exhaustion, and even depression at the prospect of this process.

In this phase, K experienced more experiential instances of her own creative coping and asserted her individual agency in healing. However, she began to realize the complexities around healing from intersecting forms of oppression. She also experienced both the positive and negative emotions/states that come from utilizing coping toward liberation in the real world. Our baseline trust allowed K to experience her own agency in session with me and also experiment with this in the real world. My continued commitment to and vigilance around our interpersonal boundaries created a sense of safety with K that allowed for her personal growth.

Phase Four: Bridging Personal Agency to Group Agency (Month Four)

K and I continued to meet weekly and we discussed the complexities of her finding her "voice," and the ups and downs of her healing, as well as discussed plans to come out to her grandmother. K mentioned several meetings, with her friend from the open mic, where the two wrote together. K revealed these meetings inspired her to start a spoken word support group where black women who are suffering could get together, share writing, and possibly perform together.

A crucial aspect of my therapeutic relationships is brainstorming with individuals ways they can find their own agency alongside of others in their community. This is derived from Fanon's intervention of "sociotherapy" (Fanon, 2018) whereby liberation is experienced when the oppressed are able to engage in culturally relevant, creative tasks at the group level. Complete social/psychological liberation is achieved when the group as a whole is liberated. In this sense, individual therapy is simply preparation work that sustains an individual's energy to do work in the broader community.

K's desire to create a support group for black women reflected her belief in her coping skills and agency in her healing/liberation. In the beginning of our work together K suggested that requesting a black therapist might be racist, an indication of the insidious nature of internalized oppression Fanon warns about. Now she felt comfortable stating she was creating a support group for black women by black women. This support group, aligned with Fanon's concept of sociotherapy, allowed K the capacity to sustain and fulfill her in ways that outlasted individual therapy.

I validated K's instinct and suggested we might use some session time to plan and organize this endeavor. I made it clear to K that I did not want to join her group, but I could assist her in thinking what a support group model would look like, offer her some pointers on group facilitation, and possibly brainstorm with her about recruiting and structure. K liked this idea but wanted to split our sessions between her own process and planning the support group.

During this phase, the black therapist returned from leave and I informed K. At this time, K said she wanted to tell me something she had been holding inside. K stated that she wanted to talk about her rape with me but she could not "find the strength" because her rapist was black and "I don't want to talk about black men like that, especially in front of you." K went on to explain it had been very difficult for her to work through the complexities of being raped by a black man. She mentioned that she felt ashamed working through this with a white person.

I thanked K for telling me this and conveyed that I understood. I also continued to validate K's healing instincts. According to Judith Herman's stages of healing, when a survivor feels completely safe, they will often transition to the second phase of remembrance and mourning or direct emotional process about the trauma. I offered to K that we could finish together in the next few weeks and she could transition to the black therapist to start direct process of the rape. I offered that we could continue with a new ground rule around avoiding talking about the rape; however, I reinforced that her instinct to process and not avoid talking about the trauma was healthy and should be facilitated. I told K we are restricted by a clinic rule that an individual could only see one clinician at a time in order to make as much availability as possible. K expressed feeling torn about this situation and mentioned she felt very uncomfortable even thinking she has to make this choice. K revealed she was scared about meeting a new therapist even though they are black and sad that our time together would end.

This was a great example of how oppression has unexpected complexities that caused deep emotions for both K and me. K could not deny we had a connection in our therapeutic relationship but she also felt great shame and anxiety in having to talk to me, a white person, about trauma she experienced at the hands of another black person. I validated K for this self and societal awareness. I also disclosed that the situation was sad for me as well. I told K that our therapeutic relationship brought me joy and although I understood the limits of cross-racial connections, it made me feel sad that I could not provide her the healing context that she needed. K and I sat in this reality for the duration of the session and grieved the limitations racial hierarchy placed on us. At the next session, K and I decided to extend our sessions for one month in order to finish planning for the support group. I explained to K what a warm hand-off to our black clinician would look like. I also offered to K that we could arrange a limited amount of sessions of co-therapy, where the black clinician and myself could be in the room together.

Epilogue

K continued trauma processing with the black clinician for several months and reported multiple benefits from this experience. She was unable to come out to her grandmother during the time she spent with our center. K's grandmother and I came to know each other on a first name basis. K got her support group up and running. I kept literature about this support group in my office and had several women reach out to K to join her group. I received several new survivors as referrals from both K and K's friend that came with her to one of our initial appointments. Through my attention to keeping and maintaining K's trust, validating her agency to heal, and encouraging her attempts at community liberation as a valid treatment goal, K and I were able to create a healing space that allowed her to feel some sense of safety in her healing context. This safety allowed her to assert her needs for healing and enter into the next phase of her healing and liberation on her terms.

In conclusion, Fanon's idea of psychotherapy as an agent of social liberation and warning that social liberation is painful are foundational to my therapeutic practice. My work with K is an example of two beings finding Fanon's "new rhythm" that will be the nourishment of the liberation process. Within psychotherapy, the rhythm is an interpersonal process whereby K, a woman of color, was able to set and affirm her own emotional boundaries with a white therapist, learn to creatively use a flexible healing process for her best interest, and take her individual agency into her community at large contributing to a collective healing movement. Fanon's indelible warning that social liberation will be painful and disruptive is essential to my practice. Understanding the disruptive force of psychological trauma has helped prepare me for the equally disruptive force of social liberation. As a white clinician working for racial liberation, Fanon has helped me to learn that my role in liberation is to be comfortable with disruption, welcome it, withstand it gracefully, and emerge a "new being".

References

Bonilla-Silva, E. (2010). *Racism without racists: Color-blind racism and racial inequality in contemporary America*. Lanham: Rowman & Littlefield.

Cross, W. E., Jr. (1995). The psychology of nigrescence: Revising the Cross model. In J. G. Ponterotto, J. M. Casas, L. A. Suzuki, & C. M. Alexander (Eds.), *Handbook of multicultural counseling* (pp. 93–122). Thousand Oaks, CA, US: Sage Publications, Inc.

DuBois, W. E. B. (1982). *The souls of Black folks: Revised and updated bibliography*. New York: Penguin.

Fanon, F. (1991). *Black skin, white masks*. New York, NY: Grove Press.

Fanon, F. (2004). *The wretched of the earth/Frantz Fanon: Translated from the French by Richard Philcox: Introductions by Jean-Paul Sartre and Homi K. Bhabha*. New York: Grove Press.

Fanon, F. (2018). *Alienation and freedom*. New York: NY: Bloomsbury Publishing.

Guthrie, R. V. (2004). *Even the rat was white: A historical view of psychology*. Boston: Pearson Education.

Herman, J. L. (1992). *Trauma and recovery: The aftermath of violence, from domestic abuse to political terror*. New York: Basic Books.

Resick, P. A., & Schnicke, M. K. (1992). Cognitive processing therapy for sexual assault victims. *Journal of Consulting and Clinical Psychology, 60*(5), 748–756.

Tatum, B. D. (2017). *Why are all the Black kids sitting together in the cafeteria? And other conversations about race*. New York, NY: Basic Books.

Wampold, B. E. (2015). How important are the common factors in psychotherapy? An update. *World Psychiatry, 14*(3), 270–277.

9 "When I Was Growing Up, It Was Important to Be Identified as a Revolutionary"

A Conversation With Community Activist Imani Bazzell

Imani Bazzell, Helen A. Neville, and Lou Turner

Most scholarly writings on Frantz Fanon and even in liberation/Black/community psychology exclude the voices of those who are in the trenches fighting for justice and access to culturally responsive mental health services. In the United States there has been different strands of political Fanonian thought (e.g., the Black Power movement and the Black Panther Party and others); there's also been a strand of thought that hasn't been engaged much. This includes professionals and community healthcare activists engaged in actual practices with people in psychiatric centers, mental health facilities, or in community settings. In this chapter, we highlight the work and influence of community activist Ms. Imani Bazzell. Her activism in general covers health and education within local African American communities, but encompasses liberation more broadly.

The focus of our conversation with Ms. Imani is on her Fanon-inspired radio show ACCESS Live. The show was part of a larger federally funded initiative (ACCESS Initiative) granted to the Champaign County Mental Health Board in Central Illinois. The radio show was designed to educate and engage the local Black community around issues of justice and mental health. ACCESS Live was on the air for three years between 2012 and 2015; about 64 of the episodes are archived online (https://archive.org/details/Access_Live_with_Imani_Bazzell_-_5-7-14). It is auspicious that we arranged the conversation in 2019, the 60th anniversary of *A Dying Colonialism*. In this text, Fanon includes a chapter explicating the role of the radio in the decolonization struggle, and its impact on the psychology of the colonized.

Ms. Imani is a well-known and respected community activist in Champaign–Urbana, Illinois—a micro-urban community in the Midwest United States. She was the founding director of SisterNet, a local network of African American women committed to health and healing. Throughout the years she has worn many hats, including directing *At Promise of Success*, a collaboration between the Champaign Public Schools, the Community Academic Support Network, and the University of Illinois. Proud mother of three, Ms. Imani has fought her entire career against racism in the schools and in health care. She advocated for the creation of spaces where Black professionals can collaborate to provide transformative and comprehensive justice-informed care for African American youth and their families.

A Revolutionary in the Making: Family Background and Early Experiences

In order to understand who someone is in the current moment, it is critical to explore their roots, the soil in which their seed was planted and grew to maturation. Born in Los Angeles and living in a number of cities across the United States, Ms. Imani spent many of her coming-of-age years in Milwaukee. Imani's life experience growing up in deeply segregated Black communities shaped her involvement in community organizing and a lifelong commitment to improving the lived experiences of those most affected by neocolonialism and racial oppression. Ms. Imani does not hold back in describing her family life as a child, which was at once filled with love, intellectual stimulation, radical foundation, and chaos.

> So, interestingly, Fanon has been attacked by feminists, Black feminists in particular. I think damn near any man, certainly in the public eye, might deserve that, but it's difficult for me, because I came up in a household that was emotionally dysfunctional, but very intellectually inclined. And so, Fanon, Baldwin, all of them were throughout [my house], no matter where we moved. We moved a lot. I'm the classic kid they write about, the classic *at-risk* kid.
>
> What was I doing with two well-educated parents? But you can have educated parents who are not plugged in. I joke that I'm not sure if they knew my name. And this is an eight-member household. Not including pets. Papa was a rolling stone. But again, I could see there were books. . . . If we didn't have anything, there were bookshelves, even if there wasn't room, one would be in the bathroom.
>
> I knew the Renaissance folks, of course, Malcolm [X], all of that. So, I would say that I came up in a leftist household. But it was communicatively dysfunctional, and my parents made sure we knew how to read and all that before we went to school. I do remember, before starting kindergarten, being forced to sit down on the floor in the living room and go through these little learning projects. Which I know other kids in my neighborhood weren't necessarily getting.

In our conversation, Ms. Imani talked about her political awakening (Fanon, 1966). She learned the cruelties of racial oppression early in life and her parents and older siblings exposed her to radical thinkers to help interpret these realities. Also, being a child of the 1960s, she was introduced to revolutionary Black politics by her older brother Barry and through her involvement with the

Black Panther Party as a teenager. These early activities planted seeds for her later community activism around education and health.

> I think I was forced into political activity through school segregation, school integration stuff. So, back as far as 12 years old, I started acting up. But before 12, you know how you don't know why you know things? And you don't know why you believe things? I think I might have told you all this little story before. When Nixon, in 1968, got elected President, I remember there was a big picture of him on the front cover of the *Washington Post*. That's when we lived in Anacostia, in southeast DC.
>
> I got my crayons out and I started drawing on Nixon's face. And I drew him into a devil. And I remember my parents looking down to see what I was doing laughing to each other. I cannot tell you who told me Nixon was not good for us. I don't know who told me Fanon should've been my hero? I don't know.
>
> I find that it is revealed to you, over time. So, who told me Nixon was against Black folks? Why was I drawing a devil on him? I don't remember anybody telling me that. It's just in the air, you know?
>
> [As I got older] I remember free breakfast programs and knocking on doors and handing out flyers. And my first job was with the People's Free Health Clinic. That was in Milwaukee. The People's Free Health Clinic was a project, of course, of the Black Panther Party. So my first job, at 14, was to knock on doors, offer free pest control, free hypertension checks, and free lead paint poisoning testing.
>
> That was in the era when all these Black kids were coming up with lead paint poisoning. The Panthers weren't against violence if required, just like Fanon said. But also, people lose the great humanity of folks. They had to break it down in Algiers. I mean, everywhere we've had to have armed struggle, it's not because people are really mean and want to kill people. It's that you want some independence. . . .
>
> [My brother, Darrell and I were away at college, with my little sister, Lori the only child left at home]; Barry, my brother, had already moved out to Oakland [to write for the paper] and work directly with Huey [Newton]. He went out and got my sister and brought her back to Oakland to be in the [Black Panther] day school. Because she didn't know how to act. So I guess the day school was going to straighten her out [and she ultimately got straighten out]. She used to fuss if there was going to be a protest or something, she wanted to hold the signs too. But her job was to pass out drinks to everybody so nobody would be thirsty. And she's like, "But I wanted to hold the signs!"
>
> It was really nice going to the 50th anniversary of the Black Panther Party . . . 2016 was the 50th Panther Party, right? To see all the sisters there who had done the work to set up the schools and clinics

After a brief discussion noting the influence of Fanon on the global Black Power Movement, including the Black Panther Party, Ms. Imani remarked on the link between Fanon and her identity as a revolutionary with an interest in challenging internalized oppression.

> You're asking me in what ways did Fanon influence [my] approach to promoting mental health among Black children, families, and communities. Mostly, what I was thinking about was that he felt it was important to be identified as a revolutionary. And when I was growing up, it was important to be identified as a revolutionary.
>
> And this thing that I just keep bringing up around historical trauma [in my professional roles], I'm using interchangeably with internalized oppression. I feel like I got that from him. I got that understanding from him. *Black Skin, White Masks* [in particular].
>
> So, it was between the SisterNet [the Black community-based Black women's health collective she founded] principles and just not really being able to explain "why Fanon" and the question that he must be identified as a revolutionary. I was told the same thing. So, I know it was that. I knew there was *Black Skin, White Masks*, which, of course, at a young age, I didn't quite understand. But again, this internalized racism piece, I knew we were not going to be free without dealing with it.

Internalized Racism and Historical Trauma

> The Negro enslaved by his inferiority, the white man enslaved by his superiority alike behave in accordance with a neurotic orientation.
>
> – Frantz Fanon

Ms. Imani's professional interests center on issues related to internalized racism. Drawing on Fanon's arguments about the sickness of (neo)colonialism on the colonized and the colonizers, Ms. Imani's community organizing has incorporated political education to help "awaken" Black people to the manifestations of the dominant racial ideologies of inferiority and superiority in daily life. The goal of such education, of course, is social action. Ms. Imani's work also has included providing racial and cultural diversity education to mainly White professionals, which stems from her understanding of the pathology of racism and how deeply it affects White people with a false sense of superiority and ignorance of the contributions of People of Color.

> It's always been really important to me that when people do racial justice training, you have to break it down into segments. People have it broken down into individual racism, institutional racism, and cultural racism. But I break it down into institutional racism, individual racism, and internalized racism. And I just don't feel the internalized racism piece gets the attention that it needs.
>
> Do we not get that the white man can take his foot off our necks any time he wants, and we would continue to walk around like this? That's called

internalized racism. That's when we're willing to do his work for him. And I've always, from a young person, felt strongly about that. . . .

I just got a text [message] today from somebody in Canada who used to be on my staff: [she writes] "[a]s for up here, based on the agenda of the United Nations for people of African descent, the government funded programs with a budget that surpasses $47 million. They now address anti-Black racism. They implement anti-oppressive practices, et cetera. But the elephant in the room is how to deal with the internalized racism." Which is what I'm saying. So, she's sort of repeating me, bless her little heart. To deal with internalized racism, and not to mention cultural chauvinism among the different islands . . . . She's from Trinidad.

Ms. Imani views internalized racism as an outgrowth of historical trauma and remaining ignorant of either further perpetuates oppressive relationships in the classroom, doctor's office, counseling session, and interpersonal relationships.

You asked me what my situations have been here in town that Black folks would have traumatic responses to these events [police killings of Black men and women].

This community is so traumatized, it doesn't know it's traumatized. And many of our people play into the trauma. We know that the way internalized oppression works is when you hate yourself, you hate people who look like you. I'm saying that to say, bad stuff happens here all the time, and people respond all the time, in small or large settings, depending upon what the issue is. It wasn't until Kiwane [Carrington a 15-year-old Black teenager shot and killed by police in Champaign, Illinois, in 2009] that [residents] started filming the police again. Otherwise, without witnessing that wasn't a tragic event.

So, I guess what I'm saying is, and I think this confirms that Black folks on some level all feel related, we all suffer from historical trauma. So, even though Treyvon [Martin] was murdered in Florida, not in Champaign–Urbana, and even though Mike Brown was murdered in Ferguson, not Champaign–Urbana, Illinois, the impact was still the same.

And so, we're all keeping ourselves in our place. On Christmas, I had Channel 3 News knocking on my door. Because there were two shooters the night before down the street from my house. The "man" didn't do that. But the "man" made the guns. The "man" makes it easy for us to get the guns, on purpose. But the "man" knows we'll shoot each other.

Until we deal with [internalized racism] and that's got to be dealt with in formal mental health settings and informal mental health settings. But if we got mental health providers who don't know what the hell it is, how are they going to be providing appropriate care to our community? So, at some point, you got to stop waiting for people who ain't coming.

Cultivating Culturally Responsive Care
Through Training

Ms. Imani regularly provides "diversity" education to teachers and mental health workers with the goal of promoting cultural humility and competencies among those working on the frontlines with African American youth and families, especially those who have been most affected by the pathology of racism and class exploitation. Ms. Imani's applied work in this area is consonant with the efforts of Fanon to uncover the ways in which "traditional" care further alienates clients and communities that come from cultures different from those in which the interventions were developed. In this portion of our conversation, Ms. Imani talks about her experiences facilitating racism awareness trainings leading up to her work on the larger ACCESS Initiative.

I didn't feel [mental health workers] understood what internalized oppression or historical trauma was when it came to Black folks. I went to the Mental Health Center a couple of times to do trainings. What is somebody without a degree, any kind of mental health degree, training mental health workers? I am the same person who ain't got a teaching degree who's always training teachers. I don't mean this in a put down way because it's going to land at the footsteps of the university [University of Illinois Urbana–Champaign]. Because it's mandatory training, some of them were resistant to being trained by me. So, I asked them one of my questions: Could they explain to me what internalized racism is, or internalized oppression. When I'm teaching about internalized oppression, I'll often use "racism" as the example, instead of repeating the same thing multiple times with sexism, et cetera, et cetera. Racism is the thing that people hate to deal with most.

I remember, I'd say, "So what is internalized oppression?" And they'd all look at each other. These are people with degrees! At minimum masters' degrees. "Oh, well, I don't know." You mean you or your parents spent this much money on a bachelor's degree for you, and you've never even heard this term? And then you got a masters' degree in counseling, or you got an MSW [Masters' of Social Work] with family counseling. I'd name all the ones they are, and you have never heard of historical trauma or internalized oppression?

So, here you are, the people who are coming to you for help need help that is informed by historical trauma, that is informed by culturally informed psychology and history, and you're saying you don't know how to treat them, because you don't know this stuff! And you know, they start crying. It's not that I'm hurting their feelings, my approach is the same approach I had with my kids when I'd be cooking dinner and they got on their little cartoons and then they come running to me and say, "Mommy, come see this!" And it's a commercial about buying them something. And I would say, "Oh, they got your mind." And then the kids would walk out the kitchen with their heads in their arms. (Laughs) And it's sort of the same thing with the mental health workers; I would just say to them, "I'm so sorry that you were robbed of an education." I would say, "Through your professional development program that you begin to study people like Fanon, that you study these terms [internalized racism, historical trauma, etc.], that you look at how they might manifest themselves in people you're already working with, and how you might think about doing your work differently, or bringing somebody else in in certain aspects of it."

I would say these things on the radio and off the radio to mental health workers. I would say them on the radio because I wanted the Black community to hear it being said! That they deserve quality, informed mental healthcare. And here are mental healthcare workers being held accountable. *You are so important. And I am showing you what courage looks like.*

Justice for the People: History and Implementation of ACCESS Live

So, as quickly as I can, I want to tell you what the history of ACCESS Live is. So, the head of the Champaign County Mental Health Board had been wanting to try to do something meaningful, in the context of making a difference in low-income and Black communities. I'd say mostly Black community, which runs simultaneously with low-income.

And there's this federal grant, right? And so, our community had written for that grant multiple times and not gotten it. And, while I was at the Urban League, they even asked me [to get involved]. I was always sort of on the periphery of [those conversations], because there aren't that many people in Champaign-Urbana who have an interest in equity and excellence in education, access to mental health care, et cetera, et cetera.

I think the reason there was as much interest as there was in access to mental health care was that there was money. You could write for money, you know? So, our mental health board gets money from Champaign County, the County Board. And they then give out small grants you can apply for in the spring. In a lot of areas, you can't do that, but in mental health you could. And so, there was this collection of people who applied every year and got it every year.

I think after the second or third time of going after this [federal] grant, Peter Tracy [the Executive Director of the Champaign County Mental Health Board at the time] was like, "Forget it. We're, we're going to get it." I thought it was smart thinking. Let's just do the work. Let's do the work, and then we'll apply again. We'll be able to write and say, "See, we understand what you're asking for. Look at what we've already done. And, this is what we want to do." I thought that was smart.

He called me in. My much more direct involvement had come because . . . Well, let me back up and say, in representing the plaintive class in the Black community against the Champaign Public Schools around educational equity, or access to education, or lack thereof, I did a lot to bring groups of folks together, and to bring some leadership and fight back about the education issue. So, there's all this overlap with people who are getting little grant monies from the mental health board.

Yes. Well, that's an aside. So, I tried to bring some creativity into even how we applied for the grant.

So, this ACCESS Live was a program of what initially was the [larger] ACCESS Initiative, which was what we started before we ever received any funding. But, the idea was to try to promote culturally appropriate mental health services, to try to have an impact on the health and well-being in the Black community. This was being run through the mental health board.

It appears the creation of a local radio show was both a platform to disseminate the work of the larger ACCESS Initiative and also to silence the "revolutionary" activist, Ms. Imani, who insisted the group remain accountable to the community that they were to provide services to and, to be honest, benefit from by having a large federal grant.

[I was allowed to develop ACCESS Live] to shut me up. So, there would be different committee meetings on the different things. So, the committee that I was most interested in was defining what we mean by trauma, and to be trauma and justice-informed. Because we would want everybody who's providing mental health services, especially to 10 to 18-year-old Black kids and their families, to know what trauma-informed means.

And so, every week, trauma-informed, trauma-informed . . . By the time the meeting was over, I would say, "I promise, I'm not trying to start anything, it's just, when do we get to the justice part?" [Inevitably someone would say] "Oh, we got to finish up this part, and then we're going to get to that part."

Every week, there was my hand again. "I get that we want to do trauma-informed. What will justice-informed look like?" Right? "How will we tie those things together?"

And then, when I couldn't get them there, I'm like, "Okay, I'll change my language." I'll say, "Okay. How about we say, 'historical trauma'?" So, if I use the term "historical trauma," then they can't get away from that. Because then they know I'm still talking about racism, sexism, etcetera, especially racism and impoverishment, because it is the history of Black folks; [it's] generational, historical trauma.

It's a given that Black folks experience historical trauma. We have this committee where we are trying to define what trauma-informed practices are. Here's my hand going up again, "Can I understand when we're going to talk about what historical trauma best practices are?"

It's interesting, because on the one hand, it's like, "Can we shut her up? Can we direct her somewhere, give her something to shut her up?" And it's interesting, the way you shut me up is giving me a platform.

Ms. Imani presented the initial idea of a radio show as a way to reach the community. The larger committee as well as the Executive Director at the time advocated for her to serve as the host, given her related experience. In the past, she hosted a local PBS television show and a two-hour a week Urban League show.

[The development of ACCESS Live as a radio show] happened because a big part of the project was an engagement project. And so, one excellent way to engage the Black community is through Black radio. Mr. Tracy [Parsons] had been the Executive Director [of the local Urban League, which has since closed]. He had some radio experience, but he wasn't going to turn around and do a radio show, too. And they knew, of course, I had experience designing shows, as well as hosting them, interviewing people, etcetera.

So, while my idea, it would've been Tracy [former Urban League supervisor] looking for some way to engage me that could help them engage the community. Tracy knew that I would bust my ass for all of them all the time, before the ACCESS Initiative, much less once the ACCESS Initiative started, and once this thing got funded.

He knew that there was no way that they could continue without finding me a significant role. I remember him saying, "Well, write something up that you'd like to do." I'm like, "And justice, right? He says, "Well, write something up." What that was about was not just ACCESS Live, it was about different ways to engage the Black community and what we're talking about.

[ACCESS Live the radio show] was an engagement mechanism [through] a Black-owned radio station . . . This point is very important. Let me say on the media question that there are very few Black-owned radio stations left in the country. I think that's important, and I think that its political. People think there are more Black radio stations than there really are. But they are stations that have been bought by white corporations that play Black music. Not to be confused with Black-owned and operated. So, WBCP, whom we've always worked with, is actually the only Black-owned radio station south of Chicago, if I have the story right.

[ACCESS Live] was supposed to be an opportunity for the different task forces, subcommittees, whomever, doing work on [the larger ACCESS Initiative]. It was supposed to be an opportunity for various ones of them to come in on a weekly basis and explain, and I say, account to the Black community on how what they are doing is making the Black community mentally healthy, stronger, and a recipient of and engaging in more justice-related activity.

As originally conceptualized, Ms. Imani expected the ACCESS Live radio show to become sustainable over time, creating a permanent mechanism to educate the Black community about health and justice. She also envisioned that the radio show would translate theory and research into accessible language for community members to consume and, in turn, the community would create an institution demanding access to trauma- and justice-informed information and services. She hoped to work in concert with Black mental health professionals and Black community members to promote healing through a "love ethic."

But the vision? The whole idea of the grant project was to put things in place that were sustainable over time. So, my thing is our media access; two-way street media access must be sustainable over time, if it's going to actually make a difference. What we think after three years is all of a sudden mental healthcare in the Black community is not stigmatized? Or that we could think about ways in which we, as family members, as friends, as co-workers, can take our understanding of how to recognize trauma in one another, and how to make referrals, etc. I was a kid during the Vietnam War. And I remember what trauma used to be called. PTSD used to be called Shell Shock. So, I remember growing up with this idea of being Shell Shocked. And when I use that term on the radio, Black folks in the community would say, "Oh! That's PTSD!" Right?

It means using different language or words. You know, I'm blessed and highly favored to have grown up in poor Black communities, because I know the language and I know the people, because they are me. And, we have every right to be self-sustaining and self-efficacious, and to recognize trauma for what it is, and to understand these from our historical experience.

I believe in our Black mental healthcare workers, who I tried to pull together an organization called "Why We Can't Wait," which is the name of the grant that I wrote to the Champaign County Mental Health Board. That essentially put the Urban League in that partnership of folks who were working on [the larger ACCESS Initiative grant]. The name of the grant proposal was called "Why We Can't Wait," referencing Martin Luther King, Jr.'s book.

The whole point of "Why We Can't Wait" was to bring Black mental health workers, social workers, whatever, together at the Urban League, to eat and talk about what does it look like for us to define these things for ourselves, and teach your white colleagues, and bring them to the Black community. Because the Black community is not finding them.

One time, Peter, you remember, he's the head of the Champaign County Mental Health Board, had somebody with him who was in town visiting and had something to do with mental health. He might even have something to do with funding. So he [Peter] knew it was a day we were going to be meeting, and talking about what Black mental healthcare should look like. He asked, "Imani, please, would there be any way possible if he and I could come to one of your meetings, if we promise just to be a fly on the wall?"

[At the end of the meeting] Peter was almost speechless and asked me to find a way to bring that conversation to the Champaign County Mental

Health Board meeting, to an upcoming board meeting. And the gentleman that he had come with him . . . was so moved, he talked about this community we were building. And he said, "What I hear you talking about and what I am so moved by is this love ethic." And that's in fact, Why We Can't Wait, and what eventually ACCESS Live would be. It is inspired by, moved by, moved forward by, every day, a love ethic.

When conceptualizing the initiative, we'd have various committees that would break down parts of the larger effort, and then we finally got the funding. Parents were supposed to be really engaged and listened to. There was particular interest around being trauma-informed. The difference between our grant proposal and other grant proposals, that may have gotten us through, is that we said we were going to be trauma- and justice-informed.

Most of these meetings happened in my workplace because it had plenty of space. I would feed them lunch or snacks or whatever. So, a lot of these meetings were happening where I worked. Everybody wanted to define [the project]. Once the money came in, then, here again, comes the Mental Health Center and all the mental health providers. They begin showing up and they're a part of it, and the juvenile detention folks, who we had already been working with, because the specific targets were 10 through 18-year-olds.

Once ACCESS Live was implemented, local and national experts were interviewed on topics relevant to the community including contemporary events that may serve as triggers for trauma, including "Black mass incarceration." And, "there's always a lot of interest in anything having to do with the police, jailing, incarceration, and things having to do with public education." Ms. Imani also included discussions about larger issues related to human rights:

> Well, once, I read an article about a sister who was operating in Washington, DC and she was doing work in the area that I felt ACCESS Live was concerned about. So, I looked her up and asked her, "Can you be on my show over the phone?" I had a lot of guests over the phone. She talked about human rights. Which is something that I tried to bring up; obviously, that's what Fanon cared about; that's what Du Bois cared about. It was the whole anti-colonial era, because, you know, I'm coming out of a Black Panther family.

When asked about the reach and impact of ACCESS Live, Ms. Imani was pleased the show reached community members as intended: "We know Black folks were listening because they were stopping me. People who you would not expect." But, she also described the project as incomplete, primarily because of the lack of institutional support.

> I think [ACCESS Live] had an incomplete impact. I think it's had a positive and important impact. One, because local cable access wanted to

film it. Two, I haven't done the show in probably three years, but I'm still stopped by people about it. And I'm not just stopped by educated people, though I am happy to know educated people were listening.

I remember one time, Ollie Watts Davis [Conductor of the University of Illinois Black choir] came up and said, "Oh, Imani! I was over on Neil Street and I was talking to somebody in front of something, then I looked at my watch and it said, 2:00. Oh, I got to run! I better get in and turn the radio on."

And so, I know it had an impact. I'm not talking about this to say something special about myself. There just were no others doing this work.

"A Crime Was Committed": Hopes, Concerns, and the Demise of ACCESS Live

Although ACCESS Live by all accounts achieved its goal of educating the local Black community about trauma and justice issues related to health—about half of the radio installments have been memorialized on the Internet—the initiative discontinued at the conclusion of the federal grant. Ms. Imani raised concerns about the lack of sustainability of the effort. And, similar to Fanon's criticism about the barriers of implementing culturally relevant sociotherapy in a Muslim men's psychiatric ward, Ms. Imani identified language and limited resources as obstacles to reaching some audience members and sustaining the program.

My hope for ACCESS Live was that it would be ongoing, because we don't stop having mental health issues after three years. My issue was the bigger funded project, and I remember saying very clearly and out loud, if after the four years of this funding, or five years or whatever it was is over, and there is not at least one strong self-efficacious, self-driving Black organization or institution in this community, a crime will have been committed. And sure enough, when the funding was over, that was the case. So, I declare a crime was committed.

ACCESS Live was a very direct opportunity for engaging the Black community.

It was a two-way street. On the one hand, it was all the people who have gotten funded, who then are already mental health workers, are already serving on committees, task forces, etcetera. People who call themselves already working with families. It was a chance for them to come and report out, or be accountable to the community, on what we're doing. . . . And it was also the other way down the street directly to the Black community, in terms of, what is the word, "de-stigmatizing" mental health care.

A big part of ACCESS Live was to de-stigmatize mental health care in the Black community. My way of trying to do that was to have people who can speak *English*. Instead of just scholars talking to each other.

[My concern was always] "How would you put this in a way that the average person who's listening to this would understand you?"

There's pressure on me to get [the guests] to engage. Because to be honest, they were not engaging the broader Black community.

Well, I'm trying to do that the whole time, and when I have scholars come in, like having you or Helen come in. I'm having you come in as scholar-activists. Not just people who can explain Freud or Jung. We didn't do that.

I was saying it was a two-way street. . . . [Many of the scholars] could not report out in ways they should have been able to report out.

And then the funding ended . . .

When the lunch money ran out, folks started disappearing.

There wasn't [enough impetus in the Black community]. Because there was no community of Black mental health workers. I was trying to help build a community of Black mental health workers.

The funding ended, but the initiative still shouldn't have because the feds who were granting the money said the idea was sustainable.

They should've been working something out with the radio station. [When the Urban League shut down, there was no one, no institution.] Exactly. See, the Urban League would've done it. The Urban League would've gotten some money for ACCESS Live.

Remember what I said earlier: If after five years, or however much longer we got this money, and there is not a Black institution that is stronger and self-sufficient, etcetera etcetera, to support this, then a crime will have been committed.

Conclusion

The trajectory of community mental health, community psychology, and different ways in which mental healthcare or psychotherapy is delivered to communities of color, within a Fanonian frame, is recovered in the psychopolitical activism of Imani Bazzell. *ACCESS Live* not only comes to mind as an innovative use of community radio for mental health messaging but because Imani Bazzell's political biography intersects some of the earliest engagements with Frantz Fanon's thought in the US Black Power and Black Panther social movements. Social movements as an educational-psychological ecosystem come closest to Fanon's *modus operandi* as a psychotherapist in colonial societies undergoing decolonization. Nonetheless there is a strand of Fanon's thought which has seldom been engaged that Imani Bazzell's media organizing also brings to mind, namely, how the sociohistorical specificity of the community setting determines the medium by which the psychopolitical message of Black liberation is delivered. For Bazzell, as for Fanon, the radio was instrumental in sustaining community resilience, or in the case of Algeria, bringing to birth a "new reality of the nation."

Section 4

Fanonian Research in Action

10 Mending a Crack in the Sky

An Evolving Community Healing Case Study Among Somali Canadians

Nkechinyelum A. Chioneso, Mahad A. Yusuf, and Shamso M. Elmi

If people come together, they can even mend a crack in the sky.

Somali Proverb

Alarming rates of primarily male youth violence among Somali Canadians have exacerbated community trauma and fragmentation. In the greater Toronto area, Somali males under 29 years of age are 23 times more likely than the general population to be homicide victims; most suffer fatal shooting deaths. Victims tend to reside in overpoliced and underserved neighborhoods populated by Somali Canadian families living below the federal poverty threshold in largely single-parent mother-led households. Somali mothers' accounts of trauma suggest many suffer from repeated trauma. First, as a result of the ongoing Somali civil war beginning in the 1980s, Somali mothers endured significant societal upheaval, family separation, and personal assaults. Seeking refuge in Canada, their families' resettlement experiences have been impaired by racist and exclusionary barriers. Then, Somali mothers began struggling with youth violence in their communities that resulted in the incarceration or premature death of their children. Eventually, Somali interfamilial blaming and distrust propelled the deterioration of community solidarity. Facing increased risk of their families developing behavioral and mental health challenges connected to multiple traumatic experiences, Somali Canadian mothers are demanding solutions to youth violence.

For over a decade, Somali mothers have led awareness campaigns to end youth violence in their communities as they seek justice for their injured, incarcerated, or murdered sons; by and large, their pleas for help have gone unheard. Through a community-based Somali social services agency, Midaynta, where mothers have established trusting relationships, we—Mahad A. Yusuf, Shamso M. Elmi, and Nkechinyelum A. Chioneso—formed a partnership with Somali mothers. This partnership led to the development of a three-phased research initiative to address youth violence in the greater Toronto area: Mending a Crack in the Sky. The initiative is designed to (1) collect data by conducting participatory action research; (2) develop a community action plan informed by research results; and (3) create a documentary film. To accomplish these goals, the initiative adopts a Fanonian lens that emphasizes the significance of oppressive sociohistorical systems in relation to the manifestation of psychosomatic illnesses and violence, while prioritizing a community's agency and lived experiences to enable the cultivation of liberatory wellness.

In this chapter, we reflect on the development and implementation of a community-based initiative that highlights voices of African mothers fighting for solutions to improve the lives of their families and communities. To contextualize our reflexive exploration, we first briefly describe the factors influencing Somali emigration and settlement in Canada, the formation of Midaynta and creation of the Mending a Crack in the Sky (MCIS) research project. Outlining the ways in which our evolving roles, responsibilities, and action steps led to the drafting of a strategic plan, we centralize Somali mothers' agency and point to the importance of their proactive ownership of the MCIS research process. We then evaluate both the barriers we encountered and the community wins achieved while implementing MCIS. Here we identify our research team's methodological limitations and internal group dynamics, and the active engagement of Somali parents in community healing. Lastly, we incorporate an analysis of the challenges and implications for future work to provide an understanding of the difficulties involved in conducting culturally informed and transformative research within oppressed communities. Much like Fanon in his evaluation of the Muslim men's ward in his first clinical paper (see Turner, 2020), later we discuss goals of the research and identify key barriers to its full implementation to date. Our examination of the MCIS project provides valuable lessons for not only working with Somali communities, but for also conducting applied research with marginalized immigrant and refugee communities.

Midaynta and the Formation of MCIS: Background and Rapport

Africans from various regions of the world fought to rid ourselves of European oppression. While the majority of us gained "flag independence" from our respective ruling colonial power(s) in the decades of 1960–1980, the masses continue to experience "life not as a flowering or development of an essential productiveness, but as a permanent struggle against an omnipresent death. This ever-menacing death," Fanon (1967b) argued, "is experienced as endemic famine, unemployment, a high death rate, an inferiority complex and the absence of any hope for the future" (p. 128). These socioeconomic and psychological push factors limit our life options. Thus, we emigrate from our neocolonial homelands seeking sustenance in Canada's exported image as a welcoming humanitarian, morally-conscious, upwardly mobile, and multicultural society—but what we seek is not what we necessarily find.

Fleeing civil war and famine, significant numbers of Somalis began arriving in Canada between the late 1980s and the early 1990s. Reportedly, 62,550 Somalis live in Canada (Statistics Canada, 2016), but unofficial estimates and our research team suggest there are over 150,000 Somali Canadian residents. Like the majority of African/Black Canadians who comprise 3.5% of the country's total population (i.e., 37 million people), Somalis primarily live in the province of Ontario (approximately 60%) and within the greater Toronto area (GTA) (Aden, Issa, Rayale, & Abokor, 2018; Jiwani & Al-Rawi, 2019).

Established in 1993, Midaynta (*unity* in Somali) Community Services was initially a Somali family reunification project that evolved into a registered non-profit organization, providing an array of settlement services and educational programming. Somali mothers in northwestern areas of Toronto bestowed an "honorary mother" title upon me, Mahad A. Yusuf, the Executive Director of Midaynta. As an honorary mother, I was granted the privilege and responsibility to act as their representative, advocate for resources, and assist in sounding the alarm about the ever-increasing rate of youth violence in Somali Canadian communities.

As racist policies and procedures remain entrenched in Canadian institutions, distressing physical and mental health trends are rising and impacting wider segments of the African Canadian populace (e. g., youth) (Coteau, 2017; Daniel & Cukier, 2015; UN Report, 2017). Eight years ago, an ambitious solution to reverse debilitating trends was proposed. African Canadian leaders representing various (healthcare, political, business, non-profit, and philanthropy) sectors were brought together to develop a "Black Health Network" with the requisite resources and strategies to improve the health outcomes of African Canadian communities in Ontario. In 2011–2012, three consecutive Black Leadership Health Network (BLHN) summits occurred across the province in Toronto (central region), Windsor (western region), and Ottawa (eastern region) to lay the groundwork for a single organization to be launched by 2013.

To fulfill my dual roles as an honorary mother and the Executive Director of Midaynta, I (Yusuf) accepted BLHN's invitation and participated in both the Windsor and Ottawa summits. I, Nkechinyelum A. Chioneso, was one of several consultants working with the BLHN initiative. At the Windsor 2011 summit, I facilitated a workshop on the priorities associated with linking research to African Canadian healthcare needs that included creating a community research agenda and outlining advocacy strategies. After the workshop, I (Yusuf) formally introduced myself to Dr. Chioneso and stated: "The Somali community needs psychologists like you to work with us. *Please*, don't read my eyes—I don't want you to see the pain they hold! The mothers are crying; they are asking for help because we have so many problems." Thus began our collegial rapport which developed during Midaynta site visits, tours of predominately Somali residential and business areas, and our involvement in the BLHN initiative. However, because of a variety of unforeseen circumstances (e.g., Chioneso's relocation to the United States) over a five-year period, our interactions became sporadic as our conversations dwindled. "Good intentions," in the absence of commitments and resources, did not materialize into a working project with the Somali mothers.

Community advocates respond to multiple emergencies daily and when their hectic schedules permit, they welcome non-urgent phone calls. Community psychologists who straddle the world of academia and community settings frequently seek to reconnect with the pulse of grassroots activism. In October 2016, I (Chioneso) reconnected with Mr. Yusuf to discuss his well-being, Midaynta's organizational development, and the status of the Somali Canadian community. By the end of our conversation, Mr. Yusuf secured my commitment to participate in the "2nd Annual Youth Radicalization: New and Emerging Issues Conference," at the Munk School of Global Affairs, University of Toronto. The November 2016 conference was hosted by Midaynta in partnership with the Ontario Institute for Studies in Education, the Office of the Consulate General of the United States, the Canadian Council of Imams, and the Mosaic Institute.

As a member of the conference panel, "Ensuring Newcomers are Settled and Fully Integrated," my (Chioneso's) presentation focused on challenges and opportunities in community engagement with African/Black communities. I used a "burning pots" image as a metaphor to capture the reported lived experiences of African Canadian research participants' health status. The photograph depicted a stark wooded wilderness with fires flaring beneath three large cast iron burning pots, each hanging on a chain along a single wood panel framework. Like being in the wilderness, participants reported feeling lost or isolated as they individually navigated social service agencies; spaces where they experienced interpersonal and institutional distrust. The fires flaring beneath the three burning pots represented constant states of duress with multiple stressors simultaneously demanding participants' attention (e.g., unemployment, food insecurity, a child's school suspensions, etc.). When grappling with major stressors and institutional barriers, participants' physical (e.g., diabetes) and mental health issues (e.g., unspoken traumas) were unseen and thus diminished concerns that transformed from acute conditions to chronic illnesses (Nestel, 2012). I posed a rhetorical question to the audience: "When African Canadians experience major stressors in their lives, how should they determine what stressor should be addressed first?" The burning pots metaphor resonated with Somali conference participants, it clarified some of the challenges their community was struggling to address.

Shamso M. Elmi, a prominent Somali mother who works as a translator and community development organizer with Midaynta, formally introduced herself to me (Chioneso) after the panel presentation. While expressing what she both appreciated *and* what was missing in the presentation, Mrs. Elmi interlaced our conversation with humorous personal stories. Together, we laughed loudly like the little girls we used to be, who metamorphosed into queen-mothers that carefully listened while playfully acknowledging each other's life journey. Later that day, a select number of Midaynta conference organizers, conference participants, and Somali mothers shared a meal. Fanon (2018) was correct, "the social act of eating and drinking, you might say, works to untie tongues" (p. 282) because a commitment was made that evening: Mr. Yusuf, Mrs. Elmi, and I (Chioneso) would lead a research project that addressed Somali mothers' concerns about youth violence. At this juncture, the flexibility of our inter-relationships allowed us to be undecided about (re)naming the problem and who owned the research process. In subsequent meetings, our newly developed seven person research team concurred that developing action steps was a necessary component to be generated by the research process.

(Re) Naming the Problem: Initial Work of the MCIS Research Project

A discrepancy exists between official data indicating approximately 50 Somali homicides in Ontario and Alberta between the years 2005 and 2015, and the Somali community's claim that hundreds of Somali youth in Ontario alone have been and are at risk of being homicide victims (Aden et al., 2018; Ibrahim, 2018; Jiwani & Al-Rawi, 2019; Livingstone, 2015). In response to Somali outcries in the GTA, the Somali Research Youth Initiative examined Somali homicides based on public data and police records from 2004 to 2016 (Aden et al., 2018). Demographic data indicated that Somali homicide victims were predominately male (95%), under the age of 29 years old (82%), and died due to shootings (62%). The Initiative also found that between 2004 and 2014, Somalis constituted 1.6% of total homicide victims in Toronto and the rate increased to 16% (i.e., 23.2 times the general population) by 2014, even though total homicides in Toronto decreased by 12% in the same decade (Aden et al., 2018, pp. 21–22). Affirming the community's perspective, the Initiative concluded that the Somali homicide rate is disproportionate to the size of the total Somali population, and increasingly, Somali homicide victims are youth below the age of 18 years old (Aden et al., 2018).

When our research team began exploring the question of what are the roots of youth violence in Somali Canadian communities, we named two salient problems: immigration settlement barriers and racism. Fanon (1967b) suggested that "an interaction must exist between the family and society at large. The home is the basis of the truth of society, but society authenticates and legitimizes the family. The colonial structure [, however,] is the very negation of this reciprocal justification" (p. 66). Within Canada's colonial structure, immigration settlement barriers and racism are contributing factors to the delegitimization of Somali families and the non-authentication of their communities manifested as youth violence (Galabuzi, 2006; Ibrahim, 2018; Jibril, 2011).

For instance, the 1997 Undocumented Convention Refugees in Canada Class (UCRCC) regulation is a discriminatory federal immigration policy that negatively impacted Somali (and Afghan) Canadians (Dryer, 1998; Kwak, 2018; OCASI, 2016; Razack, 2000). I (Yusuf) emphasized that the UCRCC targeted Somalis. As newcomers, it made it *very* difficult for our families to resettle and prevented our youth from integrating into this society! As a result of the UCRCC, thousands of Somali refugees were classified as lacking sufficient identity documentation and their experiences included: enduring mandatory five-year (rather than the average three-year) waiting periods to be eligible to apply for permanent residency; producing DNA test results as proof of biological relationships to sponsor overseas dependents; and financing protracted legal cases (Abdulkadir, 2006; OCASI, 2016). Awaiting permanent residency (for sometimes 10 years), these settlement issues became barriers to Somali family reunification, employment opportunities, postsecondary education, access to healthcare, and voting rights (Bokore, 2013; Jibril, 2011; OCASI, 2016). The majority of Somali refugees were women and children. In the absence of extended family and clan support in Canada, these mostly single-parent mother-led households (because of widowhood and spousal sponsorship barriers) bore the brunt of navigating settlement issues to obtain basic resources for their families (Abdulkadir, 2006). Very quickly, the distressed faces of Somali mothers were assigned to the colony's preexisting cast of "third-world freeloaders," while her sons' maturing faces characterized "Black criminality" (Galabuzi, 2006; Jiwani & Al-Rawi, 2019; Razack, 2000).

Naming immigration settlement barriers as a contributing factor to youth violence was not possible without also naming "racism" as a problem. Fanon (1969) argued that racism is "only one element of a vaster whole: that of the systemized oppression of a people" (p. 33); thus the "habit of considering racism as a mental quirk, as a psychological flaw, must be abandoned" (p. 38) because in principle, a "given society is racist or it is not" (p. 85). By all accounts, Canada is a racist society. Systemic racism embodied within institutional policies, programs, and practices is well documented (Fry, 2018; Galabuzi, 2006; Hampton, 2010; Khenti, 2014; Nestel, 2012; UN Report, 2017).

Encounters with systemic racism perhaps began, but certainly did not end with the immigration system for Somali Canadians. Compared to 26% of European Canadian families, 65% of African Canadian single-parent mother-led families are living in poverty (UN Report, 2017, p. 12). Struggling to obtain permanent residency for their families, Somali mothers also had tremendous difficulty accessing social services (e.g., English language programs, childcare assistance, and affordable food) to alleviate the constraints of poverty. Despite these ongoing institutional barriers, mothers firmly believed the educational system granted their children equal access to opportunities and upward mobility. Instead, Somali children reported unfair grading, low teacher expectations, administrative streamlining into non-academic programs, and religious intolerance (Aden et al., 2018; COP-COC, 2019a; Farah, 2011; Mohamed, 2015). As a result, approximately 25% of all Somali students and 33% of Somali boys withdraw from Toronto high schools without a diploma (Livingstone, 2015; Mohamed, 2015).

Some mothers did not fully understand their children's educational experiences or their seemingly irrational decisions to "give up" and leave high school. Particularly vexing are the experiences of Canadian-born children who did everything right (i.e., law abiding citizens who are community volunteers and university degree holders), yet they are unemployed. Racialized[1] men and women are 24% and 43%, respectively, more likely to be unemployed compared to European Canadian men living in Ontario (COP-COC, 2019b). Older children express feelings of sadness and worthlessness because of their inability to make financial contributions to the household or meet their family's high expectations; and observant younger siblings note that educational and career pursuits are fruitless endeavors (Daniel & Cukier, 2015; Farah, 2011; Ibrahim, 2018). While contemplating how to address her children's negative sentiments and ameliorate their self-esteem, mothers often retreat to their bedrooms overcome with headaches and neck pains (Bokore, 2013; Schuchman & McDonald, 2004). Symptoms of elevated distress (e.g., anxiety and insomnia) are further exacerbated by the frequent encounters Somali youth have with the criminal justice system.

A "school-to-prison pipeline" developed in Toronto schools attended by significant numbers of racialized student populations (COP-COC, 2019a; Daniel & Cukier, 2015). With increased armed police presence in their schools, Somali youth felt targeted by police who often intervene in student conflicts and participate in the high rates of harsh disciplinary actions, such as expulsions, experienced by African Canadian youth (Farah, 2011; Ibrahim, 2018; Mohamed, 2015). Representing 12% of the student body, 48% of all expulsions in the Toronto student population involve African Canadian students (COP-COC, 2019a). Police surveillance, random searches, and racial profiling are commonplace for Somali youth, which coincides with their high rates of incarceration (Aden et al., 2018; COP-COC, 2019c; Mullings, Morgan, & Quelleng, 2016). From 2006 to 2016, there was a 70% increase in the number of African Canadians incarcerated in federal prisons; consequently, African Canadians now comprise 10% of the federally incarcerated population despite being 3.5% of Canada's total population (McIntyre, 2016; UN Report, 2017; Warde, 2013). With the overpolicing and overrepresentation of African Canadians, including Somali youth, in the criminal justice system, Somali mothers feel helpless and abused by the legal system (e.g., exorbitant fees coupled with inadequate legal counsel).

While incarceration curtails future opportunities for Somali youth, Islamophobia eradicates their humanity. Since the September 11, 2001 attacks in the United States, there have been heightened media warnings and Canadian Security Intelligence Service (CSIS) reports about Somali youth radicalization, and their susceptibility to becoming "Muslim terrorists" aligned with al-Shabaab who threaten Canada's national security (Ahmad, 2017; Fellin, 2015; Jiwani & Al-Rawi, 2019). Overwhelmed by the devastatingly real or perceived portrayals of their youth, mothers make medical appointments with a general practitioner to address their reoccurring chest pains, congested lungs, and other ailments. Their appointments are easily forgotten tasks since getting out of bed has become increasingly burdensome (Bokore, 2013).

Panelists at Midaynta's 2nd Annual Youth Radicalization Conference offered Somali mothers a glimmer of hope. Fanon (1967b) pointed out that the "decision to kill a civilian in the street is not an easy one, and no one comes to it lightly. No one takes the step of placing a bomb in a public place without a battle of conscience" (p. 55). Similarly, panelists reminded conference participants that Muslim youth have a conscience, and we have a responsibility to "re-humanize our youth." That is, Islamophobia encourages us to forget that radicalized youth are humans who act violently when they have been wronged. They tend to be victims of psychological discrimination who seek social acceptance and desire friendships with others who share their worldview. Radicalized youth crave a sense of purpose in their lives and hope to partake in valued societal roles. Honoring their need for belongingness and providing them with cultural safety requires us to "figure out how to re-humanize our youth and shift the narrative." A panelist further emphasized that for too long, "we have allowed others to define our words—even what it means to be a 'Muslim!' Words make *worlds*. It is time for us to make a world for our children with our own words." Inspired by these convictions, Somali mothers left the conference appreciating that they were not alone in their quest to reclaim their children and prevent youth violence.

Our research team was equally committed to transforming the disparaging narrative about Somali/Muslim youth. To do so, consensus-building about naming the problem was mandatory. Although immigration settlement issues and racism were named as salient problems connected to youth violence in Somali Canadian communities, we were undecided about whether one, both, or possibly neither problem should be our focus. The difficulty in developing consensus was partially because of an implicit belief that had to be revealed. To address this issue, I (Chioneso) posed a reflection question: "Are Somali Canadian settlement issues and racist experiences worse or vastly different from the experiences of other African Canadian immigrant groups?" Our reflection exercise involved reviewing two influential government commissioned studies: the "Stephen Lewis Report on Race Relations in Ontario" by Lewis (1992) and "The Review of the Roots of Youth Violence" report by McMurtry and Curling (2008).

The Lewis (1992) report is a one-month provincial government study of race relations in response to the Toronto "Yonge Street riot." On May 4, 1992, the Black Action Defense Committee (a community-based group committed to the elimination of racism) organized a peaceful demonstration against anti-Black police violence following the fatal shooting of Raymond Lawrence, a 22-year-old African Canadian male immigrant, by Toronto police on May 2, 1992. The demonstration evolved into a mass rebellion prompting government officials to consider improving socioeconomic opportunities for impoverished youth, particularly African Canadian youth (Bradburn, 2011; Mullings et al., 2016). Lewis (1992) found that anti-Black racism not only impedes the life opportunities of African Canadians, these communities—especially the mothers—were living in fear of police encounters that often resulted in the socioeconomic death (i.e., incarceration) or physical death of their sons. Lewis (1992) wrote:

> First, what we are dealing with, at root, and fundamentally, is anti-Black racism. . . . . [E]very visible minority community experiences the

indignities and wounds of systemic discrimination throughout Southern Ontario, [but] it is the Black community which is the focus. It is Blacks who are being shot [by police], it is Black youth that is unemployed in excessive numbers, it is Black students who are being inappropriately streamed in schools, it is Black kids who are disproportionately dropping out, it is housing communities with large concentrations of Black residents where the sense of vulnerability and disadvantage is most acute, it is Black employees, professional and non-professional, on whom the doors of upward equity slam shut. . . . [R]acism cannot mask its primary target.

(p. 2)

To promote "enlightened race relations," Lewis' (1992) recommendations included: the immediate implementation of criminal justice oversight committees, employment equity initiatives, educational reforms, and community development programs.

Fifteen years later, as the life opportunities of African Canadian youth remained stagnant, youth violence escalated. With the crime rate among 15–24-year-old youth rising to three times the national average, disturbing violent crime rate trends among youth became evident. Since the 1990s, for example, violent crimes became increasingly concentrated among impoverished racialized male youth and occurred in disadvantaged neighborhoods where both victims and offenders resided. In the GTA, approximately 40% of homicide victims were African Canadian male youth; a record number of youth were charged with murder; and almost 50% of murders were committed with firearms (McMurtry & Curling, 2008). Evidently, state violence was internalized among racialized youth. That is, the "victims and survivors of vertical violence [have] . . . in turn vent their anger and frustration through horizontal violence, victimizing themselves, their relatives, and their peers" (Bulhan, 1985, p. 134). In the absence of organized community solutions, Fanon (2018) believed horizontal violence escalates because "colonialism, in its most perverse and condemnable aspect, manages to pit men against each other whom everything unites and that a shared oppression degrades" (p. 565).

In 2007, the provincial government commissioned another report to address violence involving youth among Ontario residents. This response was sparked by the Toronto high school shooting death of Jordan Manners, a 15-year-old African Canadian male, on May 23, 2007. Held in custody for four years before the acquittal of all charges, the alleged shooters were the victim's two male friends. McMurtry and Curling's (2008) one-year study identified 10 immediate risk factors as roots of youth violence. Racism and immigration settlement issues were two outlined risk factors in addition to: poverty, community design (e.g., bleak housing landscapes), the educational system, family issues (e.g., single-parent and low household income), health issues, lack of economic opportunities, denial of the youth voice, and the justice system. Throughout the province, McMurtry and Curling (2008) found risk factors were more pronounced in predominately racialized communities, and African

Canadians suffered from the most overtly noxious forms of racism. Noting the negative impact of every risk factor was intensified by racism, McMurtry and Curling (2008) concluded nonetheless that the intersectionality of racism and poverty was the strongest root factor influencing youth violence. Over 50 years prior, Fanon made a similar observation. It was apparent to him that the "effective disalienation of the black man entails an immediate recognition of social and economic realities," he argued, and if "there is an inferiority complex, it is the outcome of a double process: primarily economic; subsequently, the internalization—or, better, the epidermalization—of this inferiority" (Fanon, 1967a, p. 11).

By and large, McMurtry and Curling's (2008) findings and recommendations echoed the preceding Lewis (1992) report. After reviewing the documents, our research team agreed that every risk factor and all outlined issues in both reports apply, but are not unique, to Somali Canadian communities. In fact, the Lewis (1992) report highlighted that problems plaguing Somali Canadians existed *prior* to their arrival in significant numbers and are consistent with the ongoing problems the larger African Canadian populace confronts. In other words, the undermining settlement barriers and racism Somali Canadians experience have less to do with their individual characteristics or their embodiment of a national "Somali" consciousness.

From a Fanonian perspective, the salient issue is structural oppression/colonialism that is established through violence to benefit some people/colonizers (e.g., European Canadian and upper-class citizens) and is maintained by violence at the expense of other people/colonized (e.g., racialized immigrants and low-income residents). Therefore, as Fanon (1966) urged, "a rapid step must be taken from national consciousness to political and social consciousness" to effectively dismantle structural oppression manifesting as youth violence (p. 161). The harshness of Somali lived realities, however, made the revelation difficult to relinquish, but certain systemic reminders helped to loosen the tension. I (Yusuf) reminded the team that "most Somalis have been in this country for almost 30 years. We are not considered 'newcomers' anymore, but we still have the same problems as when we arrived." Other research team members also pointed out that the newly arriving "Syrians are Muslims like us and refugees fleeing civil war like we did—but they are getting 'the red carpet treatment!' If we were treated as well as they are, our lives would be so much better now." These reminders encouraged the unraveling of national consciousness to make room for political and social consciousness. Eventually our research team agreed that neither immigration settlement barriers nor racism should be the problem of focus for our study.

While unraveling implicit beliefs to develop consensus, we also grappled with our inability (or unwillingness) to name a problem associated with the mothers. Their stories were essential to shifting the narrative about youth violence in Somali Canadian communities. A continuous concern was maintaining the respect and confidentiality of Somali mothers. Simultaneously, a requisite flexibility in our thinking to encourage the naming of what needed to be named, and thereby brought into existence, was missing. We lacked a necessary readiness to create space for their unspoken traumas; thus, a problem floated around us, a problem waiting to be named. "There comes a time when silence becomes dishonesty," warned Fanon (1969, p. 55).

With the fragmentation of family and community bonds amplified by the loss of their youth, the consequences of dishonesty through silence demanded that *something* had to be broached. That *something* eventually came in the language of creating a "Mothers Outreach Workers" (MOWs) initiative; our first step to develop targeted mental health counseling for Somali mothers. Previous community-based efforts were made to address the Somali Canadian community's mental health challenges, particularly with the dissemination of Elmi's (1999) study that identified mental health services and support for Somalis in need were sorely lacking in the GTA. In Spring 2000, rising to the challenges Elmi (1999) documented, Midaynta partnered with mental health professionals representing eight Somali and non-Somali agencies. They initiated a Somali Family Mental Health Support Program Advisory Committee to address the need for culturally and linguistically relevant mental health services and to eliminate the stigma associated with mental health illnesses within Somali Canadian community (Nur, Dalal, & Baker, 2005). Over a four-year period, the Advisory Committee successfully obtained provincial funding and designed subgroup specific workshops (e.g., women's groups and youth groups), produced multimedia (e.g., brochures, videos, radio talk shows, etc.), organized the first Somali mental health conference in Toronto, and wrote a best practices booklet. However, because of a lack of sustainable funding and permanent staff, the Somali Family Mental Health Support Program goals were not fully realized.

Prevalent mental health challenges among Somali Canadians include depression, anxiety, recurring nightmares, angry outbursts, and substance use (Bokore, 2013; Elmi, 1999; Ibrahim, 2018). Similarly, mental health challenges among Somali communities in other recipient countries have been reported, such as in: Britain, reoccurring flashbacks of murdered individuals, anxiety, feeling lost, and high suicide rates (CSO, 2017; Palmer, 2006); New Zealand, high rates of stress and somatization disorders (e.g., chronic headaches, backaches, and insomnia) (Guerin, Guerin, Diiriye, & Yates, 2004; Mohamed, 2011); and the United States, high rates of psychoses, depression, and post-traumatic stress disorder (Kroll, Yusuf, & Fujiwara, 2011; Schuchman & McDonald, 2004). Despite a great need for services, Somalis residing in western countries are generally not accessing mental health services because of institutional barriers (e. g., racism and language obstacles), community perspectives (e.g., stigma and traditional cultural healing beliefs), and familial struggles (e.g., unemployment and navigating legal bureaucracies) (CSO, 2017; Guerin et al., 2004; Ibrahim, 2018).

Past trauma and current adjustment challenges increase the risk of Somali mothers developing behavioral and mental health problems that have largely gone untreated until long after resettlement (Elmi, 1999; Ibrahim, 2018). These mothers endured multiple losses and suffered repeated trauma coinciding with one or more life-altering events prior to resettlement, such as: family separation, death of loved ones, political persecution, famine, rape, torture, and loss of homeland. Increasingly, there is great concern that Somali mothers' traumatic experiences have had an intergenerational impact and their trauma patterns are resurfacing because of losing their children to ongoing violence and incarceration (Bokore, 2013; Ibrahim, 2018). Therefore, the proposed MOWs service model is a strength-based and community-based initiative with a focus on mental health, first aid training, and family therapy that provides language specific services. Currently, the government-funded Youth Outreach Workers (YOWs) service model provides "at-risk youth" with support, referrals, and advocacy services by front-line youth workers serving as mentors and liaisons with social service agencies (Hoskins & Meilleur, 2012). An outcome of the McMurtry and Curling (2008) report recommendations, the YOWs program aims to foster successful youth development and safer communities. Similarly, we anticipate MOWs will enhance skill development and cater to the well-being of women through a comprehensive social support network. By improving the accessibility and diversity of community workers through the recruitment of Somali mothers, the proposed MOWs initiative intends to offer more effective wrap-around services to assist affected families and prevent youth violence.

Given the importance of mothers as guardians of the home, it is possible that Somali mothers feel responsible for the delegitimization of their families and by extension, have personalized the non-authentication of their communities. In varying degrees, these feelings coupled with their past traumas and resurfacing trauma patterns, may have led to a "suffering in silence" which negates multiple aspects of their well-being (Bokore, 2013). However, addressing youth violence is not possible if mothers do not reclaim their wellness and adopt Fanon's (2018) assertion that "violence must first be fought with the language of truth and of reason" (p. 655). Speaking, listening, and acting truthfully in supportive environments that engage their stories is an opportunity for reason to flourish; an opportunity to inspire proactive community change. To this end, our research team would continue to partner with the mothers. However, it was also important for Somali mothers to embrace their central roles and responsibilities in the initiative to not only (re)name the problem(s), but also own transformative processes.

Owning the MCIS Research Process: Evolving Roles, Responsibilities, and Action Steps

Fanon (1967b) identified stereotypes of Muslim womanhood in Algeria under French colonialism that parallel existing stereotypes about Somali Canadian women who are largely Muslim practitioners: "Her alleged confinement, her lack of importance, her humility, her silent existence bordering on quasi-absence. . . . [Islam makes] no place for her, amputating her personality, allowing her neither development nor maturity, maintaining her in a perpetual infantilism" (p. 65). Contrary to these stereotypes, Somali mothers are key stakeholders in their communities' well-being. Her Muslim womanhood is an integral aspect of her identity, a source of being and belonging that helps her navigate the exclusionary harshness of Canadian society, which makes no place for her.

"We want justice!" Somali mothers consistently proclaimed, but justice as an integral aspect of liberation was not experientially evident in the abstract research process we were initially developing. Re-engaging politicians, however, was perceived as a concrete option Somali mothers wished to pursue with the research team's support. Given my (Yusuf's) honorary mother status and the organization's mission to build vibrant, socially integrated and united communities, Midaynta unhesitatingly complied with the mothers' requests. Fanon (1969) claimed that "liberation must be the work of the oppressed people" (p. 105). Bearing this in mind, I (Chioneso) relinquished my ideas about the team's research process and reoriented my role vis-à-vis the group's needs. That is, I became more flexible, making myself available to the community in ways that they requested and found beneficial. While doing so, I strongly encouraged the mothers to recruit a local Somali person who had a similar skill-set as my own in addition to an insider's perspective through language and cultural expertise to become an integral member of the team. The Somali mothers refused: "No, we choose you. To be Somali is not all that is important." Apparently, "language, culture—these are not enough to make you belong to a people. Something more is needed: a common life, common experiences and memories, common aims" (Fanon, 1967b, p. 175). Our unfolding commonalities allowed us to pursue community healing in self-determining ways.

For example, Somali mothers saw the value of advocating for community resources through Canadian politicians. A local politician accepted our invitation to meet with the mothers. At the December 2016 lunch meeting, Midaynta organized the logistics and covered all costs. I (Elmi) coordinated the participating mothers. My (Chioneso's) responsibility was to observe, take notes, and identify potential next steps. After Midaynta led the discussion that included a presentation of Somali youth homicide data, the 20 Somali mothers in attendance shared their personal stories about their murdered sons' unsolved cases. While claiming the importance of their sons' eclipsed lives, the mothers struggled to hold onto the significance of their own lives. Each testimony was a soul oppressed note in a symphony of pain. We collectively wept—hijabs, winter scarves, open palms, unscented tissues, and warm embraces caught our tears. We experienced a "collective catharsis," what Fanon (1967a) described as an important occurrence in "every collectivity, [there] exists—must exist—a channel, an outlet through which the forces accumulated in the form of aggression can be released" (p. 145). By the end of our mournful meeting, the Somali mothers suggested the government should fund a Mothers Outreach Workers (MOWs) initiative to help mothers support each other and their communities. The politician listened graciously, sympathized with the Somali mothers and promised to facilitate a meeting between the mothers and a politician whose ministerial portfolio was directly relevant to their needs.

The mothers' meeting with the politician was a success. However, I (Chioneso) challenged the team's understanding of success: "Besides meeting with the local politician and a promise to meet with another politician, what did *we gain?*" Our team spoke about the importance of politicians seeing Somali homicide data, hearing mothers' agonizing stories, and witnessing their distressful tears. While acknowledging the team's perspective, I highlighted that the politician seemed aware of the presented issues, and more importantly—power does not concede to tears. If we continue to meet with politicians, we must develop and present our demands because politicians are incapable of cultivating the solutions we seek. Anchored in this experience, our subsequent research team meetings shifted towards a greater focus on serving Somali mothers' needs.

As promised, the local politician initiated an opportunity for the Somali mothers to meet with another politician, a meeting that was negotiated through Midaynta. With only three-weeks to prepare, we agreed to host a community forum. Once again, Midaynta was responsible for all logistics, expenses incurred, advertisements, and correspondences with the politician's office. Meanwhile, Mrs. Elmi and I (Chioneso) worked with a core group of Somali mothers to develop a strategic plan that they would deliver to the politician. After their ideas were unpacked, clarified, and documented, a formal presentation was crafted. A subset of five mothers (including Elmi) was assigned to co-lead the presentation, which incorporated snippets of their personal stories. Based on group consensus, a meeting agenda that included Somali female youth workers in key supportive roles (e.g., presenting a community historical overview) was drafted and finalized. At the February 2017 mothers' meeting with the provincial politician, approximately 200 people were in attendance. Three formal requests were made:

1. Funding to support the Mending a Crack in the Sky (MCIS) community research initiative, which would include:

   a) Collecting data using a community-based participatory action research methodological approach
   b) Development and implementation of a Community Action Plan informed by community data that would identify approaches to collectively rebuild trust and heal the community (e.g., truth and reconciliation sessions, testimonial therapy, sociotherapy, etc.)
   c) A documentary film project

2. Development of a comprehensive legal team to serve Somali communities against policing and other state actions that victimize Somali youth and older residents. This would require:

   a) Recruitment of African/Black Canadian lawyers, legal staff and personnel in the areas of: criminal justice, immigration, family relations, and translation services

b) Additional services required are legal education for families and victim services (e.g., hotlines, witness protection programs, etc.)

3. Creation of targeted mental health and support services for Somali families. This should include:

a) Establishing an African/Black healing team
b) Funding, recruitment, and training of 20 Mothers Outreach Workers (MOWs) positions across the province that would include: specialized mental health services through enhanced MOWs and basic support services through standard MOWs

Impressed with the mothers' presentation and the outpouring of community support, the politician asked Midaynta to establish follow-up meetings with the politician's representatives to further discuss the strategic plan.

The purpose of the mothers meeting with politicians was to obtain governmental support for our community strategic plan. While we appreciated the support of the two politicians and continued to engage in dialogue with them, Somali mothers also demanded to speak with the provincial chief: the Premier of Ontario. In February 2016, Midaynta wrote a letter on behalf of one hundred Somali mothers of homicide victims requesting an urgent meeting with the Premier of Ontario. However, it was not until March 2018 that a delegation of 15 Somali mothers, led by me (Elmi), was better prepared to meet with the Premier at Queen's Park (the Ontario Legislative Building) equipped with our strategic plan. Once again, it was a successful meeting. However, the positive outcomes of our community engagement process made it clear to Somali mothers that the "collective building up of a destiny is the assumption of responsibility" (Fanon, 1966, p. 163). In other words, if overcoming collective adversities and ending youth violence are their major concerns, Somali mothers must ultimately own thoughtful processes that inform their action steps to achieve the justice they seek.

Implementing MCIS: An Evaluation of Barriers and Community Wins

When conducting research within oppressed communities, psychology like "psychiatry has to be political," Fanon declared (Cherki, 2006, p. 72). Participatory action research can take on any form depending on who is implementing the approach. Thus, it was important for us to grapple with the politics of power by foregrounding the structural frameworks that may impact our (in)actions. We considered the following questions: What was within our realm of control? Would we comply with institutionally established research norms? MCIS required implementation resources, who did we expect to obtain resources, from what source(s), and at what cost? How would we exert our power? By raising these issues, I (Chioneso) encouraged us to assume ownership of the initial formulation of MCIS. Both the barriers we encountered and the community wins we achieved were instructive for the viability and long-term sustainability of MCIS.

Ideally the findings in the first phase of the research would inform both the action plan and the documentary film. However, efforts to implement the participatory action research were hindered by three key factors. First, our initial articulation of the community-based participatory action research was ill-suited for this population. The methodological approach we adopted required advanced English and computer literacy skills, access to funding, and the availability of significant allotments of time dedicated to research activities. Given these requirements among a predominately refugee population whose second or third language is English and the majority of whom are impoverished and/or working multiple low-paying jobs, the initiative struggled to gain momentum.

Second, cognitive dissonance impeded our ability to develop research questions. The listening session with youth workers indicated that lack of employment, poor education, and mental health challenges led to youth violence. However, during listening sessions with separate groups of mothers and fathers, intra-Somali issues (e. g., family deterioration) surfaced as a community priority linked to youth violence; a revelation that destabilized a strongly held belief among the community that youth violence (and correlative external factors) was "the" problem. Confronting internalized oppression and/or mental health challenges as the focus of the study became an intimidating proposition.

A third impediment arose after the listening session results; the research team became divided. Young research team members (i.e., under 35 years old and non-parents) employed as youth workers disagreed with the study potentially focusing on internalized oppression and, to a lesser degree, mental health challenges. They argued systemic issues should be our focus and emphasized that peer-to-peer outreach work would fix the problem. Achieving social justice was a commonly held desire by all; however, clarifying definitions of social justice and how or when social justice is achieved was not possible because the group dynamics deteriorated (e.g., canceled meetings and the resignation of team members). Consequently, the initiative came to a standstill.

Attempting to lead the research process based on methodological principles anchored in established theories is an academic goal that rarely coincides with the research expectations and desired political outcomes of oppressed communities. In his clinical work, Fanon (2018) and his colleagues recognized that if the betterment of "people are what constitute the goal, . . . then it becomes clear, it becomes necessary, that no dose of habit, of habituation, of automatism can intervene. For people have the extraordinary quality of being in constant renewal" (p. 338). To this end, Fanon (1967a) sometimes chose to be "derelict" and left "methods to the botanists and the mathematicians [because] there is a point at which methods devour themselves" (p. 12).

Tools support goal achievement; they should not become the end-goal or supersede the process. Centering people, communities in research rather than the normative criteria of methodological rigor helps to switch our focus to curbing the tide of increasing psychological distress and socioeconomic impoverishment resulting from oppressive conditions. Therefore, a Fanonian approach encourages social scientists to engage a political standpoint that broadens opportunities for communities to (re)name the problem, own the research process, and develop action steps that lead to community wins— however small or grand. These acts of self-determination require human- ism, flexibility in thoughts and interactions to yield innovative and liberatory outcomes.

The barriers to implementing the first phase of the research project encour- aged us to be flexible and creative in our approach to MCIS. Developing action steps (phase two) was an unquestioned commitment to be generated by the research process. This commitment was informed by Fanon's (1967a) contention that to "educate man to be *actional*, preserving in all his relations his respect for the basic values that constitute a human world, is the prime task of him who, having taken thought, prepares to act" (p. 222). That is, we imagined a process whereby our participatory action research findings would direct the development of a community action plan. After establishing legiti- macy through community verification and buy-in procedures, the action plan would, in turn, outline approaches to address youth violence and collectively heal the community. However, the reality of our circumstances outlined above demanded a less linear procedure. The new process required greater elasticity and thus we opted to generate action steps in real-time rather than a future time-frame as originally planned.

Despite numerous challenges, community wins emerged as a result of the 16-month (November 2016–March 2018) research process. For example, action steps such as advocating for community needs improved. As mentioned, our meetings with politicians became better organized and specific requests were prepared in advance and clearly presented: (1) fund the Mending a Crack in the Sky community initiative; (2) develop a comprehensive legal team to serve Somali communities; and (3) create targeted mental health and support services for Somali families. With their increasing levels of self-confidence, interpersonal trust, and skill development during our research process, Somali mothers also gained a clearer sense of political purpose. They experienced "political education," what Fanon (1966) described as "opening their minds, awakening them, and allowing the birth of their intelligence" and capabilities (p. 157). Fanon further emphasized that:

> To educate the masses politically does not mean, cannot mean making a political speech. What it means is to try, relentlessly and passionately, to teach the masses that everything depends on them; that if we stagnate it is their responsibility, and that if we go forward it is due to them too, that there is no such thing as a demiurge, that there is no famous man who will take the responsibility for everything, but that the demiurge is the people themselves and the magic hands are finally only the hands of the people.
> (pp. 157–158)

To enable the "magic hands" of the people to move the community forward, the research process inspired an awakening and reconnecting of community bonds. That is, a weekly structured community reconciliation group was established to encourage fellowship (e.g., sharing meals), educate the group (e.g., guest speakers present on various topics—policies and funders' expectations), and generate ideas to address community problems. In January 2018, I (Chioneso) facilitated a community healing workshop with the Somali community reconciliation group. On that occasion and setting, a Somali mother who had not spoken for nearly two years following the murder of her son, became highly engaged, laughed throughout the session, and declared "I am healed!" at the end of the workshop. She subsequently became a more active participant within the reconciliation group and accepted a leadership role. Over the next 12 months, an inverse relationship became steadily apparent—as her sense of purpose and joy increased, her reliance on medication decreased. She is now frequently described as "one of the happiest people you will ever meet." Her experience exemplified Fanon's (2018) belief that the "medicine of the person presents itself as a deliberate choice for optimism in the face of [a dialectical] human reality" that seizes our will to overcome tragedies while delivering opportunities to be architects of our own freedom (p. 271).

At the same time, designing a community action plan became a highly embraced goal by both mothers and fathers. Among the objectives of the community action plan is to obtain government funding for the creation of a women's economic security project for the purpose of making the work of the group self-sustaining. A MOWs job description and budget were drafted and later submitted in pursuance of a federal grant. However, MOWs currently operate without outside funding, which led mothers to discuss the prospects of social entrepreneurialism by starting businesses and formally working together to make their community collaborations self-sustainable. In the meantime, I (Elmi) and other mothers are learning how to create a digital story (i.e., a 2–4 minute story that incorporates multimedia). Together, we are also visiting mothers residing in priority neighborhoods as we find ways to support MOWs with our available resources. To date, approximately 300 mothers have been recruited to become MOWs.

Lastly, creating a common vision to effectively implement and self-sustain a community action plan came to the fore following the bombing in Mogadishu, Somalia on October 14, 2017. The bombing catalyzed the organizing efforts of the community into a $500,000 fundraising initiative to aid Somalis impacted by the bombing back home. An intergenerational model was devised in which five parents and five youth formed various fundraising committees responsible for raising $15,000 each. A substantial amount of money has been raised and the Somali community successfully lobbied the government to lift sanctions that prohibited their ability to remit funds from Canada to Somalia. This initiative demonstrated how necessary it is for parents to take the first steps to eliminate the growing intergenerational divide that has contributed to Somali youth violence; highlighting Fanon's (2018) claim that "there is no need always to be on a search for the unusual. Creative intentions can emerge from out of the common" to address community problems (p. 282).

MCIS: An Analysis of Challenges and Implications for Future Work

The difficulty of conducting participatory action research (PAR) in marginalized African/Black communities is evidenced by residents often challenging researchers to go beyond "their" research questions, hypotheses, and methodological rigor. As a community psychologist, the Somali group in Toronto required me (Chioneso) to function in particular ways, such as listening to their testimonies in both Somali and English. This meant hearing and appreciating Somali, experiencing their pain, shedding tears, as well as sitting and eating with the community. As a community psychologist, it meant translating their testimonies into concise language and into a coherent narrative. This may explain why the Somali group refused to work with a Somali researcher after I pointed out the advantages of working with an "insider" (i.e., someone who spoke Somali and possessed similar skills as my own). Apparently, the Somali group preferred someone who could help them craft and deliver their message to Canadian politicians and decision makers; requests that extend beyond the scope of PAR. Hence, PAR did not effectively address Somali Canadian needs because they are grappling with issues of liberation and self-determination while suffering and dying "within" a colonial context.

Furthermore, the methodological requirements of PAR for the Somali research project posed significant challenges. For example, the Internal Review Board requirements for the Collaborative Institutional Training Initiative (CITI Program) certification incurred costs of $100.00 USD (approximately $131.00 CAD) per person for each team member to pay out of pocket, using their personal credit cards. Most team members were unwilling to pay or could not afford to pay this fee despite Midaynta's willingness to reimburse all team members. Another challenge was the significant time commitment required to read, understand, and complete the certification process. Admittedly, PAR has the advantage of collaboration with community members in the development of research ideas and questions. However, to conduct research entails recruitment of interested community members, logistics, focus groups, data analysis, all of which required funding and significant time commitments. Despite the stated importance of the project, many team members could not attend to these issues because of more pressing needs (e.g., seeking employment) and other commitments (e.g., caretaking children and/or elderly parents) (Woods, 2009).

Accessing funding, determining how the project should be funded, and negotiating how the research focus aligns with that of prospective funders were all issues that had to be addressed. Additionally, we had the task of funding the documentary film. In collaboration with filmmaker René Vautier, Fanon produced a film, *J'ai huit ans* (1961), to record his therapeutic research with

Algerian refugees in Tunis. The film captures his experimental visualization strategy whereby patients, like the well-known Algerian writer Boukhatem Farès, were asked to "visualize" and give artistic expression to their psychological problems. In Farès' case, he created a series of artwork called "Screams in the Night," and traces the development of his artistic talent to his therapeutic sessions with Fanon while he was a patient in the Tunis hospital (Mirzoeff, 2012). Like Fanon, we planned to record Somali mothers' stories and the research project. We secured a filmmaker who was prepared to work with us; however, we did not resolve our funding challenges.

Moreover, the Somali listening sessions brought distinct perspectives of youth workers who believed that unemployment, lack of education, and mental health challenges were the source of youth violence. The parents cited the same reasons, but also identified internal Somali challenges. A kind of collective cognitive dissonance developed when internal Somali issues (e.g., blame, distrust, poor relationships between women, and family deterioration) surfaced as a community priority, which many believed had to be examined if effective responses to youth violence were to be developed. This revelation destabilized the strongly held belief that youth violence was the primary issue that needed to be fixed. Although the research team was brought together to address the concerns raised by Somali mothers, younger team members resisted buying in and disagreed with the study. The perspectives of younger team members were affected by personal issues, such as feeling forced by their employer to participate, thus lacking freedom of choice or self-selection. They also felt overwhelmed by other responsibilities (e.g., completing graduate degree coursework) and youth work, which included recurring personal and work-related experiences of youth violence.

Like other members of the Somali community, younger team members were tired of doing "*another* community study." They felt that if the focus is to do youth work, then the study should focus on the problems that youth have (e.g., unemployment and lack of education) and fix those problems. Further, they strongly believed that it was "wrong to bring Somali mothers' personal issues into the public" sphere. Fanon (2018) pointed out that:

> A mother is someone who has protected us from suffering, from troubles. It was one's mother that resolved all the little matters. Whenever things are not going well, a desire arises to confide in one's mother. There thus seems to be a habit, a constant in our way of reacting to suffering: to call for one's mother . . . [because our] mother consoles, [she] caresses [our wounds].
>
> (p. 345)

Considered together, younger team members felt compelled to protect their (sole) protectors. To do otherwise, may compromise this love bond or worse, become an act of betrayal. In the end, the research team organized to study the effects associated with Somali youth violence divided and our group dynamics broke down. Despite attempts to achieve group consensus, things fell apart.

Although the Somali community initiative came to a standstill, the research team challenged the Somali mothers to ask themselves: What do we want? What does "justice" mean to us? How can we heal? Where do we go from here? A promising next step is the Community Healing and Resistance Through Storytelling (C-HeARTS) framework. *Community healing* is defined as an ongoing multilevel process whereby oppressed groups strengthen their connectedness and collective memory in ways that promote critical consciousness to achieve optimal states of justice (Chioneso et al., 2019). The C-HeARTS framework consists of three major components. First, the framework proposes that the bedrock of community healing is the principle of justice (i.e., ethical behaviors such as truth, balance, and reciprocity), which guides healing processes and informs desired outcomes. Second, culturally appropriate operational tools, such as storytelling and resistance should be intentionally utilized to direct the re-narrating of trauma and inform action steps. Lastly, strategically enhancing three psychological dimensions and related key components may foster community healing: connectedness (i.e., promote understanding, validation, and nurturing), collective memory (i.e., cultivate trust, remembering, and decolonizing the mind), and critical consciousness (i.e., increase personal empowerment, collective organizing, and advocacy for community needs). Ultimately, the C-HeARTS framework aims to foster a community's ability to transform oppressive systems. If the Somali community is receptive to this idea, the C-HeARTS framework may facilitate the reengagement of Mending a Crack in the Sky.

Conclusion

Allowing us to reconceptualize our current circumstances while reaching for optimal possibilities, Mending a Crack in the Sky was an opportunity that we granted ourselves. Key to our success was developing respectful working relationships, community buy-in, and emphasizing the strengths of Somali mothers. Our positive working relationships reinforced the commitments we hold to engage in the synergistic benefits of collaborative efforts. The supportive Somali community buy-in we achieved was grounded in Midaynta's and Mrs. Elmi's long-standing community development work. Community buy-in grew as a result of building new trusting and challenging relationships that incorporated community expertise and Somali identified goals into the project. Of utmost importance was the awakening of Somali mothers' consciousness and talents. A new open path pointed to the significance of nurturing their personal well-being and skills, exploring the dynamic interrelationship of motherhood and sisterhood, and honoring the courage required to initiate familial and community reconciliation. The strides we continue to take along this path and destinations we embark upon, remain to be seen.

Midaynta Community Services has been at the forefront of finding solutions to the problem of youth violence in African Canadian communities, particularly Somali communities, by working closely with government ministries and engaging in dialogue with politicians. While these conversations go a long way in raising awareness, Somali communities are in dire need of urgent and strategic action to stop the violence. The Toronto Somali community has multiple challenges, for which it has a central role in designing effective solutions. Mending a Crack in the Sky focused on community healing; that is, identifying roles for facilitating connectedness, recalling collective memory, and developing critical consciousness. Central to the project's community action plan is a community psychology framework that evidences important parallels with Fanon's practice of sociotherapy, and points to his conviction that:

> The search for truth in local attitudes is a collective affair. . . . [F]or the success of the decision which is adopted depends upon the co-ordinated, conscious effort of the whole of the people. . . . The collective struggle presupposes collective responsibility at the base and collegiate responsibility at the top. Yes; everybody will have to be compromised in the fight for the common good.
>
> (Fanon, 1966, p. 159)

Through a heightened critical consciousness, Fanon (1967b) encouraged us to be cognizant of the fact that "we are at the heart of the drama" (p. 125). As a result of self-determining acts of freedom, we can create new and more flexible community narratives using our own words in the making of a healthier world for the optimal development of our youth and communities.

Note

1. In 2005, the Ontario Human Rights Commission (OHRC) approved guidelines on racism and racial discrimination including terminology deemed more appropriate when collectively describing people: "Recognizing that race is a social construct, the Commission describes people as 'racialized person' or 'racialized group' instead of the more outdated and inaccurate terms 'racial minority,' 'visible minority,' 'person of colour' or 'non-White'" (OHRC, 2005, Fact sheet). With the exception of Indigenous peoples because of their distinct status as the original inhabitants of Canada, racialized persons refers to all people considered non-Caucasian in race or non-white in color.

References

Abdulkadir, R. (2006). *"Undocumented convention refugee in Canada": The implications of and rationale behind Canada's identity document requirement from convention refugees within its borders* (Unpublished master's thesis). Carleton University, Ottawa, Canada.

Aden, M., Issa, A., Rayale, S., & Abokor, L. (2018). *Another day, another Janazah: An investigation into violence, homicide and Somali-Canadian youth in Ontario.* Toronto, Canada: Youth LEAPS.

Ahmad, H. (2017). Youth de-radicalization: A Canadian framework. *Journal for Deradicalization, 12,* 119–168.

Bokore, N. (2013). Suffering in silence: A Canadian Somali case study. *Journal of Social Work Practice, 27,* 95–113. doi:10.1080/02650533.2012.682979.

Bradburn, J. (2011). There's a riot goin' on down Yonge Street. *Torontoist*. Retrieved from https://torontoist.com/2011/08/theres_a_riot_goin_on_down_yonge_street/.

Bulhan, H. A. (1985). *Frantz Fanon and the psychology of oppression*. New York, NY: Plenum Press.

Cherki, A. (2006). *Frantz Fanon: A portrait* (N. Benabid, Trans.). Ithaca, NY: Cornell University Press.

Chioneso, N. A., Hunter, C. D., Gobin, R. L., Smith McNeil, S., Mendenhall, R., & Neville, H. (2019). *Community Healing and Resistance Through Storytelling: A framework to address racial trauma in Africana communities*. Unpublished manuscript.

COP-COC. (2019a). *Fact sheet #3: Racialized poverty in education and learning*. Toronto, Canada: Colour of Poverty-Colour of Change.

COP-COC. (2019b). *Fact sheet #5: Racialized poverty in employment*. Toronto, Canada: Colour of Poverty-Colour of Change.

COP-COC. (2019c). *Fact sheet #7: Racialized poverty in justice and policing*. Toronto, Canada: Colour of Poverty-Colour of Change.

Coteau, M. (2017). *Bill 114: An Act to provide for anti-racism measures*. Toronto, Canada: Government of Ontario.

CSO. (2017). *Somalis and mental health: Raising awareness and developing interventions that improve outcomes*. London, UK: Council of Somali Organisations. Retrieved from www.coun cilofsomaliorgs.com/sites/default/files/resources/CSO-M.Health%20Report.pdf.

Daniel, L., & Cukier, W. (2015). *The 360 project: Addressing the discrimination experienced by Somali Canadians and racialized LGBTQ homeless youth in Toronto*. Toronto, Canada: Ryerson University.

Dryer, J. (1998). The undocumented convention refugees in Canada class: Creating a refugee underclass. *Journal of Law and Social Policy, 13*, 166–187.

Elmi, A. S. (1999). *A study on the mental health needs of the Somali community in Toronto*. Toronto, Canada: York Community Services & Rexdale Community Health Centre.

Fanon, F. (1966). *The wretched of the earth*. New York: Grove Press.

Fanon, F. (1967a). *Black skin, white masks*. New York: Grove Press.

Fanon, F. (1967b). *A dying colonialism*. New York: Grove Press.

Fanon, F. (1969). *Toward the African revolution*. New York: Grove Press.

Fanon, F. (2018). *Alienation and freedom*. In J. Khalfa & R. J. C. Young (Eds.), & S. Corcoran (Trans.). London, England: Bloomsbury Academic.

Farah, H. K. (2011). *Exploring the narrative experience of Somali-Djiboutian youth in and about Ottawa Public Schools* (Unpublished doctoral dissertation). University of Ottawa, Ottawa, Canada.

Fellin, M. (2015). The impact of media representations on Somali youth's experiences in educational spaces. *Landscapes of Violence, 3*, 1–32.

Fry, H. (2018). *Taking action against systemic racism and religious discrimination including Islamophobia*. Ottawa, Canada: House of Commons of Canada.

Galabuzi, G.-E. (2006). *Canada's economic apartheid: The social exclusion of racialized groups in the new century*. Toronto, Canada: Canadian Scholars's Press.

Guerin, B., Guerin, P., Diiriye, R. O., & Yates, S. (2004). Somali conceptions and expectations concerning mental health: Some guidelines for mental health professionals. *New Zealand Journal of Psychology, 33*(2), 59–67.

Hampton, R. (2010). Black learners in Canada. *Race & Class, 52*(1), 103–110. doi:10.1177/03063968103717.

Hoskins, E., & Meilleur, M. (2012). *Ontario's youth action plan*. Toronto, Canada: Government of Ontario.

Ibrahim, M. (2018). *Medical returnees: Somali Canadians seeking psychosocial and spiritual healing in east Africa* (Unpublished doctoral dissertation). Simon Fraser University, Burnaby, Canada.

Jibril, S. (2011). *"Cashberta:" Migration experiences of Somali-Canadian second generation youth in Canada* (Unpublished major research paper). York University, Toronto, Canada.

Jiwani, Y., & Al-Rawi, A. (2019). Intersecting violence: The representation of Somali youth in the Canadian press. *Journalism*, 1–35. doi:10.1177/1464884919825503.

Khenti, A. (2014). The Canadian war on drugs: Structural violence and unequal treatment of Black Canadians. *International Journal of Drug Policy, 25*(2), 190–195. doi:10.1016/j.drugpo.2013.12.001.

Kroll, J., Yusuf, A. I., & Fujiwara, K. (2011). Psychoses, PTSD, and depression in Somali refugees in Minnesota. *Social Psychiatry and Psychiatric Epidemiology, 6*, 481–493. doi:10.1007/s00127-010-0216-0.

Kwak, L. J. (2018). Still making Canada white: Racial governmentality and the "good immigrant" in Canadian parliamentary debates. *Canadian Journal of Women & the Law, 30*, 447–470. doi:10.3138/cjwl.30.3.005.

Lewis, S. (1992). *Stephen Lewis report on race relations.* Toronto, Canada: Government of Ontario.

Livingstone, A. (2015). Broken dreams in little Mogadishu: Canada's Somali community continues to struggle with higher-than-average levels of violence, unemployment and discrimination. *Broadview.* Retrieved from https://broadview.org/broken-dreams-in-little-mogadishu/.

McIntyre, C. (2016). Canada has a Black incarceration problem. *Torontoist.* Retrieved from https://torontoist.com/2016/04/african-canadian-prison-population/.

McMurtry, R., & Curling, A. (2008). *The review of the roots of youth violence.* Toronto, Canada: Government of Ontario.

Mirzoeff, N. (2012). *"We are all children of Algeria": Visuality and countervisuality, 1954–2011.* Retrieved from http://scalar.usc.edu/nehvectors/mirzoeff/jai-huit-ans-analysis.

Mohamed, A. (2011). *Religion, culture and mental health in Somali refugees in Christchurch* (Unpublished master's thesis). University of Otago, Dunedin, New Zealand.

Mohamed, S. (2015). *Failing to make the grade: Somali-Canadian students and their encounters with the Canadian education system* (Unpublished major research paper). Ryerson University, Toronto, Canada.

Mullings, D. V., Morgan, A., & Quelleng, H. K. (2016). Canada the great White North where anti-Black racism thrives: Kicking down the doors and exposing the realities. *Phylon, 53*, 20–41.

Nestel, S. (2012). *Colour coded health care: The impact of race and racism on Canadians' health.* Toronto, Canada: Wellesley Institute.

Nur, U. I., Dalal, M., & Baker, K. (2005). *Best practices: Somali Family Mental Health Support Program.* Toronto, Canada: Ontario Trillium Foundation.

OCASI. (2016). *Somali refugee resettlement in Canada.* Toronto, Canada: Ontario Council of Agencies Serving Immigrants.

OHRC. (2005). *Racial discrimination, race and racism [Fact sheet].* Toronto, Canada: Ontario Human Rights Commission. Retrieved from www.ohrc.on.ca/en/racial- discrimination-race-and-racism-fact-sheet.

Palmer, D. (2006). Imperfect prescription: Mental health perceptions, experiences and challenges faced by the Somali community in the London Borough of Camden and service responses to them. *Primary Care Mental Health, 4*, 45–56.

Razack, S. H. (2000). "Simple logic": Race, the identity documents rule and the story of a nation besieged and betrayed. *Journal of Law and Social Policy, 15,* 181–209.

Schuchman, D. M., & McDonald, C. (2004). Somali mental health. *Bildhaan: An International Journal of Somali Studies, 4,* 65–77.

Statistics Canada. (2016). *Census profile, 2016 census.* Ottawa, Canada: Government of Canada.

Turner, L. (2020). "Psychiatry has to be political": The Préterrain to a new Fanon. In *Frantz Fanon's psychotherapeutic approaches to clinical work: Practicing internationally with marginalized communities.* Abingdon, UK: Routledge.

UN Report. (2017). *Report of the working group of experts on people of African descent on its mission to Canada.* Geneva, Switzerland: United Nations, Human Rights Council.

Warde, B. (2013). Black male disproportionality in the criminal justice systems of the USA, Canada, and England: A comparative analysis of incarceration. *Journal of African American Studies, 17,* 461–479. doi:10.1007/s12111-012-9235-0.

Woods, V. D. (2009). African American health initiative planning project: A social ecological approach utilizing community-based participatory research methods. *Journal of Black Psychology, 35,* 247–270. doi:10.1177/0095798409333589.

11 Race and Recognition

Pathways to an Affirmative Black Identity[1]

Helen A. Neville, Brigitte Viard, and Lou Turner

I ask that I be taken into consideration on the basis of my desire. I am not only here—now, locked in thinghood. I desire somewhere else and something else. I demand that an account be taken of my contradictory activity insofar as I pursue something other than life, insofar as I am fighting for the birth of a human world, in other words, a world of reciprocal recognitions.

He who is reluctant to recognize me is against me. In a fierce struggle I am willing to feel the shudder of death, the irreversible extinction, but also the possibility of impossibility.

(Fanon, 1952/2008, p. 193)

Scholars have long theorized about the ways in which Black people throughout the Diaspora develop affirmative identities, even in the face of racial oppression. We began this manuscript with a quote from Fanon's (1952/2008) *Black Skin, White Masks* to highlight the connection between the concept of recognition and racial identity. Drawing on the work of philosopher G. W. F. Hegel, Fanon asserted that Black individuals desire mutual recognition as a necessary condition of "self worth, identity, and even humanity" (Bulhan, 1985, p. 103). Although all people strive to be seen as valuable, worthy human beings, the reality of racial oppression frustrates Black peoples' attainment of reciprocal or mutual recognition. The lack of recognition of humanity is reflected in the structural oppression of Black people in the U.S. and around the globe as illustrated by the health, wealth, education, and criminal justice disparities between Blacks and their White counterparts, even in countries in which Black people are the numeric majority. The recent murder of Trayvon Martin in the U.S. and the acquittal of George Zimmerman for the killing underscore the ways in which Black life is devalued in society; a fact further illustrated by the horrific Halloween costumes in which White men mocked the murder of Trayvon Martin by dressing in Black face and wearing a "blood stained" hoodie.

In this manuscript, we explore in greater detail the connection between recognition and Black racial identity. Our work is rooted in the Black radical scholar tradition (e.g., Cross, 1971; Fanon, 1952/2008; Thompson & Alfred, 2008). These scholars provide a foundation in which to conceptualize racial identity as a critical aspect of (mental) liberation. Given the vibrant racial identity research in Black psychology, there is surprisingly little empirical research on the concept of recognition as an aspect of racial identity. There is an abundance of quantitative research, however, on the link between racial pride or affirmation and a range of psychological, educational, and behavioral correlates (e.g., Telesford, Mendoza-Denton, & Worrell, 2013; Whittaker & Neville, 2010). What is lacking in the literature is an understanding of the process in which one develops an affirmative racial identity under situations in which one's humanity is called into question by external forces, not because of individual characteristics but solely because of race. Qualitative methods are needed to uncover if people do in fact identify issues of recognition as an aspect of their racial identity journey. The purpose of the current study was to address this gap by exploring if the concept of recognition emerged in Black individuals' racial life stories across multiple national contexts; the life story method allows people to narrate the complexities of their personal and social identities.

As a way of providing the context for the study, we first define recognition—both in terms of its general meaning and the way in which social group membership complicates this general meaning. Although our definition of recognition is grounded in Fanon's work, we integrate research from a range of scholars to provide a more contemporary understanding of the term. Next, we conceptually connect recognition and racial identity beliefs. Prior to outlining the purpose of the investigation, we briefly review the relevant empirical literature.

Defining Recognition

For the purposes of this manuscript, recognition consists of two primary dimensions: existential (i.e., self and other acknowledgement for one's global sense of worthiness) and social group (i.e., self- and other acknowledgement of one's sense of worthiness given one's social group membership). At its core, recognition is a process in which individuals claim or assert humanity onto themselves and others based on their beliefs. Early theorists focused on the idea that recognition involves reciprocity, that is, the notion that we exist in relation to one another (Fanon, 1952/2008; Hegel, 1931/1967). Recognizing ourselves and being recognized by others (as individuals worth valuing) is a life-long process as we are continually changing and evolving in relation to others and ourselves (Wynne, 2000). Recognition is also a dialogic process shaped by our internal evaluations of self and our interactions with the social world (Taylor, 1992). In this sense, recognition is an existential phenomenon in which one's very existence is based on being recognized. Thus, all individuals regardless of social identity strive to be seen as fully human; they strive for existential recognition.

It is when this type of existential recognition is undermined or absent that one engages in actions to affirm one's humanity and dignity. The iconic images of Black men carrying signs during the 1968 Memphis sanitation workers strike declaring "I am a Man," is symbolic of the struggle to assert one's humanity in the face of oppression. As indicated by this example, recognition is complicated by social identities (race and gender). Part of our identity is constituted by our characteristics, even those that are not chosen such as race. The ways in which personal characteristics or group membership mold our identity is dependent on recognition of them by others.

> If we take into account that my practical identity does not consist of my simply having features, but rather of my having features that I identify with, then we see how recognition can shape my identity even in cases of the innate characteristics I was born with. The role that different characteristics have on one's self-image depends on the opinions of others, because one's identifications are formed dialogically. Thus, while recognition may or may not have a role in my having the characteristics, it has a crucial role in these characteristics constituting a part of my identity.
>
> (Laitinen, 2002, p. 475)

In the above passage, philosopher Laitinen hints at recognition's role in constructing a social identity by analyzing how certain characteristics are socially affirmed (or not).

The second order aspect of recognition is social group recognition—or for the purposes of our work—racial group recognition. This conceptualization builds on Fanon's work and extends Laitinen's (2002) analysis to include Black racial identity. Black individuals develop a sense of social identity dialogically or through an exploration of both the internal views about the self on the basis of racial group membership and the external views of actors who are either racially similar or different (Taylor, 1992).

Recognition and Racial Identity

Recognition is inextricably linked to racial identity because seeking recognition from others is an aspect of self-consciousness. According to Hegel (1931/1967) "Self-consciousness exists in itself and for itself, in that and by the fact that it exists for another self-consciousness; that is to say, it is only by being acknowledged or recognized" (p. 229). Racial identity theorists such as Cross (e.g., 1971) extended the notion of individual self-consciousness to reflect a larger group consciousness process, which for Black Americans means "*self-actualization under conditions of oppression*" (p. 25).

Black people are not just reactionary. They do not primarily look to Whites for validation; but, it is difficult to deny the dehumanization of racism that exists within larger society in which Whites have economic and/or political control. Blacks look to other Blacks for comparison and recognition. According to Fanon (1952/2008), however, this type of social comparison is often tainted by European-influenced cultural norms and traditions due to White supremacy: "The Martinican compares himself not to the white man, the father, the boss, God, but to his own counterpart under the patronage of the white man" (p. 190).

And thus the desire and struggle for recognition must—as Fanon and later Cross argued—include a critical awareness of the realities of racial oppression on the lived experiences of Black people and a "fierce struggle" on the part of Blacks to assert their humanity. And as such, the process of affirming one's racial identity is stimulated in part by a desire and struggle for freedom and recognition. Nelson Mandela's comments during his 1964 trial which he later repeated upon his release from prison in 1990 beautifully capture the complexities of (a) group consciousness, (b) assertion of the ideal of a reciprocal recognition in which Black and Whites recognize the humanity in one another, and (c) a willingness to struggle to the death for this type of recognition:

> I have fought against white domination, and I have fought against black domination. I have cherished the ideal of a democratic and free society in which all persons live together in harmony and with equal opportunities. It is an ideal which I hope to live for and to achieve. But if needs be, it is an ideal for which I am prepared to die.

For Fanon, the struggle for freedom and recognition took place within the anti-colonial context and for Mandela it took place during apartheid. The struggle for freedom and recognition is still important in the current social and historical context, a moment in which many former colonial states adopt a neoliberal and color-blind perspective in an attempt to veil the persistence of racial oppression. The struggle in these countries is for social equity around a range of issues including access to quality education and jobs with living wages and eradicating negative racial stereotyping and the criminalization of Blacks.

Race, Recognition, and Research

The concept of recognition has implications for psychology, yet very few psychology researchers have examined recognition. Moreover, there are only a handful of empirical studies in related fields examining any aspect of recognition. In one of the few studies, Ford (2011) conducted face-to-face interviews with faculty across, race, gender and discipline at a large mid-western university. Findings suggested that women of color faculty felt disrespected and "misrecognized" by White students, primarily because they did not conform to these students' schema of a faculty member. Women of color participants reported incidents in which their intellectual contributions and scholarship were mini-mized or overlooked and also they identified social interactions in which their authority as professors was called into question. They were denied the same type of status and respect that their White male colleagues were afforded by virtue of their identity. The theme of (mis)recognition is further articulated in the recently published and widely publicized collection of essays, *Presumed Incompetent: The Intersections of Race and Class for Women in Academia* (Gutierrez y Muhs, Niemann, Gonzalez, & Harris, 2012).

Research on the invisibility of Black men and women is closely aligned with Ford's (2011) notion of misrecognition. Being invisible is a form of lack of recognition and refers to the depersonalization of Blacks through racial ste-reotypes and thus not being seen as three-dimensional persons (Franklin, 1999, 2006). According to Franklin (1999), Black Americans—men in particular—often experience the invisibility syndrome or the "inner struggle with the feel-ing that one's talents, abilities, personality, and worth are not valued or even recognized because of prejudice and racism" (p. 761). Emerging qualitative data provide support for the psychological toll of being perceived as "invisible" by others. For example, Tovar-Murray and Tovar-Murray (2012) interviewed 10 Black men about their perceptions of invisibility. Each of the men discussed encounters with Whites in which they felt invisible and/or discredited because of their race. Exposure to repeated racial slights during these encounters placed an "extra burden" on the men and led to feelings of helplessness and anger. The participants did not passively accept this treatment, but developed social support networks to affirm their identity and, moreover, they actively challenged racism in their immediate environment.

Surprisingly, few racial identity researchers explicitly incorporate issues of recognition—either existential or social group—into their empirical work. Sellers, Rowley, Chavous, Shelton, and Smith (1997) multidimensional model of racial identity (MMRI) is one of the few that do. MMRI consists of four dimensions of racial identity: salience, centrality, ideology and regard. Salience and centrality center on the significance of race in an individual's experience whereas ideology and regard encompass the qualitative aspects of ones identity as African American. Sellers et al.'s (1997) articulation of private (one's inter-nal evaluation of being Black) and public regard (i.e., perceived appraisal of how non-Blacks perceive Blacks) partially captures issues of recognition.

Although the general concept of regard captures a component of recogni-tion, the operational definition of the construct in the MMRI is slightly different than the way in which recognition is defined in this paper. The main difference rests in the assessment of public regard. Public regard within the MMRI frame-work refers to other racial groups' evaluation of Black people (e.g., "Blacks are not respected by the broader society," Sellers et al., 1997, p. 815). Extending the work of scholars writing on recognition, we conceptualize regard more as an "appraisal" component of our identity. That is, the way in which we perceive others' evaluation of us on the basis of our group membership (e.g., "People see me not as an individual but as a racial stereotype"). The differences in the conceptualizations may account for the equivocal empirical support for the link between regard and psychological adjustment. Not surprisingly, findings generally suggest an association between increased private regard (or reflexive appraisal) and lower psychological distress (e.g., Sellers, Copeland-Linder, Martin, & Lewis, 2006). However, findings tend to suggest that lower public regard serves as a buffer between experiences of racial discrimination and psychological adjustment (e.g., Caldwell, Kohn-Wood, Schmeelk-Cone, Chavous, & Zimmerman, 2004; Sellers & Shelton, 2003). And, thus, lower public regard from the MMRI framework does not have a negative effect on psychological well-being; in fact, it might actually enhance one's well-being. To date, we were unable to find empirical studies investigating the association between perceived external appraisal of one's racial self and well-being.

Research Purpose

Conceptually, developing a positive Black racial identity is related to issues of recognition; however, there is a dearth of empirical research exploring this association. Recognition transcends class, gender, and social location in that everyone is subject to the process of seeking recognition. We assert, however, that recognition is one of the core processes in which Black people search for and affirm their humanity within a system of racial oppression that dehumanizes all people within the system. Therefore, understanding the ways in which someone seeks recognition is a critical component of understanding their identity formation. The current qualitative study explored the concept of recognition using racial life narratives. This methodology was selected because of its flexibility in capturing identity formation within social-cultural contexts (McAdams, Josselson, & Leiblich, 2006; Polkinghorne, 1988). The life narrative approach allows researchers to explore the context in which people tell stories and the meaning they attribute to their experiences. In particular, life narratives or stories allow participants to construct meaning of their lives especially around the question of "who am I?"

In this investigation we explored if participants spontaneously discussed issues of recognition as an aspect of their racial life story. And, if the participants did discuss recognition, we wanted to describe the dimensions of recognition that were part of their racial identity.

We adopted a multinational approach with the assumption that Black individuals are similarly racialized in most settings with a history of racial oppression. We worked from the premise that race is a social construction and thus the concept of who is Black is determined by the geopolitical space of a given historical moment. This counters the reactionary notion of "race" as biology. The four sites in this study—Australia, Bermuda, South Africa, and the US—were selected because: (a) each had a history of racial oppression via chattel slavery (Bermuda, US), colonization (Australia, South Africa, US), genocide (Australia, US), and/or apartheid (South Africa); (b) the racial inequalities or stratification persists in the site as exemplified by current health, wealth, education, and/or political disparities, but (c) claims of these differences are minimized in favor of arguing for a post-racial society; (d) English is the (an) official language, and (e) personal familiarity with the context and access to community liaisons. We also wanted to collect data from sites that were predominantly White (Australia and U.S.) and from sites that were predominantly Black (Bermuda and South Africa). In the latter sites, Blacks are in political power and there are attempts to transition into a more racial egalitarian society, but racial stratification persists.

Method

Research Design

The current study is part of a larger multinational Black racial identity project. Participants in this study were asked to reflect on and share the story of one specific identity—racial identity—as opposed to sharing the themes and episodes in their entire life story. By focusing on racial experiences and the meaning one attributes to these experiences, we were able to investigate common themes about racial identity that cut across context and individuals as well as identify the unique cultural and individual contexts shaping people's understanding of what it means to be Black. For the purposes of this publication, only data pertaining to the overarching theme of recognition were analyzed.

Researchers Backgrounds

The first author is a Black American professor in counseling psychology and Black Studies. Her research over the past 20 years has incorporated quantitative and qualitative explorations of racism experiences and racial identity, particularly among Black Americans. She has traveled extensively in Australia, Bermuda, and South Africa. The second author is a Haitian-American Teach for America fellow, with B.A.s in psychology and African American Studies. She received intensive training in the area of racial identity and qualitative data analysis. The third author is an African American Fanon scholar who has written extensively on Hegel and Fanon's theories of recognition and revolution.

Interview Participants

Participants were 64 self-identified Black adults in four countries/territory: Australia (9 men and 10 women), Bermuda (7 men and 8 women), United States (7 men and 8 women), and South (7 men and 8 women). In addition to the diverse nationalities of the participants, they ranged in ethnicity as well. The largest range of ethnic group diversity was represented in the South African (8 "African" ethnic identities such as Xhosa, Zulu, 3 "Coloureds," and 4 people of Indian descent) and Australian samples (15 Aboriginals and 3 Torres Strait Islanders). At the time of the interview, participants ranged in age from 19 to mid-70s. Participants represented a range of class positions and included workers, professionals, elite, college students, and unemployed individuals; participants came from varied walks of life. Some of the participants were incarcerated at some point in their lives, others were business people with extensive life experience in other countries, some had high government type jobs, others were teenage parents, and some were students. Most of the sample was heterosexual and 7 participants identified as either gay ($n = 4$) or lesbian ($n = 3$).

Interview Protocols

The overwhelming majority of the sample ($n = 54$) participated in an individual semi-structured interview. The interview protocol was adapted from Dan P. McAdams' Life Story Interview (www.sesp.northwestern.edu/docs/Interviewrevised95.pdf). The life story interview protocol used in this study incorporated probes about general life experiences around family background. However, the bulk of the interview probes centered on participants' experiences with race and what it means to be Black; these probes included questions about critical incidents promoting an awareness of race or what being Black means throughout one's life; definition of what being Black means; and potential turning points in one's racial life story. Two participants opted to write their narrative as opposed to participate in an interview and one focus group was conducted in Australia ($n = 8$); only three broad sets of questions were posed in the group discussion: (1) What is it like for you to be Black in Australia? We are interested in hearing your stories and your experiences. (2) What does being Black mean to you? Has this understanding changed over time? (3) Has gender influenced your experiences as a Black person?

Procedures

Recruitment

The interview participants were identified through community contacts in each site and a snowball method. A purposeful sample was sought and specific attention was given to recruit diverse self-identified "Black" participants in terms of gender, class position, ideology, and sexual identity. The focus group was organized by one community contact/participant. The interviews were conducted in a number of Australian (Brisbane, Cairns, Melbourne, and Sydney), South African (Cape Town and Johannesburg), and United States cities (Chicago area, Denver, Los Angeles, and New York) and throughout the island of Bermuda.

Interviews

The first author conducted each of the individual interviews and co-facilitated the one focus group. The interviews were conducted in English; each of the participants received formal education in English. That means that the instruction in their primary and secondary schooling was in English. Participants for whom English was not their first language were currently employed in settings in which English was the primary language spoken. The majority of the individual interviews lasted about two hours (the range was from one hour to about four hours). The one focus group discussion lasted four hours. Per recommendations from qualitative researchers (e.g., Fassinger, 2005), the interview protocol was pilot tested prior to data collection, and only minor revisions were made. Interviews were audio-recorded and conducted in a location identified by the interviewee (e.g., park, place of employment, home, restaurant, etc.). Individual interview participants were given an equivalent of $30 and the focus group participants were given $5 as a small token of appreciation for their participation.

Data Analysis

The interviews were transcribed verbatim, reviewed for accuracy, and the majority of the transcripts were sent to the individual interviewees for comments, feedback, and changes. Due to confidentiality concerns, the transcript was not shared with focus group members. The first two authors immersed themselves in the data via reviewing the transcriptions, transcribing selected interviews, listening to the audio recordings, and discussing the interviews prior to analysis. Data were downloaded into ATLAS.ti, a qualitative data software program.

Data analysis for this study was primarily guided through dimensional analysis methods (e.g., Kools, McCarthy, Durham, & Robrecht, 1996; Ward, 2005). Specifically, we used open coding, mapping, and axial coding to systematically analyze the texts as related to sense of recognition. We initially loosely defined recognition as the ways in which individuals want, desire, and seek recognition/ acceptance and the actions that they use to bring this about. Each of the interviews was reviewed for any information related to "recognition." The "recognition" codes were entered into the ATLAS.ti software. Undergraduate research members of the first author's racial identity lab received extensive training on coding the data; they then recorded the coding in ATLAS.ti. The coding was double checked by the second author and a graduate research assistant also trained on the project.

Next, the first and second author retrieved and reviewed the texts that received "recognition" codes, this included codes in individual interviews, written narratives, and focus group. The first two authors independently and then collectively conducted a line-by-line analysis of the identified text. During this process, researchers independently developed codes and core dimensions of recognition. The first two authors met often to discuss their respective line-by-line analyses and emerging codes and dimensions (i.e., open coding). Convergent and divergent interpretations were discussed during these meetings. We often returned to the entire interview for a closer read and further discussion to help resolve disagreements in coding. We later used the coding meetings as peer debriefing sessions and to further refine the identification and description of the dimensions and their interconnections (i.e., mapping and axial coding). In identifying and describing the emerging themes, we tried to ensure that multiple voices in the data were represented. Notes were taken after each research team meeting, thus establishing an audit trail. The coding was shared with the third author who reviewed and commented on the initial themes. On the basis of this feedback, the coding and themes were finalized.

Results

We uncovered the central theme of Global Recognition in the interviews or the over-arching desire to be seen for one's humanity and all that entails. As shown in Figure 11.1, we also identified processes that either promoted (i.e., Racial Recognition and Acceptance) or undermined (i.e., Lack of Recognition and Acceptance) one's subjective experience of Global Recognition. Each of these processes or sub-themes contained two categories. Specifically, participants discussed experiencing (lack of) recognition and acceptance from their Communities (i.e., either in-group or out-group). Consistent with the extant literature, Invisibility emerged as an additional subtheme of Lack of

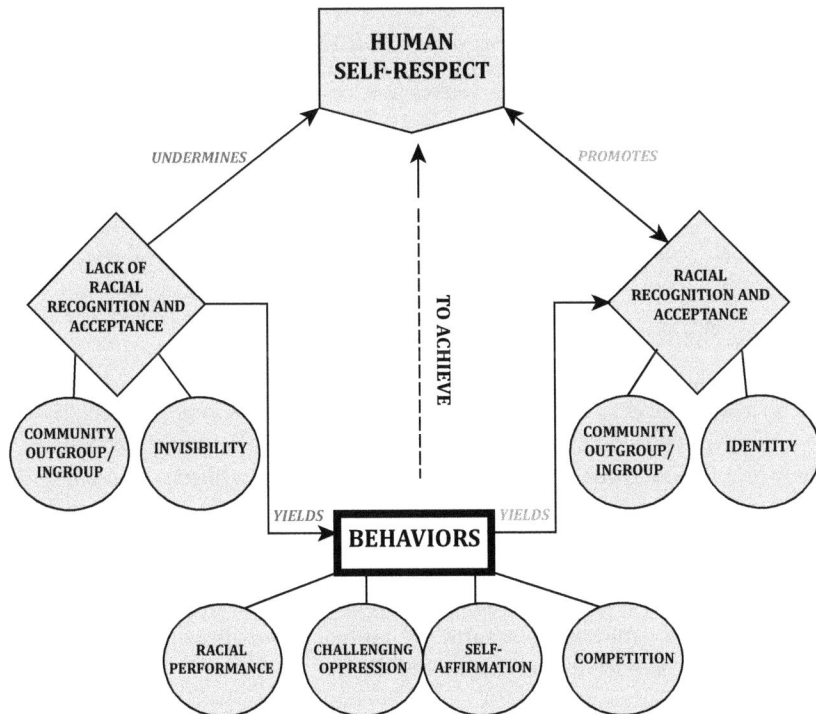

Figure 11.1 Emerging Model of Recognition as Part of Black Racial Identity

Recognition and Acceptance. Participants identified a personal affirmation of one's identity as the second sub-theme of Racial Recognition and Acceptance. In addition to these two processes, we identified four behaviors individuals who lacked racial recognition/acceptance engaged in to achieve some form of recognition: challenging oppression, competition, self-affirmation, and racial performance. The central theme, sub-themes and categories are described in detail below.

Global Recognition

In this context, Global Recognition refers to the striving for respect and acknowledgement for the complexities of being human. One participant, Merci, a "Coloured" South African undergraduate college student in her early 40s stated, "Just accept me for who I am as a person." Merci discussed the desire for being accepted simply as a human being, regardless of her ethnicity, race and the color of her skin. Even though Merci yearned for this type of Global Respect, she did not minimize or downplay her racial identity. Similarly, Buck, a businessman from the U.S. in his 20s described wanting to be accepted as a person, "I was always a person who wanted to be respected as an athlete, as a person."

Racial Recognition and Acceptance (RRA)

RRA reflects examples in the narratives in which participants perceived being respected or embraced by others on the basis of their racial identity and often how this identity intersects with other social identities such as sexual orientation. Participants identified receiving a sense of racial recognition and acceptance from members of their own racial community and also other communities; in addition, they discussed affirming their racial identity on a personal level.

Community In-Group / Out-Group RRA

Typically when participants provided an example of a Community In-group RRA, it was preceded by examples of feeling rejected by others on the basis of phenotype (e.g., too light or too dark), class position, or other social identity. For example, Ida—a Bermudian teacher in her 40s—described a high point in her racial life story in this way:

> I guess a peak experience was when I accepted that it was okay to be the Ida that I am and . . . while I had such powerful responses from my own culture folks from other cultures did no readily accept who I was until I had some significant interactions with them.

A number of participants also identified instances in which they received recognition for their accomplishments from Whites within a racialized context. CR, also in his 40s and from Bermuda, illustrated this point:

And I lost out [the speaking contest]; I didn't reach the finals. But one of the things that happened was that the eventual winner came up to me and thought that my speech was better. He was a White male. But he felt and it was quite powerful.

In this story, CR's talked about entering a debate in which he had a better speech than his opponent, but lost out because he was Black and spoke on a topic relevant to racism; the fact that the young White male "winner" acknowledged the excellence of his speech was important to CR as it provided a "reality check" attesting to the strength of his oratory skills and written word.

Racial Affirmation RRA

A number of participants described a process in which they achieved a Personal Affirmation of their identity or a sense of racial confidence, acceptance, and/or genuine pride. Nise an Aboriginal activist in her 50s captured this perspective best when summarizing her racial life story:

> I think I've had a tough life, but I've had a good life. It hasn't been easy over the years. I've been put down. I've been attacked. I've been abused. . . . You can either wallow in self-pity or you can move on with your life. And I think where I am today, I'm just very proud of where I'm at, very proud of being a black woman.

Lack of Racial Recognition and Acceptance (LRRA)

While RRA promoted a sense of Global Recognition among participants, LRRA undermined this overall notion of respect. Most of the participants identified times in which they experienced racial slights and even blatant forms of racial discrimination. We uncovered three central dimensions of LRRA: Community In-group/ Out-group and Invisibility.

Community In-Group/Out-Group LRRA

Similar to the RRA, participants perceived a Lack of Racial Recognition and Acceptance (LRRA) from other Black individuals as well as from folks outside of the Black community. Lack of recognition or acceptance was often based on some aspect of race (including phenotype) and, for some, on the intersection between race and other social identities, including gender, class, and sexual orientation. Christina, a U.S. student in her 20's felt rejected from other Blacks for various reasons throughout her life:

> It means that I am part of a community that does not accept me in multiple domains in certain ways. When I was younger I felt rejected because I was smart, which was so stupid. I mean that the most ignorant thing ever. But now it could be more because I am a lesbian, which is ignorant in a

different way (laugh). It doesn't make me as angry because I know that part of the issue is religious beliefs that people are usually stuck on.

Although participants perceived LRRA from Black individuals, they were much more likely to share stories in which people from other racial groups, primarily Whites, ignored or minimized their talents and abilities because of racial prejudice. The experiences ranged from being overlooked or ignored to more systematic levels of LRRA. Dr. E a retiree in Bermuda described how as a child she was hurt when her White neighbor refused to acknowledge her existence in the street when their paths crossed in the town when other White individuals were around. CR spoke at length about LRRA in securing a job in Bermuda.

> The [company] took so long to negotiate my contract I got to the point, "you know what I've got other things to do." And at the last minute and they said, "oh come on, no we need you." And so I decided, okay I'll do it for second year. Whether I do it for third year, I don't know. I do realize that I have options. After going to France, for instance, I got an email . . . from an . . . associate in Iran that wanted me to come and speak. But the fact of the matter is that . . . you get far more recognition when you leave Bermuda than you do here. So I've turned my goals to doing things more outside of Bermuda

Invisibility

Invisibility refers to the sense of exclusion participants felt because of their racial identity. Magenta an Aboriginal woman in her early 40's described this notion of invisibility in a professional setting:

> There's no communication. There's an invisibility of everything. The meaning let alone the actual words that I use. [I finally told a colleague] "since I have been on the faculty, I felt invisible." . . . But I can't be invisible, and when I say, that I was actually talking from a collective sense, so using the word, "I", but representing, all of those other dimensions of my experiences as an Aboriginal person, which incorporates, you know, the institution, and it's reaction to me, and it's inclusion and exclusion of me.

In her position as a university faculty, Magenta addressed her feelings of being invisible, and her colleagues' inability to recognize her worth and ability as an academic because of her race.

Behaviors

Partly in response to this lack of recognition or feeling rejected, participants identified ways in which they sought recognition and acceptance. Four main strategies emerged: challenging oppression, competition, self-affirmation, and racial performance.

Challenging Racism and Oppression

The primary way that individuals' sought recognition was through challenging racism and oppression. Many times this challenge took the form of calling people out on their racist behavior. Ms. Delilah, a Torres Strait Islander elder, shared an experience catching a bus that captured this subtle but direct type of challenge.

> And a bus pulled up here, where I was standing there was a couple that came up waiting for the bus too. . . . Anyway, I was saying to this couple, "What a lovely day, hello, what a lovely day. Good morning." And this man turned around and said to me, he looked really stern like you know, and he said to me, "What do you want from us? We do not have any money." And you know when he said that I said right away, "I don't want your money, thank you. All I'm acknowledging is that it's a beautiful day." . . . Anyway, so when we got off at the street, the bus stopped. So I got up and I was sitting right behind this couple, and I turned around and I said, "Once again, good morning and I hope you have a lovely day." And I said to them, I said "I think you're in the wrong country." So when I walked out that door the lady said, "Oh, excuse me madam. I'm sorry we just thought that," and I said, "No, you just thought what? I'm getting off the bus. I have no comment. I addressed you; I addressed the day, what a lovely day it was. So it's your problem that you went there within yourself."

Some participants like Pablo—a 50 something year old man of Indian descent from South Africa—adopted an activist stance and connected their anti-racism activism to their racial identity:

> I think what my sense of being Black is about being proud to be a South African Black man and it comes with expectations of being Black for me about being sensitive to being anti-oppressive. It's not just a skin color. It's not just a sense of history but it also comes with a sense of responsibility of what one has to do as a Black man or a Black person.

Competition

A number of participants, particularly men, countered racial oppression by viewing social interactions with Whites as a game. This type of Competition revealed itself through sports and through every day encounters. For example, 50-something-year-old Riley from Australia described his philosophy to interacting with people in power:

> You know, money speaks and it speaks louder than color. And I play the game too. Sometimes, I'll suit up and put a tie on you know . . . And they sit down at the table and they invite you and they give you a funny look,

"Oh yeah what are you doing here?" And then when you start talking to them and they ask you questions and you give answers to those questions and then you can see the little wheels in their heads turning and the lights coming on. And that's what I like. 'Cause I play my cards very close to my chest. I play it much accordingly to the way the game should be played. They put a card down and I put down a bigger, a higher card.

Self Affirmation

Some of the participants engaged in Self Affirmation as a way to counter an incident or long-standing threat to their personal worth or Global Recognition. In these instances, participants provided positive evaluations of their accomplishments or abilities. In talking about the importance of education in providing him opportunities, Buck talked about his strengths despite the stereotypes he faced:

> For me, education also did because you know I love the fact that I don't like to be put into a category, "he's this or he's that or he's an athlete." I can do anything that you can do. I have more education than the average person. I did better and I wish that people would understand I went in front of the athletic league and you know and I just kind of carried that with me, that's the kind of person I am. To just have that about myself.

Racial Performance

Racial performance is a way that individuals change themselves to fit in and be accepted. Dorothy, a US artist in her early 30s, explained as an adolescent she became a "chameleon" to try to fit in with others, particularly her Black peers.

> It was salt and pepper, it was, you know the hip-hop band, and it was putting my hair a certain way, dressing a certain way and it was even speaking differently, slang, you know, instead of how I do talk. I could see myself flipping my dialogue. The way that I spoke, it was completely different, so I became a chameleon in that way when I was around certain people, I spoke a certain way. When I was around Black people, I was like I had to prove that I'm Black; hear me talk. I think that was how I tried to be Black. Mostly in the way I speak.

Discussion

Findings from the racial life stories in this study revealed that self-identified Black individuals across age, ethnicity, geographical location, gender viewed recognition as a key dimension of Blackness. Our analysis both supports and extends research. First, consistent with theoretical writings, we found two broad types of recognition: existential recognition based on the value of being human (i.e., Global Recognition) and the second order form of recognition based on one's status group in society (i.e., Lack of Racial Recognition and Acceptance). Consistent with theoretical writings (Thompson & Alfred, 2008), participants engaged in a range of behaviors to affirm their individual and collective identities. Thus, among our participants, to be Black was to (a) have experienced both lack of recognition and acceptance from people within and outside of their community and also (b) to adopt an affirming, internalized understanding of Blackness based on recognition (i.e., self-acceptance and resistance). To be Black in this sense was consistent with Cross' (1971) self-actualization and other scholars' conceptualization of critical consciousness and collective action (Duncan, 2010; Thompson & Alfred, 2008). That is, many of the participants were aware of the ways in which they were dehumanized (lack of recognition); some participants further connected these experiences to racial oppression and took action to demand to be seen as a equally worthy.

Most of the narratives included an example of being ignored, demeaned, or rejected by Whites and other non-Black individuals, which is not at all sur-prising given the preponderance of White supremacy in each of the interview contexts. Interestingly, though, some of the participants did not explicitly con-nect these experiences with the desire to seek approval and acceptance from Whites. Instead, the racial dynamics within the society provided participants with a framework to understand and interpret their racial life narrative. Some participants identified subtle ways in which Whites encouraged them to give up their racial-ethnic identity as a tool to be accepted by others. This was particu-larly the case in Australia, where being indigenous was considered the lowest of the low. A number of Black/aboriginal participants relayed a story similar to the one Darrel told in which acquaintances often said: "why you always say you're Aboriginal, when you can get by with saying you're not, like saying you're American or something?" And, participants' response was inevitably to assert one's aboriginal identity. Thus, while some participants were encouraged to distance themselves from or denounce Blackness, participants instead chose to affirm their own Black identity outside of the White gaze. Participants expe-rienced and resisted being rejected or "misrecognized."

We also found support for the connection between invisibility and recog-nition as related to people's understanding of what it means to be Black. In addition to Franklin's (1999) conceptualization of the invisibility syndrome as an inner struggle due to the devaluation and dehumanization of one's talents because of one's racial membership, participants in this study also framed invisibility as a collective struggle. For example, Magenta framed invisibility as not being recognized for her contributions and, moreover, for the lack of inclu-sion of one's racial/ethnic contributions within the work environment. Both types of invisibility were identified as stressful, but the latter was particularly disconcerting because the work environment erased the collective contribu-tions of her ancestors. Invisibility in this sense suggests that collective recogni-tion is an aspect of how individuals come to understand their racial identity. The collective invisibility we found in our study differs slightly from Sellers and colleagues' (1997) description of public regard. Both incorporate an evaluation of the respect other groups have for one's racial group. The main difference is that in our study, collective invisibility also captures the outward manifestations of this lack of respect (e.g., lack of inclusion of contributions).

In addition to identifying lack of respect by Whites, participants discussed lack of racial recognition and acceptance from other Blacks as an aspect of understanding of what it means to be Black. Participants discussed a desire to receive recognition or validation from other Black individuals. Fanon (1952/1967) theorized about Black on Black recognition. He observed that "The Negro is comparison . . . [H]e is constantly preoccupied with self-evaluation and with ego-ideal. Whenever he comes into contact with someone else [Black], the question of value, of merit, arises . . . The question is always whether he [the other Black] is less intelligent than I, Blacker than I, less respectable than I" (p. 211). From this framework, Black individuals look to other Blacks to gauge their racial authenticity and global worth.

We uncovered this type of comparative racial self-evaluation in the interviews especially as related to issues of skin color/phenotype and wanting to be viewed as authentically Black. For example, Zha-Lei (Bermudian young adult) was ostracized and ignored for having a phenotypically ambiguous appearance and for "talking White." As a child, kids would say "oh she talks like that, she's a weirdo; leave her alone." These experiences led Zha-Lei to question whether she was Black enough and to her trying out different behaviors to fit in. She began to question what it meant to be authentically "Black."

Our findings extend beyond racial self-evaluation to include the incorporation of feeling rejected or ignored by people in their own community. Some participants wanted other Blacks in their community to accept them in their totality and not on a limited view of what it means to be Black. Similar to Christina's story, the process of developing an affirmative Black identity for some involved grappling with perceived rejection from people in their community based on other social identities or attributes such as sexual identity. Some participants thus did not compare themselves to other Blacks as a way to gauge their authenticity, but rather they looked to Blacks in their community for acceptance for their difference.

Participants' Black identity was informed by the interplay between lack of racial recognition/acceptance and racial recognition/acceptance. This iterative process is under theorized in the racial identity literature. Findings suggest that while participants disclosed painful experiences of being dismissed, these stories were countered with ones highlighting acceptance and pride; new experiences provided participants an opportunity to reflect on and gain new understanding of their identity. There were a number of accounts in which people inside and outside of the community affirmed participants' racial identity/experiences. The most interesting stories from our perspective, though, involved the process in which participants' affirmed their own racial identity and asserted pride. Like Nise, these participants at some point experienced devaluation from others for being an "outsider" within their own racial/ethnic group (e.g., not being "Black" enough) and for asserting Blackness among or being too black for Whites. Yet, later in life they redefined what being Black meant; they adopted a positive, affirmative identity characterized by pride and based on an internal definition of Blackness.

Building on the earlier works of racial identity theorists such as Cross (1971, 1995), participants identified processes connected to developing an affirmative racial identity, which in this study incorporated an assertion of recognition and dignity. In his original Nigrescence model, Cross described an encounter stage in which individuals begin to challenge previously held negative assumptions about what it means to be Black. From this framework, the encounter process can be initiated via positive experiences with other Blacks and/or a negative racist incident. This questioning is needed to develop an affirmative Black identity. Findings from the current investigation uncovered behaviors that participants engaged in to counter lack of recognition/acceptance experiences. These participants' responses did not necessarily emerge from a lack of awareness about race(ism), but instead the behaviors were designed to challenge the rejection and dismissal one received based on race. And, as such, the behaviors were designed to cope with and/or change the dehumanizing actions of others.

Consistent with other narrative research findings on coping with racism (e.g., Shorter-Gooden, 2004; Swim, Hyers, Cohen, Fitzgerald, & Bylsma, 2003), challenging oppression was one of the strategies participants used to call out and/or change the behaviors in their environments. These forms of resistance took a variety of forms ranging from naming racism in interpersonal situations to becoming involved in political action. Participants who challenged racism in general expressed greater levels of group consciousness or what Duncan (2010) described as an increased "critical analysis of the group's [Black's] relative position in the societal power hierarchy" (p. 1604). So, to be Black for some involved an awareness of being dehumanized based on their racial position and taking action to assert their humanity. Participants in the study also performed what el-Khoury (2012) called revolutions of everyday life, which include actions such as self-empowerment and self-definition.

Participants identified strategies consistent with el-Khoury's (2012) conceptualization of resistance, including engaging in competition and affirming one's talents. Several Black adults demanded respect through competition. Men in our sample were more likely to talk about asserting human dignity by beating Whites at their own game—whether through sports or life more generally—than were women. A number of athletes commented on how their athletic prowess earned them respect from others and countered some of the blatant racist attitudes directed toward other Blacks in their town. Sports also provided male participants an opportunity to smash racism. Buck (US) talked about winning football games against the predominantly White school as a response to the racism he experienced: "At the time it was just, they're racists and I want to win the game." Men in each of the four national contexts also talked about outperforming Whites in business and everyday life as a way of demonstrating they are as good as if not better than their White counterparts. Thus, winning and doing well provided men in our sample opportunities to gain respect and recognition from others and, moreover, to affirm their own dignity. The expression of competition additionally is consistent with Fanon's theory of recognition. Drawing on the work of Adler, Fanon also viewed recognition as a striving for competence and superiority. Winning embodies an expression of competence and superiority.

Participants, particularly in Bermuda, found creative ways to affirm talents that were undermined through a lifetime of rejection and dehumanization from White people and systems. People provided self-affirmations of their personal strengths and abilities. Unlike the concept of "valuing of self" in Shorter-Gooden's (2004) research in which Black American women found ways to nurture and validate themselves in the face of oppression, participants adopted a type of self-affirmation position that was not explicitly connected to the oppression they experienced; racial oppression instead served as the context in which to interpret these behaviors. Self-affirmations were perhaps more pronounced in the Bermuda because of the everyday slights and dismissal that occur in close, yet racially segregated living quarters and the long intergenerational and often "complicated" connections between Black and White families. The reluctance to hire Black Bermudian workers in the private sector and the constant fight for recognition as competent and intelligent could potentially undermine one's sense of self. One way some of the participants countered the daily barrage of racial antipathy was to provide counter narratives in which they highlighted their accomplishments and talents.

Some participants also performed race to try to fit in and gain acceptance, primarily among their Black peers. These participants changed their dialect, appearance, and mode of interacting to appear more authentically Black. Women more so than men disclosed performing race and much of the performance occurred during adolescence. This is not surprising given it is a developmental period in which teenagers are exploring the meaning of their social identities. These findings are similar to Burrell, Winston, and Freeman's (2013) concept of race-acting. Middle school youth in their study identified multiple dimensions of "acting Black," of which "style" (e.g., talking Black, listening to rap/hip hop) was most consistent with our findings. However, findings from participants in the current study suggests that performing race or "acting Black" was connected to perceived racial expectations among their peer groups as a way of being accepted into that group. Willie's (2003) exploration of acting Black among college students best captures our participants' desire for racial authenticity in environments which challenge, negate, and undermine Blackness.

Although the findings from this investigation provide interesting insights about the concept of recognition in how individuals come to understand what it means to be Black, there are number of noteworthy limitations. The focus of the larger project was on racial identity and specific questions about recognition/acceptance were not asked. Perhaps if more pointed questions were included in the interview protocol, different dimensions of recognition may have been uncovered. In addition, the interviews were retrospective and thus memory played a role in the stories that were shared. While what one remembers is critical to the meaning people attribute to events, there is no way to verify the veracity of the actual events in this study. So, our findings are particularly limited to people's recollection and interpretations of racial encounters. The findings may also be influenced by the racial-gender-nationality of the interviewer. Each interview was conducted by the same African American woman. Participants may have disclosed different information if they were interviewed by somebody of their same gender and nationality. Although an aspect of recognition emerged in the individual interviews (i.e., the primary data collection method), written narratives, and the one focus group, additional written narratives and focus groups could have been conducted to further triangulate the findings.

Findings from this investigation provide fruitful insights for additional investigation. We encourage future researchers to further explore the process in which people affirm and assert their dignity and worth in racialized contexts. In this study we uncovered a developing model describing the types of racial rejection or lack of recognition people may encounter and also the proactive strategies people use to fight for their rights as humans, which nurture their dignity. Much more information is needed on each aspect identified in the emerging model. Our findings specifically suggest that interactions with other Black people play critical roles in how we see ourselves as individuals and as racial beings. More information is needed about the ways in which we affirm people as individuals and as authentically Black. Conversely, though further exploration is also needed to document the ways we reject one another based on internalized oppression and the potentially harmful impact this may have on Black relationships and psychological adjustments.

Finally, more engagements is needed with the work of Frantz Fanon, who theorized some of the most compelling frameworks for interpreting research on Black identity and resistance. Fanon understood that a person is human to the extent that she tries to impose her existence on another for the purpose of being recognized. Because human worth depends on recognition by others, it is in the other that the meaning of life is found. The sense of inferiority that a Black individual may feel also explains the narcissistic injury someone experiences when he/she feels degraded or their sense of self-worth is undermined. One way people cope with or rebuild a sustainable sense of self is through the modes of behavior and strategies that our research has uncovered, and that Fanon's theory of recognition foreshadows.

Note

1. Reprinted with permission. Neville, H. A., Viard, B., & Turner, L. (2015). Race and recognition: Pathways to an affirmative Black racial identity. *Journal of Black Psychology, 41*, 247–271.

References

Bulhan, H. A. (1985). *Frantz Fanon and the psychology of oppression*. New York: Plenum.

Burrell, J. O., Winston, C. E., & Freeman, K. E. (2013). Race-acting: The varied and complex affirmative meaning of "acting Black" for African-American adolescents. *Culture & Psychology, 19*(1), 95–116.

Caldwell, C. H., Kohn-Wood, L. P., Schmeelk-Cone, K. H., Chavous, M., & Zimmerman, M. A. (2004). Racial discrimination and racial identity as risk and protective factors for violent behaviors in African American young adults. *American Journal of Community Psychology, 33*, 91–105.

Cross, W. E., Jr. (1971). The Negro-Black conversion experience. *Black World, 20*(9), 13–27.

Cross, W. E., Jr. (1995). *Shades of Black: Diversity in African American identity*. Philadephia: Temple University Press.

Duncan, L. E. (2010). Using group consciousness theories to understand political activism: Case studies of Barack Obama, Hillary Clinton, and Ingo Hasselbach. *Journal of Personality, 78*(6), 1601–1636. http://dx.doi.org/10.1111/j.1467-6494.2010.00664.x.

el-Khoury, L. (2012). "Being while black": Resistance and the management of the self. *Social Identities: Journal for the Study of Race, Nation and Culture, 18*(1), 85–100. http://dx.doi.org/10.1080/13504630.2012.629516.

Fanon, F. (1952/1967/2008). *Black Skin, White Masks*. New York: Grove Press (Original Work published 1952).

Fassinger, R. E. (2005). Paradigms, praxis, problems, and promise: Grounded theory in counseling psychology research. *Journal of Counseling Psychology, 52*, 156–166. doi:10.1037/0022-0167.52.2.156.

Ford, K. A. (2011). Race, gender, and bodily (mis) recognitions: Women of color faculty experiences with white students in the college classroom. *Journal of Higher Education, 82*(4), 444–478.

Franklin, A. J. (1999). Invisibility syndrome and racial identity development in psychotherapy and counseling African American men. *The Counseling Psychologist, 27*, 761–793.

Franklin, A. J. (2006). A dialogue about gender, race, and invisibility in psychotherapy with African American men. In J. C. Muran (Ed.), *Dialogues on difference: Diversity studies of the therapeutic relationship* (pp. 117–131). Washington, DC: American Psychological Association Books.

Gutierrez y Muhs, G., Niemann, Y. F., Gonzalez, C. G., & Harris, A. P. (Eds.). (2012). *Presumed incompetent: The intersections of race and class for women in academia*. Boulder, CO: Utah State University Press.

Hegel, G. W. F. (1931/1967). *The phenomenology of mind* (J. B. Baillie, Trans., 2nd ed., pp. 228–240). New York: Harper & Row.

Kools, S., McCarthy, M., Durham, R., & Robrecht, L. (1996). Dimensional analysis: Broadening the conception of grounded theory. *Qualitative Health Research, 6*(3), 312–330.

Laitinen, A. (2002). Interpersonal recognition: A response to value or a precondition of personhood? *Inquiry, 45*(4), 463–478.

McAdams, D. P., Josselson, R., & Leiblich, A. (Eds.). (2006). *Identity and story: Creating self in narrative*. Washington, DC: American Psychological Association.

Polkinghorne, D. E. (1988). *Narrative knowing and the human sciences*. Albany, NY: State University of New York Press.

Sellers, R. M., Copeland-Linder, N., Martin, P. P., & Lewis, R. L. (2006). Racial identity matters: The relationship between racial discrimination and psychological functioning in African American adolescents. *Journal of Research on Adolescence, 16*, 187–216.

Sellers, R. M., Rowley, S., Chavous, T. M., Shelton, J. N., & Smith, M. A. (1997). Multidimensional inventory of Black identity: A preliminary investigation of reliability and construct validity. *Journal of Personality and Social Psychology, 73*(4), 805–815.

Sellers, R. M., & Shelton, J. N. (2003). The role of racial identity in perceived racial discrimination. *Journal of Personality and Social Psychology, 84*, 1079–1092.

Shorter-Gooden, K. (2004). Multiple resistance strategies: How African American women cope with racism and sexism. *Journal of Black Psychology, 30*(3), 406–425. http://dx.doi.org/10.1177/0095798404266050.

Swim, J. K., Hyers, L. L., Cohen, L. L., Fitzgerald, D. C., & Bylsma, W. H. (2003). African american college students' experiences with everyday racism: Characteristics of and responses to these incidents. *Journal of Black Psychology, 29*(1), 38–67. http://dx.doi.org/10.1177/0095798402239228s.

Taylor, C. (1992). *The ethics of authenticity*. Cambridge, MA: Harvard University Press.

Telesford, J., Mendoza-Denton, R., & Worrell, F. C. (2013). Clusters of CRIS scores and psychological adjustment. *Cultural Diversity and Ethnic Minority Psychology, 19*(1), 86–91. http://dx.doi.org/10.1037/a0031254.

Thompson, C. E., & Alfred, D. (2008). Black liberation psychology and practice. In H. Neville, B. M. Tynes, & S. O. Utsey (Eds.), *Handbook of African American psychology* (pp. 483–496). Thousand Oaks, CA: Sage Publications.

Tovar-Murray, D., & Tovar-Murray, M. (2012). A phenomenological analysis of the invisibility syndrome. *Journal of Multicultural Counseling and Development, 40*, 24–36.

Ward, E. C. (2005). Keeping it real: A grounded theory study of African American clients engaging in counseling at a community mental health agency. *Journal of Counseling Psychology, 52*(4), 471–481. doi:10.1037/0022-0167.52.4.471.

Whittaker, V. A., & Neville, H. A. (2010). Examining the relation between racial identity attitude clusters and psychological health outcomes in African American college students. *Journal of Black Psychology, 36*(4), 383–409. http://dx.doi.org/10.1177/0095798409353757.

Willie, S. S. (2003). *Acting Black: College, identity and the performance of race*. New York, NY: Routledge.

Wynne, E. (2000). *Reflections on recognition: Matter of self-realization or a matter of justice?* Proceedings from Thinking Fundamentals, IWM Junior Visiting Fellows Conference, 9, Vienna.

Contributors

Imani Bazzell has worked as a community educator and organizer in the areas of racial justice, gender justice, healthcare access, educational reform, and leadership development for over 35 years. She is the founding director of *SisterNet*, a local network of African American women committed to the physical, emotional, intellectual, and spiritual health of Black women. Additionally, she serves as an independent consultant with public schools, colleges and universities, unions, non-profits, state and international agencies, and community-based organizations to promote organizational development and social justice.

Among her many community contributions, Imani produced and hosted ACCESS Live, the public engagement radio show of the ACCESS Initiative dedicated to ending stigma and increasing community awareness and engagement with mental health providers and multiple systems that indicate racial disproportionality and disparity with negative outcomes for African American youth and their families; including public education, child welfare, health, and criminal justice.

Roberto Beneduce, PhD, MD, anthropologist and psychiatrist, is Professor of Medical and Psychological Anthropology at the University of Turin, and founder of the Frantz Fanon Centre (Turin), a centre devote to research and clinical intervention in the area of migration, refugees, and asylum seekers. He is presently conducting a comparative ethnographic study on marginality, violence, and suffering, as well as on local healing knowledge in Sub-Saharan Africa and South America. His previous work includes an ethnographic study of ritual therapies and religious imaginary in Mali and Cameroon, the history of ethnopsychiatry, and the effects of mass atrocities on mental health (Eritrea and DRC). He is the author of the volumes *Un lugar en el mundo. Senderos de la migración entre violencia, memoria y deseo* (ENAH y UAT, 2015), *L'histoire au corps. Mémoires indociles et archives du désordre dans les cultes de possession en Afrique* (Academic Press, 2016), and—with Nigel Gibson—*Frantz Fanon, Psychiatry and Politics* (Rowman & Littlefield, 2017).

Erica Burman is Professor of Education, Associate Fellow of the British Psychological Society, and a United Kingdom Council of Psychotherapists registered Group Analyst (and full member of the Institute of Group Analysis). She trained as a developmental psychologist, and is well known as a critical developmental psychologist and methodologist specializing in innovative and activist qualitative research. She is author of *Fanon, education, action: child as method* (Routledge, 2019), *Deconstructing Developmental Psychology* (Routledge, 3rd edition, 2017), *Developments: child, image, nation* (Routledge, 2008), and is an associate editor of the *SAGE Encyclopaedia of Childhood and Childhood Studies* (forthcoming). Erica co-founded the Discourse Unit (www.discourseunit.com), a transinstitutional, transdisciplinary network researching the reproduction and transformation of language and subjectivity. Erica's research has focused on critical developmental and educational psychology, feminist and postcolonial theory, childhood studies, and on critical mental health practice (particularly around gender and cultural issues). Much of her current work addresses the connections between emotions, mental health, and (social as well as individual) change, in particular as anchored by representations of, and appeals to, childhood. She has co-led funded research projects on conceptualizing and challenging state and interpersonal violence in relation to minoritized women and children, and on educational and mental health impacts of poverty and "austerity." She currently leads the Knowledge, Power and Identity research strand of the Education and Psychology research group at Manchester Institute of Education (see www.seed.manchester.ac.uk/education/research/research-themes-and-projects/sean/projects/knowledge-power-identity/. For further information see www.manchester.ac.uk/research/Erica.burman/andwww.ericaburman.com). She is a past Chair of the Psychology of Women Section of the British Psychological Society, and in 2016 she was awarded an Honorary Lifetime Fellowship of the British Psychological Society in recognition of her contribution to Psychology.

Nkechinyelum A. Chioneso, Ph.D. is Assistant Professor of Psychology in the Department of Psychology at Florida A&M University in Florida, USA. With a specialty in community psychology, Dr. Chioneso seeks to promote healthy individuals within healthy communities by advancing a psychological sense of community, sustaining wellness, and building healthy systems.

As the former assistant director of public engagement in the Psychological Services Center, Department of Psychology, at the University of Illinois in Urbana-Champaign, Illinois, Dr. Chioneso provided leadership in the development and implementation of university–community engagement efforts in the local area. Previously, she consulted with community groups and nonprofit organizations seeking solutions to better address the social determinants of health, while fostering community spaces that inspire a greater and more equitable realization of our human potentials.

Shamso M. Elmi is a translator, interpreter, and community development organizer. Prior to emigrating from Somalia, Mrs. Elmi was pursuing a medical degree at Somali National University. She created three digital stories—Home Safe Hamilton, Newcomer Women, and Victim's Mother—to highlight how Canadian society treats those who are immigrants, Black, and Muslim. While working with various city agencies in Toronto and Hamilton, Canada, Mrs. Elmi also directs an after-school program for young children. She is a community leader committed to helping African Canadian mothers take preventive measures that address behavioral and mental health challenges.

Joseph Gonkapieu Gueu is an actor, comedian, and human rights activist from the Ivory Coast. He studied at the National University of Cocody and also at the National Institute of Arts and Cultural Action of Cote d'Ivoire (Ivory Coast). He holds a Master's degree in theater and a post-graduate degree in specialized cultural activities. During the sociopolitical crisis in Cote d'Ivoire, he had actively participated in the program for the "Re-integration of Youth through the Arts." He also contributed by carrying out theatrical performances in order to instruct child soldiers on how to become part of community life after conflict.

Lewis M. King, PhD, is an extraordinary original thinker, outstanding scholar, and leader. He has been the recipient of numerous honors and awards encompassing teaching, research, and community development. A *Los Angeles Times Magazine* article (10–23–2005) recognized his contribution and described him as using the skills of both a scientist and businessman to invest in human capital. Dr. King's scholarly work over the last 45 years has focused on developing evidence-based change models in the service of equity and justice for historically marginalized people and communities. These efforts have centered on emancipation consciousness and practices of humans struggling to overcome oppression. In the course of these efforts he has developed critical institutions to include a major International Research and Development Center (Fanon R&D), national models (to include Intentional Critical Civility), and powerful cultural practices (to include a Culturecology Model—utilized by the NIH in Diabetes prevention). His landmark work in 1986–87 with the US Congress led to legislation—Research Centers for Minority Institutions—RCMI, 1987. This fund (now over $300 million annually) now serves as the base research funding for over 160 Universities in the US and Puerto Rico.

Luke Molloy registered as a psychiatric nurse in Ireland in 1999. He migrated to Australia in 2004. His clinical experience has been primarily in acute mental health inpatient settings in both of these countries. Luke is currently a senior lecturer in the School of Nursing at the University of Wollongong. He also works as a registered nurse in Sutherland Hospital, Sydney. His research is focused on the care and treatment of non-Indigenous practitioners, cultural safety, and Aboriginal and Torres Strait Islander peoples.

Helen A. Neville is Professor of Educational Psychology and African American studies at the University of Illinois at Urbana-Champaign. Her research on issues of race, racism, and racial identity has appeared in a wide range of journals including the *American Psychologist, Journal of Counseling Psychology, The Counseling Psychologist, Journal of Black Studies,* and *Cultural Diversity and Ethnic Minority Psychology.* She is the lead editor of the *Handbook of African American Psychology*, a past associate editor of the *Journal of Black Psychology* and of *The Counseling Psychologist*, and she serves on the editorial boards of a number of other psychology and Black studies journals. Dr. Neville has been recognized for her research, teaching, and mentoring efforts including gaining Fellow status in the American Psychological Association, receiving the American Psychological Association Graduate Students Kenneth and Mamie Clark Award for Outstanding Contribution to the Professional Development of Ethnic Minority Graduate Students the Charles, and the Shirley Thomas Award for mentoring and contributions to African American students and community. She was also honored with the Association of Black Psychologists' Distinguished Psychologist of the Year award. Dr. Neville is a past president of the Society for the Psychological Study of Culture, Ethnicity and Race (APA Division 45).

Camille Robcis is Associate Professor of French and History at Columbia University. Her first book, *The Law of Kinship: Anthropology, Psychoanalysis, and the Family in France* (Cornell University Press, 2013), won the 2013 Berkshire Conference of Women Historians Book Prize. Her second book, *Disalienation: Politics, Philosophy, and Radical Psychiatry in France* (forthcoming, 2020) traces the history of institutional psychotherapy, a movement born after World War II that advocated a radical restructuring of the asylum in an attempt to rethink and reform psychiatric care. She received her B.A. in history and modern culture & media from Brown University, her Ph.D. in history from Cornell, and she taught for ten years in Cornell's History Department. She has received fellowships from the Penn Humanities Forum, LAPA (Princeton Law and Public Affairs), the National Endowment for the Humanities, and the Institute for Advanced Study.

Hawthorne E. Smith, PhD, is a licensed psychologist and Program Director of the Bellevue Program for Survivors of Torture. He is also an associate clinical professor at the NYU School of Medicine in the Department of Psychiatry. Dr. Smith received his doctorate in counseling psychology (with distinction) from Teachers College; Columbia University. Dr. Smith had previously earned a bachelor of science in foreign service from the Georgetown University School of Foreign Service, an advanced certificate in African studies from Cheikh Anta Diop University in Dakar, Senegal, as well as a masters in international affairs from the Columbia University School of International and Public Affairs.

Dr. Smith has facilitated a support group for French-speaking African survivors of torture for the past 23 years. He has been recognized for his work with such awards as: the Robin Hood Foundation's "Hero Award"; the "Frantz Fanon Award" from the Postgraduate Center for Mental Health;

the "W.E.B. DuBois Award" from the International Youth Leadership Institute; the "Distinguished Alumni–Early Career Award" from Teachers College; the "Man of Distinction Award" from the National Association of Health Service Executives; and the "Union Square Award for Community Advocacy" from the Fund for the City of New York.

Prior to coming to Bellevue, Dr. Smith coordinated care at a shelter for homeless families in San Francisco prior to, and in the aftermath of the 1989 earthquake. He was a youth counselor to "court involved youth" in Washington, DC during the height of the crack epidemic. Dr. Smith was also a co-founding member of Nah We Yone, Inc. (a non-profit organization working primarily with refugees from Sierra Leone, as well as other displaced Africans in New York), and helped to coordinate the International Youth Leadership Institute (IYLI), a leadership program for marginalized New York City teens.

Dr. Smith is also a professional musician (saxophonist and vocalist) with international experience.

Lou Turner is Clinical Assistant Professor in the Department of Urban and Regional Planning and in the College of Fine and Applied Arts at the University of Illinois Urbana-Champaign. As co-author of *Frantz Fanon, Soweto and American Black Thought* (1978; 1986), Turner has helped reacquaint a new generation of activists and intellectuals with the thoughts of Frantz Fanon, in the 1980s, as Steve Biko and the Black Consciousness Movement in South African were discovering him in the maelstrom of the revolutionary struggle that would end apartheid. Banned copies of Turner's work circulated in the South African underground along with banned copies of Fanon's works. Turner has published essays and book chapters on many aspects of Fanon's work, given numerous presentations on new thinking in Fanon Studies, lectured on university campuses across the US and with Helen A. Neville taught a course on Black Liberation Psychology centered on Fanon's work. Turner has also collaborated with Neville in producing one of the very few empirical studies to use Fanonian categories in its research methods. While dialectical philosophy has been a particular dimension of Turner's work in Fanon Studies, the publication of Fanon's clinical papers (2018) has refocused Turner to excavating a "new Fanon."

Maria Judith Valgoi is Assistant Professor of Psychology at Governors State University and a licensed clinical psychologist in the state of Illinois. She completed her Ph.D. in 2016 at University of Illinois Urbana-Champaign intersecting her studies in the counseling psychology and African American studies departments. Dr. Valgoi believes that to be "trauma-informed" is to be antiracist. She believes a truly trauma-informed space acknowledges legacies of racist social control through violence and provides sanctuary from current violence as well as opportunities to work toward liberation. Her research focuses around using participatory action methodologies to build trauma-informed work environments for entities that serve survivors, especially entities without formal mental health training. She currently consults with elementary schools around creating trauma-informed school communities and offers secondary trauma supervision to professionals that work with survivors.

Brigitte Viard is an early childhood educator with a passion for instilling a love of literacy in young learners. She is currently a first grade teacher at Latin School in Chicago. In her previous position as a kindergarten teacher in St. Louis, Brigitte undertook an active role in curriculum development with attention to rigor and cultural responsiveness. Brigitte also taught for 4 years as a preschool teacher in Saint Louis Public Schools. Brigitte is a proud alumni of Teach for America (STL '13). She is a licensed reading specialist and is completing a second masters in gifted education.

Mahad A. Yusuf is Executive Director of Midaynta Community Services, a registered charity organization in Toronto, Canada. Mr. Yusuf founded the Somali Immigrant Aid Organization in 1986 to assist fair and effective governmental processing of refugee claims. He was also instrumental in the establishment of other non-profit organizations: Dejinta Beesha (Somali Multi-Service Agency), Midaynta Community Services, and the Somali Community Centre of Etobicoke. Previously, Mr. Yusuf held technical support and maintenance positions in the banking industry and was later employed by IBM Global Services. He is a graduate of DeVry Institute of Technology and holds executive leadership and professional development diplomas from Ryerson University, York University, and the University of Toronto. He has over 25 years of experience in organizational development, project management, and strong creative leadership.

Index

life narratives 259; and black identity 269
Life World 90, 91
L'Information psychiatrique 33
lived experience 26, 53; of African
  Canadians 232
Lopez, Emilio Mira 73
Los Angeles: Bradley Center 104;
  Central City Community Mental
  Health Center 7, 87; community
  mental health centers 87; Fanon
  Research and Development Center
  3, 5, 6–7, 50, 51, 85, 87, 88–93,
  93–96; Frederick Douglass Child
  Development Center 7; King/Drew
  Medical Center 87–88; Suicide
  Prevention Hotline 92–93; Watts
  rebellion 7
Lumumba, Patrice 166
Lynch, Hollis 98

Macey, David 51
madness 26, 28; and colonialism 73–74;
  Fanon on 115
Mandela, Nelson 257
Mandouze, Andre 75
Manners, Jordan 237
Mannoni, Octave 60, 131
Manuellan, Marie-Jeanne 35–36
marginalized communities 13–14
Martin, Trayvon 254
Marx, Karl 25, 29, 36, 65–66
Marxian analysis of sociotherapy
  61–62
Masilela, Ntongela 98
Maspero, François 35
Mauss, Marcel 25, 34
McCord, C. 101
McCulloch, Jock 2, 51, 190
medicine: and politics 26–27; successes
  of the Fanon Research and
  Development Center 101–104
melancholy, racial 155n49, 156n56,
  156n57
Mending a Crack in the Sky (MCIS)
  229–230, 230, 233, 234, 242, 250;
  Collaborative Institutional Training
  Initiative (CITI Program) certification
  247; funding 247–248; implementing
  243–247; implications for future work
  247–249
mental healthcare 2, 4, 10; for Aboriginal
  and Torres Strait Islander peoples
  185–186, 189–190; annex care 72;
  building trust 200–207; challenges
  among Somali Canadians 239;

colonial, institutional assessment
  of 68–72; community 12; cultural
  safety 184, 188–189, 190–191;
  "Mothers Outreach Workers" 239;
  and politics 113; psychiatric nursing
  11; public service messaging 13;
  therapeutic governance 79; *see also*
  clinical papers; community mental
  health; ethnopsychiatry; interventions;
  psychiatry; Saint-Alban Hospital;
  therapy
Merleau-Ponty, Maurice 25, 77;
  Phenomenology of Perception 73
Midaynta Community Services 14,
  229, 230, 231, 232, 233, 235–236,
  241, 249
Mirzoeff, Nicholas 76
Mitterand, François 54
Mollet, Guy 23, 45
Molloy, Luke 11
Morocco, immigrant patients, treating
  132–134
"Mothers Outreach Workers" 239, 240,
  242–243, 246
multidimensional model of racial identity
  (MMRI) 258–259
Muslim men's ward, Fanon's
  sociotherapy in 6, 14, 46, 53, 55,
  56, 57, 58, 59, 60, 62, 230; *see also*
  Islamophobia

N-A-C-H-E-S 100
Nandy, Ashis 129
national culture 36
National Institute of Mental Health 7,
  88; R&D model 89
'native psychology' 31
Nazi Germany, "Action T4" 28
neocolonial trauma 11, 13
Neville, Helen A. 2, 39, 40
"new Fanon" 41, 49, 50–51
new humanism 8, 13–14, 15, 44, 111,
  114, 197, 204, 207
Nigerian sex trade 137–138, 151–152n22
Nkrumah, Kwame 86
Nobles, Wade 93, 95, 104
North Africa: Berber customary law 65;
  immigrant patients, treating 132–134;
  institutional psychotherapy 31–35;
  social contracts 67; split development
  61; storytellers 63
"North African syndrome" 26–27, 28, 65
Notre journal 32–33, 115
nursing: cultural safety 188–189;
  Fanonian practice 191–192

Milton Keynes UK
Ingram Content Group UK Ltd.
UKHW050722091123
432231UK00014B/105

9 781032 239163